Feminist Trauma Theologies

Feminist Trauma Theologies

Body, Scripture and Church in Critical Perspective

Edited by

Karen O'Donnell
and
Katie Cross

scm press

© Editor and Contributors 2020

Published in 2020 by SCM Press
Editorial office
3rd Floor, Invicta House,
108–114 Golden Lane,
London EC1Y 0TG, UK
www.scmpress.co.uk

SCM Press is an imprint of Hymns Ancient and Modern Ltd
(a registered charity)

Hymns Ancient and Modern® is a registered trademark of
Hymns Ancient and Modern Ltd
13A Hellesdon Park Road, Norwich,
Norfolk NR6 5DR, UK

978 0 334 05872 4

British Library Cataloguing in Publication data
A catalogue record for this book is available
from the British Library

Typeset by Regent Typesetting
Printed and bound by
CPI Group (UK) Ltd

This book is dedicated to our mothers – Christine and Marie – who showed us what it means to be compassionate, brave and strong.

The survivor who has achieved commonality with others
can rest from her labors. Her recovery is accomplished;
all that remains before her is her life.
(Judith Herman, *Trauma and Recovery:
The Aftermath of Violence*)

Contents

Method in Feminist Trauma Theologies

Feminist Trauma Theologies: Violence against Women

Feminist Trauma Theologies: Christian Communities and Trauma

Feminist Trauma Theologies: Post-Traumatic Remaking

List of Contributors

Rosie Andrious is currently a Research Associate within the Theology and Religious Studies Department at King's College, London. She previously worked as a chaplain and was Head of Spiritual and Pastoral Care in one of the largest NHS trusts in London. She completed her PhD under the supervision of Professor Joan Taylor at King's College, London, and was also awarded the Postgraduate Certificate in Academic Practice from the King's Learning Institute. Prior to her ordination in the Church of England in 2001, she read theology as an undergraduate at King's where she also completed a postgraduate masters in biblical studies. Previously she worked as a part-time lecturer at KCL and a Mental Health Chaplain for the South London and Maundsley NHS Trust. Her research interests include gender studies, women in early Christianity, martyrdom literature and representation of violence. She has published in the areas of biblical studies, contemporary spirituality and chaplaincy.

Kirsi Cobb is Lecturer in Biblical Studies at Cliff College in Derbyshire, UK. Her research focuses on biblical hermeneutics as well as Old Testament studies, with a particular interest in women's studies. Her recent research projects centre on the presentation and interpretation of women, especially in the Old Testament, exploring ways to read their stories in more empowering ways. Her most recent publication, 'When Irony Bites Back: A Deconstructive Reading of the Midwives' Excuse in Exodus 1:19' (in I. Fischer, ed., *Gender Agenda Matters*, Cambridge: Cambridge Scholars Press, 2015) was in part based on her PhD research (2012; forthcoming), which focused on the narrative portrayal of Miriam in Exodus 2, 15 and Numbers 12.

Natalie Collins is a gender justice specialist. She set up Spark (www.sparkequip.org) and works to enable individuals and organizations to prevent and respond to male violence against women. She is also the Creator and Director of DAY (www.dayprogramme.org), an innovative youth domestic abuse and exploitation education programme. Natalie organizes Project 3:28 (www.project328.info), co-founded the UK Christian Feminist Network (www.christianfeministnetwork.com), blogs and tweets as God Loves Women and has written a book about Christians and domestic abuse, entitled *Out of Control: Couples, Conflict and the Capacity for Change* (SPCK, 2019). She speaks and writes on understanding and ending gender injustice nationally and internationally.

Katie Cross is Christ's College Teaching Fellow in Practical Theology at the University of Aberdeen. She is (in official terms) the first woman to teach for Christ's College since its foundation in 1843. Her work and teaching are centred on theologies of trauma, suffering and disaster. Katie's PhD research was a theological engagement with issues of trauma and suffering in an increasingly non-religious UK context, and involved a qualitative study of the Sunday Assembly, a 'godless' congregation. A monograph based on this research, entitled *The Sunday Assembly and Theologies of Suffering*, will be published by Routledge in 2020.

Manon Ceridwen James is the Director of Formation for Licensed Ministry for the St Padarn's Institute, Church in Wales. Her poetry has appeared in several publications, including *Poetry Wales* and *Envoi*. She gained her PhD investigating the role that religion plays in the identity of Welsh women in 2015, and her research has been published in two edited collections of feminist theological qualitative research (*The Faith Lives of Women and Girls* and *Researching Female Faith*, both published by Routledge), and her book *Women, Identity and Religion in Wales: Theology, Poetry, Story* was published in 2018 by the University of Wales Press.

Al McFadyen is Senior Lecturer in Systematic Theology at the University of Leeds, while also a part-time (unpaid) operational officer in West Yorkshire Police. The views expressed here are his own and do not necessarily reflect those of either organization. His theological work is focused on theological anthropology and the doctrine of sin. He attempts to triangulate secular with theological thought in relation to concrete human situations where humanity is at risk. He has also published on religion and policing. His main publications are *The Call to Personhood* (Cambridge University Press, 1990) and *Bound to Sin: Abuse, Holocaust and the Christian Doctrine of Sin* (Cambridge University Press, 2000). In 2014, he was awarded an MBE for services to policing and the community.

Esther McIntosh is currently Subject Director for Theology and Religious Studies and Senior Lecturer in Religion, Philosophy and Ethics at York St John University. She is a feminist theologian and John Macmurray scholar engaged in interdisciplinary research that focuses on definitions of personhood and community, the ethics of personal relations, gender justice and the use of social media by religious communities. Representative publications include: *John Macmurray's Religious Philosophy: What it Means to be a Person* (Ashgate and Routledge, 2011); 'Belonging without Believing: Church as Community in an Age of Digital Media', *International Journal* of *Public Theology* 9:2 (2015); '"I Met God, She's Black": Racial, Gender and Sexual Equalities in Public Theology', in S. Kim and K. Day (eds), *A Companion to Public Theology* (Brill, 2017). In addition, she is currently engaged in a CUF-funded project exploring chaplaincy support for trans and non-binary staff and students in Anglican foundation universities.

Ally Moder is a feminist practical theologian whose interdisciplinary work centres on theological, spiritual and psychological understandings of trauma, mental health and human flourishing. She holds a PhD in practical theology and teaches in this field at multiple universities, in addition to speaking globally on women in leadership and ending violence against women and girls. Through her published articles and popular blogs, she also provides free faith-based resources for survivors of domestic abuse to heal. Ally brings two decades of pastoral ministry to her work as a speaker, author and consultant, and is available at www.allymoder.com.

Karen O'Donnell is the Coordinator of the Centre for Contemporary Spirituality and Programme Leader in the MA in Christian Spirituality at Sarum College, Salisbury. Karen received her PhD at the University of Exeter and is the Secretary for the Society for the Study of Theology. Her research interests are at the intersection of bodies and theologies. Karen is a feminist, constructive theologian and has published on Mariology, sacramental theology, and theologies of reproductive loss. She has previously published work on trauma in *Broken Bodies: The Eucharist, Mary and the Body in Trauma Theology* (SCM Press, 2018).

Santiago Piñón is an Associate Professor of Religion at Texas Christian University. His latest publication, 'The Box and the Dark Night of the Soul: An Autoethnography from the Force of Losing a Child in the Delivery Room' (*Online Journal of Healthcare Ethics*), addresses healthcare professionals who care for the parents who have lost a child. Dr Piñón is an advocate for gender equality in his courses by bringing to light how men contribute to the oppression of women. He is the father of a 12-year-old who became part of the family seven years ago, father of 5-year-old triplets, and father of twins who died shortly after being born (11 October 2009).

Shelly Rambo is Associate Professor of Theology at Boston University School of Theology. Her research and teaching interests focus on religious responses to suffering, trauma and violence. She is author of *Spirit and Trauma: A Theology of Remaining* (Westminster John Knox, 2010), *Resurrecting Wounds: Living in the Afterlife of Trauma* (Baylor University Press, 2017) and a co-edited volume with Stephanie Arel, *Post-Traumatic Public Theology* (Palgrave MacMillan, 2016).

Leah E. Robinson serves as Associate Professor of Religion and Practical Theology at Pfeiffer University in North Carolina, USA. She has previously held posts of University Teacher in Practical Theology and Peacebuilding at Glasgow University as well as Lecturer in Practical Theology at the University of Edinburgh. Her most recent book is *Embodied Peacebuilding: Reconciliation as Practical Theology* (Peter Lang, 2015). She is currently researching oppressive theological practices for her forthcoming book, *From Slavery to Westboro Baptist: Practical Theology as Oppression* (Jessica Kingsley, 2020).

Hilary Jerome Scarsella is Visiting Assistant Professor of Theology and Ethics at Memphis Theological Seminary and a Postdoctoral Fellow with the Louisville Institute. Currently, she is working on a book that grapples with the theological dimensions of contemporary discourse on the problem and promise of belief in the context of sexual violence. Recent publications can be found in the journal *Religion Compass*, Fordham University Press's *Trauma and Transcendence* and in Palgrave MacMillan's *Trauma and Lived Religion*.

Sonia Soans was awarded her PhD from Manchester Metropolitan University. Her primary training is in the field of psychology. A practising Anglican, she has been involved deeply in church life. Her research interests include the intersections between gender, society, violence and media. She is currently working as an Assistant Professor in Bangalore, India.

Acknowledgements

We have a great number of acknowledgements to offer at the beginning of this book. An edited volume is, invariably, the work of a whole team of people. While our names are on the front cover, we know very well that this book is as much the product of the brilliant scholars who wrote essays for the volume, as it is a product of our tenacity and imagination. We are so incredibly grateful to all our contributors: Hilary Scarsella, Manon Ceridwen James, Al McFadyen, Kirsi Cobb, Leah Robinson, Sonia Soans, Natalie Collins, Rosie Andrious, Ally Moder, Santiago Piñón and Esther McIntosh. We are also grateful to Penny Cowell Doe and Sanjee Perera, who both wanted to write chapters for this book but for various reasons were not able to do so.

We are most grateful to Shelly Rambo who generously provided a Foreword that far exceeded our expectations. Shelly has outlined a trajectory in feminist trauma theologies that situates this book so clearly in a developing pathway and an ongoing conversation. Her Foreword lends a perspective to this book that we would not have been able to articulate alone. Moreover, she was able to write this Foreword at a particularly busy time and we appreciate it so much.

We are grateful to SCM Press, and especially David Shervington, for believing that this project was important and for committing energy and resources to seeing it come to fruition. We also want to acknowledge the key role a publisher like SCM Press plays in producing a book that is aimed at both academy and church. We are very grateful that SCM Press is committed to working at this vital intersection.

We must also acknowledge that the seeds for this project were planted in a whisky-fuelled conversation at the annual conference of the Society for the Study of Theology in 2018. So we are grateful to SST for being a place where a diverse range of academics can meet, discuss theology and make plans for brilliant books over a few drinks. Cheers!

I, Karen, have a few offers of thanks of my own to make too. First, I am so thankful that I got to work on this project with Katie Cross. Not only is Katie a brilliant theologian and a compassionate and innovative thinker, but she has also become a great friend. We have worked very hard on this volume together and working with Katie has been an absolute pleasure.

I am also very grateful to my colleagues at Sarum College who have given me both encouragement and space to complete this project. With particular thanks to James Woodward – who can always be relied upon for a glass of wine and a word of encouragement – and also Jayme Reaves who has lent her biblical expertise to this book and kept me excited about this project. I am thankful, as well, to my students – past and present – who have been so enthusiastic in learning about both feminist theology and trauma theology and who keep my thinking fresh.

Finally, I am very grateful to my friends and family who have done their best to keep looking interested in this project over the last two years! With particular thanks to Sarah, Amanda, Harriet and Kristen, who are the most persistent women; to my mother – Marie – who is a constant source of encouragement; and to James – who longs for a book on a cheerful subject matter but is my favourite nonetheless.

I, Katie, would like to thank my co-editor and friend Karen O'Donnell for suggesting that we put this book together, and for being a joy to collaborate with. Karen's commitment to theology in places of pain is inspirational: hers is the work that truly matters. Her kindness (and brilliant organizational skills!) have created not only this book but a supportive and sustaining network of scholars. Thank you, Karen – I am so proud to be your friend.

I am indebted to the exceptionally brave band of women whose stories of purity culture appear in Chapter 2 of this book. They openly and generously shared their lives and their traumas with me; I hope that I have done their stories justice.

My heartfelt thanks to my colleagues at the University of Aberdeen for their wisdom and counsel, and to friends and family who have loved me through this project (and beyond!) In particular, my dad, Nicos Scholarios, for his patience and wisdom, and my brothers, Andrew and Peter Scholarios, for the colour and laughter they bring to my life! Special thanks to my husband Peter Cross, for his love, compassion and dedication to making a difference.

This book is for our mothers. For my mum, Christine – you have wrestled with and resisted damaging theologies throughout your whole life. Your compassion, your love and your fierce, inclusive faith inspire me to action in every day of mine. Thank you for all you do for other women, and thank you for all you've done for me.

Foreword

SHELLY RAMBO

After thumbing through countless pages of Reformed theology, I recall Serene Jones suggesting that we read some of the interdisciplinary research about trauma coming from scholars at Yale University. Literary scholars, psychoanalysts and historians across the University were assessing the impact of violence on persons and communities and doing so largely under the umbrella of post-Holocaust studies. These were pioneering efforts to record and preserve testimonies to the genocide of European Jews. We did not know at the time that these books would comprise an emerging canon of trauma theory.

There was no such thing as trauma theology. Within Christian theology, Rebecca Chopp, Flora Keshgegian and Serene Jones, each steeped in feminist and liberation theologies, began to integrate these studies of trauma into their work.[1] Judith Herman's *Trauma and Recovery*, published in 1992 and now a classic in the field, presented trauma as a decidedly political and feminist issue.[2] Most theologians working with early trauma theories were women – and espoused feminists. They were committed to accounting for the absence of women in sacred texts, the scarcity of women in religious leadership, and the impact of violence on the lives of women, many of whom drew life from their religious traditions. Although suffering has always been at the forefront of theological reflection, the study of trauma raised unique challenges to theology, both in content and form.[3]

As a graduate student inspired by the work of my teachers, I grew in my conviction that theology, like other disciplines, needed to respond to Cathy Caruth's invitation for disciplines to gather around the enigma of trauma 'for the truth that it tells us'.[4] Rife with truth-claims, theology needed to show up. Caruth's appeal to truth is not a religious appeal; and yet it is a deeply ethical one. She claims that the structure of traumatic experience casts a different light on how we think about history and are positioned in relationship to the past. The truths, unknown and yet transmitted, suggest that we are positioned as witnesses (not recipients in some simple and straightforward sense) to pasts we may never fully know. The challenge to the disciplines is a challenge not only to identify trauma but to bear witness to it. Caruth's appeal expands the clinical diagnosis of trauma beyond pathology and traumatic repetition to the truth that lies at the heart of existence.

Theologians working in the area of trauma vary in terms of whether or not they claim that all existence is traumatically structured or whether trauma is an exceptional experience.[5] These definitional questions are still in play, within both trauma studies and theology. The experience of trauma, as non-linear, renders empty certain long-standing notions of subjectivity, rationality and memory. Trauma does not adhere to the boundaries of space and time. We know that wounds remain, long after an experience of harm is inflicted. Trauma, while rooted in the soil of particular places, is not contained there.

The 'unlanguagability' of trauma and its curious communicability present a searing challenge to Christian theology, as it circles around the central claim that the Word takes on flesh and walks in our midst. What if this Word is rendered wordless? And what does it look like for biblical texts to provide testimonies to what cannot be spoken? Several of us targeted classic Christian doctrines to respond to trauma. My training in feminist systematic theology directed me to the site of the cross to unpack the logic of divine suffering as it mapped on to human experience. And yet trauma theories directed me beyond the cross, to the juncture of cross and resurrection.

The lineage of 'trauma theology' is deeply feminist. There was no stated break from one to pursue the other. While we were gathered around trauma, it was our shared feminist commitments that made us think that theology shaped women's lives in particular ways, and not always for the better. For many women, the language and practices of Christian faith are *both* wounding and healing. Feminist theologians know that faith-claims can cut both ways. Theological claims kept many of us from occupying positions of leadership, and yet for me and many of my peers theological reflection provided a haven and crucible for reclaiming our relationship to God and to our home traditions.

Feminist theologians empowered me to speak my truth. They offered me routes for proclamation. Theories of trauma assured me that what is unspoken will, nonetheless, be registered. Trauma surfaced the testimonial function of theology; while everything on the surface of things appears to be OK, trauma theories track the undertow of traditions and their impact on those who are afforded less representation. Analysis of trauma offers a way of accounting for the unstated and invisible forces that continue to diminish women, even as our traditions afford us greater access to positions of leadership.

This collection insists that Christian churches must reckon with their histories of harm against women. Many of us within the world of academic Christian theology recognized the challenge of being a woman in the profession and frequently analysed the workings of power within our own institutions and guilds. And yet we rarely registered this as traumatic in its effects. At some level, trauma theory provided an alternative route for us to make sense of the systems that continuously diminished us, often in ways that were difficult to see. The diagnostics of trauma provided a framework for not only theologizing suffering but for understanding the systems in which we did our theologizing. They provided another way of naming the deep roots of patriarchy.

I have emphasized the testimonial power of theology as witness to trauma in my own writings. But the essays in this volume provide a bolder public counterpoint to insidious Christian practices and modes of thought.

Many writings on trauma are not named under the rubric of theologies of trauma, and yet they must be counted as primary resources in this work. It is important to state that early theological works in trauma were written primarily by white, Christian, cis-gendered scholars from North America.[6] Classifying our theologies is a political act, so I urge us to continue to probe how classifying theology as 'trauma theology' functions. I am invested in keeping all theological efforts honest and responsive to our communities of concern and care. What does our theology do? Does it have the capacity to touch pain, or does it bypass it, move above it, or too readily sweep it up into overarching narratives of redemption and victory? Sharon Betcher reminds me that much in North American culture teaches us to turn away from pain and suffering.[7] It is our religious traditions, she says, that teach us to shore up our spiritual muscles to remain with what is most difficult. It is our spiritual mandate.

After a public presentation, a woman approached me and said: 'There is a lot of talk about fight/flight in trauma, but the missing component is freeze.' The teachings about the role of women in her religious tradition, she admitted, were instrumental to her freeze response. The admonitions about keeping silent and adhering to those in authority served to seal the experience, to lock it in, and to keep her stuck. Theology provided the authorizing glue that kept her from moving. There was no fight or flight. Only freeze.

Her testimony, and others like it, are central to this collection. This collection does something unique, as it brings together trauma and feminist theology in a more explicit way than previous works. The emergence of what is called 'trauma theology' begs the question of what is lost when the term 'feminist' drops out. Especially now, in this critical moment in which gendered violence is surging, and publicly sanctioned within some religious traditions, it is important not simply to underscore the mandate of liberation and flourishing but to own up to the ways in which Christian theology itself operates as a perpetrator of trauma. Several of the chapters in this book testify to what can be identified as religious trauma. Christian churches have not simply failed to witness trauma inflicted by others; they are sites of trauma's perpetration.

Each of the essays here are works of constructive theology, in that they continue to demand something from the texts and traditions of Christianity and insist that there is still something vital in engaging Christianity. These authors are confident in using personal narrative, expansive in their use of literatures, and strident in their critique of existing streams of authority. I often tell my students that I think they are more courageous than I am. I underscore this as I read these essays.

Notes

1 I would argue that Rebecca Chopp laid the groundwork for feminist theological engagements with trauma in several of her books, most notably *The Power to Speak*. Rebecca S. Chopp, *The Power to Speak: Feminism, Language, and God* (New York: Crossroad, 1989); Flora Keshgegian was the first to bring attention to historical trauma (the Armenian genocide) and Christian theology. Flora Keshgegian, *Redeeming Memories: A Theology of Healing and Transformation* (Nashville, TN: Abingdon Press, 2000). Serene Jones, *Trauma and Grace: Theology in a Ruptured World* (Louisville, KY: Westminster John Knox Press, 2009).

2 Judith Herman, *Trauma and Recovery: The Aftermath of Violence – From Domestic Abuse to Political Terror* (New York: Basic Books, 1992).

3 Rebecca Chopp, 'Theology and the Poetics of Testimony', in *Converging on Culture: Theologians in Dialogue with Cultural Analysis and Criticism*, ed. Delwin Brown, Sheila Greeve Davaney and Kathryn Tanner (Oxford: Oxford University Press, 2001), 56–70.

4 Cathy Caruth, *Trauma: Explorations in Memory* (Baltimore, MD: Johns Hopkins University Press, 1995), vii–viii. For the focus on ethics, see Cathy Caruth, 'Traumatic Awakenings: Freud, Lacan, and the Ethics of Memory', in *Unclaimed Experience: Trauma, Narrative, and History* (Baltimore, MD: Johns Hopkins University Press), 91–112.

5 Wendy Farley, *Tragic Vision and Divine Compassion: A Contemporary Theodicy* (Louisville, KY: Westminster John Knox Press, 1990). Although Farley does not draw specifically on trauma theory, her long-standing work on evil and radical suffering contributes to the literatures in theology and trauma. Farley stands out as someone who is more likely to claim that trauma is a dimension of human experience. Taking Simone Weil as a key resource, Farley positions radical suffering within a tragic framework, as does Kathleen Sands. See Kathleen Sands, *Escape from Paradise: Evil and Tragedy in Feminist Theology* (Minneapolis, MN: Fortress Press, 1994).

6 This raises important issues, certainly beyond the scope of this piece. For example, I consider Emilie Townes' edited volume, *A Troubling in My Soul* and M. Shawn Copeland's *Enfleshing Freedom* to be womanist responses to trauma. I would include Nancy Pineda Madrid's work here as well, although she speaks about social suffering instead of using the language of trauma. Their methodologies place contexts of suffering and trauma at their centre, although they do not work from within the framework of trauma theory. A question for this collection would be whether the use of trauma theory is contextually specific and, more pointedly, raced. Emilie Townes, ed., *A Troubling in my Soul: Womanist Perspectives on Evil and Suffering* (Maryknoll, NY: Orbis Books, 1993); M. Shawn Copeland, *Enfleshing Freedom: Body, Race, and Being* (Minneapolis, MN: Fortress Press, 2009); Nancy Pineda Madrid, *Suffering and Salvation in Ciudad Juarez* (Minneapolis, MN: Fortress Press, 2011).

7 Sharon Betcher, *Spirit and the Obligations of Social Flesh: A Secular Theology for the Global City* (New York: Fordham University Press, 2013).

Introduction

KAREN O'DONNELL AND KATIE CROSS

Feminist Trauma Theologies

These are weighty words, contested words, difficult words. Feminist.
Trauma. Theologies. None of these are uncontroversial words. These are
words that people resist. Words that are negated. Words that bring fear.
Ironically then, for us as editors, these are words that have brought hope
and have sustained and delighted us in the process of compiling this volume.
Why? Because they are words that have brought us into community; words
that have created friendships around the world; words that have opened up
difficult, powerful and significant conversations.

Both trauma and feminist theologies can be contested terms. This book
does not offer one single definition of trauma, or of what it might mean to
be feminist and *do* theology in a feminist way. And yet, all the chapters in
this book are engaged with the same kind of work.

While this is the first volume to attempt to articulate something explicit
in terms of feminist trauma theologies, we do not believe that we are the
first people to do work in trauma theology that is *feminist*. Serene Jones has
engaged with questions about the trauma of domestic abuse, the silencing
of women, the trauma of reproductive loss.[1] Shelly Rambo has written on
the trauma of Mary Magdalene, the trauma of the haemorrhaging woman,
and the questions of social justice in the aftermath of Hurricane Katrina.[2]
Phillis Isabella Sheppard has considered the lived religious experiences and
traumas of black women through a womanist psychoanalytic lens.[3] Jennifer
Beste undertook groundbreaking work around the impact of sexual abuse
on theologies of the divine.[4] However, even work in trauma theology that is
not specifically focused on women's experience of trauma is often a feminist
trauma theology.

We agree with Anne Phillips, Fran Porter and Nicola Slee when they argue
that it is 'obsolete and erroneous' to try to define a specifically feminist
research method or methodology, since feminists in all areas of research will
use any and all of the existing research methods.[5] However, it is certainly
true that many feminist scholars have embraced particular characteristics
in their work.[6] For Andrea Doucet and Natasha Mauthner, these include a
desire for research to be done *for* women and with women; methodological

innovation that challenges conventional ways of undertaking research; a concern with broader issues of social change and social justice; critical attention to power, knowing and representation; and explicitly reflexive and transparent work about the position, action and responsibility of the researcher.[7] These characteristics are present in many works on trauma theology, even where there is no explicit reference to feminist approaches.

Why should this be the case? It is certainly true that trauma theology and feminist theology are two sub-disciplines within theology that seem to be marked by a higher number of women scholars than other fields. Perhaps we should not be surprised by some overlap of approaches given that many women scholars are influenced by feminism, even if not explicitly feminist in their work. Nevertheless, it would seem that the connection between these two theologies is deeper than simply an overlap of personnel. Feminist theologians and trauma theologians are both seeking to understand people's experiences and to reshape theologies in the light of that experience, so that they do justice to the real lives of real people. Furthermore, both trauma theologians and feminist theologians recognize the way in which theologies have traditionally been constructed by those who are less likely to be women, and also by those less likely to experience trauma. Approaches that have a concern for social justice and pay critical attention to ways of knowing, questions of representation and modes of constructing knowledge are common to both feminist and trauma theologies.

If it is not possible to define a specifically *feminist* methodology in theology, what about trauma theology? In many ways, trauma is equally difficult to pin down, not least because there is a whole array of definitions of trauma from cultural, psychological, medical and theoretical perspectives. Many definitions of trauma make reference to the idea that trauma is a (missed) encounter with death.[8] This seems too prescriptive in some ways; a focus on events where one's very life is under threat negates the low-level, insidious and institutional forms of trauma that can be equally traumatic. It would seem preferable, therefore, to expand a definition of trauma to include violence that is physical, emotional and mental. In this respect, the definition of trauma given by feminist scholar Judith Herman, who offers a particularly gendered reading of the history of trauma, is most insightful:

> Psychological trauma is an affliction of the powerless. At the moment of trauma, the victim is rendered helpless by overwhelming force. When the force is that of nature, we speak of disasters. When the force is that of other human beings, we speak of atrocities. Traumatic events overwhelm the ordinary systems of care that give people a sense of control, connection, and meaning ... Traumatic events are extraordinary, not because they occur rarely, but rather because they overwhelm the ordinary human adaptations to life.[9]

Herman raises the issue of power and powerlessness alongside the over-whelming nature of trauma. Understanding trauma as that which overwhelms ordinary human adaptations to life expands our thinking about trauma and allows for the identification of a range of human experiences as traumatic.

Feminist trauma theologies can be understood, therefore, as theologies (in plurality) that seek to engage with experiences of trauma (that which overwhelms ordinary human adaptations to life) from a feminist approach that aims to pay critical attention to questions of power, knowing and representation as well as broader issues of social justice, with an eye to understanding the ways in which patriarchal societal structures both cause trauma and create the environment in which traumas can flourish. While the topics and methods represented in this volume vary widely, all of the chapters included here bear these characteristics in common.

A Question of Terminology

In many ways, then, the question of what *kind* of theology feminist trauma theologies are is a moot point. It would seem that if one cannot specific-ally define feminist trauma theologies (and identify them only by the broad characteristics they have in common) then attempting to affix a label to these theologies is useless. However, as the reader will see from the opening two chapters, the editors of this volume have situated this work in two similar and interrelated sub-disciplines of theological work.

The first type of theology we claim this work to be is in the mode of *constructive theology*. Outlined in more detail in Chapter 1, constructive theology is understood as an approach to theology that recognizes the con-structed nature of all theology and resists the 'systematization' of theology that seeks to create overarching narratives which ignore or exclude anything that does not 'fit'. Constructive theologians tend to follow a process that begins with the recognition of the insufficiency of a doctrine or theology, proceeds through a 'thick' description of the reasons for the insufficiency, and results in the construction or reconceptualization of theology in the light of this. This is certainly what many of the contributors to this volume are doing. The aim of a constructive theology is, as Paul Lakeland and Serene Jones note, not just to describe

> what theology has been; we are trying to understand and construct it in the present, to imagine what life-giving faith can be in today's world. In doing so, as with any construction job, we are attempting to build a viable structure. In our case, that structure is an inhabitable, beautiful, fruitful theology.[10]

Constructive theology aims to create something that takes the contemporary context and experience seriously as it builds a theology in which people can genuinely live and flourish.

The chapters contained in this volume might also be described as practical theology. Practical theology is a complex and varied discipline,[11] but in essence it seeks to engage critically with the dissonance between theology and lived reality. Several of the authors in this volume, such as Al McFadyen, Natalie Collins and Hilary Scarsella, deal with the ways in which theological doctrine has been used to coerce, control and subjugate women, becoming a source of trauma in and of itself. Richard Osmer suggests that practical theology is first descriptive; it asks what is happening. Practical theology is also interpretive, questioning 'why' the particular event or practice is taking place. Finally, it is pragmatic, and looks to respond in ways that are 'transformative'. This book brings to voice a number of lived experiences for the first time in print. Each chapter questions the deeper roots of women's trauma, drawing particular experiences into conversation with more widespread discussions about the pervasive nature of this kind of suffering. Don Browning adds that practical theology should involve:

> some description of the present situation, some critical theory about the ideal situation, and some understanding of the processes, spiritual forces, and technologies required to get from where we are to the future idea, no matter how fragmentarily and incompletely that idea can be realised.[12]

The project contained within these pages is, by nature, fragmented and incomplete. We cannot hope to encapsulate the suffering of people in its fullest extent in this book. We are bound by our inability to offer hope and solutions to every person who has encountered the traumas that are written about here. Nevertheless, this work is, in itself, a step towards a 'future idea'; a better and safer world. It is our hope that those who read it will feel able to join in transforming theology to make this a new reality. In this way, the volume might legitimately be described as a work of practical theology.

Why does it matter what *type* of theology feminist trauma theologies are? In lots of ways it does not matter at all. Theologians are still engaging in working in this area with no concern as to how it fits into traditional sub-categories of theology. And we recognize that any division within theology, and indeed within academic fields in general, is entirely artificial in the first place. However, there is still some value in thinking about where in the theological milieu this work might fit. Arguing that this work is both constructive and practical theology allows us to articulate a method in undertaking such work and also provides some legitimization for a field of theological research that some would consider to be 'forced' and 'giving culture too much power'.[13] Placing this work in the context of constructive and practical theology puts the contributors to this volume into community with a range of scholars with whom we share much in common.

Body, Scripture and Church in Critical Perspective

This book has the subheading Body, Scripture and Church in Critical Perspective. The volume itself is not, however, divided into these three sections. Rather, we have divided the chapters into four groups. The first group focuses on methods in feminist trauma theologies. The second is on violence against women (although, interestingly, almost all of the chapters could have gone into this section). The third group focuses on Christian communities and trauma, while the fourth section considers the modes of post-traumatic remaking with which the trauma survivor might engage.

While we have already emphasized the wide range of approaches, topics and conclusions that the contributors have brought, each and every chapter in this volume considers the body, scripture and the church in critical perspective. Indeed, critiquing the ways in which bodies, scriptures and Christian communities inflict, experience and respond to trauma is a key characteristic of feminist trauma theologies. It is in this way that these theologians raise questions of social justice and critique modes of power, authority, knowing and representation in the light of the experience of trauma.

Of course, some of these chapters engage in this critical work in very explicit ways. Kirsi Cobb's chapter takes us deep into the Scriptures in her reading of Hosea in the light of intimate partner violence. Leah Robinson critically reflects on the Church in her chapter on traumatic ordination theology. Hilary Scarsella, Manon Ceridwen James and Al McFadyen all critically reflect on the body and bodily experience of trauma in their chapters focused on violence against women. But these chapters are not devoid of the other critical perspectives too. For how can one talk of intimate partner violence and Scripture without reflecting on the bodily experience of trauma and the inability of the Church to develop a robust rejection of such behaviour? Or to think about ordination without considering the problematic nature of women's bodies in the light of Scriptures? Or to write about violence against women without considering the Scriptures and church contexts that allow such interpretations of Scripture and behaviour to go unchallenged? Such feminist trauma theologies are holistic theologies. Critical perspectives on the body, the Scriptures and the Church go hand in hand.

Time

In many ways, the time is right for this volume. In the last few years, society – including the Church (in some cases) – has woken up to the pervasive trauma experienced by women. The rise of the #MeToo movement, Black Lives Matter, #ChurchToo and #MosqueToo, post-conflict PTSD, child sexual abuse revelations (including those in the Church), have all contributed to an increased recognition of the extent of trauma experienced in ordinary twenty-first-century life. Trauma is not the experience of the few, but of the many.

So, this volume is timely. Time is a central concept in trauma theory. It is one of a number of elements that a traumatized person experiences as 'shattered' or 'disrupted' in the experience of trauma. Symptoms of PTSD are often reflections of this disruption of time so that the traumatized person finds themselves experiencing flashbacks, hallucinations and nightmares in which the past (often the distorted memory of the traumatic events) tries to repeatedly intrude on the present. The chapters in this volume are similarly, in most cases, expressions of this past continuing to press into the present as the theologians writing them try to make sense of these experiences in the light of their theological convictions and knowledge.

This book is, of course, not the last word on feminist trauma theologies, but the opening of a conversation that we hope will continue for many years. Theology has a reputation for being a long way behind trends in other academic disciplines, and even further behind theological responses to horrific events. As theologians, we need to reduce the distance between this traumatic past that wants to keep pressing forward, and the present into which it makes itself known. Practical and constructive theologies are interested in the present contexts and experiences, so turning our attention to trauma in a timely way is important.

Reading and Flourishing

This volume is a timely contribution to the discourse of trauma theology, beginning to articulate the ways in which feminist scholars might (and indeed do) work in trauma theology in deliberately and markedly feminist ways, and how trauma theologians might engage with insights and perspectives from feminist theology in the contemporary context. We recognize that trauma theology is often done 'on the spot' in the midst of suffering and that, for some, hope is an intangible and unreachable goal. At the same time, we hope that this volume brings life and hope to those who have experienced trauma and those who work with traumatized people, and to an academic discourse that is still finding its feet and establishing itself. We believe that feminist trauma theologies are critical and vital in the twenty-first century if we are to build a theology that brings life and space for people to flourish.

Special Thanks

While we are grateful to all the authors who contributed chapters to this volume, we have a particular thanks to give to the following authors: Hilary Jerome Scarsella, Kirsi Cobb, Leah Robinson, Natalie Collins,

Santiago Piñón and Esther McIntosh. Not only are their chapters brilliant contributions to the discourse of feminist trauma theologies, but they also wrote candidly about their own experiences of trauma. Their theology came from the place where it hurts. Thank you.

Notes

1 Serene Jones, *Trauma and Grace: Theology in a Ruptured World* (Louisville, KY: Westminster John Knox Press, 2009).

2 Shelly Rambo, *Spirit and Trauma: A Theology of Remaining* (Louisville, KY: Westminster John Knox Press, 2010); Shelly Rambo, 'Trauma and Faith: Reading the Narrative of the Hemorrhaging Woman', *International Journal of Practical Theology* 13, 2 (2010), 1–25; Shelly Rambo, 'Between Death and Life: Trauma, Divine Love, and the Witness of Mary Magdalene', *Studies in Christian Ethics* 18 (2005), 7–21.

3 Phillis Isabella Sheppard, *Self, Culture, and Others in Womanist Practical Theology* (New York: Palgrave Macmillan, 2011).

4 Jennifer Erin Beste, *God and the Victim: Traumatic Intrusions on Grace and Freedom* (Oxford: Oxford University Press, 2008).

5 Anne Phillips, Fran Porter and Nicola Slee, 'Introduction', in *Researching Female Faith: Qualitative Research Methods*, ed. Nicola Slee, Fran Porter and Anne Phillips (London and New York: Routledge, 2018), 6.

6 Andrea Doucet and Natasha S. Mauthner, 'Feminist Methodologies and Epistemology', in *21st Century Sociology: A Reference Handbook*, vol. 2, ed. Clifton D. Bryant and Dennis L. Peck (Thousand Oaks, CA: Sage, 2007), 40.

7 Doucet and Mauthner, 'Feminist Methodologies', 40–1.

8 See, for example, Cathy Caruth, *Unclaimed Experience: Trauma, Narrative, and History* (Baltimore, MD: The Johns Hopkins University Press, 1996).

9 Judith Herman, *Trauma and Recovery: From Domestic Abuse to Political Terror* (London: Pandora, 2001), 33.

10 Paul Lakefield and Serene Jones, eds, *Constructive Theology: A Contemporary Approach to Classical Themes* (Minneapolis, MN: Fortress Press, 2005), 1.

11 See Bonnie Miller-McLemore, 'Five Misunderstandings about Practical Theology', *International Journal of Practical Theology* 16, no. 1 (2012); Eric Stoddart, *Advancing Practical Theology: Critical Discipleship for Disturbing Times* (London: SCM Press, 2014); Richard Osmer, 'Practical Theology: A Current International Perspective', *HTS Teologiese Studies/Theological Studies* 67, no. 2 (2011).

12 Don Browning, 'Practical Theology and Political Theology', *Theology Today* 42, no. 10 (1985), 20.

13 Both comments that the editors have received from students in introducing them to this work.

How to Read This Volume

The editors of this volume have read these chapters on multiple occasions in the process of compiling the manuscript and each time have been aware of the powerful and profound impact these chapters can have upon the reader. As individual readers we have had to seek out sustainable and sustaining practices of self-care and support each other as we worked through the volume. It goes without saying that this volume comes, of course, with multiple trigger warnings, including:

- domestic violence
- coercive control
- stillbirth and death of a child
- sexual abuse
- spiritual abuse
- rape
- physical violence
- murder
- death of a parent
- death.

Despite this, or perhaps because of it, we think this volume is vital reading. Therefore, we want to encourage readers to find ways of engaging with this research that help them to flourish.

Self-care

We suggest investing in practices of self-care around reading that help you to process these chapters. Practices of self-care should be intentional and will, to some extent, be individual to each reader. However, we suggest that such practices are useful for all people (and probably for all texts – certainly those focused on trauma!), regardless of how you approach this volume. For example, you might find it easier to read just one chapter at a time and take some time away from the volume in between. You may wish to develop journalling or creative practices that help to work through these chapters and express some of the intense emotions that might accompany reading this volume.

Reading in Community

We also suggest that this book might be one that is best read in community. We, as editors, chose to work on this book together in partnership. We chose to make it an edited volume because we felt it was important this was a book created in community. It would make sense to read it in community too. This might be as simple as reading it with a friend and planning in time to talk about the various chapters as you do. But you might like to read this in a feminist reading group, with the opportunity to share your experiences with other people and hear their perspectives on the various chapters. There is much advice online about setting up such reading groups, but we would advise a few starting points:

- Make it clear what you are going to read and why. What is the aim of this group?
- Plan ahead to establish momentum.
- Plan to ask questions that mean everyone gets to say something early on.
- Set some group rules for your discussion.
- Find an accessible venue and be clear about accessibility. Why not meet at a women-owned business and support other women as you get reading!
- Pay attention to different perspectives and make sure there is a variety of voices in your group (if you only hear from one kind of person, you only get one kind of perspective).
- Start putting together a To Be Read list (a quick look at the footnotes and references in this volume will give you many other great books to read) and think about what you will read next.

Guided Reading Questions

Below are some guided reading questions that may support pedagogical or reading group discussions about this volume. These are suitable for reading individual chapters, or the volume as a whole.

What does 'trauma' look like in this volume (or particular chapter)?
- Does it bear any common themes or characteristics?
- How is it experienced in different contexts or situations?

Discuss the stories told in this volume, or in the chapter that you have just read.
- Why is it important that these stories are told?
- Is there a particular story or narrative that stood out to you? Why?

Where is God in this/these chapter(s)? What is the role of God in trauma theology?

Is there a particular theological move that an author in the volume or chapter makes that captures your imagination?
• What does the author do? What does this achieve? What impact does this have?

What is the role of Scripture in this/these chapter(s)?
• How is the Bible used and abused?
• Could the Bible be described as a 'tool of trauma' according to the lived experiences contained in these chapters? Could it be a source of redemption?

How is the Church represented in this/these chapter(s)?
• In what ways does the Church contribute to trauma?
• Can the Church be a place of refuge or safety for those who have experienced trauma?
• Does the book cause you to think about the Church differently?

What might post-traumatic remaking look like in the context of a Christian community or church? What theological resources might be beneficial in considering post-traumatic remaking?

PART I

Method in Feminist Trauma Theologies

I

The Voices of the Marys:
Towards a Method in
Feminist Trauma Theologies

KAREN O'DONNELL

Introduction

In 2016 I attended the annual conference of the Society for the Study of Theology at Durham University in the UK. One of the keynote speakers was Michelle Gonzalez Maldonado from the University of Miami, speaking on the topic 'Redeeming Race: A Theological Construction of Racialized Humanity'.[1] While the whole paper she gave was outstanding and provocative, in the discussion afterwards she said that she felt she had to do theology from the place where it hurts, that this was the theology that mattered. Her comment struck a chord in me. In the intervening years, I have mentioned this comment repeatedly as a description of the kind of theological work I am interested in and that excites me. Trauma and the experience of work with those who have been traumatized is, for me, the place where it hurts. Consequently, it is from this place that I undertake my theological work.

Theological work in the area of trauma is both a fascinating and vital area to work in. Such work attempts to overcome the tendency (now, thankfully, becoming less common) to elide the body from theological exploration. Systematic theologies have, at times, sought to abstract the body and ignore the bodily sources that have given it life. Meredith Minister, in her powerful work on the embodied God, notes:

> While the role of materiality in theological formation is increasingly recognised in the postmodern academy, it is not a given for all theologians ... Because theology comes from bodies in material contexts, assuming a disembodied theology threatens violence against the bodies that have to be excised in order to name the disembodied God.[2]

Trauma theologies, including feminist trauma theologies, take bodily experience seriously as both worthy of theological exploration and as sites of theological construction.

I wanted to contribute a chapter on method in feminist trauma theologies to this volume for a number of reasons. First, I am increasingly convinced that establishing method is important, especially in constructive theologies like feminist trauma theologies, not to impose a set of parameters on those engaged in such work, but rather to give such work a recognizable shape and to ensure that such work is not dismissed as lightweight and unrigorous. If one wants to break the rules, one must know what rules one is breaking and why. Second, there has been 20 years-worth of work done in the field of trauma theology, much of it by feminist theologians. It is rigorous, serious and powerful work. Each theologian undertaking such work has formed an implicit methodology to give shape to their work. I wanted to use this contribution to draw those methodologies together in proposing a broad outline for a method in feminist trauma theologies.

I begin by making the case for feminist trauma theologies to be considered under the umbrella term of constructive theologies, which helps determine the goals of such theological scholarship, before turning my attention to the significance of method and the varieties of methods employed in trauma theologies. In exploring a specifically feminist approach to trauma theology, I draw on the narratives of the various women named Mary in the New Testament (Mary of Clopas, Mary sister of Lazarus, Mary Magdalene and Mary, Jesus' mother) as women whose stories are layered in trauma experiences. These multiple Marian vignettes help to demonstrate the key characteristics of feminist trauma theologies and, in dialogue with methods from constructive theology and the study of spirituality, help to form my proposed method in the study of feminist trauma theologies.

Feminist and Trauma Theologies as Constructive Theology

I contend that feminist theology and trauma theology can both be considered to be constructive theologies. While scholars have a variety of ways of approaching both of these topics – and method, of course, is always connected to the goals of a piece of research – broadly speaking, both of these theologies are building something new. While 'method' in this area of theology is not necessarily well defined, the work of Susannah Cornwall – constructive theologian at the University of Exeter – is most useful. In her recent book, *Un/Familiar Theology: Reconceiving Sex, Reproduction and Generativity*, Cornwall notes:

> This book is not about the ethics of reproductive interventions – such as IVF, ICSI and embryo screening – or related technologies for aiding conception. Rather, it is about the ways in which Christian *theological* conceptions of institutions such as marriage, family, parenting and reproduction have changed and are changing, and about what resources exist within and beyond the tradition to understand these changes not as a

raging tide to be turned back, but as in continuity with goods deeply embedded in the collection of theologies concerned with the Christian faith.[3]

While this paragraph is intended as a clarificatory introduction to the text, making the scope of the work clear, Cornwall actually provides an insight into the characteristics of constructive theology in this brief paragraph. From this, I extract four principles of constructive theology: a recognition of change or development taking place; a mandate to draw on resources both within and beyond the Christian tradition; an identification of a multitude of theolog*ies*; and finally the construction of a theology that is in continuity with the goods deeply embedded in the tradition of Christian faith.

These four principles are at work in both feminist and trauma-informed approaches to theology. In both cases, there is a recognition that something has changed, that traditional theological narrative is insufficient for the demands of the twenty-first century, when it comes to the experience of women or the experience of those who have been traumatized. From this recognition, there comes a need to draw on resources wider than traditional theology. So feminist theology is an interdisciplinary endeavour that draws on work in gender studies, psychology, sociology, anthropology, economics, politics, to name but a few. Similarly, trauma theologians turn to neuroscience, psychology, trauma studies, literary theory, personal narratives – all expanding the scope of the theological work undertaken. This leads, almost inevitably, to an identification of a multitude of theologies (plural). There is no one feminist theology, just as there is no single trauma theology. These constructive theologies resist systematization of theology into completed accounts. But these theologies always hold to the goods that are deeply embedded in the rich Christian tradition, often rediscovering ancient ways of being or doing, offering deep insights into established truth-claims.

Given the constructive nature of these two theologies (feminist and trauma) in their singular instances, it makes sense to consider feminist trauma theologies (that is, specifically feminist approaches to trauma theology) to be constructive theologies also. However, as the reader will see, not all the contributors to this volume take a constructive approach to this work! There is room for multiple theologies.

Perhaps the most sustained reflection on constructive theology and the methods theologians use when undertaking such theology, has been carried out by Jason A. Wyman. Wyman has focused on the work of the Workgroup on Constructive Theology, which was founded in 1975 at Vanderbilt University and has undergone a number of instantiations since then. He notes of this kind of theology:

> Constructive Christian theology acknowledges the constitutive discursive role theologians play in constructing Christianity, rather than supposing that theology attempts to describe an objective deposit of religious truth, as systematic and dogmatic theology tend to do. It is interdisciplinary in

its approach and is employed toward progressive, social justice ends. It differs from systematic and dogmatic theology both in its method and aims.[4]

Constructive theology stands in opposition to systematic theology. This is a bold statement to make, but at the heart of constructive theology is a rejection of the idea that there can be a 'system' of theology that is complete, finished, and stands for all time. Constructive theology is perpetually ongoing.[5] Furthermore, while constructive theology admires liberal theology and takes liberationist critiques of theology seriously, it cannot be easily aligned with these methods of theology either. However, constructive theologians do not reject such works out of hand, but rather engage with it as a product of its time, and as one among many of the goods embedded in the Christian tradition.

Before moving on to briefly consider why on earth method matters in the first place, I want to draw attention to the aims of some of these constructive theologians, and indeed my own aims, in consciously constructing theology along these lines.

> We are not interested in merely describing what theology has been; we are trying to understand and construct it in the present, to imagine what life-giving faith can be in today's world. In doing so, as with any construction job, we are attempting to build a viable structure. In our case, that structure is an inhabitable, beautiful, fruitful theology.[6]

Feminist trauma theologies are not a description of what theology has been, but are an attempt to imagine what life-giving faith can be in today's world. It is an attempt to build theologies that are fruitful, beautiful and ones in which one can live.

Method Matters

Like a multitude of doctoral students before me, I can vividly recall despairing over writing my methodology for my thesis. I can remember the frustration I felt at having to find a set of rules to play by, compounded by the fact that I was working in the field of trauma theology and no one had, at that point, articulated a clear method for doing such research. Or rather, each trauma theologian I read seemed to have a different way of approaching the field.

I have since become convinced of the importance of understanding methodology both in terms of my own work and the way in which I teach my students. Method matters. It is not only an essential starting point for any new research undertaken in a particular field (even if the researcher ultimately chooses to disregard aspects of method in favour of forging their own path), but also one of the ways in which the scholar ensures the validity and usefulness of their research.

I have positioned trauma theology as a form of constructive theology that gives, as we shall see, access into a particular type of theological method. But this is not the only mode in which trauma theology can be undertaken (as we demonstrated in the Introduction to this volume), nor is it a hard and fast rule for the way in which such research might be done. Methodology, in this area of theology, is the beginning point and provides the broad parameters. It is not the imposition upon the researcher of unbreakable rules. One must, however, know what the expected conventions of a discipline are, before one decides to move beyond them. A. K. M. Adam writes of approaches to disciplinary boundaries and conventions:

> Responsible border crossers follow the laws of the country into which they have entered, so they will work hard to make their interpretations acceptable to the inhabitants of each discursive world they visit; they will study their analytic psychology or their psychoanalytic theory diligently, so that their incursions into this alien discourse meet with the approval of local officials. Other border crossers may reason that they are no more bound to local laws than to the laws that bind biblical interpreters to historical inquiries; they will pay less regard to the authority of Freud or Marx and more to the effects one can bring about with an unauthorized version of their theories. These wanton transgressors need observe no criteria other than the exhilarating thrill of an interpretive tour de force.[7]

Although he is writing in the context of biblical studies, his approach to the question of method and discipline is nonetheless widely applicable. In interdisciplinary work such as feminist trauma theologies, one can choose to follow the conventions or to forge one's own path. Either way, one must know which conventions and methods one is either working with or rejecting.

The first section of this volume is given over to a discussion of method in relation to feminist trauma theologies, as is the first section of this chapter. Why does method matter so much? It is more than a merely convenient beginning point for introducing this theological work. Reflection on method – thinking about how one might undertake *doing* theology – is vital (and not just for feminist trauma theologies). The establishment of method is the attempt to ensure the validity and ultimately the fruitfulness of the research being undertaken.[8]

Methods in Trauma Theology

Trauma theology, relatively nascent a field as it is, has already seen a variety of methods employed in the *doing* of such theology. For example, Jennifer Beste uses a qualitative method in exploring post-traumatic theologies of sexual abuse victims, drawing interviews with trauma survivors into dialogue with the theology of Karl Rahner.[9] Serene Jones opts for a mix of auto-ethnographic, historical and literary methods in her work on trauma and grace.[10] Carrie Doehring is one of the few theologians interested in trauma who has used a quantitative method (analysing statistics) in her work on post-traumatic representations of God.[11] Marcus Pound opts for a critical theory approach to trauma,[12] whereas Dirk Lange employs a mix of historical and literary criticism in shaping a theology of trauma.[13] There is room within trauma theology for a wide range of methodologies and approaches, and method is always influenced by the aim of the particular research being considered. What is often common among these theologians is that they are attempting to construct something new. More recent work in trauma theology has moved away from specifically historical or literary methods and towards a process that has more in common with constructive theology.[14] Increasingly, trauma theology seems to begin with a historical reflection (on a doctrine, an event, a figure), broaden out into critical analysis and evaluation, before highlighting the contemporary issues faced as construction of new and life-giving theology is offered.

The Marys and Characteristics of Feminist Method

Why, then, have I turned to the relatively obscure characters of the Marys in the New Testament? I am convinced, as will already be apparent, that constructive theology offers a useful methodological approach to *doing* feminist trauma theologies. The space for a plurality of theologies within this mode of research allows a variety of starting points in exploring theologies of trauma or post-traumatic theologies. I have previously explored such theologies from the twin heartlands of trauma – bodies and memory – in my book *Broken Bodies: The Eucharist, Mary and the Body in Trauma Theology*.[15] But here I want to offer a distinctly feminist approach to trauma theology. My beginning point, the historical reflection that will provide the foundations for constructing a trauma theology, is the often-neglected traumatized voices of the women named Mary in the Gospels. These are Mary the mother of Jesus, Mary Magdalene, Mary the sister of Lazarus and Martha, and Mary the wife of Clopas (who was also Jesus' aunt). These are women who have become pregnant without intercourse (which I have not described as rape, but have, nonetheless, previously argued that the Annunciation–Incarnation event is a traumatic experience[16]); who have witnessed the brutal murder of her son, her nephew, her great friend; who experienced the death of her brother when she knew he could have been saved. These are women who are interrupted, disbelieved, rebuked for being emotional, disdained for their anger, and who are afraid, but who persisted. As I write this list, I am reminded of the recent testimony of Christine Blasey Ford in the Brett Kavanaugh Supreme Court justice nominations, who was interrupted, disbelieved, rebuked, disdained and afraid in front of the confirmation committee, and indeed the wider world. Blasey Ford began her testimony by saying that she was standing before the committee not because she wanted to, she admitted, 'I am terrified.'[17] Similarly, in the confirmation of Jeff Sessions as Attorney General of the United States, the phrase 'nevertheless, she persisted' was used to silence Senator Elizabeth Warren's objections to Sessions's confirmation on the grounds of his disgraceful record on civil rights issues.[18] The voices of these Mary characters are the voices of traumatized women throughout history. What better starting point for feminist trauma theologies than the experiences and words of these women?

Marian Vignettes

I will take each of these four characters in turn and explore both their experience and their post-traumatic voice (or lack thereof) in order of increasing textual significance in the Gospel writings, beginning first with Mary the wife of Clopas. This Mary is only mentioned by name in John 19.25,[19] where she is identified as being one of the women standing at the foot of the cross at the crucifixion of Jesus, along with Mary the mother of Jesus and Mary Magdalene (both of whom we will consider later). Some interpretations also consider her to be the 'other' Mary mentioned in the Gospel of Matthew (28.1–10) who goes with Mary Magdalene to visit Jesus' tomb. And while there is some discussion as to whether she is Jesus' paternal aunt, his maternal aunt, his cousin or his sister, we can certainly conclude that she is a close relative of Jesus and one whose care and love for him and his family brought her first to an execution and then to a graveside. This Mary is never alone but always seen with other women. Perhaps we can imagine her as an older woman who supports her sisters through difficult times; a strong shoulder to lean on; a practical woman who knows when she is needed. Though she witnesses the murder of her relative on bogus charges, we do not hear of her distress. She is silent in the Gospels, but she is there.

The second Mary to which we turn is Mary the sister of Martha and Lazarus. The raising of Lazarus from the dead, while a familiar narrative, is mentioned only in John's Gospel. Here Mary is introduced as 'the one who anointed the Lord with perfume and wiped his feet with her hair' (John 11.2), which is significant as the anointing account comes *after* the resurrection account. Had her extravagant gesture (rather than her status as friend or sister) already become her primary identifier by the time John's Gospel was written? Jesus arrived four days after Lazarus died, coming too late to save him. We might imagine Mary to be heartbroken in her grief for the death of her brother, and furious that Jesus (who loved her) had not come in time. She believed he could have saved Lazarus. Mary refuses to come out to meet Jesus (John 11.20). When she does go to see him, she falls to the floor and weeps, rebuking Jesus with the words 'Lord, if you had been here, my brother would not have died' (John 11.32). Her tears disturbed Jesus' spirit and deeply moved him, and so he raised Lazarus back to life.

The writer of the Gospel of John identifies this Mary as the woman who anoints the feet of Jesus with extravagant perfume, wiping his feet with her hair (John 12.3). Although this event is recorded by all four Evangelists (Matthew 26.6–13; Mark 14.3–9; Luke 7.36–50; John 12.1–8), only the Johannine writer names her as Mary and connects her to Lazarus and Martha. While anointing is not an unusual event in Scripture, the use of hair to wipe away the excess perfume is particularly distinctive. Teresa Hornsby notes that there is no parallel in literature contemporary to or preceding the Gospels of hair being used in this manner.[20] She cites it as an act undertaken 'in defiance of all convention', drawing parallels with similar parodies in the later text of Petronius' *Satyricon* (AD 61).[21]

The woman who anoints Jesus with perfume is sometimes assumed to be Mary Magdalene. There is no textual evidence to support this. Nonetheless, Mary Magdalene is a perennially popular figure in the Gospels. One of Jesus' followers and the first evangelist who, upon meeting the risen Jesus, tells the other disciples, 'He is not here; for he has been raised!' (Matthew 28.6), Mary stands with the other women at the foot of the cross and watches her great friend being executed. Various Gospel accounts tell how she went with Mary the mother of Jesus or the other Mary to Jesus' tomb to anoint his body for burial. Indeed, Mary Magdalene is almost always seen in the inter-generational company of other women. Furthermore, the writer of John notes that she stands outside the tomb weeping.

It is, however, the *voice* of Mary Magdalene that I am most interested in for the purposes of this chapter, particularly her post-traumatic voice. If, once again, we might imagine this woman, we might imagine a loyal friend; a devoted follower who loved Jesus. We might imagine a woman who is broken at seeing her friend, the one whom she followed, murdered in such a brutal fashion. How can witnessing something like that not be traumatizing? And yet, in her post-traumatic utterances, she is not believed. No one believes her when she tells them her dear friend is no longer dead but is, somehow, risen from the dead! Why would she make up such a story, when it could so easily be discredited? And why would the group of people she had spent so much time with refuse to believe her? The same questions are asked by rape victims all the time.

The final Mary to which we turn is the most well known – Mary the mother of Jesus. Her story, as we see it in the Gospels, turns on two traumatic events. At the beginning of the narrative, Mary finds herself suddenly, unexpectedly, complicatedly and problematically pregnant. I do not argue, as some have done, that Mary was raped[22] (either divinely or humanly) as her *fiat* is consent to the work of God within her. But nonetheless, we can only imagine that this experience was traumatic for her. In the aftermath of this first traumatic event, the author of Luke constructs the words of the Magnificat on the lips of Mary. In these verses Mary offers a testimony to the work of God within her.

> 'My soul magnifies the Lord
> and my spirit rejoices in God my Saviour,
> for he has regarded the low estate of his handmaiden.
> For behold, henceforth all generations will call me blessed;
> for he who is mighty has done great things for me,
> and holy is his name.
> And his mercy is on those who fear him
> from generation to generation.
> He has shown strength in his arm,
> he has scattered the proud in the imagination of their hearts,
> he has put down the mighty from their thrones
> and exalted those of low degree;
> he has filled the hungry with good things,
> and the rich he has sent empty away.
> He has helped his servant Israel,
> in remembrance of his mercy,
> as he spoke to our fathers,
> to Abraham and to his posterity for ever.' (Luke 1.46–55, RSV)

These familiar words – sung every day at Evensong, lisped out on the lips of primary school children each December – are the construction of Mary's testimony post-trauma. In the mode of post-traumatic remaking, she constructs a narrative that allows her to make sense of her experience and move forward with it. The Magnificat is a profoundly political statement; in the first instance, it is a radical declaration of the mode of God's interaction with the world, in which God is on the side of the poor and oppressed. In this sense, the selection of this text for daily recitation at evening prayer is a revolutionary act. Each day it declares God's intention to disrupt the established order. Singing it daily reminds believers that God is a God of revolution. Furthermore, the Magnificat as Mary's (post-traumatic) testimony is at once private, public and political. Researchers who have worked with refugees expressing their own trauma narratives note that, in the telling of their story, the narrative of trauma becomes a testimony.[23] Testimony, in this context, 'contains both connotations of something subjective or private, and of something objective, judicial, or political'.[24] The second part of the Magnificat takes on this political and juridical flavour of public testimony; Mary reframes her trauma as an experience in which the justice of God is being made known.[25] Joel Green notes:

> It is difficult to imagine a more powerful reflection on the significance of the coming of Jesus than Mary's prophetic words in Luke 1.46–55, the Magnificat or Mary's Song. Images of the divine warrior and gracious God coalesce in this celebration of the advent of salvation in Jesus. Here, Mary identified the shape of Israel's restoration as it will be narrated in the words and deeds of Jesus in subsequent chapters, and invites others, her audience in and outside the narrative to make their home in this redemptive vision.[26]

The meaning of this traumatic event has been reframed into public, political and judicial terms and now sits in both the private, confessional sphere and in the public, political realm. Mary's words, in response to the trauma of the Annunciation–Incarnation event, both reshape her framing of that event and articulate a vision of social justice.

Some 30 years later, Mary watches as the child she rejoiced in God for is nailed to a cross and executed. She stood at the foot of the cross with her female friends and relatives, perhaps with only one male companion from the band that had followed her son so fervently. This beloved disciple is instructed to care for Mary after Jesus' death (John 19.25–26). A couple of days later, still with her female companions, Mary goes to prepare the body of her son for his burial (Mark 16.1–8). Upon entering the tomb:

> They saw a young man sitting on the right side, dressed in a white robe; and they were amazed. And he said to them, 'Do not be amazed; you seek Jesus of Nazareth, who was crucified. He has risen, he is not here; see the place where they laid him. But go, tell his disciples and Peter that he is going before you to Galilee; there you will see him, as he told you.' And they went out and fled from the tomb; for trembling and astonishment had come upon them; and they said nothing to anyone for they were afraid. (Mark 16.5–8, RSV)

Because we know the end of this narrative, it is easy to overlook the very real emotions these women (including Mary the mother of Jesus) experienced. Because we know the figure is a post-resurrection Jesus or an angel, we forget the fear and distress that this mother must have felt upon going to the tomb of her son in the first place, and then finding the grave disturbed, strange figures there, no body and a seemingly impossible statement. Mary does not speak in this episode, so we can only imagine her distress and horror at the sight she witnesses. Perhaps we can imagine that, in this experience, her trauma renders her silent.

Features of Feminist Trauma Theologies

Sometimes they speak, and sometimes they are silent, but the 'voices' of the Marys (whether spoken or silent) speak volumes about the nature of feminist trauma theologies and point theologians towards a method; how do we *do* feminist trauma theologies? In this section, I highlight five aspects of feminist trauma theologies, exploring each in turn, before directing our attention towards a resulting method.

Drawing on the 'voices' of the Marys, it is clear that feminist trauma theologies begin from a place of honest confrontation with God. We see this in Mary's rebuke of Jesus for failing to come quickly enough to save her brother. We see it in Mary's question of God at the Annunciation–Incarnation event when she asks, 'How can this be?' (Luke 1.34). A feminist trauma theology is not afraid to challenge God, to express disappointment, fury, disbelief at the turn of events. None of these women immediately smile beatifically and trot out toxic[27] verses like Jeremiah 29.11 or Romans 8.28 – both verses that are abused and used, often in a church context, to minimize an individual's experience of pain and trauma. Like the psalmist before them, these women are not afraid to question God and to ask God, through tears and rage, how God could let this happen. These feminist trauma theologies are constructed as they overcome fear and refuse to be silent, passive or frightened any more. Even as they are terrified. Once again, I am reminded of the testimony of Christine Blasey Ford who began her testimony before the Supreme Court Confirmation Committee with the words, 'I am not here today because I want to be. I am terrified.'[28] Such words could be the beginning of many feminist trauma theologies. Honest and terrified and necessary.

A second key feature of these feminist trauma theologies is that they are porous. They allow space for divine interruption into faith, experience and theology. In so many of the stories of the Marys we encountered in the previous section, these women experience a divine interruption. Jesus interrupts their despair, their conversation, their experience, in order to change the trajectory or alter the perspective. Feminist trauma theologies, like all constructive theologies, are not complete and finished systems of theology, but rather are open, porous, unfinished theologies that hold to the goods of Christian tradition, while allowing space for something new to be spoken.

The third striking feature of these feminist trauma theologies is the way in which such theologies construct narratives that have the flavour of testimony and function in the public and political spheres of life. One only has to cast an eye down the content list of this volume to note that so many of these feminist trauma theologies draw from the experience of the author. Experience is one of the hallmarks of the feminist approach. Furthermore, as the contents of this volume also demonstrate, the feminist trauma theologies on offer here cannot be consigned to the realm of a private faith or experience, but rather function in the public (and often political) sphere.

The consequence of taking trauma seriously in the theological context, not least feminist accounts of trauma, is an impact that reaches far beyond the personal. Such theologies call for radical changes in the way we listen to those who are traumatized, particularly women, but also other vulnerable and marginalized people groups. Such theologies call for a radical over-throw of the status quo and a rejection of toxic cultures that do not care for all people, but rather privilege the experience and testimony of only those in and with power.

The fourth characteristic of feminist trauma theologies is that they, like the Marys in the vignettes, defy convention and seek to disrupt the estab-lished order. Like Mary the sister of Lazarus, who wiped oil from the feet of Jesus with her hair, these theologies are not interested in the 'done' thing or the usual way of behaving. Rather, they are concerned with the 'right' thing as expression of their focus on social justice and theologies that allow people to flourish. Like Mary the mother of Jesus, who declares the divine disruption of the established order, these feminist trauma theologies declare the concern of God for the vulnerable and the traumatized. These theologies are, therefore, unsettling and unsettlers of tradition.

The final element that I want to highlight from these various Marian vignettes that I am using to characterize feminist trauma theologies is the sense of community. These women are rarely alone, but almost always in the company of other women. They stand shoulder to shoulder at the foot of the cross. They go together to anoint Jesus' body at the tomb. They value sisterhood (Mary and Martha) and extended family (Mary, Elizabeth, Mary of Clopas) and the wider group of Jesus' disciples. Their testimonies, their voices, are spoken in community. This community element is significant and is one reason why this book is edited by two women rather than one, and why this is an edited volume rather than a single-authored monograph. This kind of theology is a community endeavour.

The voices of the Marys, these New Testament women, offer some key concepts that might inform our approach to feminist trauma theologies. They begin from an honest confrontation with God and the overcoming of fear. They are porous and incomplete, allowing space for divine interrup-tion. They construct narratives that function as public, political testimony. They defy and disrupt tradition and the established orders of things. This construction is undertaken in community.

A Proposed Method

For the last 20 or so years (since the late 1990s), theologians interested in trauma have been engaging its study without necessarily articulating a defined method. This does not, of course, mean that they were not utilizing methodologies in trauma theology. Like all constructive theologies, a specific method, relevant to each instantiation of trauma theology, can be difficult to pin down. However, with the benefit of 20 years' worth of work in the area, alongside contemporary reflection on method in constructive theology more broadly, as well as in cogent sub-disciplines such as the study of spirituality, it is possible to begin to articulate a method in feminist trauma theologies.

As I noted earlier, in reflecting on the history of the Workgroup on Constructive Theology, which has been in existence since the mid-1970s, Wyman has examined the implicit method in the kind of constructive theology the members of this workgroup have been undertaking as he charts the formation of constructive theology as its own category. Wyman notes that:

> methodologically constructive theology forgoes magnum opus, systematic accounts of Christianity, often seen as the ideal expression of systematic or dogmatic theologies. Its aims are open-ended, fallible, revisable imaginative constructions of what it means to be Christian in the world today, confronting contemporary crises and mobilizing against Christianity's past mistakes and injustices.[29]

Working out of the texts produced by this workgroup, Wyman identifies a threefold method that begins with reflection on the historical context of a doctrine or theological question. This is then followed by some form of critical reflection and analysis of the doctrine or theological question, often drawing it into dialogue with contemporary issues. Finally, constructive theology focuses on *constructing* theology in the present day. To quote Lakefield and Jones once more:

> We are not interested in merely describing what theology has been; we are trying to understand and construct it in the present, to imagine what life-giving faith can be in today's world. In doing so, as with any construction job, we are attempting to build a viable structure. In our case, that structure is an inhabitable, beautiful, fruitful theology.[30]

Historical reflection, in this context, serves as the building blocks of something new and fresh, something that is always ongoing, as the contemporary context never stands still and is never finished.

This threefold method bears marked similarities to the hermeneutical method proposed by Sandra M. Schneiders in the study of spirituality. Schneiders highlights that the study of spirituality is, like trauma theology, an interdisciplinary field and advocates a threefold hermeneutical method as helpful in approaching the study of spirituality. This method begins with 'thick' description of the phenomenon or phenomena under investigation, followed by critical analysis that might draw on other disciplines widely (as appropriate), and resulting in constructive interpretation.[31] She concludes by proposing that 'studies in spirituality are, ideally, neither purely descriptive nor merely critical but also constructive'.[32] While spirituality and trauma theology are by no means the same discipline, the study of the two clearly bears much in common as they seek to use interdisciplinary approaches to critique previous theological work and build something new.

Drawing the Marian vignettes, as access points into feminist trauma theologies, into dialogue with these methodological approaches to cogent disciplines, it is clear that feminist trauma theologies often begin with 'thick' description and reflection on experience – what *has* happened. This experiential approach is theologically honest in its tone and may speak with a trembling voice, but nonetheless experience is the beginning point, as it is in so much feminist work. This basis in experience means that there will never be a finished theology of trauma, that is completed once for all time; rather, there will only be multiple theologies of trauma that speak to particular experiences, at particular times and in particular contexts. Such trauma theologies will, of course, inform one another and resonate across time and space. They are, after all, porous and open to divine interruption.

Feminist trauma theologies are critical, in both senses of the word. They are critical in their reflection on traumatic experiences and the way these are perceived and understood in contemporary contexts. They are critical of the ways in which trauma and bodies are elided or perfected in traditional theological narratives and doctrines. Such critical theologies have the flavour of testimony, and function in the public, political context. But they are also *critical*. They are essential. Feminist trauma theologies are necessary in the twenty-first century as trauma becomes an ever more common experience and contemporary culture is still trying to work out how to deal with such experiences well (or at all).

Finally, like an Amish barn-raising, feminist trauma theologies are a community building project. They work together, with sisters and brothers, to build a new shelter, new theologies that bring life and sustain those who have both constructed them and those who were standing in a storm, desperately seeking a place of refuge. These feminist trauma theologies are places of plurality, of community and of ongoing dialogue. Such theologies must not remain isolated in the academy, but must make the connection to Christian communities, churches, pulpits, prayer groups and bedside tables if they are to offer hope and liveable, flourishing theology for people who have experienced trauma. These theologies are never finished, but are remodelled, extended, gutted, redecorated, rewired, replumbed and even torn down, as the project of constructive theology is ongoing.

Conclusion

I set out, in this chapter, to establish a movement towards a methodology in the study of feminist trauma theologies, highlighting from the very beginning both the subjective and flexible nature of this methodology. I have situated it in the realm of a constructive theology, which is where I situate myself as a trauma theologian, but one could make a case for trauma theology working as a different mode of theology or even as an individual type of interdisciplinary theological work. Wherever such work is situated, it is clear that trauma theologies, especially the feminist trauma theologies presented in this volume, are significant and vital to contemporary theological work.

In drawing on the often-overlooked voices of the various Marys and their companions in the New Testament, I sought to highlight some of the key features of feminist trauma theologies, many of which are evident throughout this volume. Feminist trauma theologies are places of honest confrontation with the divine, overcoming fear and choosing to speak anyway. They are theologies that have within them space for divine interruption and encounter – open to God doing something new, even as they hold to the goods of the Christian tradition of which they are part. These feminist trauma theologies construct narratives that have the flavour of testimony and function in the public and political sphere(s). They do not simply describe, but they testify, they bear witness, they speak unspoken truths, they claim power. These testimonies expect to be heard, expect to have impact and expect to make a difference. They expect to defy convention and disrupt the established order of things – they unsettle the status quo. Finally, feminist trauma theologies are done in community. One of the reasons for putting together a co-edited volume focused on this topic, rather than a single-authored monograph, was to highlight the communal nature of this theological endeavour. It speaks with many voices and to many issues. It stands shoulder to shoulder with others who similarly testify. It hears the stories of sisters and brothers and acknowledges their power and solidarity. This is not a work accomplished alone but rather a communal effort. It is not one person's system of theology – complete and closed – but it is a community building project – one with such big plans, and an ongoing drive to provide enough shelter for those who need it, that it is always under construction.

References

Adam, A. K. M., *What is Postmodern Biblical Criticism?*, Minneapolis, MN: Fortress Press, 1993.

Agger, Inger and Soren B. Jensen, 'Testimony as Ritual and Evidence in Psychotherapy for Political Refugees', *Journal of Traumatic Stress* 3 (1990), 115–40.

Arel, Stephanie N. and Shelly Rambo, eds, *Post-Traumatic Public Theology*, Cham, Switzerland: Palgrave Macmillan, 2016.

Beste, Jennifer Erin, *God and the Victim: Traumatic Intrusions on Grace and Freedom*, Oxford: Oxford University Press, 2008.

Bruni, Frank, 'Christine Blasey Ford's Riveting, Persuasive Testimony', *The New York Times*, 27 September 2018, sec. Opinion. www.nytimes.com/2018/09/27/opinion/christine-blasey-ford-kavanaugh-testimony.html.

Cornwall, Susannah, *Un/Familiar Theology: Reconceiving Sex, Reproduction and Generativity*, London: Bloomsbury T&T Clark, 2017.

Doehring, Carrie, *Internal Desecration: Traumatization and Representation of God*, Lanham, MD: University Press of America, 1993.

Green, Joel B., 'Blessed is She Who Believed: Mary, Curious Exemplar in Luke's Narrative', in *Blessed One: Protestant Perspectives on Mary*, ed. Beverley Roberts Gaventa and Cynthia L. Rigby, Louisville, KY: John Knox Press, 2002, 9–20.

Hornsby, Teresa J., 'Anointing Traditions', in *The Historical Jesus in Context*, ed. Amy-Jill Levine, Dale C. Allison and John Dominic Crossan, Princeton, NJ: Princeton University Press, 2006, 339–42.

Jones, Serene, *Trauma and Grace: Theology in a Ruptured World*, Louisville, KY: Westminster John Knox Press, 2009.

Kane, Paul and Ed O'Keefe, 'Republicans Vote to Rebuke Elizabeth Warren, Saying She Impugned Sessions's Character', *The Washington Post*, 8 February 2017: www.washingtonpost.com/news/powerpost/wp/2017/02/07/republicans-vote-to-rebuke-elizabeth-warren-for-impugning-sessionss-character/?noredirect=onandutm_term=.82fec6cba732.

Lakefield, Paul and Serene Jones, eds, *Constructive Theology: A Contemporary Approach to Classical Themes*, Minneapolis, MN: Fortress Press, 2005.

Lange, Dirk G., *Trauma Recalled: Liturgy, Disruption, and Theology*, Minneapolis, MN: Fortress Press, 2010.

Makers, 'Christine Blasey Ford in Her Own Words: "I Am Terrified"', *Makers* (blog), 26 September 2018. www.makers.com/blog/survivor-christine-blasey-ford-written-testimony-sexual-assault-allegation-supreme-court-nominee-brett-kavanaugh?guccounter=1.

Maldonado, Michelle Gonzalez, 'Redeeming Race: A Theological Construction of Racialized Humanity', in *Redeeming Human Nature*, Society for the Study of Theology, Durham University, 2016.

Minister, Meredith, *Trinitarian Theology and Power Relations: God Embodied*, New York: Palgrave Macmillan, 2014.

O'Donnell, Karen, *Broken Bodies: The Eucharist, Mary and the Body in Trauma Theology*, London: SCM Press, 2018.

Petronius, *Satyricon*, trans. Michael Heseltine, Cambridge, MA: Harvard University Press, 1975.

Pound, Marcus, *Theology, Psychoanalysis and Trauma*, London: SCM Press, 2007.

Rambo, Shelly, *Resurrecting Wounds: Living in the Afterlife of Trauma*, Waco, TX: Baylor University Press, 2017.

—— *Spirit and Trauma: A Theology of Remaining*, Louisville, KY: Westminster John Knox Press, 2010.

Schaberg, Jane, *The Illegitimacy of Jesus: A Feminist Theological Interpretation of the Infancy Narratives*, San Francisco: Harper and Row, 1987.

Schneiders, Sandra M., 'Approaches to the Study of Christian Spirituality', in *The Blackwell Companion to Christian Spirituality*, ed. Arthur Holder, Oxford: Blackwell, 2005, 15–33.

—— 'A Hermeneutical Approach to the Study of Christian Spirituality', in *Minding the Spirit: The Study of Christian Spirituality*, ed. Elizabeth A. Dreyer and Mark S. Burrows, Baltimore and London: The Johns Hopkins University Press, 2005, 49–60.

Wyman, Jason A., 'Interpreting the History of the Workgroup on Constructive Theology', *Theology Today* 73, no. 4 (January 2017), 312–24.

Notes

1 Michelle Gonzalez Maldonado, 'Redeeming Race: A Theological Construction of Racialized Humanity', in *Redeeming Human Nature* (Society for the Study of Theology, 2016, Durham University, 2016).

2 Meredith Minister, *Trinitarian Theology and Power Relations: God Embodied* (New York: Palgrave Macmillan, 2014), 3.

3 Susannah Cornwall, *Un/Familiar Theology: Reconceiving Sex, Reproduction and Generativity* (London: Bloomsbury T&T Clark, 2017), 1. Italics in original text.

4 Jason A. Wyman, 'Interpreting the History of the Workgroup on Constructive Theology', *Theology Today* 73, no. 4 (January 2017), 313.

5 Wyman, 'Interpreting the History', 322.

6 Paul Lakefield and Serene Jones, eds, *Constructive Theology: A Contemporary Approach to Classical Themes* (Minneapolis, MN: Fortress Press, 2005), 1.

7 A. K. M. Adam, *What Is Postmodern Biblical Criticism?* (Minneapolis, MN: Fortress Press, 1993), 65.

8 Sandra M. Schneiders, 'Approaches to the Study of Christian Spirituality', in *The Blackwell Companion to Christian Spirituality*, ed. Arthur Holder (Oxford: Blackwell, 2005), 15.

9 Jennifer Erin Beste, *God and the Victim: Traumatic Intrusions on Grace and Freedom* (Oxford: Oxford University Press, 2008).

10 Serene Jones, *Trauma and Grace: Theology in a Ruptured World* (Louisville, KY: Westminster John Knox Press, 2009).

11 Carrie Doehring, *Internal Desecration: Traumatization and Representation of God* (Lanham, MD: University Press of America, 1993).

12 Marcus Pound, *Theology, Psychoanalysis and Trauma* (London: SCM Press, 2007).

13 Dirk G. Lange, *Trauma Recalled: Liturgy, Disruption, and Theology* (Minneapolis, MN: Fortress Press, 2010).

14 See, for example, Shelly Rambo, *Spirit and Trauma: A Theology of Remaining* (Louisville, KY: Westminster John Knox Press, 2010); Shelly Rambo, *Resurrecting Wounds: Living in the Afterlife of Trauma* (Waco, TX: Baylor University Press, 2017); Karen O'Donnell, *Broken Bodies: The Eucharist, Mary and the Body in Trauma Theology* (London: SCM Press, 2018); Stephanie N. Arel and Shelly Rambo, eds, *Post-Traumatic Public Theology* (Cham, Switzerland: Palgrave Macmillan, 2016); Jones, *Trauma and Grace*.

15 O'Donnell, *Broken Bodies*.

16 O'Donnell, *Broken Bodies*, 167–9.

17 Frank Bruni, 'Christine Blasey Ford's Riveting, Persuasive Testimony', Opinion, *The New York Times*, 27 September 2018, www.nytimes.com/2018/09/27/opinion/christine-blasey-ford-kavanaugh-testimony.html.

18 Paul Kane and Ed O'Keefe, 'Republicans Vote to Rebuke Elizabeth Warren, Saying She Impugned Sessions's Character', *The Washington Post*, 8 February 2017, www.washingtonpost.com/news/powerpost/wp/2017/02/07/republicans-vote-

to-rebuke-elizabeth-warren-for-impugning-sessionss-character/?noredirect=
onandutm_term=.82fec6cba732.

19 All biblical references in this chapter are taken from the New Revised Standard Version unless otherwise indicated.

20 Teresa J. Hornsby, 'Anointing Traditions', in *The Historical Jesus in Context*, ed. Amy-Jill Levine, Dale C. Allison and John Dominic Crossan (Princeton, NJ: Princeton University Press, 2006), 341.

21 Petronius, *Satyricon*, trans. Michael Heseltine (Cambridge, MA: Harvard University Press, 1975).

22 Jane Schaberg, *The Illegitimacy of Jesus: A Feminist Theological Interpretation of the Infancy Narratives* (San Francisco: Harper and Row, 1987).

23 Inger Agger and Soren B. Jensen, 'Testimony as Ritual and Evidence in Psychotherapy for Political Refugees', *Journal of Traumatic Stress* 3 (1990), 115–40.

24 Agger and Jensen, 'Testimony as Ritual', 115.

25 O'Donnell, *Broken Bodies*, 177.

26 Joel B. Green, 'Blessed Is She Who Believed: Mary, Curious Exemplar in Luke's Narrative', in *Blessed One: Protestant Perspectives on Mary*, ed. Beverley Roberts Gaventa and Cynthia L. Rigby (Louisville, KY: John Knox Press, 2002), 16.

27 By 'toxic' I am referring to the dangerous ways in which such verses are often used within churches to deny lament and sorrow over events and insist upon a positive outlook. While both of these verses may be true, neither are helpful in the experience of trauma.

28 Makers, 'Christine Blasey Ford in Her Own Words: "I Am Terrified"', *Makers* (blog), 26 September 2018, www.makers.com/blog/survivor-christine-blasey-ford-written-testimony-sexual-assault-allegation-supreme-court-nominee-brett-kavanaugh?guccounter=1.

29 Wyman, 'Interpreting the History', 313.

30 Lakefield and Jones, *Constructive Theology*, 321.

31 Sandra M. Schneiders, 'A Hermeneutical Approach to the Study of Christian Spirituality', in *Minding the Spirit: The Study of Christian Spirituality*, ed. Elizabeth A. Dreyer and Mark S. Burrows (Baltimore and London: The Johns Hopkins University Press, 2005), 56–7.

32 Schneiders, 'Hermeneutical Approach', 57.

2

'I Have the Power in My Body to Make People Sin': The Trauma of Purity Culture and the Concept of 'Body Theodicy'

KATIE CROSS

Sofia sits in her kitchen, facing her laptop screen. She is restless: clasping and unclasping her hands, running her thumbnail along the computer's edge, shifting in her seat. At the other end of the call, I sit in silence, listening as her story unfolds. It is a story of pain and trauma, one in which the body is made enemy and adversary. For much of her young life, Sofia was held captive by evangelical purity culture, and made to believe that sexual virtue was her highest calling. During this time, her church told her that God would love her less if she had sex before marriage. Later, members of the same church implied that Sofia had been raped because she had grown 'distant' from God. While Sofia has now left the church in question, her body bears the scars of dangerous and distorted theology. The trauma of her experience persists in the present, in her body, in her relationships and in her sense of self.

Sofia's story is not an isolated case. In the era of #MeToo,[1] we have experienced a cultural moment of recognition and articulation about the harrowing, pervasive and frighteningly 'ordinary' nature of sexual trauma and violence against women. Journalist Sandi Villarreal writes that while dialogue about the 'harmful, sometimes PTSD-like' consequences of adopting a purity ethic has been occurring for some time, 'the rise of the #MeToo movement in 2017 and the #ChurchToo movement soon after offered many the impetus to speak out'.[2] The latter, attributed to justice activist Emily Joy,[3] critiques inter alia the phenomenon of 'purity culture', and aims to dismantle a particular set of evangelical theologies pertaining to female decency.

Purity culture is difficult to define but does create enough of a pattern to be loosely explained, at least for the purposes of this chapter. Generally speaking, purity culture manifests most clearly in conservative Christian communities. It is deeply ensconced and established in evangelical traditions, primarily in the United States but also in the United Kingdom.[4] The central tenants of purity culture include (but are not limited to) the restriction of all sexual activity to heterosexual marriage, an emphasis on modesty and sexual purity, and abstinence-only education. While both young men and women are exposed to these teachings, American feminist writer Jessica Valenti suggests that women and sexual minorities are disproportionately targeted and affected by them, due to their heteronormative and hetero-patriarchal roots.[5]

In methodological terms, doing feminist theological work after the water-shed 'moment' of #MeToo necessitates the centring of women's narratives in this important conversation. To do that, we must first listen to them. Accordingly, this chapter is one that contributes to conversations around the methodology of feminist trauma theology, providing one example of how such research might be undertaken. It is centred on empirical work, consist-ing of a series of research interviews with women who are bound together by the common traumatic experience of purity culture. Practical theologian Heather Walton suggests that 'hearing about humanity from a female per-spective entails asking fundamental questions of the master discourses' in the discipline of theology.[6] Here, I ask questions of the 'master discourse' pertain-ing to the problem of evil and the practice of theodicy. I suggest that women living with trauma as a result of purity culture experience this theological doctrine in physical and *bodily* ways. Trauma theologian Shelly Rambo points to the way in which trauma 'persists in the present ... in symptoms that live on in the body'.[7] I argue that theodicy, historically conceptualized as a theological attempt to defend the love and goodness of God in a world of evil and suffering, can be understood as something that becomes trapped or embedded in women's bodies as a result of purity culture. This occurs where the theological accusation is made that women suffer due to the 'sin' of 'sexual impurity'. I name this phenomenon *body theodicy*.

To understand this is to begin to do the feminist work of centring and listening to women who have been deeply hurt both by their churches and by theology. Feminist practical theologian Elaine Graham writes that 'out of the concrete, embodied and dynamic stories of life – and in particular, out of women's pursuit of words and deeds that empower and bring to speech those formerly rendered silent and invisible – new theological voices are making themselves heard'.[8] Listen carefully: the voices of women who have been traumatized by purity culture[9] have much to say.

Methodology

For this study, I chose to undertake theological research on trauma in a feminist manner. To that end, it may be described as a work of 'feminist trauma theology'. As Karen O'Donnell notes in the previous chapter, the methodology of feminist trauma theology is both 'flexible' and 'subjective'. What follows is one example of feminist trauma theology research, which is located within the discipline of practical theology, and draws on the wisdom of feminist and qualitative research models.

Practical theology seeks to explore the dissonance between theology and lived reality, looking to test the authenticity of doctrinal claims against the lives of real people.[10] Writing about feminist practical theology, Walton states: 'women have something different to say to practical theology ... having a woman's body places us in a particular cultural location from which to make political judgements and interventions'.[11] Her words hold significance for the current post-#MeToo context, and point to the importance of women undertaking theological research about women. But what makes this research intrinsically *feminist*? Maureen McHugh and Lisa Cosgrove argue that feminist research must examine the gendered context of women's lives and, in doing so, expose inequalities.[12] The disproportionate way in which purity culture affects women and girls is something that is explored in this chapter. For Maeve Landman, feminist research asserts that 'consciousness-raising is a legitimate way of seeing and is therefore a methodological tool' in and of itself.[13] In other words, the simple act of amplifying women's voices can make research a feminist undertaking. Finally, McHugh and Cosgrove strongly iterate that feminist research is not just about women, but *for* women. By these assertions, the research contained within this chapter is feminist because of the platform it provides for women's stories to be heard, and the space it creates for these traumatic experiences to be listened to in theological conversation.

The research contained within this chapter is based on a series of qualitative research interviews with ten women. Each woman self-identified as having experienced trauma through purity culture.[14] Initial recruitment took place on Twitter,[15] and the women[16] were interviewed over Skype.[17] These interviews lasted from one to two hours, and sometimes longer. I asked each woman about her experiences of purity culture, using open-ended and non-directive questions to allow space for individual interpretation.[18] The answers they gave to those questions[19] form the basis of this chapter.

Purity Culture in Practice: Theodicies of Blame

The most recent resurgence of purity culture in the USA can be distinguished as a movement occurring in the 1990s and 2000s, although its historical roots run deeper than this. In *Virgin Nation*, Sara Moslener presents modern purity culture as the latest iteration of a historical trend that has connected 'sexual immorality with national insecurity and impending apocalypse'.[20] Valenti concurs that morality and sexuality have often been conflated in the US context, creating 'a juggernaut of unrealistic sexual expectations for young women'.[21] Indeed, the culture of purity that emerges from these factors demands that women remain sexually 'chaste', or otherwise be blamed for their supposed promiscuity or immorality.

What, then, does purity culture look like in practice? I suggest that it is underpinned by a sense of blame and responsibility, levelled at young women in particular. This is evident in several of the key tenets of purity culture, as explored in research interviews and described below by the women I spoke with.

'Crushed petals and torn paper hearts': purity metaphors

Purity culture rhetoric is built on metaphors, intended to convey that sex before marriage causes women's bodies to devaluate. At youth groups, or meetings of organizations like True Love Waits[22] or Silver Ring Thing,[23] physical objects are used as part of these illustrations, and are crushed, torn or partially destroyed to symbolize the 'dangers' of pre-marital sex. As Sarah explains:

> There are all these different metaphors ... like the chewing gum one is ... if you sleep with people, you're like a piece of chewing gum that's been in different people's mouths, and nobody's going to want you ... which makes you into something that is valuable until a man has you.

Natalie recalled a paper heart being passed around in a circle at her youth group. Each person in the circle was invited to tear a piece of the heart off, so that it ended up 'completely torn apart and unrecognizable'. Rosa became tearful as she spoke of a similar example used at her church:

> They'd get a flower, and everyone stands in a circle ... I'm going to cry, this is so brutal ... and then you hand it around, one by one, and crush it as hard as you can. And when it gets to the other end they say *Look, it's ruined. Look at all the people who touched this, and now it's dirty and broken and gross.*

In each case, a similar story is being told. These metaphors imply that a woman's value is inherently tied to her sexual behaviour and that if she has sex before marriage, she is to blame for later being 'unwanted' by others. They also infer that women's bodies are 'broken' or 'tainted' and made lesser by pre-marital sex.

'Pure and blameless': I Kissed Dating Goodbye

Similar messages and metaphors can be found in *I Kissed Dating Goodbye* (1997) by Joshua Harris. The book popularized the concept of 'courting' as an alternative to mainstream dating and contains advice about how to remain 'pure and blameless'.[24] While not the only book of its kind,[25] *I Kissed Dating Goodbye* was arguably the most significant text in the purity canon. Harris's manual was such an influential aspect of purity culture that all ten of the women I interviewed for this project, regardless of location, denomination or context, had read or been exposed to it. Here, Stephanie describes the impact the book had on her:

> *I Kissed Dating Goodbye* … really skewed my ideas of relationships. So like basically, it was about not dating. It said you should only couple up with someone when you are ready to get married. Then you should say you are courting, not dating. It's like a pre-engagement from the get-go. And there would be no touching … [Harris] really was a proponent of not kissing until you were engaged, even on your wedding day. Listening to that and trying to follow the rules made me unhappy. It made me depressed. It was impossible.

Readers have since publicly shared their experiences of unhealthy expect-ations of marriage, anxiety and even post-traumatic stress disorder,[26] and in recent years the book has been subject to extensive criticism. Sociologists Sara Moon and Jo Reger suggest that works like *I Kissed Dating Goodbye* 'reinforce sexist attitudes – such as benevolent sexism … and traditional gender role attitudes that correlate with rape myth acceptance, while ignoring autonomy and consent, and blurring the lines between rape and consensual sex'.[27] Similarly, Kathryn Klement and Brad Sagarin argue that Harris's book contains a 'rape supporting message',[28] as it limits women's autonomy by focusing so intently on the end-goal of marriage, perpetuat-ing blame on anyone who refuses to conform to its strict standards. Lisa fell silent after mentioning the book in her interview with me. She pulled it down from her shelf. The spine was cracked, the cover worn, the pages marked with brightly coloured tabs and highlighted sections; a window on to Lisa's purity culture past. 'This thing,' Lisa shuddered, gripping its edges so her knuckles turned white, 'this thing is pure terror.'

'I felt like my body was a crime': modesty rules

Modesty rules concern how women dress and present physically. In *I Kissed Dating Goodbye*, Harris writes:

> You may not realise this, but we guys most commonly struggle with our eyes. I think many girls are innocently unaware of the difficulty a guy has in remaining pure when looking at a girl who is dressed immodestly. Now I don't want to dictate your wardrobe, but honestly speaking, I would be blessed if girls considered more than fashion when shopping for clothes … you can help by refusing to wear clothing designed to attract attention to your body … Take responsibility of guarding [your] brothers' eyes.[29]

As Sarah explains, 'Girls were just expected to cover up. Shorts had to be long enough for fingertips to touch, no tank tops were allowed.' Abigail's clothing was all 'loose, below the knee, high collar' so that 'there was no way you could see the silhouette of [the] body'. If young girls did not comply with these modesty rules, they were blamed for sexually tempting men. Stephanie's church echoed Harris's teachings: 'They'd tell us, *You have to dress modestly, or you'll cause your brothers to stumble.*' Joanna adds, 'A lot of it was based on responsibility on girls to keep men from lusting. To the point where ... I felt like my body was a crime.'

'You'll cause others to stumble': theodicy and responsibility

Across all of the research interviews conducted for this study, *blame* was a recurring theme. Within the framework of purity culture, women's bodies are viewed as inherently sinful. They are to be covered, minimized, silenced and controlled. As we have seen, purity culture in practice is underwritten by strict codes of conduct. If these are not adhered to, women are blamed. They are told any suffering they experience in relationships is a direct repercussion of their behaviour; the way they dress, the dating rules they adhere to, and even the company they keep. If they do engage in sex before marriage, they are 'broken', 'cheapened' and 'used up'. As Anna explained, 'They would tell you at church, *God can't fix you once you've had sex*. Like you're irreparable once you've done it.'

Theologically, the blame targeted at these women might be described as a kind of theodicy. The practice of theodicy historically emerged as a theological attempt to solve the problem of evil and defend the love and goodness of God in a world of constant suffering.[30] In doing so, it became a way of excusing God's role in suffering by turning the blame back towards humans. Augustinian theodicies in particular assert that evil is a privation of good, and the result of human misuse of free will (accordingly, God is not held to be directly responsible for evil, and thus divine goodness and benevolence is upheld).[31] Irenaean theodicy also emphasizes the place of free will in relation to evil but promotes suffering as a necessary prerequisite for human spiritual growth and development.[32]

In the context of purity culture, theodicy reveals itself in both Augustinian and Irenaean forms. Women are expected to conform to standards of purity and, where they do not, they are chastised and branded 'sinful'. Further, as will become evident in due course, their suffering is pedagogical. If they experience, for example, an abusive relationship or a break-up, this is configured as something that is their fault. Any suffering that they go through is something to be learned from. In the lived experience of the women of this study, the practice of theodicy becomes more than simply a 'teaching moment'. The fear-based messages that they are exposed to embed themselves, both in their minds and in their bodies.

'Body Theodicy'

'It was March 2018 and I found myself doubled over the toilet at my favourite breakfast cafe, vomiting and crying while the woman I was on a date with unknowingly ate her blueberry pancakes outside,'[33] writes Hannah Brashers in a *HuffPost* article entitled 'How An Evangelical Dating Guide and Purity Culture Gave Me an Anxiety Disorder'. Hannah recounts the 'panic attacks, constant nausea and a total loss of appetite'[34] that plagued her after she left her small fundamentalist Baptist church. Having detached herself from the ideologies of purity culture and embraced her sexuality and agnosticism, she believed that she was ready to date again – but within weeks she was experiencing a sense of 'mounting terror'. It was then that she 'truly began to realise the deep impact that purity culture had had on mind and body'.[35]

> Dating and sex had felt dangerous and sinful for so long – not to mention the biblical implications of dating a *woman*. I had trained myself to shut down all bodily desires and now that my desire had awakened, a fight or flight response had been activated. I couldn't seem to convince my body that dating was safe. I realized that while I'd been convinced during my youth that *I* was making the choice to not date or have sex, I had actually been stripped of bodily agency. The fundamentalism of my upbringing had terrified me into submission.[36]

Distressingly, Hannah's story is not a rarity. Far from being unique, it is one that I recognize from the experiences of my own research participants. In psychological terms, the symptoms that Hannah exhibits might be referred to as post-traumatic stress disorder (PTSD). In theological terms, I suggest that this particular conflation of trauma resulting from purity culture might be termed *body theodicy*. Theodicy has the potential to shift from being an idea or set of arguments (an external experience of being told that your suffering is your responsibility) to a piece of theology that becomes trapped within the body (hence '*body* theodicy'); an internal process of blame and condemnation of the self. The trauma that these women experienced as a result of purity culture is not ascribed to God, but to their own actions and to their inherently 'sinful' bodies. Here, I turn to two narratives in particular which illustrate this concept more fully: Jane's story of bodily trauma and vaginismus, and Sofia's experiences of rape and abuse. Each woman has her own unique story to tell. At the same time, both are woven together by their traumatic experiences at the hands of purity ideology.

Jane's story

Jane has pink hair, a nose ring and a broad, infectious smile. She lives with her husband in the American north-west. Like many of the participants in this study, she grew up in a conservative non-denominational church, and did not receive any sex education at church or at school. 'All we were told was that sex was for marriage, and between a man and a woman,' Jane explains. 'It was all very heteronormative.' When she was 13 years old, Jane's father took her to dinner and presented her with a specially made purity ring. He wrote out vows for her to sign, and made his own vows too, specifically to 'guide her through purity until marriage'. There were rules about contact with the opposite sex: 'no hugging, no sitting too close'. Jane remembers attending a youth retreat one Easter, where she participated in a reflection. Everyone was instructed to write down their 'biggest sin' on a small piece of paper, and these were then nailed to a large, wooden cross. On her piece of paper, Jane wrote down 'struggling with sexual sin'. As she recalls this story, she hangs her head: 'I just believed I was *thinking* about sex too much.'

Jane continued to feel similar shame throughout much of her young adolescence. She remembers feeling 'massively guilty' about kissing her first boyfriend, and about going on dates at university. When she married her husband, their combined sexual history was, in Jane's words, 'almost non-existent'. Even so, they had been promised that sex within marriage would bind them together and would be pleasurable for both of them. The reality of their early days of marriage was very different:

> When we got married, on the wedding night, we already decided before-hand that we'd be too tired to try anything. So we just cuddled. But then we went on honeymoon, and we kind of made a plan to have sex, like *This is when we will do it* ... and we were both so nervous. Like we hadn't seen each other naked before! There were so many nerves. And for me, the nerves went to guilt, because even though we were married ... I started just feeling terrible. I was really scared of my husband's body; I was afraid to touch him. I felt sick, just awful, dirty, like what I was trying to do was wrong. We couldn't get through it, we had to stop.

The next day, Jane called a friend for help. Her friend gave her some advice, and some biological information that Jane admits she had never heard before:

> So we tried having sex again, and we got the point of [penetration], but I was in so much pain. I was crying so much ... It felt like everything was on fire. And we kept trying ... but nothing worked. I felt so, so guilty. My husband had waited for sex his whole life so that I could give it to him ... and I couldn't. I felt like I couldn't perform my *wifely duties*.

Back at home, Jane and her husband kept trying to have sex, but Jane explains that she 'felt so dirty, awful, overwhelmed with guilt – I didn't want to do it'. Eventually, they stopped; in part because it was causing both of them a lot of guilt and trauma, and also because Jane was suffering from severe pain during penetrative sex. She confided in a friend about this, who encouraged her to make an appointment with a gynaecologist to try and understand the pain that she was feeling. The first gynaecologist that Jane visited diagnosed her with 'pelvic floor muscle spasms'. While trying unsuccessfully to follow his treatment plan, Jane came across the term 'vaginismus' in an online forum and explains that 'the symptoms exactly fit what I was feeling'. Vaginismus is a condition in which involuntary muscle spasm prevents vaginal penetration, and often results in pain with attempts at sex. According to research scientist Jennifer Gosselin, writing on vaginismus in particular (and sexual dysfunction more widely): 'Cultural and religious beliefs, practices and expectations may ... play a role in sexual difficulties, such as views that women should be subordinate to men and should not enjoy sex [and] the discouragement of bodily exploration.'[37]

As we have seen in this chapter, purity culture teachings disproportionately impact women and discourage any bodily exploration outside marriage. It is therefore entirely plausible that Jane's body trauma in the form of vaginismus was directly caused by her exposure to purity culture. The messages of blame that she was exposed to for much of her life brought her a great deal of guilt and shame; recall her assertion that sex was one of her expected 'wifely duties'. Indeed, Jane herself made the link between purity culture and her condition:

> Some of my friends helped me buy a workbook on vaginismus online ... I started going through the workbook and I was finding out that purity culture was basically the cause of all of this ...'bodily trauma', I guess you could call it. The workbook talked about preconceived notions of sex, and I realized that so much of the baggage I was carrying around sex came from those experiences of purity culture.

Jane has since sought treatment, attending therapy sessions and finding help for her condition. Her story also draws attention to the heteronormativity of purity culture, which leaves no space for those it targets to present as anything other than heterosexual. On her journey through therapy, Jane has realized: 'I suppressed my sexual views, my orientation. I realized I wasn't straight, I was attracted to girls too, and I had been in the past.' This is yet another aspect of Jane's body trauma; the way in which she felt forced to have her body partake in sexual experiences that felt unnatural to her.

Jane's story is also one that speaks to the messiness around dismantling purity culture; one that resists discussion of a new sexual ethic, because she is still suffering in the present:

Even now, even after deconstructing so much, I can feel guilty. I can still get caught up in feelings of shame and guilt. I'm trying so much to be aware of my feelings and emotions … I have a new therapist now who works with me physically … Therapy was good for my emotions, but it didn't fix my body. Mentally, the understanding is there … but there's still a lot of physical pain. My body has a lot to process still. I graduated from physical therapy about two weeks ago now. And now I know I'm bi[sexual] … what does that mean for me? Is sex with a man what I want? There have been a lot of sleepless nights, there's been crying … I worry about my husband leaving me if I don't have sex with him.

Jane's story makes for difficult reading, especially because it lingers outside any sphere of resolution. She has left the denomination that shamed her, made new friends and sought therapy. She has recently removed her purity ring; a small symbolic gesture which has had a profound impact on her thinking. And yet, as I write, Jane is still suffering at the hands of purity culture. This distance from it has not healed her body trauma. This is because 'body theodicy' is insidious; it lives within long after the initial trauma has passed. As Linda Kay Klein suggests, the psychological effects of purity culture can follow women into their adult lives. This can lead to mental and physical side effects similar to symptoms of post-traumatic stress disorder.[38] Even now, Jane continues to live with messages of guilt and blame trapped within her body.

Sofia's story

I began this chapter with the image of Sofia, sitting at her kitchen table, her voice breaking as she relayed her traumatic past. While this chapter contains some very difficult narratives, Sofia's is perhaps the most jarring of all. She grew up in the south-west of the USA, in a culturally Catholic Mexican family. Beyond her early years, she did not attend church much as a young child. At the age of 11, a school friend invited Sofia to visit her evangelical church, a church Sofia remained at until three years ago. At the church in question, sex education was 'fear-based'. Modest dressing was mandated, and there were extensive rules for young girls ('long shorts, no tank tops, wear a t-shirt over your one-piece at the pool'). As a person of colour, Sofia experienced these rules in a disproportionate way. She explains that her 'curvy, Mexican body' was policed as she went through puberty, and that she was made to cover her silhouette more than the other white girls in her youth group.

At the age of 17, Sofia had her first relationship. She describes how her boyfriend oscillated between 'big romantic gestures' and manipulative behaviour, cutting her off from family and friends and controlling her appearance. He was verbally, sexually (and, on occasion, physically) abusive towards her. Sofia was being raped; but the structures that purity culture had put in place prevented her from reporting this:

> I didn't know how to communicate that to a responsible party, because all I could think of was the shame aspect of it – *They'll know I had sex.* When, in reality, I was being raped. They'd think I was sinful, like now I was a chewed-up piece of gum and no one would want me. So I think that like … it's hard to admit, but in a lot of ways the particular belief structure of the youth group I was in really kind of groomed me to be in that relationship, and then kept me there because I didn't feel like I would be shown grace, or that I'd be shown understanding or that I would be heard. My boyfriend, too … he'd say things to me like, *Oh you're such a tease, I can't help myself,* and all of that. It played into this purity culture idea of, it's my responsibility to stop men lusting over me. And whatever I was doing wasn't stopping him. I know now it's bullshit … but at the time I couldn't escape it.

Sofia continued to blame herself for this relationship long after it ended. Because of the messages that purity culture had instilled in her, she felt that she hadn't been a 'good Christian', and that she had been responsible for the way her partner behaved as a result:

> I was told that if I kept things covered, I wasn't causing guys to lust after me … They would tell you that you were a sexual object for guys to lust after, but also not to sexualize yourself? It wasn't that big of a jump from this idea of *I have the power in my body to make people sin* … It's not a big leap in logic to think that I'm making him feel this way. If only I could do XYZ, he wouldn't belittle me, he wouldn't harm me.

It took Sofia a long time to come to terms with the fact that she had been raped by her partner; that there were many times when she had not consented to sex with him. By this time, she was married. Sofia and her husband made the decision to seek counselling for this, and attended sessions at a different church. But, as Sofia explains, this was a 'huge mistake':

> It perpetuated all of the horrible ideas that I already had about my part in [the abuse]. I remember the pastor telling me … I remember crying and asking him why this has happened to me. And I remember him saying, *You have to remember that sometimes God allows bad things to happen for a purpose.* And he used the example of Jesus being crucified and said that that couldn't have been easy for God, but that Jesus' suffering was for … a better cause, a higher purpose. He asked me when I was with my ex, *Were you walking in your faith? Were you strong in your faith, or were you far away from the church?* If you draw a line from point A to point B, basically, what he was saying … was that I was being unfaithful to God, so God allowed me to be raped so I would come back to him.

This shame lived in Sofia's body for a long time. Her marriage brought a great deal of 'pressure' to have sex with her husband; she explains that she felt 'forced' to have sex with him, too. Sofia recalls her mother-in-law, who did not know about her past traumas, explaining to her that she was responsible for 'taking care' of her husband's needs: 'She basically said, *When your husband wants to do it, you have to submit.*'

Sofia's story encapsulates the concept of 'body theodicy'. Her experiences are an extreme (but tragically all too common) example of the blame that purity culture perpetuates, to the extent that resulting trauma becomes embedded within a woman's experience, and even within her body. This trope of God 'allowing' bad things to happen for a higher purpose is insidious and damaging. Worse still, it is the lie of theodicy that breeds guilt and shame among women who are already vulnerable to such teachings. It is lazy theology, choosing to point the finger of blame at those who are already marginalized and lack the power to challenge this within such tightly controlled structures. Ultimately, this theology harms women not only spiritually, or psychologically, but in bodily ways. A piece of doctrine designed in the abstract thus has actual and concrete repercussions.

Turning Away From Purity Culture

In 2019, there was a discernible movement away from purity culture, both within and outwith evangelical church circles. A number of books critiquing purity culture have been published in recent years, including *Pure* by Linda Kay-Klein, *Shameless* by Nadia Boltz-Weber, and *Damaged Goods* by Diana Anderson. 'True Love Waits' and 'Silver Ring Thing', two programmes that encouraged adolescents to make chastity pledges at their events,[39] have since been rebranded. Silver Ring Things' website redirects to Unaltered Ministries, which appears to focus on purity in all aspects of one's life.[40] In 2016, Joshua Harris indicated a partial retraction of his original message in *I Kissed Dating Goodbye*.[41] In 2019 Harris disavowed the book entirely, calling for an end to its publication. His personal life has also suffered; he has announced that his marriage is over and that he has lost his faith.[42]

It is significant that the writer of such an authoritative work of purity culture doctrine has since recanted his teachings. This, coupled with the rebranding of some key purity organizations, would appear to indicate a partial understanding of the damage that purity culture ideology can cause. However, while these organizations have reinvented themselves, their messages of abstinence and purity have remained the same. Further, Harris in particular has been criticized for his lack of concern. Brashers writes that Harris's apologies have failed to acknowledge the damaging legacy of purity culture: 'There is little representation for those, like myself, who find ourselves decades later, unpacking the trauma that his book and purity culture inflicted upon us.'[43]

Towards a new sexual ethic?

This chapter aims to provide a place for conversations regarding purity culture to begin. It is self-consciously a feminist piece, and so its underlying intention is to elevate women's voices so that they might be taken seriously in a theological realm. There is power in narrative-building, and in naming experience. Klein's book *Pure* promotes the importance of conversation around purity culture. As part of her initiative 'Break Free Together', Klein and trained facilitators meet with church congregations to host dinner conversations and story exchanges, examining what people learned about sexuality growing up and how these messages impact their adult lives. 'If we don't do that deep internal work,' warns Klein, 'we're going to end up inadvertently passing on what we're raised with via what we don't talk about, via how we treat people, via the choices we make that young people watch us make, and so on.'[44] In other words, breaking the cycle of trauma caused by purity culture begins with listening, reflecting and communicating. It begins with pieces of work such as this one.

What comes next? A number of thinkers, writers and theologians have begun to offer suggestions for a new sexual ethic beyond purity culture. These offerings tend to be framed generally; they are not specific to any one context or denomination. Nevertheless, they are worth some consideration here.

In her book *Shameless*, Lutheran Pastor Nadia Bolz-Weber proposes 'a sexual revolution'. She suggests a guiding principle for a new sexual ethic: first showing concern for self and for our neighbours. Bolz-Weber adds that human beings should be held above doctrinal ideas: 'we should not be more loyal to an idea, a doctrine, or an interpretation of a Bible verse than we are to people.'[45] Her words might be interpreted as a criticism of the very issues that have been discussed in this chapter, including the use of theodicy to incite blame and fear. Diana E. Anderson, writer of *Damaged Goods: New Perspectives on Christian Purity*, places an emphasis on recovery from shame. She advocates for sex education framed around mutual pleasure and consent, and the importance of not harming others in sexual situations.[46] Anderson's vision is that this should be supported by open communication in church circles. Adolescents should not be encouraged to wait to have sex until marriage, but until they are ready (which could be before, after or some time during marriage). This approach is intended to be individually tailored; the result of discussion in the community, and in the sexual partnership. Similarly, Bromleigh McCleneghan suggests that 'sexual sin is less about particular acts or the way they're carried out than the way partners treat each other; sexual sin is about a lack of mutuality, reciprocity, and love'.[47]

She suggests that any new sexual ethic should be based on mutual respect. LGBTQ+ rights activist and public theologian Vicky Beeching is largely in agreement with these sentiments, reminding us that 'sex is incredibly sacred, and that the Church has good things to say about sex to the world'.[48] At the same time, she warns that 'we [also] need to revisit our repressive culture ... and just figure out how we can actually create a situation where people are feeling comfortable and safe and can flourish in their relationship'.[49] All of these suggestions are based on principles of Christian love and community, and underline the importance of communication and consent.

Conclusion: Bodies Whole, Holy and Loved

I hesitate to name a single way forward or new sexual ethic here. This chapter is intended first and foremost as a feminist, consciousness-raising piece of work. It is a space in which the reader can sit in contemplation of the damage that purity culture has inflicted, and the way in which theological doctrine can mutate into something inherently harmful. It has also presented one example of how research in the area of feminist trauma theology might be configured in methodological terms; what methods might be used, and how such research might carefully be approached.

While the #MeToo and #ChurchToo movements compel us towards solutions, they also create space for people's stories of suffering to be heard. In a short meditation titled *Writing in the Dust*, Rowan Williams explains that hasty dialogue and theological solutions are the very antithesis of what is required after a trauma occurs.[50] He suggests that Christians should avoid the temptation to gravitate towards the most immediate option of response, as this may not necessarily be correct or helpful to those who have experienced (or are experiencing) the trauma first hand. If Williams is to be believed, we must take care not to rush towards new solutions until we have first heard the stories of those who have been hurt by purity culture. In listening to them, we discover that a new sexual ethic will come too late to dispel the suffering that is already embedded within the bodies of traumatized women. There may be hope for the future, but this hope is bittersweet; it is not for those whose lives and bodies have already been subjected to damaging theological messages.

It should come as no surprise that the theology we create and perpetuate impacts our bodies. How can it not, when we *do* theology in our bodies? Nevertheless, while human-made theologies can wound and hold our bodies back, this is not the final word. Elaine Graham writes that 'bodily practice is the agent and the vehicle of divine disclosure'.[51] If this is true, then there is holiness inherent in all human bodies. Purity culture dictates that the body is in some way 'broken' or 'damaged' when sex takes place outside marriage, but this theology fails to consider the deep-rooted divine worth intrinsic to human bodies. Sex before marriage cannot cancel out this divine imprint.

Sofia, who once felt 'too broken' for God to love her, now recognizes that 'God loves me and is in communion with me, always'. Bodies created in God's image are never 'damaged' or 'unwanted'. Further, bodily holiness is not something that can be achieved; not by way of modest dressing, fear-based metaphors, forced abstinence or coerced sexuality. It is innate within us all. It exists deeper within our beings than any theodicy or blame is able to permeate. The final word does not lie with that which is fallible and human made; with distorted doctrines or recanted teachings; but with the love of God that made us and holds us and exists within our bodies: whole, holy and loved.

References

Anderson, Diana, *Damaged Goods: New Perspectives on Christian Purity*, Nashville, TN: Jericho Books, 2005.

Beeching, Vicky, 'God was still my highest priority and my greatest love', *Church Times*, 22 June 2018: www.churchtimes.co.uk/articles/2018/22-june/features/features/god-was-still-my-highest-priority-and-my-greatest-love-vicky-beeching.

Bolz-Weber, Nadia, *Shameless: A Sexual Reformation*, Norwich: Canterbury Press, 2019.

Brashers, Hannah, 'How An Evangelical Dating Guide and Purity Culture Gave Me An Anxiety Disorder', *HuffPost*, 19 February 2019: www.huffpost.com/entry/i-kissed-dating-goodbye-trauma_n_5c66fedbe4b05c889d1f158e.

Evans, G. R., 'Augustine', in *The First Christian Theologians*, ed. G. R. Evans, Oxford: Blackwell, 2004.

Gosselin, Jennifer T., 'Sexual Dysfunctions and Disorders', in *Psychopathology: Foundations for a Contemporary Understanding*, ed. James E. Maddux and Barbara A. Winstead, New York: Routledge, 2012, pp. 307–46.

Graham, Elaine, 'Words Made Flesh: Women, Embodiment and Practical Theology', *Feminist Theology*, 7, no. 29, 109–21.

Guerra, Cristela, 'Where'd the #MeToo initiative really come from? Activist Tarana Burke, long before hashtags', *Boston Globe*, 17 October 2017.

Harris, Joshua, *I Kissed Dating Goodbye: A New Attitude Towards Relationships and Romance*, Colorado Springs, CO: Multnomah, 1997.

—— '"I Kissed Dating Goodbye" author: How and why I've rethought dating and purity culture', *USA Today*, 26 November 2018: https://eu.usatoday.com/story/opinion/voices/2018/11/23/christianity-kissed-dating-goodbye-relationships-sex-book-column/2071273002/.

Klein, Linda Kay, *Pure: Inside the Movement that Shamed a Generation of Young Women and How I Broke Free*, New York: Touchstone, 2008.

Klement, Kathryn and Brad Sagarin, 'Nobody Wants to Date a Whore: Rape-Supportive Messages in Women-Directed Christian Dating Books', *Sexuality and Culture* 21, no. 1, 2017, 205–23.

Landman, Maeve, 'Getting Quality in Qualitative Research: A Short Introduction to Feminist Methodology and Methods', *The Proceedings of the Nutrition Society* 65, no. 4, 2006, 429–33.

McClenghan, Bromleigh, *Good Christian Sex: Why Chastity isn't the Only Option – and Other Things the Bible Says about Sex*, New York: HarperCollins, 2016.

McGrath, Alister E., *Christian Theology: An Introduction*, Oxford: Blackwell, 2007.

—— *Theology: The Basics*, Oxford: Blackwell, 2008.

McHugh, Maureen. C. and Lisa Cosgrove, 'Research for Women', in *The Work of Women*, ed. D. Ashcraft, New York: Haworth Press, 1998, 19–43.

Moon, Sarah and Jo Reger, 'You Are Not Your Own: Rape, Sexual Consent and Evangelical Christian Dating Books', *Journal of Integrated Social Sciences* 4, no. 1 (2014), 55–74.

Moslener, Sarah, *Virgin Nation: Sexual Purity and American Adolescence*, Oxford: Oxford University Press, 2015.

Osmer, Richard, 'Practical Theology: A Current International Perspective', *HTS Teologiese Studies/Theological Studies*, 67, no. 2 (2011).

Rambo, Shelly, *Spirit and Trauma: A Theology of Remaining*, Louisville, KY: Westminster John Knox Press, 2010.

Sherwood, Harriet, 'Author of Christian Relationship Guide Says He has Lost his Faith', *Guardian*, 29 July 2019: www.theguardian.com/world/2019/jul/29/author-christian-relationship-guide-joshua-harris-says-marriage-over.

Smith, Jonathan, Michael Larkin and Paul Flowers, *Interpretative Phenomenological Analysis: Theory, Method and Research*, London: SAGE, 2009.

Valenti, Jessica, *The Purity Myth: How America's Obsession with Virginity is Hurting Young Women*, Berkeley, CA: Seal Press, 2010.

Villarreal, Sandi, 'Their Generation was Shamed by Purity Culture. Here's What They're Building in Its Place', *Sojourners*, 11 March 2019. https://sojo.net/interactive/their-generation-was-shamed-purity-culture-heres-what-theyre-building-its-place.

Walton, Heather, 'The Wisdom of Sheba: Constructing Feminist Practical Theology', *Contact* 135, no. 1 (2001), 3–12.

Williams, Rowan, *Writing in the Dust: Reflections on 11th September and Its Aftermath*, London: Hodder and Stoughton, 2002.

Notes

1 The hashtag 'Me Too' was first used on MySpace to promote 'empowerment through empathy' among women of colour who had been sexually abused. Its early usage should be attributed to African-American civil rights activist Tarana Burke. In 2017, #MeToo was co-opted for use on social media in 2017 by actress Alyssa Milano. See Cristela Guerra, 'Where'd the #MeToo initiative really come from? Activist Tarana Burke, long before hashtags', *Boston Globe*, 17 October 2017, www.bostonglobe.com/lifestyle/2017/10/17/alyssa-milano-credits-activist-tarana-burke-with-founding-metoo-movement-years-ago/o2Jv29v6ljObkKPTPB9KGP/story.html (accessed 1 August 2019).

2 Sandi Villarreal, 'Their Generation was Shamed by Purity Culture. Here's What They're Building in Its Place', *Sojourners*, 11 March 2019, https://sojo.net/interactive/their-generation-was-shamed-purity-culture-heres-what-theyre-building-its-place (accessed 1 August 2019).

3 See Emily Joy's blog about #ChurchToo: http://emilyjoypoetry.com/church too (accessed 1 August 2019).

4 To a lesser but still significant extent, purity culture has also made its way to the UK. Two participants in this study, Anna and Rosa, grew up in the purity movement in British churches. Anna remarked that UK purity culture has typically been 'less zealous' than its US counterpart, and that she often felt 'envious' of US Christians for whom purity culture was more prominent and accessible: 'They had it much easier.'

5 Jessica Valenti, *The Purity Myth: How America's Obsession with Virginity is Hurting Young Women* (Berkeley, CA: Seal Press, 2010), 5.

6 Heather Walton, 'The Wisdom of Sheba: Constructing Feminist Practical Theology', *Contact* 135, no. 1 (2001), 7.

7 Shelly Rambo, *Spirit and Trauma: A Theology of Remaining* (Louisville, KY: Westminster John Knox Press, 2010), 2.

8 Elaine Graham, 'Words Made Flesh: Women, Embodiment and Practical Theology', *Feminist Theology* 7, no. 29, 110.

9 While I am aware that not all women who are exposed to purity teachings feel that they have been harmed by them, and that this is important to recognize, this chapter focuses primarily on narratives of trauma.

10 Richard Osmer, 'Practical Theology: A Current International Perspective', *HTS Teologiese Studies/Theological Studies* 67, no. 2 (2011), 3.

11 Heather Walton, 'The Wisdom of Sheba', 6.

12 Maureen McHugh and Lisa Cosgrove, 'Research for Women', in *The Work of Women*, ed. D. Ashcraft (New York: Haworth Press, 1998), 19.

13 Maeve Landman, 'Getting Quality in Qualitative Research: A Short Introduction to Feminist Methodology and Methods', *The Proceedings of the Nutrition Society* 65, no. 4 (2006).

14 The particular qualitative framework for this study is interpretive phenomenological analysis (IPA). This approach is committed to the exploration of personal experience. It 'endeavour[s] to uncover meaning' and pays great attention to individual stories, seeking to access the 'inner worlds' of participants by drawing out 'thick', rich description of their experiences). It leaves space for the phenomenon (in this case, purity culture) to exist as subjective, and for the researcher to learn from the story of each participant. In the context of this study, an emphasis on remaining faithful to individual accounts and experiences ensures each woman's story is held as valuable in its own right and context. Even when subsequent cross-case analysis takes place, IPA is designed to remain faithful to individual accounts. In this way, it can be used to illustrate both the immediate cases of respondents, and the way in which their lives align with more general themes. As will become evident, the experiences of women in this study, sometimes called 'life worlds' in IPA rhetoric, are both rich in their individual respects and also combine to illustrate and call to attention some important truths about the capacity for theodicies to become harmful and cause trauma. See Jonathan Smith, Michael Larkin and Paul Flowers, *Interpretative Phenomenological Analysis: Theory, Method and Research* (London: Sage, 2009), 56–8.

15 Having identified that I wanted to speak to women about their experiences of purity culture and knowing that much of this takes place in the USA, I elected to advertise my study on Twitter for the greatest geographical reach possible. The wording of my call for participants did not contain any particular mention of trauma but, as previously explained, the language of 'purity culture' is generally sufficient to indicate at least a critical perspective.

16 A brief note on demographics: of the ten women I interviewed, eight were from the USA and two from the UK. Six were white, two were Latinx and two were black. Two of the participants identified as LGBTQ+. One identified as disabled. While there is not space in this chapter to fully explore the particularities of purity culture with regards to race, sexuality and disability, it is important to note the following: purity culture is not an experience confined to white, heterosexual, able-bodied women, and people of colour, LGBTQ+ people and disabled people experience purity culture in disproportionate ways which relate to their marginalized status.

17 Video conferencing software offered the best possible method of contacting geographically dispersed participants. It also allowed me to see participants in real time so that I could read body language, nonverbal gestures and other cues to help me identify the meaning and emphasis of their words.

18 Jonathan Smith and Mike Osborn, 'Interpretative Phenomenological Analysis', in *Qualitative Psychology: A Practical Guide to Research Methods*, ed. Jonathan Smith (London: Sage, 2008), 61.

19 Examples of questions asked include: What did (or does) purity culture look like in your religious context? How would you define it? How would you describe your own involvement in, or experiences of, purity culture? Has purity culture had an impact on your relationships? Has purity culture impacted your faith?

20 Sara Moslener, *Virgin Nation: Sexual Purity and American Adolescence* (Oxford: Oxford University Press, 2015), 4.

21 Valenti, *The Purity Myth*, 9.

22 True Love Waits was a US-based Christian abstinence programme produced by LifeWay Ministries. See: www.lifeway.com/en/product-family/true-love-waits (accessed 1 August 2019). Attendees at True Love Waits events were invited to make an abstinence pledge, worded as: 'Believing that true love waits, I make a commitment to God, myself, my family, those I date, and my future mate to be sexually pure until the day I enter marriage.' See www.washingtonpost.com/wp-dyn/articles/A48509-2005Mar18.html (accessed 1 August 2019).

23 Silver Ring Thing was a virginity pledge programme. During their gatherings, participants were invited to commit to a vow of sexual abstinence until marriage by purchasing and wearing silver rings. See Christine Gardner, *Making Chastity Sexy: The Rhetoric of Evangelical Abstinence Campaigns* (Berkeley, CA: University of California Press, 2011).

24 Joshua Harris, *I Kissed Dating Goodbye: A New Attitude Towards Relationships and Romance* (Colorado Springs, CO: Multnomah, 1997), 24.

25 See also the following books, which were mentioned by research participants in this study: Elisabeth Elliot, *Passion and Purity* (Grand Rapids, MI: Revell, 1994); Haley Di Marco, *Technical Virgin* (Grand Rapids, MI: Revell, 2006); and Ed and Gaye Wheat, *Intended for Pleasure* (Grand Rapids, MI: Revell, 1977).

26 Hannah Brashers, 'How an Evangelical Dating Guide and Purity Culture Gave Me an Anxiety Disorder', *HuffPost*, 19 February 2019, www.huffpost.com/entry/i-kissed-dating-goodbye-trauma_n_5c66fedbe4b05c889d1f158e (accessed 1 August 2019).

27 Sarah Moon and Jo Reger, 'You Are Not Your Own: Rape, Sexual Consent and Evangelical Christian Dating Books', *Journal of Integrated Social Sciences* 4, no. 1 (2014), 55.

28 Kathryn Klement and Brad Sagarin, 'Nobody Wants to Date a Whore:

Rape-Supportive Messages in Women-Directed Christian Dating Books', *Sexuality and Culture* 21, no. 1 (2017), 205.

29 Harris, *I Kissed Dating Goodbye*, 107.

30 Alister E. McGrath, *Christian Theology: An Introduction* (Oxford: Blackwell, 2007), 232.

31 G. R. Evans, 'Augustine', in *The First Christian Theologians*, ed. G. R. Evans (Oxford: Blackwell, 2004), 238. See also St Augustine of Hippo, *The City of God* (London: Penguin, 1972) and *Confessions* (London: Penguin, 1961).

32 Alister E. McGrath, *Theology: The Basics* (Oxford: Blackwell, 2008), 14.

33 Brashers, 'Evangelical Dating Guide'.

34 Brashers, 'Evangelical Dating Guide'.

35 Brashers, 'Evangelical Dating Guide'.

36 Brashers, 'Evangelical Dating Guide'.

37 Jennifer T. Gosselin, 'Sexual Dysfunctions and Disorders', in *Psychopathology: Foundations for a Contemporary Understanding*, ed. James Maddux and Barbara Winstead, 3rd edn (New York: Routledge, 2012), 314.

38 Linda Kay Klein, *Pure: Inside the Movement that Shamed a Generation of Young Women and How I Broke Free* (New York: Touchstone, 2018), 16.

39 Lifeway Ministries, which created True Love Waits, presents its own 'biblical' mandate for abstinence, drawing on Jesus' words from Matthew's Gospel (5.28): 'I say to you that everyone who looks at a woman with lust has already committed adultery with her in his heart.'

40 See www.unaltered.org/whatisunaltered (accessed 1 August 2019).

41 Joshua Harris, '"I Kissed Dating Goodbye" Author: How and Why I've Rethought Dating and Purity Culture', *USA Today*, 26 November 2018, https://eu.usatoday.com/story/opinion/voices/2018/11/23/christianity-kissed-dating-goodbye-relationships-sex-book-column/2071273002/ (accessed 1 August 2019).

42 Harriet Sherwood, 'Author of Christian Relationship Guide Says He has Lost His Faith', *Guardian*, 29 July 2019, www.theguardian.com/world/2019/jul/29/author-christian-relationship-guide-joshua-harris-says-marriage-over (accessed 1 August 2019).

43 Brashers, 'Evangelical Dating Guide'.

44 Linda Kay-Klein, in Sandi Villarreal, 'Their Generation was Shamed by Purity Culture'.

45 Nadia Bolz-Weber, *Shameless: A Sexual Reformation* (Norwich: Canterbury Press, 2019), 5.

46 See Diana E. Anderson, *Damaged Goods: New Perspectives on Christian Purity* (Nashville, TN: Jericho Books, 2005).

47 Bromleigh McClenghan, *Good Christian Sex: Why Chastity isn't the Only Option – and Other Things the Bible Says about Sex* (New York: HarperCollins, 2016), 69.

48 Vicky Beeching, 'God was Still My Highest Priority and My Greatest Love', *Church Times*, 22 June 2018, www.churchtimes.co.uk/articles/2018/22-june/features/features/god-was-still-my-highest-priority-and-my-greatest-love-vicky-beeching (accessed 1 August 2019).

49 Beeching, 'God was Still my Highest Priority'.

50 Rowan Williams, *Writing in the Dust: Reflections on 11th September and Its Aftermath* (London: Hodder and Stoughton, 2002), 7.

51 Graham, 'Words Made Flesh', 109.

PART 2

Feminist Trauma Theologies: Violence against Women

3

Belief: A Practice of Resistance to the Alchemy of Reality into Incoherence

HILARY JEROME SCARSELLA

Ten years ago, I sat in a library lobby across from someone important in my life, preparing to tell them for the first time that, though neither my memory nor my knowledge of the events was complete, I thought I was sexually abused as a child by a person we both had trusted. I had been working up to this day for years. My nerves were so amped it's a wonder my bones didn't rattle apart right there and drop to the floor. For as long as I could remember, I had lived with the traumatic repercussions of sexual abuse without ever feeling confident that my life had, in fact, included this violence. I had coped with the abuse by convincing myself I had made it up. Nothing had happened to me. It was silly children's make-believe. The egregious nature of its content was evidence that I was a terrible child. A terrible person. It didn't and could not mean that the nightmares in my head were put there by someone beloved.

Several months prior to walking into that library, I had coaxed myself to consider for the first time that, just maybe, I felt traumatized by sexual violence because I was. It was a new and strange idea.

One afternoon, sitting on the couch in a close friend's living room, I had noticed that my mind began its familiar routine of flipping frantically through still frames of childhood memories that, though innocent enough, always left me with a chill. For 20-odd years my habit had been to push them out of my mind as quickly as possible and pretend that there was nothing significant about the fact that this exact collection of frozen frames kept repeating itself across my vision. That afternoon, however, I changed my pattern. I closed my eyes and concentrated on one of the frames. I tried to remain open. I didn't push it away.

The frozen image – of child me in a place I knew well, toys scattered about – began to move. A door opened and a man stepped into the room. I saw his shoes.

Then, with a swift crack, my vision blurred. Eyes open or closed, all I could see was the colour red, every direction was a flood of red. I felt my mind splitting down the middle, as though it would rather self-destruct than stay in that room with that man. Something (someone?) in me I had not met, and over which I had no control, took the reins and shut the moving

43

still frame down. I was sure that I would be obliterated in the process. I thought I was going to die.

The next thing I remember, I was standing on the opposite side of my friend's living room, a blanket wrapped around my shoulders, my friend in front of me, looking concerned, hands on my arms, telling me in a soothing voice that I was all right. I don't know how much time I lost or what happened in the interim. I never asked.

As terrifying as this experience was, the gift it gave to me was that I could no longer explain away the repercussions of violence in my life as the result of my own, simple, childhood make-believe-run-amok. At that time, I still did not have clear declarative memory of abuse, but I knew that I did not fabricate the near split of my psyche. I did not pretend to dissociate. And this was a piece of reality that felt concrete enough to grasp and hold to for stability while, at a pace that didn't threaten my sanity, I faced the voice in my head long determined to convince me that I had made it all up and to keep me from knowing what I knew.

That's how I found myself at the library, months later, finally ready to tell someone who mattered that I was newly, precariously of the mind that the violence I thought I had imagined was real.

They listened to me. They were quiet for a moment. And then they said, 'You could be having false memories. In the 1990s lots of people thought they were sexually abused as children, but their memories were wrong. Couldn't you be wrong?'

My bones didn't just drop to the floor. They broke into tiny, jagged shards and blew away like sand. All of the confidence I had built in my knowledge of the violence in my life disintegrated on the spot. This person who mattered to me didn't believe me, and immediately, as if the work I had done to know myself had been of no thicker a substance than vapour, I could no longer believe me.

As survivors of childhood sexual abuse go, I am remarkably unexceptional. In my academic, ministerial and advocacy roles, I partner with more survivors than I can count whose stories mirror the one I just told.[1] The reason I begin this chapter with a small piece of my own life is because it is a piece that offers a glimpse into a phenomenon experienced by innumerable others: sexual violence can obliterate survivors' confidence in our own ability to discern what is real from what is not, what happened from what didn't. Survivor advocates emphasize the need for hearers to believe survivor accounts of sexual violence, in part, because belief mediates action. A survivor's access to safety, care, support and justice is measured in no greater proportion than the degree to which they are believed. Another reason, however, is that those who live with the traumatic, reality-bending, world-upending repercussions of sexual violence often struggle to believe *ourselves*. Disbelief from friends, family, employers, communities of faith, intellectual discourse and culture writ large exacerbates this dynamic of sexual violence trauma: the alchemy of reality into incoherence.

Due Process vs Believe All Women

It is with this concern in mind that I turn to popular attention on the ethics of extending belief to survivor testimony of sexual violence. Since the explosion of #MeToo in late 2017, whether and under what conditions survivor accounts of sexual violence ought to be believed has been a topic of constant angst. Popular discourse on the subject has taken on the shape of a trenchant dualism. One side is characterized by what I call the *due process* lens. This lens says we should not believe a survivor's testimony of abuse if we do not have corroborating evidence that would be admissible in a court of law. For as long as such evidence is lacking, this lens says it is unethical – even outside court – to believe an allegation of sexual violence because doing so amounts to socially convicting the accused without affording them a fair trial.[2] The second side of the dualism is constituted through what I will refer to as the *believe all women* lens. This lens treats the automatic and immediate extension of belief as ethically necessary in response to every allegation of sexual violence. It argues that, since we know that false allegations are statistically rare and that not believing survivors both enables continued abuse and inflicts further traumatic harm on the one whose testimony is denied, all who disclose experiences of sexual violence should, as a rule, be believed.[3]

Given the snapshot of my own lived experience with which I opened this essay, the reader will not be surprised that I consider the *believe all women* lens unquestionably preferable to the *due process* lens.[4] However, while diverse and nuanced variations of these two positions abound, in their most culturally ubiquitous forms I am concerned that neither enables the kind of solidarity with sexual violence survivors necessary for a thick resistance to the harms of abuse. The *due process* lens is incapable of validating the majority of sexual violence experiences, because the kind of evidence it requires for belief tends to be unavailable in situations of sexual violence. Twenty years after the fact, I did not have one piece of the kind of evidence that would be requested in court to support my account. Because the *due process* lens cannot validate experiences of sexual violence in the absence of such evidence even when no legal proceeding is at issue, its ability to hold perpetrators accountable and motivate systemic change is weak. Its potential for aggravating the trauma of sexual violence by further undermining survivors' sense of reality is high.

The *believe all women* lens, on the other hand, holds validating survivors' experiences of sexual violence as its explicit intention. Perhaps, if the person I spoke with in that library had been more committed to its mandate, our conversation would have had somewhat better prospects for success. But the *believe all women* lens can only validate survivors' sense of reality in general for as long as no example of a false or mistaken testimony is available to invalidate the idea that all accounts of sexual violence are inherently historically accurate. When one survivor's testimony is called into question, as happened in 2015 when *Rolling Stone* retracted a story it published on an alleged rape at the University of Virginia, the *believe all women* lens inadvertently calls all survivors' testimonies into question.[5] My library conversation partner used exactly this logic to throw my self-knowledge into doubt. In the 1990s, a collection of people who thought they had experienced childhood sexual abuse had, according to popular media, been wrong; so why wasn't I?[6]

Tracing the Problem in Western Discourse

The roots of the *due process/believe all women* dualism that characterizes the contemporary situation wind deep in the soil of Western culture. Excavating that soil and examining its sources of nutrients grants us an opportunity to understand what energizes the system. One such source of energy, I contend, can be traced to late nineteenth- and early twentieth-century development of the burgeoning discipline of psychiatry and, more specifically, psychoanalysis. In his lifetime, Sigmund Freud composed two basic and fundamentally incompatible theories of the link between sexuality and psychological distress: the seduction theory and the Oedipal theory of childhood sexuality. Both theories are constructed, at least in part, through Freud's own extension or withholding of belief from his patients' accounts of childhood sexual abuse. In terms I freely admit are overly simplified to fit within the limited scope of this chapter, the seduction theory rests on a foundation of belief, and the Oedipal theory is constructed through disbelief.[7] The seduction theory treats patients' memory of sexual abuse as historically representative. The Oedipal theory tends towards reading purported memory of sexual violence in terms of fantasy (children's make-believe?) rather than history.

In the two following sections of this chapter I relate Freud's shift between the seduction theory and the Oedipal theory to contemporary approaches to sexual violence such that the inadequacy of today's dualism between the *due process* lens and the *believe all women* lens becomes legible as culturally resonant with the opposition between Freud's two theories. I read the *believe all women* lens as resonant with the kind of thought that characterizes Freud's seduction theory. I read the *due process* lens as resonant with the kind of thought we find in Freud's replacement of the seduction theory with the Oedipal paradigm.

In turning to Freud, my argument is not that Freud is responsible for the configuration of the contemporary dualism or that the two sides of today's debate are identical replications of Freud's two theories. Rather, the fact of resonance between contemporary discourse and Freud's treatment of belief and sexual violence helps us to see that the dualistic frame I have named is a long-standing characteristic of Western formulations of thought regarding the ethics of belief in the wake of sexual violence testimony. In other words, my argument is that the opposing positions put forward in Freud's two theories, on the one hand, and the opposing positions expressed in *believe all women* and *due process* debates today, on the other, are two instances in which larger patterns of Western thought on the appropriateness of belief as a response to survivor testimony are visible. In Freud's time and now, the dualistic frame of the conversation fails to produce approaches to receiving accounts of sexual violence that support the possibility of solidarity with survivors.

The failure of each side of the dualism, I argue, stems from its theorizations of the relationship between memory, history and trauma in the light of sexual violence. What one thinks about the relationship between memory, history and trauma informs one's approach to believing survivors. Those of the mind that memory works like a digital store of historical data will be far more likely to believe that what a survivor remembers historically occurred. To those who maintain that memory is most often mistaken about the past, belief will not seem as wise. My hope is that becoming clear on Freud's theorization of memory, history and trauma in the seduction theory and in his transition to Oedipal theory will help to illuminate the problematics of contemporary thought on extending belief to survivor testimony and suggest a trajectory for composing more helpful frameworks for conceptualizing and recommending belief.

Given the number and volume of feminist critiques of Freud, I will say a word about why I have chosen to ground this chapter in reflection on Freudian theories and their import for contemporary problems. I want to challenge the idea that the humanities, the study of religion, the psychological disciplines or the West in general has moved beyond Freud to the extent that it is no longer necessary to ask how our ways of thinking are either impacted or illuminated by the cultural appropriation of his thought. Freud is a figure who contributed significantly to the shape of modern, Western reflection on the psychological dimensions of the human.[8] Novel advances beyond Freud abound, but I am committed to the position that it is an error to believe that the bulk of these innovations in no way carry forward the trace of Freudian frameworks. Precisely because Freudian thought has been so widely appropriated into modern, Western world views, been central to the development of trauma theory, and has been revealed as both useful and problematic by feminist, womanist, queer and other critics, focusing attention on the Freudian trace within contemporary crises has the potential to contribute to disciplinary and cultural self-awareness that can fund the kinds of interventions we now need.

Freud's Seduction Theory and *Believe All Women*

The pertinent history begins in 1895 when Freud wrote a letter to his friend and confidant, Wilhelm Fliess, in which he claimed to have finally solved the problem of hysteria – the medical quandary of his era.[9] *Hysteria* is a term that comes from the Greek word for uterus. It was originally used in connection with a belief in ancient Greek medical thought that unexplained maladies in women were caused by the uterus leaving its customary place in the lower abdomen and wandering about in the body.[10] From that point on, the diagnosis was applied over the ages to a wide range of symptoms, the unifying principle usually being that these symptoms were seen to be women-specific, though men were diagnosed with hysteria in fewer numbers as well. In the modern era, the list of symptoms the diagnosis covered included, among others, 'convulsions, irregular speech or mutism, loss of hearing, sexual dysfunction, and gastrointestinal or genitourinary complaints'.[11] Freud's early work on hysteria affirms these and adds several more – catatonia, haemorrhages, paraplegia and panic attacks, to name a few. Not least because the possible symptoms of hysteria seemed both endless and physiologically untraceable, the condition was confounding for generations of physicians.

Confident that he had found, once and for all, the etiological source of hysteria, Freud announced his discovery to the European medical community. The position Freud took in his three 1896 expositions of the subject was that hysteria was caused by sexual seduction in early childhood.[12] For Freud, *seduction* is a term that connotes sexual passivity, an experience in which one's genitals are acted upon by an adult or older child. At this point in his career, Freud did not have a concept of children's non-abusive sexual play. Nor is it entirely clear the extent to which he differentiated the apparently common practice of putting children to sleep by stroking their genitals[13] (which we would today call abusive) from, for example, the accidental stimulation of a child's genitals a caregiver might trigger while changing a child's diaper or giving him a bath (acts to which we might today attribute psychological significance but not categorize as abuse). For this reason, it would be incorrect to consider the contemporary concept of abuse a direct parallel to Freud's meaning of the word *seduction*. And yet, it is quite clear that Freud's seduction theory understood the kind of childhood sexual experience that led to hysteria as traumatic, frightening, dominating, and characterized by the absence of the child's consent. In his 1896 papers, Freud used the terms *abuse* (Missbrauch), *rape* (Vergewaltigung), *assault* (Attentat, the French term), *attack* (Angriff), *aggression* (Aggression), *traumas* (Traumen) and *seduction* (Verführung) interchangeably to describe the infantile experiences etiologically responsible for hysterical symptoms.

To support his claim that hysteria was caused by seduction, Freud emphatically stated that every one of his hysterical patients of the previous year in which he was testing his hypothesis had, indeed, been seduced as children, and that their hysterical symptoms could be traced back to experiences of their sexual passivity. Freud gives several examples of what it means for hysterical symptoms to be traced to experiences of childhood seduction. In one case, a man who, as a child, was forced to sexually pleasure an adult woman with his foot, developed neurotic fixation on his legs and hysterical paraplegia in early adulthood. Though unaware of the abuse he experienced in childhood, his unconscious self-reproach for having complied with his abuser's sexual demands manifested through a chain of memories and associations as simultaneous fixation on and dissociation from the part of his body that betrayed him. In another instance, Freud tells of a woman who developed severe anxiety attacks that would resolve only when a particular sister of hers came to her side and stayed with her. It was discovered through analysis that this woman was sexually abused as a child and that her abuser would ask her each time he was about to begin an assault if this sister was home. The sister's presence or absence made the difference between whether or not the abuser would carry out his plan. Thus, when unconsciously reminded of her childhood abuse, this sister's presence was all that could produce a sense of safety in the patient.[14]

Without hesitation, the seduction theory takes Freud's patients' recollections of childhood seduction to be historically representative even though they are representative symbolically. Memories of abuse, in other words, are considered to meaningfully reflect real experiences, and those experiences are taken to be the traumatic cause of his patients' hysterical symptoms later in life. The memory, history, trauma triad is projected as a framework that stabilizes each of its three legs by constructing a correspondent, causal relationship between them. Memory corresponds to history. History causes trauma. Access to any one leg of the triad is taken to reliably reveal the content of the other two.[15]

Judith Herman, a trauma and sexual violence specialist, describes Freud's seduction theory as evidence of Freud's original empathic commitment to his women patients. In her words, 'His [early] case histories reveal a man possessed of such passionate curiosity that he was willing to overcome his own defensiveness, and willing to listen.'[16] Even in comparison with contemporary trauma research, Herman finds Freud's seduction theory to be 'brilliant, compassionate, eloquently argued, [and] closely reasoned'.[17] For her, the genius of the seduction theory is that it is grounded, first, in closely listening to and believing that patients' memories of abuse correspond to real experiences and, second, in insistence that real experiences of early childhood sexual trauma drastically impact psychic functioning. In other words, she finds the seduction theory to be valuable because it treats memory as reliably representative of history and history as causally related to trauma.

It is one thing to say that a person who remembers being abused was abused. It is another thing to say that a person's memory of abuse is historically accurate in detail – the date of the assault, time of day, what the perpetrator was wearing, the placement of furniture in the room. Memory researchers, from Elizabeth Loftus, who is sceptical of survivor testimony, to Lenore Terr, who defends the reliability of traumatic memory, have demonstrated that memory is far from infallible with respect to this kind of detail.[18] Freud does not argue that memory is infallible in this detailed sense. He views memory as symbolic rather than as a video reel that plays back pristine data. Yet, within the structure of his argument that his patients' memories of seduction should be considered true in a historical sense, he does not deal with how it is possible to insist on the correspondence of memory with history in general without also demanding the same level of correspondence between memory and history's details.

The seduction theory infuses survivors' memory with authority, but that authority depends on a nearly impossible standard: that survivors' memories of sexual abuse will in fact correspond. This is a consequence of Freud's argument, not a central or perhaps even intentional feature. A tight correspondence is the shape of memory's relationship to history that his seduction theory implicitly recommends, and he did not build theoretical scaffolding that would enable another option. The problem, then, with Freud's seduction theory is that it takes the categories of history and memory at a kind unnerving face value. In his articulation of the seduction theory Freud leaves these categories uninterrogated. His under-theorization of the concepts and of the relationship between history and memory in sexually traumatic circumstances is what renders the seduction theory unable to ultimately support robust solidarity with survivors of this kind of violence.

In the contemporary *believe all women* approach to sexual violence, we can identify a similar problem. Those who report sexual violence are to be immediately believed. Survivor testimonies of sexually violent experiences are to be accepted as meaningfully correspondent with the historical events to which they refer. Like Freud's seduction theory, this lens intends to authorize the testimonies of sexual violence survivors as reliable sources of knowledge about history. And yet, because *believe all women* does not interrogate the way that traumatic memory works in the lives of survivors or articulate the *kind* of truth it reveals about history and experience, any instance of a false or mistaken report made by one alleged survivor calls the authority of every survivor's testimony into question. If one woman can be shown to be undeserving of belief, the legitimacy of the *believe all women* lens is in jeopardy. If memory is shown *not* to be historically representative in a correspondent sense then, in the seduction theory and *believe all women* frameworks, it becomes difficult to continue to talk about that memory as authoritative at all. Like Freud's seduction theory, the *believe all women* lens leaves the categories of memory and history, their relationship to one another, and their relationship to trauma under-thought. Consequently, it cannot account for the complexity with which these manifest in survivors' lives. Since traumatic memory has been shown to be far more complex than a lens of correspondence can support, both Freud's seduction theory and the *believe all women* position prove unable to fully authorize sexual violence survivors' testimony.

Freud's Oedipal Theory and *Due Process*

For reasons widely debated in psychoanalytic history,[19] Freud confessed privately to Wilhelm Fliess in 1897 that he had lost confidence in his seduction theory.[20] After several years of relative silence on the topic, Freud published *Three Essays on the Theory of Sexuality* in which he formally distanced himself from the seduction theory, first attempted to explain the reasons for its error, and laid the foundation for a new theory that would endure prominently in his thinking and practice for the rest of his life: the theory of infantile sexuality framed in terms of the Oedipal complex.[21]

Freud justified his move away from the seduction theory, in part, by stating that the hysterical patients whom he had originally believed were sexually seduced in childhood were, in fact, not seduced.[22] He explained, rather, that in at least some cases his patients' recollections during analysis of scenes in which they were passively sexually engaged were reproductions of their own fantasies and not representative of history.[23] Centred on the Oedipus myth and committed to a cis, binary and heterosexual conceptualization of gender and sexuality, Freud's new theory proposed that the development of the psyche is shaped as children grow to sexually desire a parent of different sex and competitively revile a parent of same sex.[24] However, since incest is taboo, a child may come to banish conscious knowledge of her desire for her father and replace it with a fantasy in which she is the passive recipient of his active sexual attention. Hence, Freud argued, his patients, whom he had believed during his development of the seduction theory were remembering real experiences of sexual abuse had, in some cases, been remembering the fantasy form of their own repressed sexual desire and *not* an event that had historically occurred.

The Oedipal theory drastically revises Freud's thought on the relationship between memory, history and trauma. Without dissociating each from the others completely, the theory opens such an expanse between the three legs of the triad that they struggle to support weight when confronted with an actual instance of childhood sexual abuse. The Oedipal theory tells us that history – what has happened to a person – is not as likely to be the cause of trauma as one's own intrapsychic conflict. The child's simultaneous desire for her father and disgust with herself for desiring her father is taken to be the root of hysterical symptoms. A hysterical patient's suffering, in other words, is no longer conceived as a response to external, intersubjective experience. It is taken to be self-inflicted.

The Oedipal theory proposes that the relation of memory to history is not direct (as the seduction theory had assumed) but, rather, mediated by fantasy. Contemporary trauma and memory research suggests that a sophisticated approach to the interplay of intrapsychic and historical influences in traumatic memory is necessary if clinicians are going to develop the capacity to sensitively and accurately interpret what their clients bring with them into treatment. To demonstrate the danger he sees in Freud's original seduction theory assertion that memory is correspondent with history, psychoanalyst K. R. Eissler recounts a case in which a middle-aged woman born with female sex organs recalled that her mother had cut off her penis when she was a child. Eissler argues that because we know that what this client recollects could not have happened in reality – the woman never had a physiological penis for her mother to remove – we cannot support a theory that insists memory is always historically true in a correspondent sense.[25] We do need some way of accounting for the fact that memory is itself a constructive and interpretive endeavour. And yet, because Freud's Oedipal theory does not provide a way of determining where fantasy begins and ends, it cannot tell us of that which presents itself as memory reflects history and what has been constructed through intrapsychic fantasy. Without denying the significance of memory for history completely, the Oedipal theory leaves that significance always open to doubt. And, when it comes to memory of childhood incest, Freud makes the necessity of this doubt absolute:

> and if in the case of girls who produce such an event [seduction] in the story of their childhood their father figures fairly regularly as the seducer, there can be no doubt either of the imaginary nature of the accusation or of the motive that has led to it. A phantasy of being seduced when no seduction has occurred is usually employed by a child to screen the auto-erotic period of his sexual activity. He spares himself shame about masturbation by retrospectively phantasying a desired object into these earliest times.[26]

This excerpt is taken from a larger section in which Freud articulates both his confidence that a significant portion of seduction memories are false and his continuing belief that some are memories of real, historical events. His Oedipal emphasis on the potential for recollections of childhood sexual abuse to be ahistorical does not eliminate the possibility that such a recollection does reference an event that happened. However, it also does not protect against the relation between memory and history becoming so destabilized that the significance of memory for history can be selectively denied. In other words, fantasy, which mediates the relation between memory and history in the Oedipal theory, threatens to replace both, and survivors of sexual violence are left vulnerable to the claim that what they believe they have experienced is a fabrication of their minds.

Just as there are resonances between the seduction theory and the *believe all women* lens, a number of the theoretical moves that characterize Freud's shift to the Oedipal paradigm share features with *due process* logic. The most obvious point of resonance is that neither considers an alleged survivor's memory of a sexually violent experience necessarily reliable for determining what occurred. A survivor's memory, alone, does not warrant belief. External forms of evidence are needed if one is to determine whether or not any particular account of sexual violence indeed happened.

While the Oedipal theory makes the relationship between any memory and the history to which it refers an open question, memory of sexual abuse in childhood becomes the quintessential example of Oedipal fantasy in disguise. This particular kind of memory then – memory of sexual abuse – is vulnerable in Freud's Oedipal framework to being understood as especially suspect and prone to distortion. Proponents of the *due process* lens express precisely this kind of attitude towards memories of sexual violence. The *due process* lens does not tend to emphasize the need for scepticism of memory in general or for external corroborating evidence as a warrant for believing all mnemic claims. It is concerned about the specific unreliability of memories of sexual violence. The *due process* lens rests on a fundamental concern that there is an unbridgeable chasm between memories of *this* kind and the histories to which they refer. Its perception that memories of sexual violence are uniquely dubious helps to justify its claim that external corroborating evidence is an ethical prerequisite for believing survivor testimony.

In another point of resonance, the Oedipal framework sees the suffering of hysterics as produced internally, not externally imposed. Hysterics are considered, in a sense, responsible for their suffering. Proponents of the *due process* position tend also to emphasize the responsibility of alleged victims of sexual violence. For example, *due process* proponents are concerned that those who claim to have experienced sexual violence are not, in making such a claim, shirking responsibility for 'their part' in the sexual encounter.[27] To extend belief to a testimony of sexual violence, the *due process* lens requires evidence not only that the event an alleged survivor remembers did, in fact occur, but evidence also that the alleged survivor did everything in their power to resist and escape assault. In the absence of such evidence the suffering of the survivor is considered pitiable, but of their own making.

Likewise, in fantasies of seduction, what presents as distressing (the patient's memory of sexual abuse) is theorized as the fantasy form of the patient's own sexual desire. Though memory of the fantasy produces affective horror in the patient, that horror indicates internal conflict around the primary fact of the unconscious *pleasure* she takes in the sexually abusive scene. The *due process* lens, in turn, expresses something like this in the form of an anxiety: it worries that those who claim to be victims make false accusations out of a sense of guilt for their own, freely chosen sexual behavior. Caitlin Flanagan, a writer for the *Atlantic* who frequently takes the *due process* position in popular discourse, represents this anxiety when she argues that a survivor whose account of sexual assault Flanagan does not find worthy of belief was motivated to tell her story out of a sense of shame for having wanted something from a man that he denied her: 'She wanted affection, kindness, attention ... What she felt afterward – rejected yet another time, by yet another man – was regret.'[28] This regret for wanting and participating in an unsatisfying sexual encounter, Flanagan supposes, was the survivor's true motive for making an accusation of assault. Before evidence is given that proves an alleged survivor's motives for coming forward are pure, those testifying to experiences of sexual violence are suspected of having wanted what they claim was traumatic for them.

Thinking *Belief* Outside the Frame

Freud's replacement of the seduction theory with the Oedipal paradigm was well received by Freud's peers and by the subsequent psychoanalytic tradition that developed largely from Freud's Oedipal theory of child sexuality. In the 1990s, however, Freud's renunciation of the seduction theory became a matter of contention, particularly in the wake of that decade's focus on the credibility of childhood memories of sexual abuse.[29] The broad affirmation that Freud's theory switch enjoyed up to that point was challenged by a minority group of psychoanalysts and psychologists allied with survivors of sexual violence, and a debate broke out between the majority who continued to view Freud's renunciation of the seduction theory as the scientifically and clinically right choice for him to have made and a new minority who argued that this choice amounted, in one way or another, to an abandonment of sexual violence survivors.[30] Those who viewed Freud's theory switch unfavourably expressed positions characteristic of the *believe all women* lens. Those who defended Freud's replacement of the seduction theory with the Oedipal paradigm expressed views consistent with the *due process* lens. The resonance between Freud's two theories and the two sides of the contemporary debate was viscerally apparent.

The terms of the contemporary debate, however, are not identical replications of the positions that Freud's two theories recommend regarding whether and when testimonies of sexual violence ought to be believed. What I have argued, rather, is that in spite of real and undeniable differences between the nature of these two attempts to parse the believability of survivor testimony, something critical of the basic frame of the conversation stays the same. One side posits memory, history and trauma as so fused together that when brought to bear on actual survivors the lens it creates can only repudiate the complexity it finds in survivors' lived realities. The other posits such destabilized relations between memory, history and trauma that no claim that memory reveals history or that history is to blame for trauma can gain reliable traction. What I have aimed to suggest by holding contemporary discourse up to a Freudian mirror is that a tendency for discourse on believing survivor testimony to fall into one of these two frames is culturally persistent. It is a dualistic frame that repeats itself through multiple iterations of Western thought.

There are serious repercussions here for theology; when we think theologically about sexual violence and ethical modes of resistance, response and support for survivors, we are preconditioned to think in the terms presented by this dualistic frame.[31] A vulnerability to thinking within one conceptual frame or the other is written into Western cultural ways of processing the appropriateness of belief in response to sexual violence. This poses a problem for theology because neither frame is constructed in a way that meets the challenge of conceptualizing belief or on terms that account for the complex interplay of memory, history and trauma in survivors' experience. It is not enough for theology to state that survivors ought to be believed. We need approaches to belief that are self-conscious of the inherent pressure in Western thought to fall into the dualistic frames and committed to avoiding the trap. We are obliged to construct alternative conceptual frames for belief and embodied practices of belief that bear full witness to what it means to live as a person who has experienced the world's attempt to erase them.[32]

To make an intervention into the problem and shift contemporary discourse in a helpful direction, then, we might consider taking a step back and focusing, first, on articulating what kind of relationship between memory, history and trauma enables thick, committed, solidarity-in-action with survivors. How, for example, would theology conceptualize and validate the kind of memory I brought with me into that library where I first told someone important to me that I feared the violence of my childhood I thought I had fabricated was real? What sense can theology make of the lines that twist back and forth between reality and its incoherence in survivors' shifting knowledge of themselves and the violence they have lived? How can theology hold space for, honour and learn from the survivor who enters the library confident that she was mistreated *and* the survivor who leaves the library equally sure that she is responsible for her suffering after all? What kind of belief can theology recommend that will affirm this survivor's experience of abuse without erasing or ignoring the persistence with which reality, for her, shifts ground?

Perhaps, the question, then, is this: *what makes for a robust concept and practice of belief in the wake of persistent uncertainty?* This is a question theology is prepared to speak to. It resonates with a dilemma Christians have been wrestling with for millennia – how can we have knowledge of God when certain evidence of God's existence and nature is seemingly unavailable? How can we be confident enough in our knowledge of God to build a life on its foundation when we cannot prove that what we take to be our knowledge of God is not mistaken? What warrants belief in God in this uncertain epistemological landscape? There are important differences between belief in God and belief with respect to survivor testimonies of sexual violence. And, yet, the wealth of theological reflection on religious belief in the absence of evidence or certainty offers creative possibilities for approaching knowledge of sexual violence and affirming survivors' testimonies.

Theological approaches to belief that treat belief in God as simple cognitive assent to an intellectual position (that is, that God exists and is good) will not get us far. Belief-as-cognitive-assent reproduces the terms of the dualism we are trying to think around. More promising, however, are theological approaches to belief in God that conceptualize belief as a practice. Teresa of Avila is one theologian to whom we might turn for direction.[33] Belief-as-practice is cultivated. It is both process and commitment. Like love or justice, it is something we do in the world and enact, over time, in our relationships. On the one hand, belief in this sense means carving space in which to live meaningfully – know oneself, build relationships, make decisions, take action – in the midst of uncertainty instead of as a result of uncertainty's defeat. To *believe survivors* in this sense would require the development of methods for holding perpetrators and enablers account-able that intervene in the cycle of violence but remain honest about the possibility that memory and history will not correspond. In another sense, belief-as-practice can be conceptualized as a daily discipline of embodied attunement to sources of wisdom on which belief is sustained. Believing sur-vivors in this way would mean focusing one's daily attention on cultivating intellectual, spiritual and relational resources that enable one, over time, to recognize truth when it is revealed through survivor testimony.

I started this chapter by focusing on the capacity of sexual violence to upend survivors' fundamental sense of reality. I called this the traumatic alchemy of reality into incoherence. This alchemic power demands our atten-tion not only because it threatens the lives of individual survivors, although it does do that. It demands our attention also because it is one of the sly mechanisms through which sexual violence perpetuates itself. If survivors are not sure of themselves, and if the world requires certainty as a foun-dation for action, resistance to a form of violence that does its work through blurring the lines between fact and fiction is ill fated. As I rehearsed the shape of Western approaches to discourse on the appropriateness of believ-ing survivor testimony, my concern was to show precisely this. We seem to be culturally conditioned to think about believing survivors through a per-sistent, dualistic frame, and the terms of the dualism threaten to sabotage our sincerest efforts to resist sexual violence and transform its harm. This is a theological problem, in part, because theology is not beyond the reach of the dualism. But it is also a problem into which theology is positioned to speak a unique word because it is, ultimately, a problem rooted in concepts and practices of belief. And *belief* is a theological concept. When the theo-logically minded among us bring the tools of the discipline to bear on the task of constructing belief as a practice of resistance to the alchemy of sur-vivors' reality into incoherence, we will have made a critical step towards resisting the power of sexual violence to perpetuate itself among us.

References

Bonomi, Carlo, '"Sexuality and Death" in Freud's Discovery of Sexual Aetiology', *International Forum of Psychoanalysis* 3, no. 2 (2007), 63–87.

Cooper-White, Pamela, 'Denial, Victims, and Survivors: Post-traumatic Identity Formation and Monuments in Heaven', *Journal of Pastoral Theology*, 22, no. 1, 2-1-2-16, DOI: 10.1179/jpt.2012.22.1.002.

Crumpton, Stephanie, *A Womanist Pastoral Theology against Intimate and Cultural Violence*, New York: Palgrave Macmillan, 2014.

Eissler, K. R., *Freud and the Seduction Theory: A Brief Love Affair*, Madison, CT: International Universities Press, 2001.

Ellis, Carolyn, Tony Adams and Arthur Bochner, 'Autoethnography: An Overview', *Forum: Qualitative Social Research/Sozialforschung* 12, no. 1: www.qualitativer-esearch.net/index.php/fqs/article/view/1589/3095.

False Memory Syndrome Foundation, accessed 25 January 2019: www.fmsonline.org/.

Flanagan, Caitlin, 'Babe Turns a Movement into a Racket', *Atlantic*, 19 January 2019: www.theatlantic.com/entertainment/archive/2018/01/how-a-movement-becomes-a-racket/551036/.

—— 'The Conversation #MeToo Needs to Have', *Atlantic*, 29 January 2018: www.theatlantic.com/politics/archive/2018/01/the-right-conversation-for-metoo/551732/.

—— 'The Humiliation of Aziz Ansari', *Atlantic*, 14 January 2018: www.theatlantic.com/entertainment/archive/2018/01/the-humiliation-of-azizansari/550541/.

Freud, Sigmund, 'Aetiology of Hysteria', in *The Standard Edition of the Complete Works of Sigmund Freud*, vol. 3, ed. and trans. James Strachey and Anna Freud, London: The Hogarth Press, 1962, 191–221.

—— 'Further Remarks on the Neuro-Psychoses of Defense', in *The Standard Edition of the Complete Works of Sigmund Freud*, vol. 3, ed. and trans. James Strachey and Anna Freud, London: The Hogarth Press, 1962, 157–85.

—— 'Heredity and the Aetiology of the Neuroses', in *The Standard Edition of the Complete Works of Sigmund Freud*, vol. 3, ed. and trans. James Strachey and Anna Freud, London: The Hogarth Press, 1962, 141–56.

—— 'My Views on the Role of Sexuality in the Etiology of the Neuroses' (1906), in *The Standard Edition of the Complete Works of Sigmund Freud*, vol. 7, ed. and trans. James Strachey and Anna Freud, London: The Hogarth Press, 1953, 271–82.

—— 'On the History of the Psycho-Analytic Movement' (1914), in *The Standard Edition of the Complete Works of Sigmund Freud*, vol. 14, ed. and trans. James Strachey and Anna Freud, London: The Hogarth Press, 1957, 7–66.

—— 'The Interpretation of Dreams' (1899), in *The Standard Edition of the Complete Works of Sigmund Freud*, vols 4 and 5, ed. and trans. James Strachey and Anna Freud, London: The Hogarth Press, 1957, 7–66.

—— *The Origins of Psychoanalysis: Letters to Wilhelm Fliess, Drafts and Notes, 1887–1902*, ed. Marie Bonaparte, Anna Freud and Ernst Kris, London: Imago, 1954.

—— 'Three Essays on the Theory of Sexuality' (1905), in *The Standard Edition of the Complete Works of Sigmund Freud*, vol. 7, ed. and trans. James Strachey and Anna Freud, London: The Hogarth Press, 1953, 135–243.

Good, Michel, 'Karl Abraham, Sigmund Freud, and the Fate of the Seduction Theory', *Journal of the Psychoanalytic Association* 43, no. 4 (August 1995), 1137–68.

Hartmann, Margaret, 'Everything We Know about the UVA Rape Case [Updated]', *New York Magazine*, 30 July 2015: http://nymag.com/intelligencer/2014/12/everything-we-know-uva-rape-case.html.

Herman, Judith, *Trauma and Recovery: The Aftermath of Violence – From Domestic Abuse to Political Terror*, New York: Basic Books, 1992.

Hollander, Jenny, 'Why "Believe Women" Means Believing Women Without Exception', *Bustle*, 21 November 2017: www.bustle.com/p/why-believe-women-means-believing-women-without-exception-5532903.

Into Account – Support for Survivors Seeking Justice, Accountability, and Healing in Christian Contexts. Blog: https://intoaccount.org/category/into-account/ (accessed 25 January 2019).

Keshgegian, Flora A., *Redeeming Memories: A Theology of Healing and Transformation*, Nashville, TN: Abingdon Press, 2000.

Loftus, Elizabeth, *The Myth of Repressed Memory: False Memories and Allegations of Sexual Abuse*, New York: St Martin's Press, 1994.

Loftus, Elizabeth and John Palmer, 'Reconstruction of Automobile Destruction: An Example of the Interaction between Language and Memory', *Journal of Verbal Learning and Verbal Behavior* 13 (1974), 585–89.

Masson, Jeffrey, *The Assault on Truth: Freud's Suppression of the Seduction Theory*, New York: Penguin Books, 1984.

McClure, John S. and Nancy J. Ramsay, eds, *Telling the Truth: Preaching Against Sexual and Domestic Violence*, Cleveland, OH: United Church Press, 1998.

McNally, Richard J., *Remembering Trauma*, Cambridge, MA: Harvard University Press, 2005.

Our Stories Untold: www.ourstoriesuntold.com/ (accessed 25 January 2019).

—— Stories: www.ourstoriesuntold.com/stories/ (accessed 25 January 2019).

Poling, James Newton, *The Abuse of Power: A Theological Problem*, Nashville, TN: Abingdon Press, 1991.

Pope, Kenneth, 'Memory, Abuse, and Science: Questioning Claims about the False Memory Syndrome Epidemic', *American Psychologist* 51, no. 9 (September 1996), 957–74.

Rambo, Shelly, *Resurrecting Wounds: Living in the Afterlife of Trauma*, Waco, TX: Baylor University Press, 2017.

Randazza, Marc, 'Should We Always Believe the Victim?', *CNN*, 7 December 2014: www.cnn.com/2014/12/05/opinion/randazza-uva-rapeallegations/index.html.

Teresa of Avila, *The Interior Castle*, New York: Paulist Press [1588] 1979.

Terr, Lenore, *Unchained Memories: True Stories of Traumatic Memories, Lost and Found*, New York: Basic Books, 1994.

Van der Kolk, Bessel, *The Body Keeps the Score*, New York: Penguin Books, 2014.

Vienna Psychoanalytic Society meeting, 24 January 1912. Proceedings published in *Minutes of the Vienna Psychoanalytic Society*, vol. 4 (1912–18), ed. H. Nunberg and E. Federn, trans. Marianne Nunberg in collaboration with Harold Collines, New York: International University Press, 1962–75.

Walsh, Kira, 'Hysteria', in *Cultural Sociology of Mental Illness: An A–Z Guide*, Los Angeles: Sage Publications, 2014.

Walton, Heather, *Writing Methods in Theological Reflection*, London: SCM Press, 2014.

Notes

1 Some of the survivors to whom I refer have published accounts that can be read online through Into Account at https://intoaccount.org/blog/ and through Our Stories Untold at www.ourstoriesuntold.com/ and www.ourstoriesuntold.com/stories/.

2 An example of the *due process* argument includes Caitlin Flanagan, 'The Conversation #MeToo Needs to Have', *Atlantic*, 29 January 2018, www.theatlantic.com/politics/archive/2018/01/the-right-conversation-for-metoo/551732/.

3 An example of the *believe all women* argument: Jenny Hollander, 'Why "Believe Women" Means Believing Women Without Exception', *Bustle*, 21 November 2017, www.bustle.com/p/why-believe-women-means-believing-women-without-exception-5532903.

4 In her book *Writing Methods in Theological Reflection* (London: SCM Press, 2014), Heather Walton's account of autoethnography speaks to the method by which I use this chapter's opening anecdote to support the development of my theological argument. Walton defines autoethnography according to Ellis, Adams and Bochner's 2011 definition: 'an approach to research and writing that seeks to describe and systematically analyse (*graphy*) personal experience (*auto*) in order to understand cultural experience (*ethno*)' (Walton, 3).

5 For a summary of the UVA case, see Margaret Hartmann, 'Everything We Know About the UVA Rape Case [Updated]', *New York Magazine*, 30 July 2015, http://nymag.com/intelligencer/2014/12/everything-we-know-uva-rape-case.html. For an example of this case being used in arguments against believing survivors, see Marc Randazza, 'Should We Always Believe the Victim?' *CNN*, 7 December 2014, www.cnn.com/2014/12/05/opinion/randazza-uva-rape-allegations/index.html.

6 In the early 1990s, childhood sexual abuse gained massive media attention as several high-profile survivors came forward and reported to have repressed and recovered memory of the abuse they experienced. In response, a group of psychologists and other interested parties developed what is now called the false memory syndrome movement. They argued that repressed memory is universally false, and mounted campaigns to discredit claims of recovered memory (and the survivors who made them) in popular, legal and psychological discourse. Trauma research now affirms multiple forms of traumatic memory in which memory might be lost and regained at different periods, but the false memory syndrome movement remains culturally influential. The crux of its argument can be found at the website for the False Memory Syndrome Foundation (accessed 25 January 2019), www.fmsfonline.org/. Elizabeth Loftus popularized the argument in her writings, for example, *The Myth of Repressed Memory: False Memories and Allegations of Sexual Abuse* (New York: St. Martin's Press, 1994). An early argument against the claims of the false memory syndrome movement can be found in Lenore Terr's *Unchained Memories: True Stories of Traumatic Memories, Lost and Found* (New York: Basic Books, 1994), and collections of relevant research on traumatic memory are referenced throughout Bessel van der Kolk's *The Body Keeps the Score* (New York: Penguin Books, 2014). Himself a trauma and abuse specialist, van der Kolk was fired from his position as medical director of the Brookline Trauma Center in 2018 for bullying and denigrating employees.

7 Though another full chapter could be devoted to the complexities of Freud's approach to believing accounts of childhood sexual abuse in each of his theories,

one clarification must be stated alongside my generalization linking the seduction theory with belief and the Oedipal theory with its withholding. That is: though Freud's replacement of the seduction theory with the Oedipal paradigm is characterized by a shift away from extending belief to accounts of childhood sexual abuse, he insists at every point in his career that clinicians understand that such abuse does occur. Freud does not deny the reality of sexual abuse. It is, rather, the terms that warrant believing any particular recollection of abuse that are at issue for him.

8 I mean both that Freud's own thought was influential and that his thought was changed, appropriated and popularized in ways that have been influential even as they fail to accurately reflect Freud's own positions. This chapter is concerned as much (if not more) with this latter form of influence as with the former.

9 Sigmund Freud, *The Origins of Psychoanalysis: Letters to Wilhelm Fliess, Drafts and Notes, 1887–1902*, ed. Marie Bonaparte, Anna Freud and Ernst Kris (London: Imago, 1954), 215–18.

10 Kira Walsh, 'Hysteria', in *Cultural Sociology of Mental Illness: An A–Z Guide* (Los Angeles: Sage Publications, 2014), 404.

11 Walsh, 'Hysteria', 403.

12 Sigmund Freud, 'Aetiology of Hysteria' (1896), in *The Standard Edition of the Complete Works of Sigmund Freud (SE)*, vol. 3, ed. and trans. James Strachey and Anna Freud (London: The Hogarth Press, 1962), 191–221; 'Further Remarks on the Neuro-Psychoses of Defense' (1896), *SE*, vol. 3, 157–85; 'Heredity and the Aetiology of the Neuroses' (1896), *SE*, vol. 3, 141–56.

13 Carlo Bonomi, '"Sexuality and Death" in Freud's Discovery of Sexual Aetiology', *International Forum of Psychoanalysis* 3, no. 2 (December 2007), 69.

14 Freud, 'Aetiology of Hysteria', 215.

15 While I am emphasizing that Freud drew a causal and correspondent relationship between the three points in the memory, history, trauma triad it is worth noting that he is doing so perhaps less directly than his contemporaries who left no room in their understanding of hysteria for the involvement of the psychic apparatus at all. In his historical context, by claiming that the psyche transforms memory into *symbols* of trauma prompted by history, Freud can be seen as creating a degree of separation between memory and trauma already in his seduction theory.

16 Judith Herman, *Trauma and Recovery: The Aftermath of Violence – from Domestic Abuse to Political Terror* (New York: Basic Books, 1992), 13.

17 Herman, *Trauma and Recovery*, 13.

18 Elizabeth Loftus and John Palmer, 'Reconstruction of Automobile Destruction: An Example of the Interaction between Language and Memory', *Journal of Verbal Learning and Verbal Behavior* 13, no. 5 (1974), 585–9. Lenore Terr, *Unchained Memories: True Stories of Traumatic Memories, Lost and Found* (New York: Basic Books, 1994).

19 For a review of the debate, see Michel Good, 'Karl Abraham, Sigmund Freud, and the Fate of the Seduction Theory', *Journal of the Psychoanalytic Association* 43, no. 4 (August 1995), 1137–68; Jeffrey Masson, *The Assault on Truth: Freud's Suppression of the Seduction Theory* (New York: Penguin Books, 1984); K. R. Eissler, *Freud and the Seduction Theory: A Brief Love Affair* (Madison, CT: International Universities Press, 2001); and Judith Herman, *Trauma and Recovery*, 7–32.

20 Freud, *The Origins of Psychoanalysis*, 215–18.

21 Sigmund Freud, 'Three Essays on the Theory of Sexuality' (1905), *SE*, vol. 7, 135–243.

22 This is not to say that Freud's belief that some of his clients' memories of abuse were not historically unrepresentative is the only reason he gives for renouncing the seduction theory. He explains his theory switch in numerous ways throughout his career.

23 See, for example, Sigmund Freud, 'My Views on the Role of Sexuality in the Etiology of the Neuroses' (1906), *SE*, vol. 7, 274; Sigmund Freud, 'On the History of the Psycho-Analytic Movement' (1914), *SE*, vol. 14, 17; and Freud's contributions to the Vienna Psychoanalytic Society meeting, 24 January 1912, in *Minutes of the Vienna Psychoanalytic Society*, vol. 4 (1912–18), ed. H. Nunberg and E. Federn, trans. Marianne Nunberg in collaboration with Harold Collines (New York: International University Press, 1962–75).

24 Freud first articulated the Oedipus complex in 'The Interpretation of Dreams' (1899), *SE*, vols. 4 and 5.

25 Eissler, *Freud and the Seduction Theory*, 283.

26 Sigmund Freud, 'Introductory Lectures on Psycho-Analysis' (1916–17), *SE*, vol. 16, 369.

27 For example, Caitlin Flanagan expresses this concern in the first of three consecutive articles that take the *due process* position in resistance to early 2018 support for an anonymous survivor who accused actor and comedian Aziz Ansari of sexual assault. Those three articles are 'The Humiliation of Aziz Ansari', *Atlantic*, 14 January 2018, www.theatlantic.com/entertainment/archive/2018/01/the-humiliation-of-aziz-ansari/550541/; 'Babe Turns a Movement into a Racket', *Atlantic*, 19 January 2019, www.theatlantic.com/entertainment/archive/2018/01/how-a-move ment-becomes-a-racket/551036/; and 'The Conversation #MeToo Needs to Have', *Atlantic*, 29 January 2018, www.theatlantic.com/politics/archive/2018/01/the-right-conversation-for-metoo/551732/.

28 Flanagan, 'The Humiliation of Aziz Ansari'.

29 Kenneth Pope's 1996 address to the American Psychological Association offers both summary and analysis of the 1990s debate. It was subsequently published as 'Memory, Abuse, and Science: Questioning Claims about the False Memory Syndrome Epidemic', *American Psychologist* 51, no. 9 (September 1996), 957–74.

30 See Eissler, *Freud and the Seduction Theory*; Herman, *Trauma and Recovery*, 7–32; Masson, *The Assault on Truth*.

31 I would argue that in theological treatments of sexual violence and the matter of belief, theology tends to favour the *believe all women* frame. This does not, by any means, discount the important contributions made by such texts. Rather, it points to the need for these foundational theological contributions to discourse on sexual violence to be built upon. Examples include James Newton Poling's *The Abuse of Power: A Theological Problem* (Nashville, TN: Abingdon Press, 1991), contributions to John S. McClure and Nancy J. Ramsay's *Telling the Truth: Preaching against Sexual and Domestic Violence* (Cleveland, OH: United Church Press, 1998), and Pamela Cooper-White's 'Denial, Victims, and Survivors: Post-traumatic Identity Formation and Monuments in Heaven', *Journal of Pastoral Theology* 22, no. 1, 2-1-2-16.

32 I do not know of work that intentionally takes up this mandate, but a number of resources exist within feminist and womanist theology for doing so. I would mention, especially, Stephanie Crumpton's *A Womanist Pastoral Theology against Intimate and Cultural Violence* (New York: Palgrave Macmillan, 2014), Flora A. Keshgegian's *Redeeming Memories: A Theology of Healing and Transformation*

(Nashville, TN: Abingdon Press, 2000), and Shelly Rambo's *Resurrecting Wounds: Living in the Afterlife of Trauma* (Waco, TX: Baylor University Press, 2017). I attempt to flesh out what taking up this mandate might look like in an article from *The Other Journal* titled 'Testimony and Witness as Liberative Praxis: Authority Refigured', https://theotherjournal.com/2019/05/30/testimony-and-witness-as-liber-ative-praxis-authority-refigured/.

33 Teresa of Avila, *The Interior Castle* (New York: Paulist Press [1588] 1979).

4

Body Remember: Reflecting Theologically on the Experience of Domestic Abuse through the Poetry of Kim Moore[1]

MANON CERIDWEN JAMES

> I don't know exactly what a prayer is.
> I do know how to pay attention.[2]

Feminist theologians have referred to women's literature as an alternative canon of sacred texts for women,[3] where difficult and painful experiences can be explored. The Cumbrian poet Kim Moore has a sequence that forms the heart of her collection, *The Art of Falling*, exploring her own experience of an abusive and coercive relationship. By deep reflection on this sequence I hope to draw out the theological implications in her writing, as well as gain insight and a deeper understanding of the traumatic experience of violence and abuse within a relationship.

Heather Walton[4] argues that literature is a place where we can learn about the trauma in women's experience, in contradiction to those theologians who see literature simply as idealized or abstract spaces, glimpses of divine encounter and of beauty, wisdom and transcendence.[5] Those with stigmatized identities have also found literature to be a place that has given them a theological voice, denied them by traditional doctrinal theology.[6] She further argues for a method of interrogating theology with literature, in order to empower those who have been silent.[7] This also reflects the concerns of Riet Bons-Storm,[8] who has also argued that women have felt silenced and their pastoral concerns ignored by the Church and its leaders, because their experiences are considered to be unspeakable by the Church and male clergy.

The use of poetry for theological reflection and theological research is a growing field. Nicola Slee has shown that poetry has potential as a research method for understanding female faith within a practical theological and qualitative framework, arguing that poets can be considered to be 'ethnographers' in that they enter the lives and seek to give voice to the people they live among.[9] Poets, she maintains, also employ methods that are similar to ethnography and she refers to the poet Alice Oswald's *Dart*,[10] a collection that reflects the voices of those who lived along the river of the same name. During the preparation for this collection, Oswald entered into the lives of those who lived there for three years, almost as a participant observer in ethnographic terms.[11] In my own study of Welsh women's identity, I also examined the memoirs and poetry of Welsh women in order to enrich my data gained from life-story interviews.[12] This chapter might be characterized as a theological reading of a body of work,[13] or even as an ethnographic exploration in order to inform theological and pastoral practices and theories, if ethnography is, as Martin Stringer maintains, a holistic, in-depth study of human experience that attempts to discover 'what lies beneath the surface'.[14] Or simply, this chapter could be seen as, Mary Oliver comments above, paying attention.[15]

Poetry and Spirituality

Mark Pryce argues that poetry and Christian faith are intimately linked, because of the creativity present in poetry, echoing the creativity of the Creator as every human is made in the image of God. Furthermore, theology has a 'poetic character' and poetry has a 'particular theological validity'.[16] Mark Oakley argues that 'poetry is the language that most truly reflects the life of the soul'.[17]

As someone who both reads and writes poetry, I argue that poetry is an essentially spiritual activity. Spirituality as a word has several different meanings, depending on context. Sometimes it is even a synonym for religion, at other times it is used in contrast to religion, which is seen as institutionalized and restricting.[18] Ironically, the clearest definitions of spirituality can be seen in official documents, especially within the world of medicine and health. According to a training document by NHS Scotland, spirituality is a broad term encompassing religious and non-religious affiliation and is closely related to meaning-making and the experience of being human:

> Spirituality is made up of so many parts and can be described in so many ways that it cannot be delineated. Human creativity, relationships, hopes, fears, guilt, happiness, religion, belief, life, death and spirituality encompass all of life.[19]

However, poetry is not spiritual in the sense of only being concerned with meaning, truth and beauty, as opposed to the body or the concrete world. Poetry holds in tension ultimate human meaning and values while at the same time being intensely rooted in the particular as well as subjective. It is both a space to explore values and important questions and a deep attentiveness to the world around us in its particularity. This would be my own definition of spirituality, that it is about holding together the eternal and the immediate and that spirituality, paradoxically, is about recognizing transcendence, values and human meaning-making in concrete and embodied experiences, often mundane.

The connection between spirituality and poetry is identified by Robert Wuthnow in his portrait of the poet Jon Davis, one of the many artists he interviewed in order to inform his understanding of the spirituality within creativity. He explains Davis's own method for writing:

> Davis tries not to begin writing with an idea in mind but in a spirit of emptiness that can be filled from beyond himself. 'Writing poetry is an emptying and a waiting rather than a thinking or a planning,' he says. Writing poetry is like prayer – indeed, often is prayer – insofar as he tries to listen and be attentive to whatever may be imparted to him.[20]

However, for Davis, this spirituality is a struggle. The mere act of writing will not automatically disclose truth, the meaning is found in this ambivalence and engaging with questions rather than answers: 'On many occasions, he still feels that the gods have fled. But he also believes that the essence of spirituality is present in the mystery of life. Sometimes his poetry gives him a connection with that mystery.'[21]

In this chapter, I explore a sequence from Kim Moore's poetry in which it could be argued that 'the gods have fled', but still attempt a theological reading of a body of work, if (as I am maintaining) poetry is innately 'spiritual'.

Poetry and the Poet

Kim Moore was born in 1981 in Leicester and now lives in Cumbria. She has published an award-winning pamphlet, *If We Could Speak Like Wolves*,[22] and a collection, *The Art of Falling*,[23] was published by Seren in 2015, winning the Geoffrey Faber Memorial Prize.[24] One of the poems, in this sequence, 'In That Year' was shortlisted as one of the best single poems in the Forward Prize in 2015.[25] She is currently working on a PhD at Manchester Metropolitan University on everyday sexism.

Although there is something of the 'death of the author' in the reading and interpretation of poetry, in that once a poem has been written it is up to the reader to interpret, there is no sense that there is a right and wrong way of interpreting a poem (despite what we may have been taught at school). Don Paterson refers to this as the 'flexibility of interpretation', where the reader meets the poem half way, making it their own.[26] Kim Moore is open in her blog that the sequence explores her own experience as a younger woman of a controlling and abusive relationship, and says it's about:

> what makes it possible for things like domestic violence to take place, what are the conditions in our society that mean some men become perpetrators and some women become victims/survivors/resisters or just lucky (if they don't experience it).[27]

She also reveals that some poems she avoids reading in public because they feel too personal and painful, referring to the poem 'I Know': 'This is the other poem in the sequence that I don't usually read out loud.'[28]

However, her blog also allows the poems to speak for themselves – there is no description of the abuse in any detail apart from what is in the poem. As Moore herself says about the poem 'I Know':

> Part of trauma theory talks about part of you remaining in the time and place where the trauma took place. I hadn't read anything around trauma theory when I wrote this poem though.
>
> Poetry can go back to that place and put a fence and a border around it, can contain it a little, so it isn't just leaking out into and onto everything else.
>
> All of these poems did this for me. I often describe them as my shields that I put between myself and the world.[29]

According to Gregory Orr, poetry is a way of translating the difficult experience into language:

> we shift the crisis to a bearable distance from us – we have removed it to the symbolic but vivid world of language ... we have actively made and shaped this model of our situation rather than passively endured it as a lived experience.[30]

In personal communication with me, Moore said that this sense of language translating a crisis and creating a 'bearable distance' has been helpful to her in reflecting on the writing of the sequence.[31]

There is no sustained description of the abuse; however, the metaphors and tropes explore very deeply how it feels to be hurt, controlled and manipulated. The lack of detail or narrative account reveals that the experience of domestic abuse is difficult and painful to articulate. There is a convention in writing about poetry that the poetic voice in the poem is not identified with the poet themselves, as if it is the poet always writing about her own experience.[32] However, as Moore has been open in her blog about the poems describing her own experience of trauma, for the purposes of this chapter I will be describing the poems as Moore's own experiences.

Although it is common to think of spirituality within poetry, poetry also often utilizes mythical tropes and stories, of which Scripture is also a part.[33] Moore's work does not have many references to faith or religion, although there are some. For example, her collection *The Art of Falling* opens with a poem entitled 'And the Soul' and with a quote from Plato, a poem about scaffolders (for her father, and the collection's name alludes to this poem) is called a psalm for the scaffolders, and there are two poems about being present in a religious building or service 'The Messiah St Bees Priory' and 'Hartley Street Spiritualist Church'. This last poem allows for the possibility of a spiritual experience, and God is also mentioned in 'The Art of Falling', again as an entity (person?) who may or may not exist. This poem directly leads into the sequence with the ending: 'And not falling apart at the sound/ of your name, which God/ help me sounds like falling.'[34] The God here almost sounds like a curse, and the mention of naming both echoes a poem within the sequence ('Your Name') and the creation myths which reference the power of naming someone or something. In the sequence, the poem 'When Someone is Singing' has a reference to the carol 'In the Bleak Midwinter'. However, her main influence within this sequence is Ovid's 'Metamorphoses', and the idea of transformation of the self by another person as being the ultimate act of violence.

Body Remember

One of the most moving poems in the sequence is 'Body Remember'. The title echoes that of Cavafy's famous poem 'Body Remember',[35] a poem that in old age looks back with affection and joy on youthful sexual experience. In Moore's poem, however, the poet is asking her body to remind her of previous experiences of abuse in order to keep her safe in the present and future. This contradiction, the joy and pleasure described by Cavafy compared to the pain and fear described by Moore, contributes to the sense of the bewildering and distressing experience of domestic abuse. What should be loving and supportive is the opposite, and this is disorientating as well as painful. Although the poet is pleading with her body to 'remember', the poem explores how the body does in fact remember past experience of abuse, and that trauma is a visceral experience that continues into the present.

Body, Remember

Body, remember that night you pretended
it was a film, you had a soundtrack running
through your head, don't lie to me body,
you know what it is. You're keeping it from me,
the stretched white sheets of a bed,
the spinning round of it, the high whining sound
in the head. Body, you remember how it felt,
surely, surely. You're lying to me. Show me
how to recognise the glint in the eye of the dog,
the rabid dog. Remind me, O body, of the way
he moved when he drank, that dangerous silence.
Let me feel how I let my eyes drop, birds falling
from a sky, how my heart was a field, and there
was a dog, loose in the field, it was worrying

the sheep, they were running and then
they were still. O body, let me remember
what it was to have a field in my chest,
O body, let me recognise the dog.[36]

The urgency of the writing ('show me', 'remind me', 'let me feel') and the accusatory tone ('don't lie to me', 'you're lying to me') convey powerfully the feeling of a past trauma affecting the present and of an overwhelming sense of anxiety. The active verbs (running, spinning, whining, worrying, running) in comparison to the words 'drop' and 'still' at the end also reflect the feeling that in an abusive situation the driving anxiety and desire to get away eventually can give way to a passivity in order to withstand the traumatic experience ('they were running and then/ they were still').

The poem evokes irritating sound as well as a feeling of physical agitation. The film 'soundtrack', enabling the poet to distance herself as if it is happening on screen to someone else, is combined with the 'high whining sound' to create constant background noise, a lack of peace.

Karen O'Donnell explores what trauma might mean for an individual:

This sense of being overwhelmed is a helpful one when considering trauma. In the experience of trauma, almost all victims experience severe emotional distress, and most experience frequent flashbacks or nightmares – the intrusion of past memory into the present.[37]

This seemingly contradictory experience of unreality as well as detailed memory is reflected in the poem 'Body Remember'. However, the overwhelming sense in the poem is fear, and a desire to keep safe. O'Donnell writes that the process of trauma recovery is in three stages,[38] and they are reflected in the poem. The first is what she calls establishing 'body integrity', that is, the establishment of safety, which is a thread throughout the poem. The second is making sense of the story of the traumatic experience, again something that is explored in the poem. The third stage is represented by the act of writing the sequence, that is, reconnecting with the world and offering the poems as a 'gift' to those who want to understand this or their own experience better. The poem also illustrates O'Donnell's claim that the trauma is a bodily event and that the memory of trauma is a somatic memory.[39]

Liminality

What O'Donnell describes as the feeling of being overwhelmed during and after trauma is conveyed very effectively by Moore in this sequence. There is a liminal tone to the writing, and this adds to the feeling of unreality, transition and diminished identity that is part of the experience of the abused woman, which Moore skilfully conveys. Liminal metaphors include monuments and follies ('In That Year'), animals are represented that echo fairy tales and myth, for example crows ('When I was a Thing with Feathers'), ravens and woodcutters ('The Knowing'). There is also a prayer to be turned into a flower or tree ('Translation'), echoing a common mythical trope (as well as a story from 'Metamorphoses'). In fact, prayer is always in this sequence a desperation in longing for the situation to change, not a connection or experience of the divine.

In the poem 'In That Year', we also see this liminal tone, combined with inherent contradiction, which is also evident in 'Body Remember'. This poem is significant within the sequence because many of the lines also appear in the other poems – for example, 'the language of insects' becomes the title of one of the later poems:

In That Year

And in that year my body was a pillar of smoke
and even his hands could not hold me.

And in that year my mind was an empty table
and he laid his thoughts down like dishes of plenty.

And in that year my heart was the old monument,
the folly, and no use could be found for it.

And in that year my tongue spoke the language
of insects and not even my father knew me.

And in that year I waited for the horses
but they only shifted their feet in the darkness.

And in that year I imagined a vain thing;
I believed that the world would come for me.

And in that year I gave up on all the things
I was promised and left myself to sadness.

And then that year lay down like a path
and I walked it, I walked it, I walk it.[40]

The other liminal metaphors not mentioned above also contain the inherent contradiction I have already written about in Moore's work. She describes her body as a 'pillar of smoke' and the path that she is walking as a path of sadness. This could allude to Exodus[41] where God is depicted as a pillar of smoke (or the 'fiery cloudy pillar' of the hymn 'Guide Me, O Thou Great

Redeemer'). However, the pillar of smoke she refers to speaks of her own diminished identity, not being led out of a difficult situation. In popular culture, and even poetry, walking a path is often to freedom (for example Nelson Mandela's *Long Walk to Freedom* or even Robert Frost's 'The Road not Taken'). Ironically, for Moore, walking a path is to be stuck in a situation.

Another inherent contradiction is seen in the second couplet, the table and the 'dishes of plenty'. This has resonances of the harvest table and the cornucopia (the horn of plenty), depicted in Greek mythology as Zeus' goat's horn (Amalthea) who nourished and fed him with a never-ending supply of food.[42] However, in this poem she has nothing to be thankful for, and the nourishment is the abuser's empty words.

The repetition of 'in that year' and the lack of commas after this repeated phrase adds to the driven tone of the poem. Being in a relationship of abuse is therefore described as hopeless, unreal and destabilizing. What should be life-giving is life-denying. There is also a disturbing effect on identity, and the victim's sense of self.

Identity

Victor Turner describes the liminality of the individual in this way:

> Liminal entities, such as neophytes in initiation or puberty rites, may be represented as possessing nothing. They may be disguised as monsters, wear only a strip of clothing, or even go naked, to demonstrate that as liminal beings they have no status, property, insignia, secular clothing indicating rank or role, position in a kinship system – in short, nothing that may distinguish them from their fellow neophytes or initiands. Their behavior is normally passive or humble; they must obey their instructors implicitly and accept arbitrary punishment without complaint.[43]

This excerpt is very resonant of the experience Moore describes, of abuse making the victim into a liminal being, overwhelmed, barely functioning and obedient and controlled, leading to a diminished identity. She elaborates in her blog:

> Transformation of the self by another – maybe it is the most violent thing that can happen.
> It is not as easily undone.
> And afterwards, the knowledge that the self can be transformed, and what to do with that self, now it has changed, and whether it is a self at all, or something else, something not-self.[44]

This shows the impact of Ovid's *Metamorphoses* on the sequence. This not-identity is described in several ways. The poet refers to herself as a 'mimic and could only sing what I'd heard'.[45] Size is also an effective way in which identity is enlarged and made smaller. Although a slightly more empowering poem, 'The World's Smallest Man' (towards the end of the sequence) refers to how the poet has made the abuser smaller in her head. Similarly, the poem 'Language of Insects' explores how such an experience almost annihilates the abused person's identity until they are small and silenced, as this excerpt shows:

> there are spiders that eat one another,
> there are ants that follow each other
> in a spiral, smaller and smaller
> until they take the life from one another,
> a black fist, all I know creeps to the edges
> of rooms, the flies on the windowsills,
> the buzzing, the buzzing that made it begin.[46]

The poem in the sequence that explores this most fully is 'Translation', which alludes to the story of Echo and Narcissus from Ovid's *Metamorphoses*, where we see the silencing explored starkly. The metaphors from this epic Roman poem (Echo, Europa, Zeus, Medusa and Daphne) adds to the liminal tone, as does the possibly most religious metaphor in the sequence of a cross nailed to the wind alluding to R. S. Thomas's poem 'In Church', where God is silent, and the cross 'untenanted'. There is no one who can come to help.

Translation

> Don't we all have a little Echo in us, our voices stolen,
> only able to repeat what has already been said:
> *you made me do it* he says and we call back *do it, do it.*
>
> Wouldn't any of us, if pushed, sit on the riverbank
> and comb snakes from our hair, or think that in our grief
> we could become a sea bird, our outstretched bodies
>
> like a cross nailed to the wind? Who amongst us
> hasn't sat astride a man more bull than man
> as he knelt in the dirt, for no good reason we can speak of?
>
> There was a time when I was translated by violence,
> there were times I prayed to be turned into a flower
> or a tree, something he wouldn't recognise as me.[47]

The transformation is complete – the poet wants to disappear in order to remain safe. Her identity is gone, and she is choosing this for herself, in order to keep safe.

If domestic abuse leads to the victim/survivor feeling that their identity is annihilated and that the physical pain is not just present in the moment but lives on in somatic memory, what are the implications here for theology?

The Uncontrolling God

> We learn not to look for religious echoes, doctrinal subtexts, or symbolic residues but to ask about how a text proposes a world whose internal connections are deeper and more troubling than the world as it is, as it has been made; we bring to bear a certain familiarity with the kinds of connection that are perceptible in a world related radically to gift and absolution, a theologically informed world; we read the lives of poetic speakers, fictional figures, dramatic voices with this familiarity in mind, restlessly asking to what extent this is a glass in which we see ourselves more fully, how far it takes us forward in 'coming to ourselves'.[48]

In this excerpt from Rowan Williams' essay on the theological reading of literature, we see a desire for theology to learn from and be challenged by literature in order for theology to be more true to itself. In this sequence of Moore's, we have gained some insight into the experience of domestic abuse, but it is a world very far from that of absolution and gift. A feminist theological approach would want to remain with the trauma and genuinely to listen to the experience, and not to hurry on to any form of resolution (or even healing), quite yet. Shelley Rambo would urge us to attend to the 'redemption from the middle'[49] where traumatic experiences are not 'glossed over',[50] and in this way we can truly understand the meaning of redemption and hope:

> This transformation, this redemption in the abyss of hell, is not about deliverance from the depths but, instead, about a way of being in the depths, a practice of witnessing that senses life arising amid what remains. The middle story is not a story of rising out of the depths, but a transformation of the depths themselves.[51]

My first response to this exploration of Moore's poetry is therefore to urge theologians as well as church members and leaders to take time to hear the experience that is reflected in these words, to question our own theology and practices and to seek out other writings that explore similar trauma, so that we have a more informed understanding, to make sense of our own lives and to be better equipped to respond to the trauma in the lives of others.

However, for the purposes of the chapter, I unfortunately do need to make connections with both theology and practices and not simply stay with the poems. In fact, there are similar themes within feminist theologians' work. The self that is annihilated is reflected in the 'soluble self' identified by Catherine Keller (ironically using another myth, that of Penelope and Odysseus) where women have subjugated themselves to the needs of men and, in a double oppression, also to God.[52] In pastoral terms, this is identified by Susan Dunlap as depression, where the self has gone, as if it was never there in the first place.[53]

Grace Jantzen critiques the 'masculinist necrophilic bias of Western theology'[54] with its emphasis on salvation and mortality, and proposes in its place a renewed emphasis on the more positive biblical metaphors of natality and flourishing. This 'imaginary of death'[55] has gone hand in hand with the capitalism and colonialism of the modern period that is predicated on subjugation and control. At the very least, a theology influenced by flourishing would be concerned with people's material lives and their well-being, as there is always a danger that a theology influenced by the salvation metaphor is overly concerned with life after death, rather than present experiences.[56] Though, if Rambo is correct, salvation can only be understood properly if we attend to a theology of 'remaining' with trauma.[57]

If theology is looking into the glass of the experience of domestic abuse, how can this help it 'come' to 'itself' as Williams suggests? There is a direct challenge here to theologies and practices that promote coercive control of the many by the few, or those that lead to forced transformations of identity or lack of acceptance of identity, as in traditional teachings about sexuality and gender. This teaching has conflated guilt (for actions) with shame (about identities), leading to the rejection and pain inflicted on those with stigmatized identities. Arguably the Christian faith has played a major part in creating and maintaining this stigmatization in the first place, as Stephen Pattison comments, who has written about his experiences of childhood trauma:

> My working hypothesis is that Christianity, like other social institutions engenders and promotes shame, often to enhance order and control. Shame can be used as a very effective means of manipulating people into obedience and compliance in the interests of the powerful who identify those interests with the will of God.[58]

In this final section, I have proposed some theological resources that are building blocks to create a different theology that would enable churches and Christian institutions to be more helpful in responding to domestic abuse, and not contribute to its perpetuation. The Church surely must put its own house in order first and address theologies that promote a controlling and identity-diminishing environment both within its own cultures and in its contribution to the cultures in which churches are situated.

The final building block could be a renewed engagement with the doctrine of God. Thomas Oord argues that God's love is unconditional and, furthermore that God is uncontrolling. God is not an autocrat, pulling strings behind the scenes. We have complete freedom and agency. Although God might act miraculously (but in 'non-coercive ways'), God guides and calls us towards flourishing and love, but does not coerce or control: 'To put the analogy succinctly: mermaids cannot run marathons because a mermaid's nature includes leglessness. God cannot create controllable creatures because God's nature is uncontrolling love.'[59] This again challenges our traditional doctrines of Almighty God, who takes over our identity and will so that we no longer have our own identity, because our identity is 'in Christ' and God demands obedience. This theology of God is unhelpful particularly to those living with, or who have survived, domestic abuse, as it has real echoes of the abuse they are suffering, or have suffered.

Moore's God is silent, impotent and unable to rescue her from her abusive relationship, despite her prayers. Maybe only when we accept that God is uncontrolling and is not the rescuer can we dismantle a theology that promotes coercive control and, in its place, continue to develop a theology that enables the happiness and flourishing of people of all identities, in their everyday lives, building on the work of Jantzen, Pattison and others. This theology would also need to respect and listen deeply to the experience of trauma, as Rambo argues, in order to fully engage with a pastorally helpful as well as more theologically rich understanding of salvation and hope.

And yet, we also need to sit with the experience that Moore describes for a while, even if a chapter in a book demands a conclusion and theological engagement. There is power and even healing in articulating this experience, as an example of what bell hooks would call a 'talking back'.

> Moving from silence into speech is for the oppressed, the colonized, the exploited, and those who stand and struggle side by side a gesture of defiance that heals, that makes new life and new growth possible. It is that act of speech, of 'talking back,' that is no mere gesture of empty words, that is the expression of our movement from object to subject – the liberated voice.[60]

Literature creates a space for different voices to be heard, and even a place where we can reimagine a different world.[61] Therefore, the act of writing or of reading about traumatic experiences can help the process of beginning to come to terms with trauma. The poem 'The World's Smallest Man' outlines what this reimagining could be like:

> Today I make you into the world's smallest man.
> You are so small I open my hand and you dance
> On the great landscape of my palm.

The poem ends with an acknowledgement that traumatic experiences are a part of who we are, with a stanza that is ambivalent as to whether this is in fact a healing or simply an acknowledgement of living with trauma:

> I think of all the places I could leave you
> now you are smaller than the lightest
> water boatman, but you keep shrinking
>
> till you are less than a grain of salt,
> so small you are living on my skin.
> And, once I breathe, I breathe you in.[62]

Moore's 'liberated voice'[63] challenges the Church in both theology and practice to lay aside theologies of power and control, of shaming and stigmatization, and to listen with humility and respect to voices speaking from a place of 'redemption from the middle'.[64] In this way, theology can learn from poetry what redemption and transformation really means.

References

Bons-Storm, Riet, *The Incredible Woman: Listening to Women's Silences in Pastoral Care and Counselling*, Nashville, TN: Abingdon Press, 1996.

Caball, Marc and David. F. Ford, eds, *Musics of Belonging: The Poetry of Micheal O'Siadhail*, Dublin: Carysfort Press, 2007.

Cavafy, Constantine P., 'Body Remember': www.poemhunter.com/poem/body-remember/ (accessed 27 June 2019).

Davie, Grace, *Religion in Britain: A Persistent Paradox*, Oxford: Wiley Blackwell, 2015.

Delahunty, Andrew and Sheila Dignen, *A Dictionary of Reference and Allusion*, Oxford: Oxford University Press, 2012.

Dunlap, Susan J., *Counselling Depressed Women*, Louisville, KY: Westminster: John Knox Press, 1997.

hooks, bell, *Talking Back*, New York: Routledge, 2015.

James, Manon Ceridwen, *Women, Identity and Religion in Wales: Theology, Poetry, Story*, Cardiff: University of Wales Press, 2018.

Jantzen, Grace M., *Becoming Divine: Towards a Feminist Philosophy of Religion*, Manchester: Manchester University Press, 1998.

Keller, Catherine, *From a Broken Web: Separation, Sexism and Self*, Boston, MA: Beacon Press, 1988.

Llewelyn, Dawn, *Reading, Feminism and Spirituality: Troubling the Waves*, Basingstoke: Palgrave Macmillan, 2015.

Moore, Kim, *The Art of Falling*, Bridgend: Seren, 2015.

—— *If We Could Speak Like Wolves*, Sheffield: Smith Doorstop, 2015.

—— 'Poetry Blog': https://kimmoorepoet.wordpress.com/tag/16daysofaction/ (accessed 1 July 2019).

NHS Scotland, 'Spiritual Care Matters: An Introductory Resource for all NHS Scotland Staff': www.nes.scot.nhs.uk/media/3723/spiritualcaremattersfinal.pdf (accessed 29 January 2019).

Oakley, Mark, *The Splash of Words*, London: Canterbury Press, 2016. Kindle edition.

O'Donnell, Karen, *Broken Bodies: The Eucharist, Mary and the Body in Trauma Theology*, London: SCM Press, 2019.

Oliver, Mary, *New and Selected Poems*, Boston, MA: Beacon Press, 1992.

Oord, Thomas J., *The Uncontrolling Love of God: An Open and Relational Account of Providence*, Downers Grove IL: IVP Academic, 2015.

Orr, Gregory, *Poetry as Survival*, Athens, GA: University of Georgia Press, 2002.

Oswald, Alice, *Dart*, London: Faber and Faber, 2010.

Padel, Ruth, *The Poem and the Journey*, London: Chatto and Windus, 2007.

Paterson, Don, *The Poem: Lyric Sign Metre*, London: Faber and Faber, 2018.

Pattison, Stephen, *Shame: Theory, Therapy Theology*, Cambridge: Cambridge University Press, 2000.

Rambo, Shelly, *Spirit and Trauma: A Theology of Remaining*, Louisville, KY: Westminster: John Knox Press, 2010. Kindle edition.

Roberts, Stephen, 'Beyond the Classic: Lady Gaga and Theology in the Wild Public Sphere', *International Journal of Public Theology* 11 (2017).

Slee, Nicola, 'Poetry as a Feminist Research Methodology', in Nicola Slee, Fran Porter and Anne Philips, *Researching Female Faith: Qualitative Research Methods*, Abingdon: Routledge, 2018, 37–52.

—— '(W)riting Like a Woman: In Search of a Feminist Theological Poetics', in *Making Nothing Happen: Five Poets Explore Faith and Spirituality*, ed. Gavin D'Costa, Eleanor Nesbitt, Mark Pryce, Ruth Shelton and Nicola Slee, Farnham: Ashgate, 2014, 9–47.

Stringer, Martin D., *Contemporary Western Ethnography and the Definition of Religion*, London: Continuum, 2008.

Turner, Victor, *The Ritual Process: Structure and Anti-Structure*, London: Taylor and Francis [1965] 2017.

Walton, Heather, *Literature, Theology and Feminism*, Manchester: Manchester University Press, 2007.

—— *Writing Methods in Theological Reflection*, London, SCM Press: 2014.

Williams, Rowan, 'Theological Reading', in *The Cambridge Companion to Literature and Religion*, ed. Susan M. Felch, Cambridge: Cambridge University Press, 2016, 21–33.

Wuthnow, Robert, *Creative Spirituality: The Way of the Artist*, Berkeley and Los Angeles, CA: University of California Press, 2001. Kindle edition.

Notes

1 The poems in this chapter are reprinted with permission from *The Art of Falling* by Kim Moore (Bridgend: Seren, 2015). I would like to thank Kim Moore for all her help with this chapter and for generously allowing me to use her poems. I would also like to thank Stephen Roberts for his help in thinking through reflecting theologically on popular and other forms of culture with me, and for sharing his wisdom.

2 Mary Oliver, from 'The Summer Day', in *New and Selected Poems* (Boston, MA: Beacon Press, 1992).

3 Dawn Llewelyn, *Reading, Feminism and Spirituality: Troubling the Waves* (Basingstoke: Palgrave Macmillan, 2015), 10.

4 Heather Walton, *Literature, Theology and Feminism* (Manchester: Manchester University Press, 2007), 35.

5 As Ford, in his introduction to essays on the poetry of Micheal O'Siadhail, comments: '[Poetry] can be a primary way to go deeper and more broadly into questions of meaning, truth, goodness, beauty and wisdom and [can be] involved in the shaping of our lives and of our world.' Marc Caball and David F. Ford, eds, *Musics of Belonging: The Poetry of Micheal O'Siadhail* (Dublin: Carysfort Press, 2007), 21.

6 Walton, *Literature, Theology and Feminism*, 26.

7 Walton, *Literature, Theology and Feminism*, 36.

8 One of the most influential feminist pastoral theology works – Riet Bons-Storm, *The Incredible Woman: Listening to Women's Silences in Pastoral Care and Counselling* (Nashville, TN: Abingdon, 1996).

9 Nicola Slee, 'Poetry as a Feminist Research Methodology', in *Researching Female Faith: Qualitative Research Methods*, ed. Nicola Slee, Fran Porter and Anne Philips (Abingdon: Routledge, 2018), 38.

10 Alice Oswald, *Dart* (London: Faber and Faber, 2010).

11 Slee, 'Poetry as a Feminist Research Methodology', 38–9.

12 Manon Ceridwen James, *Women, Identity and Religion in Wales*: *Theology, Poetry, Story* (Cardiff: University of Wales Press, 2018).

13 See Stephen Roberts, 'Beyond the Classic: Lady Gaga and Theology in the Wild Public Sphere', *International Journal of Public Theology* 11 (2017), 163–87, who refers to a 'theological reading' of Lady Gaga's work.

14 Martin D. Stringer, *Contemporary Western Ethnography and the Definition of Religion* (London: Continuum, 2008), 19.

15 Mark Oakley also maintains that 'poetry is a form of attention, a literal coming to our senses, a turning aside from convention and memory', Mark Oakley, *The Splash of Words* (London: Canterbury Press, 2016), Kindle, 394.

16 Mark Pryce, *Poetry, Practical Theology and Reflective Practice* (Abingdon: Routledge, 2019), 40.

17 Oakley, *The Splash of Words*, 337.

18 Grace Davie, *Religion in Britain: A Persistent Paradox* (Oxford: Wiley Blackwell, 2015), 161–7.

19 NHS Scotland, 'Spiritual Care Matters: An Introductory Resource for all NHS Scotland Staff', www.nes.scot.nhs.uk/media/3723/spiritualcaremattersfinal.pdf (accessed 29 January 2019), 12.

20 Robert Wuthnow, *Creative Spirituality: The Way of the Artist* (Berkeley and Los Angeles, CA: University of California Press, 2001), Kindle, 449–51.

21 Wuthnow, *Creative Spirituality: The Way of the Artist*, Kindle, 227–9.

22 Kim Moore, *If We Could Speak Like Wolves* (Sheffield: Smith Doorstop, 2015).

23 Moore, *The Art of Falling*.

24 'The Geoffrey Faber Memorial Prize', Faber and Faber, www.faber.co.uk/geoffrey-faber-prize (accessed 27 June 2019).

25 'Forward Prizes 2015', Forward Arts Foundation, www.forwardartsfounda tion.org/forward-prizes-for-poetry/about/forward-prizes-2015/ (accessed 27 June 2019).

26 Don Paterson, *The Poem: Lyric Sign Metre* (London: Faber and Faber, 2018), 17.

27 Kim Moore's Poetry Blog, entry 10 December 2017, https://kimmoorepoet. wordpress.com/tag/16daysofaction/ (accessed 29 January 2019).

28 Moore, entry 7 December 2017, https://kimmoorepoet.wordpress.com/tag/ 16daysofaction/ (accessed 29 January 2019).

29 Moore, entry 7 December 2017.

30 Gregory Orr, *Poetry as Survival* (Athens, GA: University of Georgia Press, 2002), 19.

31 Kim Moore, email message to author, 29 January 2019.

32 Ruth Padel, *The Poem and the Journey* (London, Chatto and Windus, 2007), 56.

33 'It is notable that many contemporary poets, most of them without overt religious faith, frequently employ religion or liturgical forms to address weighty matters, investing them with new secular meaning at the same time as calling on and utilizing their ancient, totemic power for their own meanings and ends.' From Nicola Slee, '(W)riting Like a Woman: In Search of a Feminist Theological Poetics', in *Making Nothing Happen: Five Poets Explore Faith and Spirituality*, ed. Gavin D'Costa, Eleanor Nesbitt, Mark Pryce, Ruth Shelton and Nicola Slee (Farnham: Ashgate, 2014), 14, 15.

34 Moore, *The Art of Falling*, 27.

35 Constantine P. Cavafy, 'Body Remember': www.poemhunter.com/poem/ body-remember/ (accessed 27 June 2019).

36 Kim Moore, *The Art of Falling*, 32. Used with permission.

37 Karen O'Donnell, *Broken Bodies: The Eucharist, Mary and the Body in Trauma Theology* (London: SCM Press, 2019), 4.

38 O'Donnell, *Broken Bodies*, 7.

39 O'Donnell, *Broken Bodies*, 11.

40 Kim Moore, *The Art of Falling*, 31. Used with permission.

41 Exodus 13.1.

42 Andrew Delahunty and Sheila Dignen, *A Dictionary of Reference and Allusion* (Oxford: Oxford University Press, 2012), 91.

43 Victor Turner, *The Ritual Process: Structure and Anti-Structure* (London: Taylor and Francis [1965] 2017), 95.

44 Moore, entry 8 December 2017, https://kimmoorepoet.wordpress.com/tag/ 16daysofaction/ (accessed 29 January 2019).

45 Moore, *The Art of Falling*, 45. Used with permission.

46 Moore, *The Art of Falling*, 37. Used with permission.

47 Moore, *The Art of Falling*, 44. Used with permission.

48 Rowan Williams, 'Theological Reading', in *The Cambridge Companion to Literature and Religion*, ed. Susan M. Felch (Cambridge: Cambridge University Press, 2016), 33.

49 Shelly Rambo, *Spirit and Trauma: A Theology of Remaining* (Louisville, KY: Westminster John Knox Press. 2010), Kindle, 144.

50 Rambo, *Spirit and Trauma*, 147.

51 Rambo, *Spirit and Trauma*, 172

52 Catherine Keller, *From a Broken Web: Separation, Sexism and Self* (Boston, MA: Beacon Press, 1988), 39.

53 Susan J. Dunlap, *Counselling Depressed Women* (Louisville, KY: Westminster John Knox Press, 1997), 52.

54 Grace M. Jantzen, *Becoming Divine: Towards a Feminist Philosophy of Religion* (Manchester: Manchester University Press, 1998), 159.

55 Jantzen, *Becoming Divine*, 159.

56 Jantzen, *Becoming Divine*, 169.

57 Rambo, *Spirit and Trauma*, 157.

58 Stephen Pattison, *Shame: Theory, Therapy Theology* (Cambridge: Cambridge University Press, 2000), 229.

59 Thomas J. Oord, *The Uncontrolling Love of God: An Open and Relational Account of Providence* (Downers Grove, IL: IVP Academic, 2015), 148.

60 bell hooks, *Talking Back* (New York: Routledge, 2015), 9.

61 Heather Walton, *Writing Methods in Theological Reflection* (London, SCM Press: 2014), 138–9.

62 Moore, *The Art of Falling*, 45. Used with permission.

63 bell hooks, *Talking Back*, 9.

64 Rambo, *Spirit and Trauma*, 144.

5

'I Breathe Him in with Every Breath I Take': Framing Domestic Victimization as Trauma and Coercive Control in Feminist Trauma Theologies

ALISTAIR MCFADYEN

Introductions

Domestic abuse and violence were significant informants in the construction of feminist trauma theories.[1] To date, however, there has been little direct, sustained attention to domestic violence in feminist trauma theologies. This reflects feminist theology more generally, where direct, sustained (and specifically theological) discussion of domestic violence is rare. Where domestic violence is mentioned, it is often as one form among others of male violence against women and girls; one context among others in which women are victimized by men. Emphasis tends to be on the important work of identifying Christian complicity in promoting gendered structures of relation that increase risk of domestic victimization.[2] Domestic victimization is seen as a key indicator of the nature and prevalence of violence against women and of women's oppression more generally; hence, it features explicitly with some frequency in feminist theological discussion to this purpose (and is an assumed background presence even when not explicitly mentioned). Consequently, there is more attention paid to the generic reality and extensiveness of male violence and female oppression; relatively little to the significance of the specificities of the domestic context for an understanding of the experience of victimization, except perhaps as an intensifier of what is otherwise the case in non-domestic contexts (for example, marital rape compared with stranger rape). Nevertheless, the domestic context has always played a significant role in feminist theologies; sometimes explicitly and in the foreground, otherwise implicitly and assumed in the background. In theological as in secular feminisms, the domestic sphere is crucial to the distribution and internalization of patriarchal power structures, symbol systems, value; it is where appropriate behaviours are learned; responsibility and agency distributed and identities shaped; where we find the personal and political interfacing – most obviously, in the way in which marriage is institutionalized and parenting codified. We find this not least embedded in the earliest, programmatic articulations of modern feminist theology. A recurrent, central feature has been exploration of the ways in which sub-mission and potent agency are learned and internalized in gendered ways,[3] so significant in how we learn to be male or female: husbands, wives, part-ners, brothers, fathers, mothers, sisters, grandparents, nieces, nephews, uncles, aunts. So despite the relatively infrequent, sustained attention paid to domestic violence, feminist theologies' domestic context is structured by and mediates the energized dynamics of patriarchal oppression through its normal and normalizing, humdrum, everyday routines.

What is the relationship between the everyday normality of domestic relationships and domestic victimization? Conventional trauma theory is likely to frame domestic victimization as an extreme experience that it inter-rupts normality, shocks and overwhelms.[4] On the face of it, it looks unlikely to draw our attention to the everyday, routinized reality of domestic abuse. Trauma theory was developed to help us understand the ways in which experiencing terrifying, extremely violent or degrading events can lead to physiological and psychiatric symptoms long afterwards. These are events of such exceptional extremity that they cannot readily be interpreted through existing patterns of social meaning (so can be isolating); nor processed and integrated with psychological, emotional, spiritual constructs already in place. The intrusive symptoms of trauma (flashbacks, nightmares, fugue states, extreme negative emotions, hyperarousal, hyper-anxiety, numbing, avoidance[5]) often have the effect of overwhelming the person in the present, transporting the traumatic event through time and into new social con-texts and relationships. These symptoms are involuntary and maladaptive, intrusive echoes of a traumatic event that was – and through these and other symptoms[6] continues to be – an interruption of normality.[7] Viewing domestic victimization through a trauma lens seems, therefore, likely to focus attention on specific incidents of sufficiently extreme, unusual char-acter to engender traumatizing sequelae,[8] for which our yardstick is likely to be (severe) physical violence.

In what follows, I explore the connection between domestic victimization and the everyday, normal routines of a domestic relationship by reflecting on the recent introduction of an offence of coercive control in England and Wales. By tracing incremental shifts in UK government understanding that led to this piece of legislation, I show that it is not just the addition of a new offence, but represents a comprehensive shift in the way domestic victimization is framed and understood. On the face of it, coercive control stands in some tension with an incidental model of domestic victimization; a tension heightened both by an emphasis on violence and by the applica-tion of trauma theory – if that signs us exclusively towards the exceptional and extreme. Coercive control need not be violent. Neither is it the episodic, incidental *interruption* of everyday normality; it *is* normality. At its heart, coercive control represents the routine patterning of life in a permanently abusive direction; the insinuation of abuse into the everyday fabric of living in a way that incorporates victims' agency in acting and willing counter to their own flourishing.

It is this apparent tension that I explore here: between an understanding of domestic victimization framed as coercive control and one framed by a (violent) incident model that, when viewed through the lens of trauma theory, emphasizes extreme acts that disrupt and intrude into the normal routines of life and prevailing relational structure. I say 'apparent' tension to signal that the matter may not be entirely straightforward. For we find some of the defining and distinctive aspects of coercive control that escape consideration in conventional trauma theory identified in one of the texts most influential in contemporary discussions: Judith Herman's brilliant *Trauma and Recovery: From Domestic Abuse to Political Terror*. Herman's work might be considered the foundation of specifically feminist trauma theory and has been very widely taken up and cited in the creative, imaginative use of trauma theory in feminist theologies. Her work extends trauma theory to consider gendered phenomena such as rape, while giving new interpretation to previous psychoanalytic descriptions of 'female' symptoms such as hysteria that takes account of the experience of victimization.[9] The subtitle alerts readers to one of her most significant findings: that experiencing traumatic incidents in some (including domestic) contexts could so modify the experience and resultant symptoms of traumatization that they required a new and distinct symptomatology that she termed Complex Post-Traumatic Stress Disorder.[10] It is the combination of two features common to these contexts that proved significant, both of which are at the core of coercive control: duration and closure. Like hostage-taking or imprisonment in a torture camp, traumatizing incidents of domestic abuse often do not happen only once, but over a prolonged period during which they are repeatedly experienced. They can have that elongated duration because the victim is somehow trapped and prevented from leaving.[11]

Considering the changed frame of domestic victimization represented by coercive control in the context of trauma theory draws our attention to the specifically feminist contribution that takes into account both the experience of victimization and the domestic context. Herman's account of Complex PTSD is built out of a composite of common elements of several otherwise quite different contexts of traumatization, of which the domestic is but one. In many significant ways, it anticipates and has influenced the development of a distinct concept of coercive control. In some important respects, however, aspects of the specific experience and effects of coercive control in a domestic context deserve more prominence and somewhat different articulation than they receive in a more composite picture. Most significant in this regard is the way in which abuse is incorporated into everyday routines of life and carried into other relational contexts, repatterning not only behaviour but also subjectivity. In closing, I make some outline suggestions as to how feminist trauma theologies might at the same time both helpfully take account of the phenomenon of coercive control and help to map its pathological dynamics. Feminist theologies (especially of sin) have, in fact, already developed a deep, rich, nuanced understanding of damaged relational selfhood and of victim agency that are already well suited to this task. One important aspect of the experience of coercive control, however, is not so well captured in feminist theological discussion: the eclipse of transcendence. In suggesting that be addressed through a redescription in terms of idolatry, feminist discussion of sin is drawn into more explicit theological idiom. Put together, one of the potential consequences of this engagement of coercive control with trauma theory is to note the significance of feminist trauma theologies being both specifically feminist and specifically theological.

Introducing Me: My Context

Domestic victimization always takes place in, is experienced, institutionally and discursively framed and interpreted in a highly specific context. And I write out of that context, located in it and in relation to domestic victimization in specific ways. That is why my delineation of coercive control is focused on official government understanding expressed in legislation, rather than on (apparently) context-neutral accounts (that have nonetheless influenced the legislation). Context is constituted, not only through more vague, ethereal, cultural forces, but through the highly specified codes, policies and practices of concrete institutions and communities of practice in this place at this time. And I am embodied, embedded in it; positioned in relation to, experiencing and interpreting domestic victimization in specific ways. I am male, a husband, father, grandfather, brother; an academic theologian; a serving officer in one of the UK's largest police forces.[12] As a police officer, I routinely and regularly encounter the reality of domestic victimization in its violent, non-violent, traumatizing and coercively controlling forms. As a member of that community of practice, I do not just experience, but literally embody and enact (officially sanctioned) public identification, understanding and ways of framing domestic victimization. The frame I work with determines what I see; the questions I ask; what others disclose; how I interpret that and the actions I take. I routinely re-enact and communicate a codified understanding of what counts as domestic abuse and how its risks should be addressed and managed by police and/or partner agencies. Through my 17 years of policing experience, however, I have also enacted significant shifts in that codified understanding, which might be characterized as a move away from a model that hermeneutically privileged violent incidents.[13] Tracking this shift from a (primarily violent) incident model to the introduction of an offence of coercive control in England and Wales is instructive in understanding its nature and significance. For this is not simply the introduction of a specific offence. Rather, the legislation belongs to a process of reframing domestic victimization through the lens of coercive control in a way that better reflects the experience of victims and survivors (achieved largely through the insistent agitation of women survivors, victims and advocates[14]); that better captures the risk associated with both non-violent and violent abuse.[15]

Introducing Tracey

When I met Tracey[16] she was seven months pregnant. She had been provided refuge in a maternity unit she had attended following an assault by her long-term partner, concerned her baby may have suffered harm. She called her sister, who with staff at the unit had persuaded her to remain as an in-patient and call police. When I met her, police were still trying to locate and arrest her partner. She appeared extremely agitated, distressed and watchfully fearful that he would find her, become angry and exact vengeance. Other people approaching or passing by her room startled her. She interrupted our conversation several times to check whether he had been arrested. She told me that he had held her by the throat against a wall while screaming abuse directly into her face, making threats to kill her and her unborn child. Still holding her neck in a stranglehold, he had swung her around the room before releasing her to crash into (fortuitously soft) furnishings. He had then left with the two friends who had stood by and watched, making further threats as to what could happen on his return and ordering her to clean up the detritus left by him and his friends drinking, snacking, taking drugs and playing computer games. Tracey was exiled to the bedroom, criticized or threatened for leaving it except when called on to serve refreshments or go to the shops to buy the boys cigarettes or drink. Her time of return and movements would be closely regulated and monitored through software on her phone. She believed his threats against her and calculated that she was at risk of serious harm or even death at his hands, though more likely unintentionally than intentionally on her assessment. What persuaded her to seek first medical and then police help and to remain at the hospital, however, was not so much the risk to her as the risk to her unborn child.

Tracey's story lends itself to interpretation through the lens of trauma theory because of the character of the violence used against her, which has potential to cause classically recognized symptoms of PTSD. Being choked or strangled is potentially fatal. Alongside a fear of death, it often creates a sense of shocked helplessness and complete subjugation; of being entirely and literally at the assailant's disposal; of belonging to him; of living only by virtue of his will and permission. It violates normal behavioural limits. Especially in a domestic context, it shatters the normal patterns of trust, love and care that we place in others, particularly partners and family members. A threshold has been crossed.[17]

This way of framing Tracey's story draws attention to significant features of her story, but also to the potential significance of some of her behaviour and affect in telling it. Our attention is drawn to the significance of the violent incident she reports – to its capacity to overwhelm and create a sense of helplessness that is not easily processed and also not easily shared with others in the confidence they will understand it and its effects.[18] In giving her account of the assault, Tracey exhibited a hyper-alert, fearful watchfulness; periodically, she appeared to go into a trance-like state as she recalled painful features of this and previous incidents to memory; she showed a sense of shame, and anticipated disbelief and blame. Trauma theory would have some real descriptive and interpretive (maybe also predictive) power in relation both to the incident and its fairly immediate effects on her.

However, there are several aspects of the initial telling of her story, the significance of which the lens of trauma theory does not illuminate so well. In her initial account of that single incident of assault, she indirectly tells us something of the character of the relationship – the everyday, routine, normal conditions of their life together. She tells us of his threats, regulation and monitoring of her behaviour, and she tells us something also of her behaviour in response. It is those aspects that reframing domestic victimization as coercive control illuminates and renders significant. Following the traces in government documents of the latter part of the journey towards specific legislation criminalizing coercive control will help us understand the nature and comprehensiveness of this reframing, placing us in a better position to explore how feminist trauma theologies might most constructively engage and be engaged by the phenomenon.

Moving on from a Violent Incident Model

We begin our journey with the 2004 UK cross-government definition of domestic violence that prevailed until 2013. It defines domestic violence as:

> any incident of threatening behaviour, violence or abuse [psychological, physical, sexual, financial or emotional] between adults who are or have been intimate partners or family members, regardless of gender or sexuality.[19]

Definitions of this kind have significant heuristic function. They directly pattern recognition (and experience) of domestic abuse and response to it by statutory and other agencies, while indirectly patterning experience and understanding of those involved in or addressing domestic victimization. The inclusion of 'abuse' as well as actual or threatened violence in its opening line – coupled with the parenthetical recognition that such abuse might be psychological, financial or emotional as well as physical – suggests the beginnings of a move towards a more expansive understanding. Nonetheless, such a move is effectively constrained within what is still clearly here a violent-incident model of domestic victimization. Violence (actual and threatened) is foregrounded in both the title of the definition and in its substance, while the opening line anchors the definition in an incident-based representation of that violence.[20]

An incident-based frame represents domestic victimization as episodic interruptions (paradigmatically here involving actual or threatened violence) of everyday, non-abusive normality to which partners, ex-partners or other family members[21] return afterwards. Where these acts are sufficiently extreme in character, the violent-incident model maps well on to conventional understandings of trauma. A violent-incident model is a representation focused on (predominantly male) perpetrator behaviour presented as discrete, episodic, paradigmatically violent *acts*: what the abuser does at the points at which he engages in specific, identifiable actions. That is what we find in the cross-government definition: abuse is defined in relation only to his agential action – she[22] is being abused when he threatens her; acts violently against her; otherwise abuses her. The temporal duration of abuse itself is entirely coincident with the duration of his sequential, episodic abusive actions. It may leave its imprint in subsequently experienced symptoms of trauma, but these are the effects of an incident of violence that has stopped. It is not strictly the abuse that is carried forwards in time, but its consequences. When his actions cease, so does the abuse: she is no longer being abused when he is not abusing her. She is in the picture as the passive recipient of abusive acts.

If we return to the narration of Tracey's experience presented earlier, we can see that a violent-incident model does helpfully frame several significant aspects of the incident she was reporting. As a heuristic device, it would assist clinical staff and attending officers to identify and investigate this as an incident of domestic violence and to assess some of the immediate risks and identify the potential for later symptoms of trauma to be experienced. In this incident, Tracey was subject to a physical assault that could be experienced as extreme, that was accompanied by denigrating, derogatorily abusive verbal commentary and followed by threats of further violence. Actual and threatened physical violence fit the frame of a violent-incident model most obviously. Both can be recognized as forms of assault in English law. That is because apprehension of the possibility of violence is understood to cause harm either directly corresponding to (especially compared with more minor tactile contacts that leave no physical injury) or else analogous to physical assaults. The fear itself can be considered psychological injury. Similarly, a violent-incident heuristic can recognize and disclose as abusive victimizations other forms of non-tactile abuse, including the sort of verbal abuse Tracey reported accompanying her assault. The basis of that recognition is the extent to which the behaviour or its consequences are analogous either to violent abuse or to physical injury. That standard of reference is similarly capable of identifying and expressing the ways in which the consequences of abuse, including psychological trauma, can endure after an incident has come to an end and the abuser has stopped abusing: that the effects attributable to a specific abusive incident may be carried forward in time in the form of physical or analogous psychological injury. Hence, a violent-incident model of domestic victimization carries a significant amount of descriptive and disclosive power extending beyond the strict confines of the momentary, incidental application of physical violence.

Nevertheless, the circumference of its descriptive and disclosive power is significantly restricted in its range of application: what it screens in; how that is interpreted through its frame; what it fails to attend to and notice as potentially significant; in the end, how it calibrates, understands and conveys the nature of abuse and victimization from the victim's point of view and in respect of her agency.

Responding to questions framed by an alternative model of victimization centred on the phenomenon of coercive control, Tracey disclosed that she had been subject to several other violent assaults by her partner at intervals throughout their relationship. Police had been called by neighbours to two of these, but on one occasion Tracey had denied that any assault had taken place; on the other, she had made a formal complaint but later withdrew her statement. She had not previously disclosed the other incidents and was only making disclosures now with the support of her sister and because her pregnancy had recalibrated her sense of responsibilities. In passing, she mentioned as well the almost constant derogatory remarks. Some of these comments were screamed at her in the context of an argument or an assault. But most were at the level of routine negations informing her that she was useless and incompetent, incapable of surviving without her partner; they were delivered in a normal tone of voice in the form of supposedly rational – even sometimes seemingly supportive – commentary. These she considered to be trivial.

Between them, Tracey and her sister disclosed that they had not seen each other or been in any other contact for over a year. Tracey had not been in contact with her mother or other family members longer than that, about the time that Tracey had dropped out of education and given up on the idea of going to university like her sister, persuaded by her partner that she was being a snob and needed to earn money to support them both. Tracey explained that her partner easily became jealous when she formed or maintained other relationships, even insisting on meeting her in her breaks at work – often turning up unannounced (he did not work). She regarded this as a sign of his love. He regarded Tracey's family as snobbish and self-righteous, representing their concerns about her relationship with him as controlling.

It was clear from her account that Tracey had significantly modified her behaviour in order to avoid criticism, abuse or violence, and not only in response to specific threats or incidents of abuse. Her sister said more than once that it was as though Tracey had become a different person through her relationship with her partner.

It took several hours for Tracey to give this detailed account of her relationship. Periodically, she would become ruminative, almost in a dissociative state, stuck on some painful detail. At several points, she appeared to become breathless, complaining that the atmosphere in the ward had become stuffy. She went outside for fresh air, combined with a cigarette break. On returning from one of these 'breathers', she movingly and revealingly articulated what it was like to narrate her relationship, which she immediately recognized as a description of her relationship: 'It's like I am breathing him in with every breath.' For Tracey, the abuse was not episodic but constant; she was never free from it, whoever she was with, whatever she was doing; it was present in every decision she made and anxious alertness to the ever-present (but not always predictable) negative consequences was a constant companion.[23]

There are several aspects of Tracey's narrative that a violent-incident heuristic and classical trauma theory would separately and together fail to bring to attention. Where domestic abuse is framed as violent acts, and especially as significantly traumatizing assaults, we are likely to be blinded to the connective tissue between the acts of violence themselves (especially if infrequent): the everyday relational context in which they are in fact embedded; with which they stand in continuity; of which they are expressions. In a violent (especially traumatic) incident model, physical assaults tend to be misrepresented as infrequent interruptions of a healthy, non-abusive everyday, from which they are disembedded and with which they are discontinuous. That is so because they are also likely to blind us to the significance and abusiveness of an everyday routine of incessant, 'low-level', non-violent abuse (such as constant negative and negating commentary on competence, behaviour, appearance, intellect) and its cumulative effects as experienced by victims. Where we judge abuse on the basis of harm analogous to significant physical injury and trauma, and where we examine discrete acts and incidents for this level of harm, we are likely therefore to miss the significance, abusiveness, harmfulness and risk of the background relational context. For that very reason, we are likely also to mischaracterize and underestimate the severity and risk of the violent physical acts themselves.

As a consequence, the nature of perpetrator agency is easily missed in the very act of making it the focal point. That, in turn, risks colluding with perpetrator narratives that frequently downplay the seriousness and severity of specific, discrete incidents while misattributing responsibility. By rendering the pattern of consistent conduct and the abusive character of the relationship less visible, the violence looks atypical and is to be explained, not by reference to his character or his structuring of the relationship, but to something she has done to provoke such an atypical reaction that interrupts the relationship's normal equilibrium for one or more discrete, unconnected moments.[24]

Finally, both the actuality and significance of Tracey's own agency will either be missed or severely downplayed, especially in relation to the temporal duration and transportability of abuse into other contexts, entirely distinguishable from the involuntary, passively received intruding mechanisms of trauma: the ways in which she makes decisions; regulates (curtails) her life and behaviour; cuts herself off from relationships with others who might provide alternative commentary on her worth, on what is right, natural, normal and good.

Reframing Through Coercive Control

The introduction in England and Wales of a specific offence of coercive and controlling behaviour (S.76 of the Serious Crime Act 2015[25]) was preceded two years earlier by a revised cross-government definition: this time, significantly, of domestic violence *and abuse*. This broadening of the definition is in large part a consequence of its explicitly incorporating and foregrounding the phenomenon of coercive control, using it effectively to frame all forms of domestic victimization.

In its 2013 iteration, the cross-government definition defines domestic violence and abuse as:

> any incident or pattern of incidents of controlling, coercive, threatening behaviour, violence or abuse between those aged 16 or over who are, or have been, intimate partners or family members regardless of gender or sexuality. It can encompass, but is not limited to:
>
> - psychological
> - physical
> - sexual
> - financial
> - emotional.
>
> Controlling behaviour is: a range of acts designed to make a person subordinate and/or dependent by isolating them from sources of support, exploiting their resources and capacities for personal gain, depriving them of the means needed for independence, resistance and escape and regulating their everyday behaviour.
>
> Coercive behaviour is: an act or a pattern of acts of assaults, threats, humiliation and intimidation or other abuse that is used to harm, punish, or frighten their victim.[26]

This general reframing of domestic violence and the understanding of coercive control conveyed within it lies behind the 2015 statute that created a specific criminal offence of controlling or coercive behaviour in an intimate or family relationship in England and Wales. The language of the legislation itself is, of necessity, less discursive. It is also focused on the agential behaviour of the perpetrator, since what is being criminalized are his specific, identifiable actions. Nevertheless, both in framing abuser behaviour as controlling or coercive and in characterizing abuse as repeated or continuous, a significant move is signalled away from the idea of domestic abuse as discrete, episodic acts disconnected from one another and disembedded from the relationship.[27] In bringing to expression that the victim is subject to control and coercion, there is implicit reference both to the ongoing structuring of relationship and to the current and future behaviour of the *victim* that is being regulated. The very notion of coercive control entails recognition that the abusive relationship, and not just behaviour, extends and is transported through time and space, both physical and social. To 'breathe him in with every breath' meant for Tracey that the abuse, its effects and meanings, constituted the comprehensive and all-containing atmosphere of her whole life: no matter what she was doing, where she was, in his presence or not – she took it and him with her, internalizing him and the abuse in patterns of watchfulness, behaviour adjustment, intrusive thoughts and feelings. Potentially, the future behaviour of the victim is subject to coercion and control after any abusive acts have finished and in situations where the abuser is not present (continuing sometimes even after his death).[28] That is partly – but only partly – accounted for by the quality and nature of the abuser's acts.

Significantly, the legislation's recognition that behaviour is coercive or controlling is calibrated against the effects the behaviour has on the victim – not, as in the Definition, in relation to perpetrator intentions.[29] Repeated or continuous behaviour is taken to be coercive or controlling if it has a 'serious effect' on the victim. A 'serious effect' is defined as being subject to or in fear of violence on 'at least two occasions' or caused 'serious alarm or distress which has a substantial adverse effect on ... usual day-to-day activities'.[30] This is the codification into criminal legislation of what the Definition represents as the effects of abuser behaviour that deprive victims of 'the means for independence, resistance and escape that results in victims regulating their everyday behaviour'.[31] The legislation rightly recognizes that being routinely subjected to the use or threat of violence can – and, indeed, is likely to – insinuate itself into victims' patterning of everyday life. But a major aim of this legislation was precisely and expressly to recognize that the cumulative impact of repeated *non*-violent interactions – even those that might appear unremarkable or even benign – could also have precisely the same effects, including engendering feelings of fear, alarm or distress, over-dependence on affirmation that lead to coercion and the exercise of control.[32]

In other words, the phenomenon of coercive control refers not only to the repeated behaviour of the abuser (understandably the focus of criminal legislation), but to the habitually repeated behaviour of the victim (and indirectly to what underlies and directs victim agency). Despite the explicit reference to violence and to 'serious alarm or distress', it is the cumulative impact on the fabric of victims' everyday routines of life that constitute and are the measure of coercive control and in relation to which its harmfulness is to be calibrated. Habitually repeated patterns of victim behaviour (and hence victim agency) are more significant in identifying and understanding victimization than the frequency and reiteration of acts of abuse, although the latter may explain the former. Whether and how extensively the victim repeatedly enacts her will by directing behaviour to avoid further abuse, to placate the abuser or seek affirmation: that is the measure of the nature, existence and severity of coercive control, not the nature, frequency and severity of abuser action. Thereby, she orders her life around strategies of harm-reduction, but thereby also repeats and embeds her victimization.

Attentiveness to victim behaviour helps explain why it need not require many (or any) repetitions of abusive acts in order to elicit control. What is necessary is for the victim to feel such concern to avoid repetition or triggering of threatened or otherwise unwelcome consequences (or to seek positive affirmation) that other desires and intentions are overwhelmed and displaced.[33] Concern will be elevated where the abuse or future threat represents a risk of severe physical, emotional or spiritual harm or cost. We can, perhaps, most easily visualize that in relation to acts of physical violence that are potentially lethal, life-changing or unbearably painful.[34]

That might easily mislead us into thinking that coercive control is a consequence purely of the nature, severity and potency inherent in the act itself. In omitting consideration of victim situation and relational structure, that is seriously misleading. Like other forms of abuse, coercive control is predicated on and exploits asymmetries of power in the relationship – albeit asymmetries that might first have to be established where they are not pre-existing. What makes abuse sufficiently traumatizing to lead the victim to regulate her behaviour is not the inherent potency contained in abuser action considered in isolation; rather, the disparities in power, capacity and resource between abuser and victim, combined with difficulties in escaping the domestic relationship or avoiding repeat contact (difficulties that the abuse might create and intensify). These disparities might be physical, emotional, spiritual, social, economic, legal, cultural, religious, cognitive, for instance – but, most likely, several at least of these in combination. It is these disparities that lend the abuser and his behaviour the power to exercise coercive control over the victim. Or, to put it better from the perspective of the victim: it is these disparities that make adaptive regulation of her own behaviour either appear or actually to be a more viable option than resisting, leaving or renegotiating the relationship.

Again, there is potential to be misled if we model the pathological dynamics of coercive control through the lens of physical force and violence. While the literature around coercive control does often refer to it as a 'capture crime' or as 'entrapment', what is happening to the victim has a different quality from a physical imprisonment where she is held captive through direct application of force to restrain or regulate her movement. That entirely displaces her agency. (In terms of criminal offences, false imprisonment would be a more appropriate offence for law enforcement and prosecutors to consider here.) Coercive control leaves her agency intact, but colonized and in the service of the abuser's perceived or actual needs and agenda; sequestered, that is, by the dynamics of abuse. She is not physically tied to a chair, locked in a room, imprisoned in a house or handcuffed to the abuser, exerting physical control over her every movement and interaction. Coercive control is far more insidious than that. Like the Cross-Government Definition, the legislation concentrates on behaviour. It does not bring to direct expression the phenomenon that it nevertheless assumes: the abusive regulation of behaviour is achieved by colonizing the victim's internal, subjective capacities for self-direction, the living of life from a personal centre whence her own values and representation of the good informs and shapes desire, will and thereby action. Instead, as the definition expresses well, under the conditions of coercive control all personal energies are directed towards service of the abuser.[35]

Coercive control almost always involves the internalization of abuse since it involves the constant or repeated self-regulation of behaviour. The victim is not passive, but active. Her will and agential capacity are utilized and directed in ways that serve and make primary the abuser's desires, agenda and interests, which have the effect of actively reorienting the direction of life-intentionality (including will, desire, value, sense of what is good and makes for flourishing) under the dominating gravitational pull of the dynamics of abuse. The process of internalization and the achievement of entrapment go together. Both are facilitated where access to alternative ways of framing and evaluating the relationship are impeded. That is rendered especially difficult where the normal or natural prioritization and subordination of their respective desires, needs and projects are supported by or at least in some continuity with, authorized and normalized by more widely shared religious, cultural, legal frames, whether formal or informal.[36] But where this is not the case, some further impediment is required to restrict effective access to or to disempower alternative sources of evaluation and accounts of what is normal, acceptable, desirable. Both the legislation and the Cross-Government Definition draw attention to the way in which the victim might be isolated by restricting her contact with others, her ability to form and maintain other relationships or involvements beyond the domestic situation (social isolation is similarly identified as an intensifier of traumatization in trauma theory – the cause is different; the effects, very similar).[37] Just as important in this regard, they also draw attention to the way in which the abuser can generate a sense of being constantly monitored, so that even when apart and away from the domestic context, she is never really apart from the abuser, nor the dynamics of the abusive relationship: she has constantly to monitor and regulate everything she says and does for fear that he will know. These dynamics of isolation are both a product of and achieve entrapment in the relationship as well as foster internalization. This is a form of entrapment that, because it is internalized, is transported with the victim into other relationships. Isolation from alternative frames of reference make it more likely that whatever rationalizations and normal-ization is given by the abuser explicitly, are implicit in the abuse or are contained in prevailing cultural, religious, societal mores, will be positively internalized. The domestic context is already one likely to have heightened significance for the construction and maintenance of identity, self-worth, sense of what is normal, right and good in relationships – whether we are considering intimate partners, siblings or trans-generational relationships. It is also one where the abuser has intimate and intricate knowledge of the victim, including her vulnerabilities. It is also a context easier to shield from external scrutiny and one harder to escape (and to face escaping) completely for ever. All of those aspects make coercive control both more likely and more dangerous.[38]

Unlike some offences that involve similar dynamics of colonization and control, coercive control of adults in the domestic context need not neces-sarily (though very often does) involve internalization of the values of abuse, and acceptance of abuser justification, however. It is quite possible for a resistant value system to be maintained, but for the victim to feel impotent or actually lack the capacity to escape, resist or seek intervention, assistance or support from third parties.[39] Nevertheless, the net effect of hypervigilance in constantly monitoring and adjusting behaviour to ensure coordination with the abuser's expressed or anticipated wishes or to avoid threatened or anticipated consequences represents even here an internal-ization of the power of the abuse and the abuser to redirect the victim's internal, agential energies. This is not, then, strictly an internalization of the values of the abuse in terms of a shared sense of what is right, or the worth of her identity, needs and desires. Nevertheless, her will is engaged and behaviour is controlled internally – not because she has internalized values that subordinate her in the service of his needs and desires, but because the power differential in the relationship, combined with his behaviour, makes her so fearful of the consequences of doing otherwise that she changes her behaviour accordingly. In a way, the power of coercive control is more tell-ing in its ability to coerce victims into acting *against* what they know to be in their own interests, or to be just, good or right than in the internalization of abusive meaning and values whereby she believes the relationship to be appropriately structured and the behaviour and expectations natural, right, reasonable, just. This is not, however, a displacement or substitution of the will. Rather, the resistant will remains intact but trapped in a situation where she has insufficient power to enact it; where her willing cannot be free from the dynamics of abusive, coercive control; cannot be free from abuser and abusive relationship. In those circumstances, her will towards her own full flourishing separately or in a relationship structured around appropriate recognition of her worth and needs is not displaced; rather, it is truncated, colonized and reoriented in the form of willing and acting to safeguard herself the best she can in a relationship she is unable to escape. Ironically, even when the victim reaches such levels of desperation that she resists control and abuse by acting decisively, we might see symptoms of the invasive colonization in an ironically reversed form if this means acting in a way out of sync with her core values and her character. This is most obviously evidenced where victims, after prolonged periods of coercive control, resist in an extreme act of violence.[40]

Feminist Trauma Theologies and Coercive Control: Sketching Some Suggested Outline Coordinates

How might feminist trauma theologies take account of this reframing of domestic victimization through the lens of coercive control that replaces the portrait of psychological deterioration at the centre of the current victimization narrative with a picture of an affirmative femininity that victims vigorously defend against illegitimate authority? By framing the controller's oppression as an attempt to co-opt and deconstruct a woman's personhood, it reaffirms what many victims themselves feel, that they are living in a conscious and self-determining relation to domination, albeit a relation that is severely constrained by objective limits on their choice and action, the idea expressed by the notion that they exercise 'control in the context of no control'.[41]

Victim agency in feminist theologies

Feminist theological anthropologies (including theologies of sin) have since the 1960s developed nuanced and rich accounts of victim agency and of wounded subjectivity that are likely to prove central for feminist trauma theologies turning to consider the specificities of domestic violence reframed as coercive control. Two interrelated elements are likely to prove most significant: critique of patriarchy as ideology, and constructive reinterpretation of the sin of 'sloth'.[42] Both are suffused by an understanding of human being and of sin as intrinsically relational. Both take the risk of thematizing women's role as active agents under conditions of victimization.[43] This is agency exercised as a result of injured and disoriented subjectivity as *victims*; in theological terms, the sin of the sinned-against.[44]

The domestic situation plays a significant role in feminist analysis of women's situation and in the function of patriarchy as ideology, both in relation to the distribution of roles and responsibilities in it and a significant locus, structured by prevailing cultural norms and codes that in turn are internalized, shaping and directing subjectivity, desire, will and therefore behaviour in all other contexts.[45] Crucially, in this process, women are represented as exercising will and active agency, variously represented by verbs in the infinitive: failing,[46] hiding,[47] refusing,[48] abdicating,[49] abnegating,[50] denying,[51] fleeing,[52] participating,[53] being complicit,[54] acquiescing,[55] accepting,[56] consenting,[57] complying[58] and cooperating.[59] Women are not passive in their oppressive victimization, since the mode of victimization is a highly energized dynamic that does not supplant will and the conditions of agential action.[60] Rather, it coerces, reorients and colonizes subjectivity, sequestering powers of active life-intentionality, including the will and desire, under a comprehensive misrepresentation of what is good, natural, true and right.[61]

Theological feminism represents these gendered dynamics as tending to produce a strongly centred sense of self in males and a fragmented, diffuse, decentred sense of self in females, oriented towards servicing the needs and interests of others and prone to collapse identity into relationships or through over-identification with another. Represented as 'self-loss' in feminist theological anthropologies generally and as 'sloth' in feminist hamartiologies, it is not strictly a loss but distortion and active disorientation of selfhood. It is a mode of sin rendered invisible in the tradition by an over-emphasis on the sin of pride as the paradigmatic sin (so all self-assertion is sin; correspondingly, humility and self-sacrifice are always virtuous). Pride as a form of potent, over-assertive, overreaching, over-weaning, domineering selfhood represents the situation of the perpetrator; stereotypically, in feminist understanding, the existential situation, experience and behaviour of dominant, domineering men. It does not express so well the situation of victims, nor the stereotypical situation of women and of female subjectivity under the conditions of patriarchal oppression. What feminist theologians mean by the complementary sin of sloth addresses the situation of those lacking the kind of power and autonomy characteristic of moral agency, whose energy and capacity for personal centredness and therefore for acting and relating – being for oneself, others, God – as oneself in relation are both dissipated and disoriented. The sin of sloth recognizes that victims, precisely as victims, are not simply passive in their own oppression, but exercise will and agency. However, victims' willing is not free, but sequestered, coerced or otherwise cooperating with their own victimization; the expression of a damaged, disordered and disoriented subjectivity. In feminist hamartiologies, sloth names subjectivity and behaviour together with victimization – what has happened to victims to condition and bend their will and so behaviour, such that they participate personally, though not freely, in their own oppression.[62]

These constructions of wounded, damaged and disoriented subjectivity provide helpful tools for bringing the experience of victimization through coercive control to an expression more appropriate to its reality than that suggested by trauma theory. Trauma theory tends to represent the victim being overwhelmed into helpless passivity (by the original trauma and also by intrusion of traumatic symptoms). In coercive control, damaged subjectivity (possibly alongside symptoms of trauma) is the vector through which the abuse is carried through a victim's intentional actions as she regulates and modifies her behaviour in order to avoid anticipated consequences or to seek alternative, positive outcomes, such as affirmation. The present tense is intentional here and significant. Trauma theory represents symptoms of trauma as present consequences of a past, finished event. Coercively controlled behaviour is not a simple consequence of abuse that has finished. It is better considered an active, present continuation of abuse that further embeds and energizes itself in repeated and habitual patterns of victim behaviour, through which the victim is continually re-victimized. In this highly energized dynamic, the victim is a victim, but retains agential capacity, which is not free in an individualistic, libertarian sense. For she is victimized through redirection, sequestration, colonization of the subjective conditions (will, intentionality, desire) through which she directs and exercises agency.[63]

These feminist theological constructions of damaged subjectivity and disoriented victim agency help us to understand the limitations of an individualistic, libertarian representation of the abusive nature of coercive control and the harm it causes. The descriptions of patriarchal oppression and of the damaged subjectivity represented by feminist reinterpretation of sloth are deeply relational: actively expressed and intensified in pathological ways of relating – to self, others (and God) – that could be characterized as over-dependent, subservient, as lacking self-centredness. And that could mislead as to the nature of what is damaged and damaging, of the pathology and of what 'corrected', healthy, healed subjectivity might look like. Is relational selfhood, an orientation on others, the problem; is harm calibrated against the yardstick of the separately centred, asocial, unrelated subject? Is that what has been attacked and lost in being subject to coercively controlling behaviour, to be restored therapeutically or through criminal justice intervention? Coercive control could be judged in those terms – as a liberty crime, an attack on the capacity for free choice and the autonomous mode of subjectivity that underlies that. It is tempting to see the harmfulness of heteronomous captivity and decentring of the self as the denial of autonomy, construed as the centring of personal life on an asocial inner core.[64]

That feminist hamartiologies identify exactly that understanding of autonomy and its corresponding mode of selfhood (pride) as well as self-loss (sloth) as sin, as pathological ways of being a self-in-relation, suggests something rather different. Both pride and sloth are pathological, judged by the yardstick of 'right relation': variously imaged in feminist theologies, this form of relationality always involves the deepest mutuality.[65] What is envisioned is a form of community in which the energies of personal life are mutually oriented and thereby focused in a highly energized, dynamic, mutual empowering of each partner's integrity and autonomy (construed as the power to live from a personal centre, directing personal energy towards the empowerment of others and being empowered through that relating). Coercive control attacks, damages and disorients personal (psychological, emotional, spiritual) integrity by exploiting and abusing the relational basis of subjectivity and selfhood. It deconstructs the structural conditions of right relation. Personal energies are pulled into an orientation towards the abuser that decentres because it is exclusive and unreciprocated, no longer circulating in mutual empowerment of the relational integrity and autonomy of both. The victim's will, desire and action service and empower his enclosed identity, integrity and interests. This is not a position of helplessness or inaction, or the loss of subjectivity or personal energies; rather, it is their colonization by being forced into the gravitational pull of building up the personal centredness of the abuser, never to return in a way that also assists the building up of a self that can be centred on oneself directed towards others and vice versa. Abuse is abuse of the conditions of relationality, an attack on the conditions of being a self in right relation.

Feminist theologies are therefore already equipped to assist feminist trauma theologies in addressing domestic violence and abuse reframed as coercive control. I suspect that the reality of domestic victimization will be near the surface of these descriptions of women's oppression and victimization under patriarchal conditions even when it is not an explicit theme. But it is significant that what is represented here is not primarily a description of what happens to women when they are subject to extreme, unusual or specifically targeted abuse. This is a description of women's experience under normal, not exceptional, conditions. That it maps so well on to the contours of domestic victimization framed through the lens of coercive control is powerfully suggestive of the deep continuities to be found between abusive behaviours and domestic relationships on the one hand and socially accepted, prevailing patterns of behaviour in relationship between males and females on the other.[66] Those continuities between the normal, everyday and the abusive bring to powerful expression two observations already made in passing that are worthy of note at this late stage in the discussion: first, why coercive control appears almost exclusively a gendered phenomenon; second, why it can be so difficult (for witnesses, investigators and victims alike) to detect and distinguish coercive control from 'normal', 'acceptable' behaviour: 'how to distinguish the "coercive" element from the normative ways in which men micro-manage women's enactment of gender roles (such as how they cook or clean) by default, simply because they are women'.[67]

The Eclipse of Transcendence: Breathing Him in With Every Breath, or Being in Bondage to an Idol

Coercive control is a form of entrapment achieved in part by blocking effective access to external sources of evaluation, empowerment, intervention. The perpetrator might effect this through a number of strategies already mentioned (for example, violence, threats, fostering over-dependency, excessive monitoring, providing rationalizations for the controlling behaviour and the distribution of value in the relationship). But coercive control is defined not by what the abuser does but by what happens to the victim's agency and how it is directed – what she does constantly to manage the risks to her well-being, selfhood and life. Control is defined by what she does, but her behaviour is a response to the controlling domination of the perpetrator. Her behaviour is an enactment of the extent and effectiveness of his coercive control; his power comprehensively to coercively reorient her decision-making and action: her active life-intentionality (will, desire, subjectivity). That control – in effect, the abusive relationship and abuser – are transported into other contexts and relationships where the abuser is not present. In a sense, we might say these other contexts, situations and relationships are not experienced as outside the abusive relationship at all. There is no outside. Coercive control is inherently totalitarian. The relationship with the abuser is the ultimate context within which all other relationships, contexts and actions take place and in relation to which they are evaluated: do they pose a risk or challenge? Will he find out? Am I enacting an alternative set of values? Will he like/approve of this and me if I do this/say this/am here? However control is coerced, achieved and exercised, the effect is always to increase the bonds (bondage) to the abuser, to raise the abuser and abusive relationship to ultimate and overriding significance for the victim. Moreover, there cannot be any outside, for the abusive relationship and the abuser have been internalized (are 'breathed in with every breath') in the organs of subjectivity through which the victim exercises will and directs her behaviour in ways that have to be permanently mindful of serving and not threatening the demands and needs of the abuser and abusive relationship. These are the means by which the abusive relationship and abuser are transported into every other context of interaction and relation.

This blocking of transcendence combined with raising to ultimate significance represents two related aspects central to the phenomenon of idolatry. Re-describing the core dynamics of coercive control through the specifically theological language of idolatry is my final suggestion for a coordinate that might prove helpful for feminist trauma theologies engaging domestic violence and abuse through the frame of coercive control. I make this suggestion for two reasons. First, naming coercive control as a form of idolatry both helpfully identifies and helpfully re-describes significant aspects of its core pathology. Second, I think this move might make helpful connections with some of the creative, constructive, imaginative currents already evident in and underlying recent feminist trauma theologies.[68]

To re-describe the dynamics of coercive control through the specifically theological lens of idolatry is to characterize it as misdirected worship (significantly, worship of a joyless kind). Worship here indicates the way we enact the prioritization of a reality as having absolute value for us. We are concerned here with behaviour (and behaviour that is coerced), rather than with ideas (what we think we worship; the values we consciously assent to): what we centre our lives on in practice; what we spend our time doing and thinking about; what becomes the criterion of value whereby we assess the worth of everything else; what pulls all our energies and agency into its service. The phenomenon of coercive control is inadequately rendered as an abuse, an attack or disorientation of subjectivity. It is a comprehensive spiritual disorientation and abuse that comprehensively disorients the whole person away from what is good and life-giving, that can sustain the ecology of joy in self, others and God, or the genuinely good that is the foundation of individual and communal flourishing.

In a way, blocking transcendence already has the effect of raising the domestic context to ultimate significance for the victim.[69] It becomes the very breath she breathes. We see that effect exaggerated and how the whole of the victim's subjectivity, her life-intentionality, is actively oriented towards servicing the needs, expectations, desires, arbitrary regulations and interests of the abuser. In extreme forms, it is not going too far to say that functionally the abuser has become the ultimate 'good'. His needs and his anticipated response are the arbiter and criterion of value.[70] Behaviour, interests and orientations are judged good according to their utility in servicing abuser needs, expectations and standards. These become the ultimate destination, orientation, horizon for the victim's committed life-intentionality and action. Neither she nor her acts, nor other relationships, are good in themselves. They are good only in coordination with and pulled into service of (or limited by) the ultimate good represented by the abuser's needs. Represented as idolatry, the pathological reality of coercive control is better illuminated: comprehensive disorientation and disaffection from what is genuinely both good and the source of all goodness, against which all other goods can be evaluated and should be coordinated. It is a disorientation of the proper pattern of worship of the true God, which grounds and energizes the abundant and mutually enriching possibilities of joy in and love of self, others and God.[71]

On my reading, just this sort of understanding of the potential of specific, explicit theological mediation of the energies and possibilities of abundant life in relation to trauma undergirds and energizes the work and orientation of a number of recent feminist trauma theologies.[72] Their vibrant promise is vested in their trying to make sense of, and mediate grace to counter, the fragmentation, brokenness, damage and rupture of trauma that disrupts the conditions of human flourishing, of right relation to self, others and God.[73] They seem to be assuming an as yet unarticulated underlying understanding of the nature and dynamics of idolatry that constrain, disorient and disrupt the energies of abundant life in right relation: joy in oneself directed to and received from others and God. By bringing trauma to theological consideration and articulation, feminist trauma theologies might bring the energies of healing and abundant life to bear on those situations where the power of 'death' is experienced as overcoming, disabling and interrupting what cuts us off from the energy and sources of abundant life.[74] There is searing, careful attentiveness to the reality and experience of trauma that forces the reader to sit with the reality of its wounds long enough to appreciate its nature, severity and damaging power. That ensures that grace makes contact with this broken and damaged reality in all its fullness, the more effectively to relate it to a more expansive sense of joyous, abundant possibility as the closed system of trauma might be broken open, so behaviour, will, desire, sense of reality and of self-worth will no longer be subject to the controlling intrusions of a traumatic past. My tentative suggestion is that, should feminist trauma theologies engage with the phenomenon of coercive control, our understanding of trauma theory and of coercive control might both be significantly enriched.

References

American Psychiatric Association, *Diagnostic and Statistical Manual of Mental Disorders (DSM-5)*, 5th edn, Arlington, VA: American Psychiatric Association, 2013.

Anderson, Kristin L., 'Gendering Coercive Control', *Violence against Women* 15, no. 12 (2009), 1444–57.

Berry, Wanda Warren, 'Images of Sin and Salvation in Feminist Theology', *Anglican Theological Review* 60, no. 1 (1979), 25–54.

Beste, Jennifer Erin, *God and the Victim: Traumatic Intrusions on Grace and Freedom*, Oxford: Oxford University Press, 2007.

—— 'Recovery from Sexual Violence and Socially Mediated Dimensions of God's Grace: Implications for Christian Communities', *Studies in Christian Ethics* 18, no. 2 (2005), 89–112.

Bishop, Charlotte and Vanessa Bettinson, 'Evidencing Domestic Violence, Including Behaviour that Falls under the New Offence of "Controlling or Coercive Behaviour"', *The International Journal of Evidence and Proof* 22, no. 1 (2018), 3–29.

Brock, Rita Nakashima, *Journeys by Heart: A Christology of Erotic Power*, New York: Crossroad, 1992.

Brown, Joanne Carlson and Carole R. Bohn, eds, *Christianity, Patriarchy and Abuse: A Feminist Critique*, New York: Pilgrim Press, 1993.

Bussert, Joy M. K., *Battered Women: From a Theology of Suffering to an Ethic of Empowerment*, Minneapolis, MN: Lutheran Church in America, 1986.

Callaghan, Jane E. M., Joanne H. Alexander, Judith Sixsmith and Lisa Chiara Fellin, 'Beyond "Witnessing": Children's Experiences of Coercive Control in Domestic Violence and Abuse', *Journal of Interpersonal Violence* 33, no. 10 (2018), 1551–81.

Chopp, Rebecca S., *The Power to Speak: Feminism, Language, God*, New York: Crossroad, 1991.

Claassens, L. Juliana M., 'Calling the Keeners: The Image of the Wailing Woman as Symbol of Survival in a Traumatized World', *Journal of Feminist Studies in Religion* 26, no. 1 (2010), 63–77.

Controlling or Coercive Behaviour in an Intimate or Family Relationship: Statutory Guidance Framework, London: Home Office, 2015.

Cross-Government Definition of Domestic Violence – a Consultation: Summary of Responses, London: Home Office, 2012.

Daly, Mary, *Beyond God the Father: Towards the Philosophy of Women's Liberation*, London: The Women's Press, 1986.

Dunfee, Susan Nelson, 'The Sin of Hiding: A Feminist Critique of Reinhold Niebuhr's Account of the Sin of Pride', *Soundings* 65, no. 3 (1982), 316–27.

Eastman, Susan Grove, *Paul and the Person: Reframing Paul's Anthropology*, Grand Rapids, MI: Eerdmans, 2017.

Fiorenza, Elisabeth Schüssler, 'Ties that Bind: Violence against Wo/Men', in *Transforming Vision: Explorations in Feminist the*Logy*, Minneapolis, MN: Fortress, 2011.

Fortune, Marie, 'The Transformation of Suffering: A Biblical and Theological Perspective', in *Violence against Women and Children: A Christian Theological Sourcebook*, ed. Carol J. Adams and Marie M. Fortune, New York: Continuum, 1995, 36–59.

Fortune, Marie M., 'Faith is Fundamental to Ending Domestic Terror', *Women's Rights Law Reporter* 33, no. 4 (2012), 463–70.

—— 'The Nature of Abuse', *Pastoral Psychology* 41, no. 5 (1 May 1993), 275–88.

Grey, Mary, *Redeeming the Dream: Feminism, Redemption and Christian Tradition*, London: SPCK, 1989.

Hamberger, L. Kevin, Sadie E. Larsen and Amy Lehrner, 'Coercive Control in Intimate Partner Violence', *Aggression and Violent Behavior* 37 (2017), 1–11.

Hampson, Daphne, 'Luther on the Self: A Feminist Critique', in *Feminist Theology: A Reader*, ed. Anne Loades (London: SPCK, 1990), ch. 18.

—— 'Reinhold Niebuhr on Sin: A Critique', in *Reinhold Niebuhr and the Issues of Our Time*, ed. Richard Harries, London: Mowbray, 1986, 46–60.

—— *Theology and Feminism*, Oxford: Basil Blackwell, 1990.

Herman, Judith Lewis, *Trauma and Recovery: From Domestic Abuse to Political Terror*, reprint with new Afterword, London: Pandora [1992], 2001.

hooks, bell, *Feminist Theory: From Margin to Center*, Boston, MA: South End, 1984.

Huang, Luping, *Women and Pride: An Exploration of the Feminist Critique of Reinhold Niebuhr's Theology of Sin*, Carlisle: Langham Monographs, 2018.

Hunsinger, Deborah van Deusen, 'Bearing the Unbearable: Trauma, Gospel and Pastoral Care', *Theology Today* 68, no. 1 (2011), 8–25.

Johnson, Michael P., *A Typology of Domestic Violence: Intimate Terrorism, Violent Resistance, and Situational Couple Violence*, Boston, MA: Northeastern University Press, 2008.

Johnson, Michael P. and Janel M. Leone, 'The Differential Effects of Intimate Terrorism and Situational Couple Violence: Findings from the National Violence against Women Survey', *Journal of Family Issues* 26, no. 3 (2005), 322–49.

Jones, Serene, *Call It Grace: Finding Meaning in a Fractured World*, London: Viking.
—— *Trauma + Grace: Theology in a Ruptured World*, 2nd edn, Louisville, KY: Westminster John Knox Press, 2019.
Katz, Emma, 'Beyond the Physical Incident Model: How Children Living with Domestic Violence are Harmed by and Resist Regimes of Coercive Control', *Child Abuse Review* 25, no. 1 (2016), 46–59.
Keshgegian, Flora A., *Redeeming Memories: A Theology of Healing and Trans-formation*, Nashville, TN: Abingdon Press, 2000.
Lee, Dorothy, *Flesh and Glory: Symbol, Gender, and Theology in the Gospel of John*, New York: Crossroad, 2002.
Marsden, Daphne, 'The Church's Contribution to Domestic Violence: Submission, Headship, and Patriarchy', in *Rape Culture, Gender Violence, and Religion: Christian Perspectives*, ed. Caroline Blyth, Emily Colgan and Katie B. Edwards, Cham: Palgrave Macmillan, 2018, ch. 5.
Martin, Bernice, 'Whose Soul is It Anyway? Domestic Tyranny and the Suffocated Soul', in *On Losing the Soul: Essays in the Social Psychology of Religion*, ed. Richard K. Fenn and Donald Capps, Albany, NY: SUNY, 1995, ch. 3.
McFadyen, Alistair I., *Bound to Sin: Abuse, the Holocaust, and the Christian Doctrine of Sin*, Cambridge: Cambridge University Press, 2000.
McFague, Sallie, *Metaphorical Theology: Models of God in Religious Language*, London: SCM Press, 1982.
Nelson, Andrew Sung Park and Susan L. Nelson, eds, *The Other Side of Sin: Woundedness from the Perspective of the Sinned-Against*, New York: SUNY, 2001.
Nelson, Susan L., 'Soul-Loss and Sin: A Dance of Alienation', in *On Losing the Soul: Essays in the Social Psychology of Religion*, ed. Richard K. Fenn and Donald Capps, New York: SUNY, 1995, 97–116.
NICE, *Post-Traumatic Stress Disorder: Nice Guideline*, National Institute for Clinical Excellence.
O'Donnell, Karen, *Broken Bodies: The Eucharist, Mary and the Body in Trauma Theology*, London: SCM Press, 2018.
Parker, Joanne and Rebecca Carlson Browne, 'For God So Loved the World?', in *Violence against Women and Children: A Christian Theological Sourcebook*, ed. Carol J. Adams and Marie M. Fortune, New York: Continuum, 1995, 36–59.
Plaskow, Judith, *Sex, Sin and Grace: Women's Experience and the Theologies of Reinhold Niebuhr and Paul Tillich*, Lanham, MD: University Press of America, 1980.
Rambo, Shelly, 'Introduction', in *Post-Traumatic Public Theology*, ed. Stephanie N. Arel and Shelly Rambo, Cham: Palgrave Macmillan, 2016.
Richards, Laura, *Domestic Abuse, Stalking and Harassment and Honour Based Violence (DASH, 2009) Risk Identification and Assessment and Management Model*, London: Association of Chief Police Officers, 2009.
Robinson, Amanda L., Andy Myhill, Julia Wire, Jo Roberts and Nick Tilley, *Risk-Led Policing of Domestic Abuse and the DASH Risk Model*, London: College of Policing, 2016.
Ruether, Rosemary Radford, *Sexism and God-Talk*, London: SCM Press, 1983.
—— 'The Western Religious Tradition and Violence against Women in the Home', in *Christianity, Patriarchy, and Abuse: A Feminist Critique*, ed. Joanna Carlson Brown and Carole R. Bohm, Cleveland, OH: Pilgrim Press, 1989, 31–41.

Saiving Goldstein, Valerie, 'The Human Situation: A Feminine View', *The Journal of Religion* 40, no. 2 (1960), 100–12.

Sharp, Shane, 'Escaping Symbolic Entrapment, Maintaining Social Identities', *Social Problems* 56, no. 2 (2009), 267–84.

—— 'Resisting Religious Coercive Control', *Violence against Women* 20, no. 12 (2014), 1407–27.

Siu-Maliko, Mercy Ah, 'A Public Theology Response to Domestic Violence in Samoa', *International Journal of Public Theology* 10, no. 1 (2016), 54–67.

Stark, Evan, *Coercive Control: The Entrapment of Women in Personal Life*, New York: Oxford University Press, 2007.

—— 'Looking Beyond Domestic Violence: Policing Coercive Control', *Journal of Police Crisis Negotiations* 12, no. 2 (2012), 199–217.

Stark, Evan and Marianne Hester, 'Coercive Control: Update and Review', *Violence against Women* 25, no. 1 (2019), 81–104.

Starr, Rachel, *Reimagining Theologies of Marriage in Contexts of Domestic Violence: When Salvation is Survival*, Abingdon: Routledge, 2018.

Strickland, Pat and Grahame Allen, *Domestic Violence in England and Wales*, London: House of Commons Library, 2018.

Suchocki, Marjorie Hewitt, *The Fall to Violence: Original Sin in Relational Theology*, New York: Continuum, 1994.

'Symptoms – Post-Traumatic Stress Disorder (PTSD)', updated 27 September 2018: www.nhs.uk/conditions/post-traumatic-stress-disorder-ptsd/symptoms/ (accessed 27 June 2019).

Thomas, Kristie A., Manisha Joshi and Susan B. Sorenson, '"Do You Know What It Feels Like to Drown?": Strangulation as Coercive Control in Intimate Relationships', *Psychology of Women Quarterly* 38, no. 1 (2014), 124–37.

van der Kolk, Bessel and Alexander C. McFarlane, 'The Black Hole of Trauma', in *Traumatic Stress: The Effects of Overwhelming Experience on Mind, Body, and Society*, ed. Bessel van der Kolk, Alexander C. McFarlane and Lars Weisaeth, New York: Guildford Press, 1996, 3–23.

Vasko, Elisabeth T., 'The Difference Gender Makes: Nuptiality, Analogy, and the Limits of Appropriating Hans Urs Von Balthasar's Theology in the Context of Sexual Violence', *The Journal of Religion* 94, no. 4 (2014), 504–28.

Walby, Sylvia and Jude Towers, 'Untangling the Concept of Coercive Control: Theorizing Domestic Violent Crime', *Criminology and Criminal Justice* 18, no. 1 (2018), 7–28.

Wiener, Cassandra, 'Seeing What Is "Invisible in Plain Sight": Policing Coercive Control', *The Howard Journal of Crime and Justice* 56, no. 4 (2017), 500–15.

Williamson, Emma, 'Living in the World of the Domestic Violence Perpetrator: Negotiating the Unreality of Coercive Control', *Violence against Women* 16, no. 12 (2010), 1412–23.

Notes

1 See especially Judith Lewis Herman, *Trauma and Recovery: From Domestic Abuse to Political Terror*, reprint with new Afterword (London: Pandora, 2001), ch. 2, 5.

2 For example, Rachel Starr, *Reimagining Theologies of Marriage in Contexts*

of Domestic Violence: When Salvation is Survival (Abingdon: Routledge, 2018); Joy M. K. Bussert, *Battered Women: From a Theology of Suffering to an Ethic of Empowerment* (Minneapolis, MN: Lutheran Church in America, 1986); Marie M. Fortune, 'The Nature of Abuse', *Pastoral Psychology* 41, no. 5 (1 May 1993); Marie M. Fortune, 'Faith is Fundamental to Ending Domestic Terror', *Women's Rights Law Reporter* 33, no. 4 (2012); Elisabeth T. Vasko, 'The Difference Gender Makes: Nuptiality, Analogy, and the Limits of Appropriating Hans Urs von Balthasar's Theology in the Context of Sexual Violence', *The Journal of Religion* 94, no. 4 (2014); Mercy Ah Siu-Maliko, 'A Public Theology Response to Domestic Violence in Samoa', *International Journal of Public Theology* 10, no. 1 (2016); Joanne Carlson Brown and Carole R Bohn, eds, *Christianity, Patriarchy and Abuse: A Feminist Critique* (New York: Pilgrim Press, 1993); Rosemary Radford Ruether, 'The Western Religious Tradition and Violence against Women in the Home', in *Christianity, Patriarchy, and Abuse: A Feminist Critique*, ed. Joanna Carlson Brown and Carole R. Bohm (Cleveland, OH: Pilgrim Press, 1989); Marie Fortune, 'The Transformation of Suffering: A Biblical and Theological Perspective', in *Violence Against Women and Children: A Christian Theological Sourcebook*, ed. Carol J. Adams and Marie M. Fortune (New York: Continuum, 1995); Daphne Marsden, 'The Church's Contribution to Domestic Violence: Submission, Headship, and Patriarchy', in *Rape Culture, Gender Violence, and Religion: Christian Perspectives*, ed. Caroline Blyth, Emily Colgan and Katie B. Edwards (Cham: Palgrave Macmillan, 2018); Elisabeth Schüssler Fiorenza, 'Ties that Bind: Violence against Wo/men', in *Transforming Vision: Explorations in Feminist The*logy* (Minneapolis, MN: Fortress Press, 2011); Joanne Carlson Brown and Rebecca Parker, 'For God So Loved the World?', in *Violence Against Women and Children: A Christian Theological Sourcebook*, ed. Carol J. Adams and Marie M. Fortune (New York: Continuum, 1995).

3 Valerie Saiving Goldstein, 'The Human Situation: A Feminine View', *The Journal of Religion* 40, no. 2 (1960).

4 Jennifer Erin Beste, 'Recovery from Sexual Violence and Socially Mediated Dimensions of God's Grace: Implications for Christian Communities', *Studies in Christian Ethics* 18, no. 2 (2005), 91, n. 8; L. Juliana M. Claassens, 'Calling the Keeners: The Image of the Wailing Woman as Symbol of Survival in a Traumatized World', *Journal of Feminist Studies in Religion* 26, no. 1 (2010), 68ff.; Deborah van Deusen Hunsinger, 'Bearing the Unbearable: Trauma, Gospel and Pastoral Care', *Theology Today* 68, no. 1 (2011), 10–14; Jennifer Erin Beste, *God and the Victim: Traumatic Intrusions on Grace and Freedom* (Oxford: Oxford University Press, 2007), 5–8; Karen O'Donnell, *Broken Bodies: The Eucharist, Mary and the Body in Trauma Theology* (London: SCM Press, 2018), 3ff.

5 Herman, *Trauma and Recovery*, 33–47; Serene Jones, *Trauma and Grace: Theology in a Ruptured World*, 2nd edn (Louisville, KY: Westminster John Knox Press, 2019), 16ff.; NICE, *Post-traumatic Stress Disorder: NICE Guideline*, NG116 (National Institute for Clinical Excellence); 'Symptoms – Post-traumatic Stress Disorder (PTSD)', updated 27 September 2018, www.nhs.uk/conditions/post-traumatic-stress-disorder-ptsd/symptoms/ (accessed 27 June 2019); Bessel van der Kolk and Alexander McFarlane, 'The Black Hole of Trauma', in *Traumatic Stress*, ed. Bessel van der Kolk, Alexander McFarlane and Lars Weisaeth (New York: Guildford Press, 1996); American Psychiatric Association, *Diagnostic and Statistical Manual of Mental Disorders (DSM-5)*, 5th edn (Arlington, VA: American Psychiatric Association, 2013).

6 Such as: persistent negative mood; persistent negative beliefs about self and others; cognitive distortions associated with irrational blame or self-blame; avoidance behaviour; especially self-destructive recklessness. See American Psychiatric Association, *DSM-5*.

7 Michael P. Johnson, *A Typology of Domestic Violence: Intimate Terrorism, Violent Resistance, and Situational Couple Violence* (Boston, MA: Northeastern University Press, 2008), 42; Herman, *Trauma and Recovery*, 33–47.

8 Evan Stark, *Coercive Control: The Entrapment of Women in Personal Life* (New York: Oxford University Press, 2007), 124–8; Charlotte Bishop and Vanessa Bettinson, 'Evidencing Domestic Violence, Including Behaviour that Falls under the New Offence of "Controlling or Coercive Behaviour"', *The International Journal of Evidence and Proof* 22, no. 1 (2018), 10ff.; Herman, *Trauma and Recovery*, 33f.; Evan Stark, 'Looking Beyond Domestic Violence: Policing Coercive Control', *Journal of Police Crisis Negotiations* 12, no. 2 (2012).

9 Herman, *Trauma and Recovery*, 11–20.

10 Herman, *Trauma and Recovery*, especially ch. 6. Cf. Johnson, *A Typology of Domestic Violence*; Michael P. Johnson and Janel M. Leone, 'The Differential Effects of Intimate Terrorism and Situational Couple Violence: Findings from the National Violence against Women Survey', *Journal of Family Issues* 26, no. 3 (2005), 41f.

11 Herman, *Trauma and Recovery*, 74.

12 The views represented here are my own and do not necessarily reflect those of West Yorkshire Police.

13 In my service, I have seen how legal and procedural changes requiring attending officers perform specified actions have led to marked changes in culture, attitudes, experience and interpretation of domestic abuse and violence. Most significant among these changes is heightened sensitivity to the risks of non-violent abuse and to the complexities of victim decision-making and agency – both decisive in understanding coercive control. (On this and the more general discussion, see Amanda L. Robinson, Andy Myhill, Julia Wire, Jo Roberts and Nick Tilley, *Risk-Led Policing of Domestic Abuse and the DASH Risk Model* (London: College of Policing, 2016).) It is very many years since I have heard colleagues express dismissive bewilderment about a victim repeatedly going back to an abusive partner or refusing to make a criminal complaint or give a statement. It is far more likely now to be interpreted as an indicator of risk and a potential sign of perpetrator control. This development in relation to domestic victimization has, I think, been accelerated by parallel legislative advances in understanding the entrapment of will and agency in relation to offences such as sexual grooming of children, forced marriage and, more recently, grooming of young children into criminal activity (especially drug supply and trafficking) by organized crime groups (in the UK, known as the county lines phenomenon). That this change in police culture and understanding has been achieved in some significant part through required adjustments in routine practice and actions at domestic incidents should come as no surprise to a theologian already attuned to the significance of routinely repeated performance, not least in a ritual context. It has heightened significance, of course, in the context of a discussion of coercive control, where to some extent it mirrors how routinely behaving in certain ways becomes internalized. Cf. Cassandra Wiener, 'Seeing What is "Invisible in Plain Sight": Policing Coercive Control', *The Howard Journal of Crime and Justice* 56, no. 4 (2017).

14 Wiener, ' "Invisible in Plain Sight"', 501.

15 Johnson finds that the level of violence used in the context of coercive control is higher than in non-controlling relationships: Johnson, *A Typology of Domestic Violence*, 39.

16 Names and other details have been changed to protect identity.

17 Its position in the DASH risk assessment form used by police and other agencies is of particular note: Laura Richards, *Domestic Abuse, Stalking and Harassment and Honour Based Violence (DASH, 2009) Risk Identification and Assessment and Management Model* (London: Association of Chief Police Officers, 2009), p. 128. On the effect on the victim, see also Kristie A. Thomas, Manisha Joshi and Susan B. Sorenson, '"Do You Know What It Feels Like to Drown?": Strangulation as Coercive Control in Intimate Relationships', *Psychology of Women Quarterly* 38, no. 1 (2014).

18 See, for example, Shelly Rambo, 'Introduction', in *Post-Traumatic Public Theology*, ed. Stephanie N. Arel and Shelly Rambo (Cham: Palgrave Macmillan, 2016), 3ff.; Herman, *Trauma and Recovery*, 1f., 8f., 51f.; Beste, *God and the Victim*, 10ff.

19 *Cross-Government Definition of Domestic Violence – A Consultation: Summary of Responses* (London: Home Office, 2012), 3.

20 Emphasizing the violence involved in domestic victimization and foregrounding it in the way we frame it has been a deliberate strategy to ensure that every time we name it, we are reminded of the prevalence of actual or threatened physical violence and the attendant risks of serious physical injury or death that are far too frequently realized. There is justified concern that framing it through the more general label 'domestic abuse', of which domestic violence is then a subset, risks drawing attention away from the underlying and actual violence that overwhelmingly characterizes domestic victimization of all kinds and so significantly misrepresents the seriousness and severity of risk. In questioning the emphasis on violent incidents, I am intending to heighten the sense of risk and violation in both physical and non-physical forms of abuse, as well as highlighting their interconnectedness in structuring and defining an abusive relationship. See, for example, Fortune, 'The Nature of Abuse', 275ff. But see her later comments specifically in relation to coercive control: Fortune, 'Faith Is Fundamental to Ending Domestic Terror', 463f.

21 It should be noted and appreciated that this earlier UK government definition is already more expansive than many government, scholarly or public discussions or definitions of domestic abuse and violence in not restricting itself to intimate partners, but extending to relationships and interactions between other adult family members. Hence, the definition is already sufficiently extensive to cover honour-based violence, forced marriage and female genital mutilation (provided the victim is 18 or over).

22 I adopt the convention of using female pronouns for victims and male for abusers, hoping not to render male victimization invisible, but to make the gender disparity and gender base of domestic victimization more visible (even more pronounced when it takes the form of coercive control). On the parenthetical point, see, for example, Evan Stark and Marianne Hester, 'Coercive Control: Update and Review', *Violence against Women* 25, no. 1 (2019), 5, 82f., 86; Stark, *Coercive Control*, 6, 16, 213ff., 367f., 102, ch. 6; Sylvia Walby and Jude Towers, 'Untangling the Concept of Coercive Control: Theorizing Domestic Violent Crime', *Criminology and Criminal Justice* 18, no. 1 (2018), 24ff.; Kristin L. Anderson, 'Gendering Coercive Control', *Violence against Women* 15, no. 12 (2009); L. Kevin Hamberger,

Sadie E. Larsen and Amy Lehrner, 'Coercive Control in Intimate Partner Violence', *Aggression and Violent Behavior* 37 (2017); Johnson, *A Typology of Domestic Violence*, 14, 18–23; Bishop and Bettinson, 'Evidencing Domestic Violence', 8f.

23 Stark, *Coercive Control*, 83ff.

24 Cf. here Stark and Hester, 'Coercive Control', 83.

25 The maximum possible sentence is five years imprisonment plus a fine.

26 *Cross-Government Definition of Domestic Violence – A Consultation: Summary of Responses*, 19. In a recently proposed amendment, the more general term 'economic' replaces 'financial' abuse to signal that the control over 'access to basic resources like food and clothing' is being controlled. See Pat Strickland and Grahame Allen, *Domestic Violence in England and Wales Briefing Paper Number 6337 S.5.1* (London: House of Commons Library, 2018).

27 Serious Crime Act 2015, S.76 (1) (a).

28 Emma Williamson, 'Living in the World of the Domestic Violence Perpetrator: Negotiating the Unreality of Coercive Control', *Violence against Women* 16, no. 12 (2010); Bernice Martin, 'Whose Soul is It Anyway? Domestic Tyranny and the Suffocated Soul', in *On Losing the Soul: Essays in the Social Psychology of Religion*, ed. Richard K. Fenn and Donald Capps (Albany, NY: SUNY, 1995), 78f.

29 The Act itself moves further away from the language of intent than official commentary, in fact – including statutory guidance. The Act states that the offence is made out if the offender repeatedly or continuously behaves in a way that is controlling and coercive, the behaviour causes harm and the offender knows or should know that it would do so. That does require at a minimum some consciousness or culpable negligence, but it is a far cry from the *mens rea* of purposeful, deliberated intent. See Serious Crime Act S.76 (1). The statutory guidance reflects that well at some points, but in others interprets the Act as requiring chosen, purposeful behaviour *intended* to achieve the exercise of control. Cf. *Controlling or Coercive Behaviour in an Intimate or Family Relationship: Statutory Guidance Framework* (London: Home Office, 2015), S.1, para. 3; S.2, paras 10f. The assumption of intent is made in most of the literature on coercive control, for example, Johnson, *A Typology of Domestic Violence*, 141of.; Hamberger, Larsen and Lehrner, 'Coercive Control in Intimate Partner Violence'; Shane Sharp, 'Resisting Religious Coercive Control', *Violence against Women* 20, no. 12 (2014).

30 Serious Crime Act, S.76 (1) (c), (4).

31 Judith Herman recognizes the significance of lack of opportunity for resistance and escape in relation to trauma. See especially Herman, *Trauma and Recovery*, 34, 74ff.

32 *Domestic Violence in England and Wales*, para.10. By contrast, both Johnson and Stark (at least in his earlier work) appear to assume that coercive control is the relational context of repeated violence; that controlling relationships (almost) always include actual violence (Bishop and Bettinson, 'Evidencing Domestic Violence', 9f.; Johnson, *A Typology of Domestic Violence*, 45ff.). Examples of such 'low-level' behaviours that might be difficult to distinguish from acceptable, reasonable or even benign ones include, for example, systematic patterns of helpfulness or intervention that might be well intentioned but displace the victim's agency, fostering a sense of inadequacy and correlate dependence. Where a victim is isolated from external sources of affirmation, pathologically low self-esteem (either pre-existent or fostered through abusive behaviour in the relationship) is likely to create the conditions for over-dependence on the abuser's appraisal of her worth, whether that is

positive or negative. The desire to seek affirmation and approval might be as likely to regulate her behaviour as the desire to avoid criticism, blame or other forms of negative evaluation (Bishop and Bettinson, 'Evidencing Domestic Violence', 11f.; Martin, 'Whose Soul is It Anyway?', 80f.). Behaviour might include: asking for a full account of her day; frequently commenting on appearance; monitoring use of time; frequently calling 'to check welfare'; constant texting; turning up unannounced at work; monitoring movements through social media or phone-tracking software; reading texts or other messages; discouraging contact with friends or family; commenting on spending. Exemplary lists are given in *Controlling or Coercive Behaviour in an Intimate or Family Relationship: Statutory Guidance Framework*, S.2, para. 12. Lists of risk behaviours can also be found in the Domestic Abuse, Stalking and Harassment risk assessment form used by UK police forces, statutory bodies and other partner agencies.

33 Johnson, *A Typology of Domestic Violence*, 88–91.

34 And possibly (perhaps with the assistance of trauma theory) such considerations might lead us to question whether we have to wait for repetition of the act in order to find coercive control. I have met more than one victim for whom being subjected to a single, severely traumatizing action proved sufficient to habitually and repeatedly re-enact strategies of harm reduction; for their behaviour to be regulated and controlled by the dominating fear and desire to avoid further abuse, risk to life or to psycho-spiritual well-being.

35 Bishop and Bettinson, 'Evidencing Domestic Violence', 10f.

36 Relevant here are specific formal codes such as inheritance rights, marriage vows, regulation of divorce, and less formal gendered or age-related expectations that might legitimate micro-management and regulation of other family members' behaviour or create expectations about subservience and prioritization of needs. Cf. Stark and Hester, 'Coercive Control', 87, 92. Social (especially religious) codes and symbols can intensify the dynamics of (symbolic) entrapment and sense of social transgression (and loss of social identity) implicit in non-compliance. At the same time, they can also license communal regulation of victim behaviour by third parties, as well as internalized rationalizations about legitimate boundaries for the exercise of her agency (especially in leaving) the relationship. Shane Sharp, 'Escaping Symbolic Entrapment, Maintaining Social Identities', *Social Problems* 56, no. 2 (2009). See also Sharp, 'Resisting Religious Coercive Control'.

37 This is likely reinforced by commentary or behaviour that reduces the capacity to gather and centre personal resources, undermining her sense of competence and confidence to act to leave, especially in being able to look after herself or children on her own. Johnson, *A Typology of Domestic Violence*, 38. The converse is also true – that escaping the entrapment requires (in addition to seeing her situation as one of abusive, coercive control) gathering the energy to leave and to visualize surviving leaving. Her economic situation will be a significant consideration in this, which may be controlled directly or indirectly (e.g. by forbidding her to work or by controlling access to education or undermining her confidence in seeking better-paid work; directly or indirectly making it difficult to go into work – having to explain visible injuries; the injuries themselves being sufficient to require repeated absence). Johnson, *A Typology of Domestic Violence*, 39.

38 Cf. here the discussion of Stark, *Coercive Control*, 205ff., 76.

39 Katz's research on the effects of coercive control on children documents some of the ways in which abused mothers covertly resist, sometimes conspiratorially

involving children. Emma Katz, 'Beyond the Physical Incident Model: How Children Living with Domestic Violence are Harmed By and Resist Regimes of Coercive Control', *Child Abuse Review* 25, no. 1 (2016). See also Jane E. M. Callaghan et al., 'Beyond "Witnessing": Children's Experiences of Coercive Control in Domestic Violence and Abuse', *Journal of Interpersonal Violence* 33, no. 10 (2018).

40 Johnson, *A Typology of Domestic Violence*, 40ff.

41 Stark, *Coercive Control*, 215.

42 I offer here a highly truncated account. For a fuller account, see Alistair I. McFadyen, *Bound to Sin: Abuse, the Holocaust, and the Christian Doctrine of Sin* (Cambridge: Cambridge University Press, 2000), especially ch. 7 and 216–21.

43 The risk is of being misinterpreted as blaming victims. In modern, Western culture we are attuned to interpret the exercise of will in directing agency to connote the freedom of potent subjectivity and thereby also moral culpability – a person fully centred on themselves, whose will expresses their asocially formed intentionality free of determining external influences with sufficient power to act accordingly. If the will is always free, then saying that victims exercise will in relation to their abuse is to blame them for their own victimization. This free, potent, essentially unrelated subject is, for secular and theological feminists alike, a patriarchal fiction that reflects how deeply embedded are male-centred perspectives in our default constructions of reality.

44 See, further, Andrew Sung Park and Susan L. Nelson, eds, *The Other Side of Sin: Woundedness from the Perspective of the Sinned-Against* (New York: SUNY, 2001).

45 See, for example: Rebecca S. Chopp, *The Power to Speak: Feminism, Language, God* (New York: Crossroad, 1991), 12ff., 25, 101–15; Mary Daly, *Beyond God the Father: Towards the Philosophy of Women's Liberation* (London: The Women's Press, 1986), 10, 33, 48ff., 122, 126; Sallie McFague, *Metaphorical Theology: Models of God in Religious Language* (London: SCM Press, 1982), 142–52; Rosemary Radford Ruether, *Sexism and God-Talk* (London: SCM Press, 1983), 37, 164, 73; bell hooks, *Feminist Theory: From Margin to Center* (Boston, MA: South End, 1984), 86; Rita Nakashima Brock, *Journeys by Heart: A Christology of Erotic Power* (New York: Crossroad, 1992), ch. 1; Dorothy Lee, *Flesh and Glory: Symbol, Gender, and Theology in the Gospel of John* (New York: Crossroad, 2002), 190–6; Fiorenza, 'Ties that Bind'.

46 Plaskow, *Sex, Sin and Grace*, 3, 35, 64f., 68, 85f., 90, 92, 114, 138; Hampson, 'Reinhold Niebuhr on Sin', 51.

47 Dunfee, 'The Sin of Hiding'.

48 Ruether, *Sexism and God-Talk*, 181.

49 Plaskow, *Sex, Sin and Grace*, 3, 65, 67, 93.

50 Hampson, 'Reinhold Niebuhr on Sin', 49.

51 Plaskow, *Sex, Sin and Grace*, 92, 118.

52 Plaskow, *Sex, Sin and Grace*, 92, 118.

53 Mary Potter Engel, 'Evil, Sin, and Violation of the Vulnerable', in *Lift Every Voice: Constructing Christian Theologies from the Underside*, ed. Susan Brooks Thistlethwaite and Mary Potter Engel (San Francisco: Harper and Row, 1990), 152–64, 156f.; Sharon D. Welch, *Communities of Resistance and Solidarity: A Feminist Theology of Liberation* (Maryknoll, NY: Orbis Books, 1985), 49.

54 Ruether, *Sexism and God-Talk*, 180f.; Daly, *Beyond God the Father*, 52;

Engel, 'Evil, Sin and Violation of the Vulnerable', 155f., 180; Plaskow, *Sex, Sin and Grace*, 64f.; Welch, *Communities of Resistance and Solidarity*, 49.

55 Engel, 'Evil, Sin and Violation of the Vulnerable', 155f., 180; Ruether, *Sexism and God-Talk*, 113f., 160–4, 180–3; Ruether, *Gaia and God: An Ecofeminist Theology of Earth Healing* (New York: HarperCollins, 1992), 141 (and cf. her understanding of confession in *Women-Church: Theology and Practice* (San Francisco: Harper and Row, 1985), 131f.); Grey, *Redeeming the Dream*, 15, 19, 27, 107f.; Mercadante, *Victims and Sinners*, 38.

56 Daly, *Beyond God the Father*, 50; Gudorf, *Victimization*, 2.

57 Daly, *Beyond God the Father*, 2.; Mercadante, *Victims and Sinners*, 41.

58 Ruether, *Sexism and God-Talk*, 186.

59 Ruether, 180ff.; Mercadante, *Victims and Sinners*, 41.

60 Herman, *Trauma and Recovery*, 115f. Herman explicitly rejects the applicability of 'complicity' and 'cooperation' to describe victims' situation since she holds them to connote freedom of choice, noting that they do not have the same meaning in situations of captivity – it is precisely that changed meaning that is carried forward into feminist use of these and analogous infinitives.

61 Cf. Susan Grove Eastman, *Paul and the Person: Reframing Paul's Anthropology* (Grand Rapids, MI: Eerdmans, 2017), ch. 4.

62 See, for example: Wanda Warren Berry, 'Images of Sin and Salvation in Feminist Theology', *Anglican Theological Review* 60, no. 1 (1979); Daly, *Beyond God the Father: Towards the Philosophy of Women's Liberation*, ch. 2; Susan Nelson Dunfee, 'The Sin of Hiding: A Feminist Critique of Reinhold Niebuhr's Account of the Sin of Pride', *Soundings* 65, no. 3 (1982); Mary Grey, *Redeeming the Dream: Feminism, Redemption and Christian Tradition* (London: SPCK, 1989), 15–19, 27, 91; Daphne Hampson, 'Reinhold Niebuhr on Sin: A Critique', in *Reinhold Niebuhr and the Issues of Our Time*, ed. Richard Harries (London: Mowbray, 1986); Daphne Hampson, 'Luther on the Self: A Feminist Critique', in *Feminist Theology: A Reader*, ed. Anne Loades (London: SPCK, 1990); Daphne Hampson, *Theology and Feminism* (Oxford: Basil Blackwell, 1990), 121–6; Judith Plaskow, *Sex, Sin and Grace: Women's Experience and the Theologies of Reinhold Niebuhr and Paul Tillich* (Lanham, MD: University Press of America, 1980); Valerie Saiving, 'The Human Situation: a Feminine View', *The Journal of Religion* 40 (1960); Marjorie Hewitt Suchocki, *The Fall to Violence: Original Sin in Relational Theology* (New York: Continuum, 1994), 26, 31ff., 39f., 43f, 83f., 96; Luping Huang, *Women and Pride: An Exploration of the Feminist Critique of Reinhold Niebuhr's Theology of Sin* (Carlisle: Langham Monographs, 2018).

63 Cf. Martin, 'Whose Soul is It Anyway?'

64 Stark, *Coercive Control*, viii, 13, 16, 165f., 262, 363, 80; Sharp, 'Resisting Religious Coercive Control', Stark's discussion immediately connects restriction of choice to notions that are stretching towards a notion of lost or damaged selfhood-in-relation. Cf. Martin, 'Whose Soul is It Anyway?', 73ff.

65 See, for example, Susan L. Nelson, 'Soul-Loss and Sin: A Dance of Alienation', in *On Losing the Soul: Essays in the Social Psychology of Religion*, ed. Donald Capps and Richard K. Fenn (New York: SUNY, 1995). Daly, *Beyond God the Father*, 32, 159, 172; Carter Heyward, *The Redemption of God* (Lanham, MD: University Press of America, 1982); Carter Heyward, *Touching Our Strength: The Erotic as the Power and Love of God* (San Francisco: HarperCollins, 1989), 96f., 104f., 192f.; Carter Heyward, *Our Passion for Justice: Images of Power, Sexuality*

and Liberation (New York: Pilgrim, 1984); Grey, *Redeeming the Dream*, 106–8; Nakashima Brock, *Journeys by Heart*, ch. 2; Sharon D. Welch, *A Feminist Ethic of Risk* (Minneapolis, MN: Fortress Press, 1990), 135; Letty M. Russell, *Human Liberation in a Feminist Perspective: A Theology* (Philadelphia, PA: Westminster, 1974), 107, 110, 121, 146, 152ff., 160, 163; Mary E. Hunt, *Fierce Tenderness: A Feminist Theology of Friendship* (New York: Crossroad, 1991); Mary Grey, *The Wisdom of Fools: Seeking Revelation for Today* (London: SPCK, 1993), ch. 4. See further McFadyen, *Bound to Sin*, 158–63.

66 Fiorenza, 'Ties that Bind'.

67 Stark and Hester, 'Coercive Control', 87. Referring to Bishop and Bettinson, 'Evidencing Domestic Violence', 8ff.

68 I make this suggestion mindful of long-standing and widespread suspicion of transcendence in feminist theology, not least in the feminist theologies I have mostly drawn on in the discussion so far. That suspicion will be intensified in relation to phenomena such as coercive control, since in so much of the tradition, divine transcendence has been read in ways that validate and legitimate hierarchy and domination in human relations reflecting the pattern of divine–human relationship. See further McFadyen, *Bound to Sin*, chs 9–10. Moreover, the transcendent, omnipotent God looks like a projection of the dominant, domineering, essentially unrelated, abstract, disembodied stereotypical male, disembedded from nature and relationships (and so also disembodied).

69 Martin, 'Whose Soul is It Anyway?', 92f., n.1.

70 Williamson, 'Living in the World of the Domestic Violence Perpetrator', 1418; Johnson, *A Typology of Domestic Violence*, 50.

71 For the proper grounding of this trinitarian understanding of idolatry, see further McFadyen, *Bound to Sin*, ch. 9.

72 Beste, 'Recovery from Sexual Violence and Socially Mediated Dimensions of God's Grace: Implications for Christian Communities', 89; Claassens, 'Calling the Keeners'; Beste, *God and the Victim*.

73 Beste, 'Recovery from Sexual Violence and Socially Mediated Dimensions of God's Grace: Implications for Christian Communities', 94ff.; Flora A. Keshgegian, *Redeeming Memories: A Theology of Healing and Transformation* (Nashville, TN: Abingdon Press, 2000); Hunsinger, 'Bearing the Unbearable: Trauma, Gospel and Pastoral Care'; Beste, *God and the Victim*, 13ff.

74 Beste, *God and the Victim*, 4, ch. 7.

6

Reading Gomer with Questions:
A Trauma-informed Feminist Study of How the Experience of Intimate Partner Violence and the Presence of Religious Belief Shape the Reading of Hosea 2.2–23

KIRSI COBB

'God is God. Surely he can do whatever he likes, right?' 'It is only a metaphor. Should we be careful not to read too much into it?' These questions are a sample of the kinds of queries I often encounter when teaching the book of Hosea in undergraduate classes. Most of my students are young adults and confessing Christians with some experience of reading the Bible within an evangelical church setting. Coming from a similar background myself, I am well acquainted with the 'love story' of Hosea/Gomer and God/Israel: the distraught husband[1] chases after his wanton wife and after desperate threats/acts of punishment, seeks loving reconciliation.[2] If Hosea was the first prophet to portray God through marital imagery,[3] Hosea 2 may well provide us with an unprecedented image of a vulnerable and broken-hearted man, 'an image in classic literature usually reserved for women'.[4] But is this all there is to the story?

In light of current data relating to domestic violence, one might be cautioned against reading Hosea 2 with such rose-tinted glasses. Recent statistics in England and Wales show that the majority of domestic violence homicide victims are female (73 per cent), with a male partner or an ex-partner as the most likely perpetrator.[5] Men, however, are more likely to be killed by other men in both non- and domestic incidences,[6] and make up 88 per cent of victims of non-domestic homicides.[7] The prevalence of male violence in and outside the home is astounding, but the gendered nature of the victims and perpetrators even more so. As noted in a recent monograph by Nancy Nason-Clark et al., patriarchal social structures often lurk behind 'context-specific social constructions of gender', exerting pressure on women to accommodate gender roles that leave them 'in subordinate positions of power to men'.[8] Such constructions, when combined with economic or even religious factors, often leave women vulnerable to intimate partner violence.[9] Male violence cannot be treated as an isolated problem or even something that must be tolerated. 'Boys will be boys' is simply not a good enough explanation when lives are at stake, be they ancient or contemporary.

As a survivor of domestic violence, these statistics make me very uncomfortable and reading Hosea 2 does little to ease it. While we must attempt to understand the text and not simply superimpose our contemporary standards on to it, we must also 'take into full account our fissured and disconcerting moment in time'.[10] In fact, our 'disconcerting moment in time' might be of benefit in illuminating aspects of biblical texts not previously emphasized, as has been illustrated in the recent rise of biblical trauma studies. If trauma, as in the oft-quoted definition by Cathy Caruth, is broadly understood as a belated and even intrusive response to an overwhelming catastrophic and/or sudden experience,[11] our contemporary context of unspeakable violence might broaden 'our historical imagination' by illuminating 'typical lingering effects of disaster'[12] in biblical texts that might have received their final form under circumstances of trauma. Although to get an exact comparison might be well beyond our reach,[13] a deeper understanding might well be within it. With this in mind, the purpose of this chapter is to explore Hosea 2.2–23 and to tentatively enquire as to what kind of insights can be gained if read against an actual lived reality of a survivor of a traumatic experience, in this case that of domestic violence.

Hosea and Metaphor

'Metaphors can hurt. Metaphors can distort. Metaphors can kill. Metaphors can oppress.'[14] This statement from Renita Weems is all too true when it comes to the marriage metaphor[15] in the book of Hosea. Although Hosea 2.2–23 seemingly connects the violence depicted to the affairs between God and Israel rather than that of Hosea and Gomer (vv. 13, 16, 20), it is questionable whether the sting of the metaphor is any less for doing so. As noted by Katharine Doob Sakenfeld, if the 'prophetic acted sign' of Hosea's marriage was intended also to display how God would respond to Israel's unfaithfulness, actual harm done to Gomer becomes 'a chilling possibility'.[16] This possibility becomes even more chilling when we recognize that Israel became a victim to military invasion, in which case Hosea's prophecies cease to be mere threats[17] and seep into the world of reality.

Although an exhaustive analysis of metaphor theory cannot be presented in this chapter, for our purposes it is significant to acknowledge that by using the marriage metaphor, the author of Hosea introduces us to a world of meaning-making where differing concepts or terms 'are brought together in order to achieve a special meaning'.[18] This 'special meaning' has the ability to go 'beyond the ordinary meaning of words or concepts'.[19] In interactive approaches to metaphor,[20] more is achieved by this than simply a substitution of one phrase for another. Rather, a metaphor remains a 'two-way traffic in ideas',[21] where the interaction between the two terms is able to reorganize the way we perceive both subjects.[22] Moreover, as both concepts also bring with themselves a *'system of associated commonplaces'*[23] – in other words, culture and/or context-specific assumptions about both terms – an indeterminate number of new and/or even shocking meanings[24] can be brought into existence. The marriage metaphor in the book of Hosea thus leaves neither human nor divine untouched. Rather, by manipulating his audience's cultural/social understanding of the subjects with the use of rhetoric and/or propaganda,[25] the author of Hosea creates a new understanding where the human and divine collide head-on, leaving a whole host of associated descriptions in its wake.

This also indicates that by the application of the marriage metaphor, the author does much more than simply introduce a novel idea. As Sharon Moughtin-Mumby notes, metaphors *'create* meaning', where 'connotations surrounding any metaphorical word are intrinsic to its meaning, and cannot be differentiated from this'.[26] This indicates that, even if Hosea's message gained its meaning from warfare imagery and/or covenantal curses,[27] or was targeted against (mostly) men and/or the male-dominated world of foreign or domestic policies,[28] the gendered nature of the metaphor remains and cannot be separated from its message.[29] By playing to established patriarchal conventions of marriage as well as gender stereotypes, the metaphor works precisely because it references accepted social and cultural norms, ideals or even fantasies[30] regarding the marriage itself, as well as the possibility of retributive punishment.[31] This applies even if we view the marriage between Hosea and Gomer not as historical reality but as a creation of a patriarchal mind. The metaphor relies in either case on depictions of masculinity and female sexuality that the implied audience would have been trusted to recognize and, in the case of the husband, even to have sympathy with.

Metaphors have the power to persuade, to change and affect our understanding of the world;[32] they can indeed hurt, distort, kill and oppress. In the world of Hosea's marriage metaphor, historical or otherwise, the line between the affairs of the divine and those of flesh and blood husbands is but a stone's throw away, if even that.

Methodology

This chapter started as a qualitative project. My intention was to interview 12 women with faith commitments, half of whom had experienced intimate partner violence. I intended to study their response to Hosea 2.2–23 and compare how their differing backgrounds affected their reading. However, getting ethical approval proved problematic due to concerns regarding the safety of the six survivors: how was I going to make sure that while they were reading and/or discussing the text, they would not experience flashbacks or other symptoms during or after the interview? This, in fact, is the conundrum facing a researcher engaged with personal narratives of trauma: while re-traumatization of research participants remains a real possibility, unless their stories are told and explored, the research community will remain largely ignorant of the impact of trauma on the lives of many. The solution to this dilemma is to carefully construct the study to ensure that comprehensive support mechanisms are in place, and this unfortunately was not possible with this study.

This chapter therefore became autoethnographic in nature, and was written in dialogue with Rachel Starr, a colleague and an author on domestic violence although not a survivor herself.[33] The focus of the project thus remained the same but the method changed.

As interactive interviewing encourages building a relationship with the dialogue partners and emphasizes collegiality,[34] this method seemed most appropriate for the study. Starr and myself are of similar age, long-term friends, teach at Bible colleges in the UK[35] and profess a faith commitment over several years, all of which provided some needed common ground.[36] In addition, as both of us are self-described feminist biblical scholars, the use of reflexivity, 'listening and looking for difference' and grounding our research firmly in the realm of our (women's) experience[37] were also important in our approach. However, I must confess that my interest in these methods, or my choice of a dialogue partner, were not done purely out of scholastic interest. As soon as I decided on an autoethnographic route, I wished my dialogue partner to be someone who would be sympathetic to reading Hosea 2 in light of domestic violence. In short, as a survivor of domestic abuse I felt vulnerable and wanted, or rather needed, an empathetic ear.

The dialogue took place over one hour about two months into the research project. It loosely followed the pattern of a semi-structured interview with a set of questions, and the passage concerned prepared and seen by both of us in advance. The interview was recorded and Starr was given the opportunity to read and respond to the transcript as well as to the summary of the dialogue present in this chapter.[38] She also gave permission for her name, as opposed to a pseudonym, to be used in this context.

Before moving on to the actual dialogue, I wish to focus on two further issues pertinent to my methodology. The first is to acknowledge the presence of other studies that have used biblical texts to study women's experience.[39] While various methods have been employed in these and other studies, autoethnography and/or interactive interviewing have not been prevalent. Regarding the book of Hosea, authors have often reflected on domestic violence when coming across appropriate passages without the exact use of the methods utilized in this chapter.[40] This chapter intends to bridge some of this gap by engaging the interaction of two 'real readers'[41] of Scripture. It is my purpose to illustrate some of the hope and frustration present when a person of faith is faced with a discourse that, in the words of Gracia Fay Ellwood, puts out 'the fires of violence and oppression by day while relighting them by night'.[42] It is important to demonstrate the honest, gut-wrenching struggles that often ensue when faced with the 'dark side' of the biblical corpus; however, I also wish to illustrate how engagement with such texts can be meaningful without brushing over the very real issue of violence present in them.

The second issue is the relationship between trauma studies and domestic violence and my placement within it. I had never sought nor felt the need for counselling for my experience, which might well put me outside the 'battered woman syndrome'[43] or PTSD as a medical diagnosis attested in some theories of trauma. However, Evan Stark has argued that the description of 'battered women' as victims of trauma and/or PTSD might not always be appropriate; rather, some of the coping strategies developed could be more accurately described as reasonable choices among limited alternatives when living under the circumstance of coercive control.[44] Indeed, if we allow trauma to speak to prolonged and chronic suffering without the need for an exact medical diagnosis, we may find in survivor stories that which in biblical trauma studies has been named trauma and/or survival literature. As trauma literature, the book of Hosea is an interpretation of prolonged suffering and unspeakable atrocities; yet, it is also a 'war-torn' artefact filled with hope, 'intended to help devastated communities survive massive loss'.[45] In this way Hosea 2 and I, as a survivor, have much in common. Both of us are attempting to explain the unexplainable and create meaning in the midst of its collapse. Although we might not always understand one another or even get along, we might find we have more in common than we think. It is these struggles, triumphs and hopes with the text that I now describe as I summarize the dialogue that took place between me and Starr on Hosea 2.2–23.

The Dialogue

'I feel ridiculously nervous' are some of my first words when the dialogue begins. I want to let Starr know right at the outset that what we are about to do is a daunting prospect for me. However, Starr is very supportive, checking some of the safeguards I have already put in place, and in about ten minutes we are talking about the passage. We decide to begin with anything we find difficult in the text.

'Even if you take out the idea that it [Hosea 2] represents some kind of ideal or positive relationship with God, even if you just take it as a man ... talking about a female partner, its hugely woven through with different types of violence,' Starr begins. She picks up on several abusive patterns, such as the husband's control of the wife's religious activities (Hosea 2.11, 13, 17), the threat of physical and sexual violence (v. 3) as well as the use of family members to punish Gomer (vv. 2, 4). To this list, I add the mention of the public humiliation of the woman in Hosea 2.10; however, the one aspect to which I pay special attention is Starr's mention of name-calling: how Gomer is described as a 'whore' and perceived in this light throughout the entire episode. Starr describes a slogan on a poster she owns that states (in Spanish), 'No woman is born a whore'. Being a 'whore' is not a chosen vocation or 'a job you go into', yet this is how you are perceived in society.

Her observation provokes a deep response in me as I had not paid any attention to name-calling in the text. Starr later notes how in biblical scholarship there has been a shift from labelling Gomer as a prostitute to questioning if she was involved in illicit marital relationships, and hence labelling her a 'whore' could be a form of emotional abuse. This, in fact, was my experience. My boyfriend called me a whore if I put on red lipstick or looked at another man with an 'adulterous look', whatever that meant. Overall, I was made to feel that 'I'm some sort of uncontrollable sexual object, that unless I'm wearing a sackcloth and ashes I'm going to be in trouble', a statement that certainly resonates with the description of Gomer in Hosea 2. Yet even with a background of domestic violence, I had not noticed that describing Gomer's actions as 'whoring' might have been name-calling: I was so occupied with the literal/historical meaning of the phrase that it being labelled emotional abuse had not even occurred to me.

As we discuss the passage further, Starr and I are beginning to fall into something akin to a rhythm: 'I [Cobb] feel like you [Starr] are picking out all the patterns, and then when I'm looking at it [Hosea 2.2–23] I'm almost filling in the blanks of what it looks like.' To this, Starr readily agrees. We are in fact seeing the same issues, just with different hues. This helps to relax me further as I now feel that I can talk about my experience with domestic violence without sounding 'hysterical' or adding something 'extra' to the text.

Next we talk about survival strategies in the passage. Starr mentions the woman's claims to autonomy through the use of her body; however, at the same time the woman's only option to survive seems to be to submit to her husband's demands. This is something I can readily identify with. I recollect incidences where I would go along with my boyfriend's demands simply to keep the peace, and yet at other times I would instinctively 'rebel' in order to gain autonomy. Here I refer to Stark's research on coercive control. It was a huge revelation to me when I realized that a lot of my 'disobedient' ways were in fact me trying to create what Stark calls 'safety zones',[46] in other words, areas that would help me keep at least an illusion of control of some parts of my existence.

It is at this point that some of my anger and grief towards the author's portrayal of marriage starts to surface. In Hosea 2, it is 'his [God's/Hosea's] way or the highway, and ... both are abusive patterns from which there is no escape'. If you rebel, you 'get what is coming to you', but if you submit, you remain in the clutches of an abuser. I confess that I would happily burn these passages from the Bible. To my surprise, Starr also notes that if she was writing the Bible today, she would not include these texts. However, since rewriting the Bible is not really an option for two confessing Christians, we discuss various alternative ways that we could read Hosea 2. Starr suggests using the text as a point of conversation to recognize and challenge violence, as well as imagining the roles of Gomer and God reversed. What provokes my interest is her description of a piece by Walter Brueggemann where he describes the God in the Bible as a statue under a sheet, whom we can only glimpse gradually as the sheet is pulled or lifted away.

This brings us to discuss biblical trauma studies. We both agree that signs of trauma and violence are ingrained in the text. Starr remarks how she does not think 'for one minute that this [how the author of Hosea presents God] is what God is like ... this is a writing about a collective experience of violence and trauma. It imagines that this [trauma] is taking place at the hands of God' and seeks a way to portray it so that the audience can still 'believe that God is ... in control'. To this I bring the evidence of my own experience. I had kept some of the correspondence between my boyfriend and me and had found an intriguing letter in which he confessed that the way he behaved was more to do with his fear of rejection than my conduct. I wonder if Hosea 2 could be 'much more about the men of their time and their understanding of God rather than it being about God himself'.

This brings me to reflect upon other images of God found in the Bible where he has been quite willing to relinquish control over his subjects, for example in the story of the prodigal son. I wish that in Hosea 2, instead of God/Hosea controlling the female with whatever means necessary, he would simply say, 'Okay, if you want to go: go!' The question of autonomy in relationships is a topic that both Starr and I find interesting and distinctly lacking in Hosea 2. From her extensive research into marriage and domestic abuse, Starr claims that unless we can turn the covenant of marriage into 'a covenant of friendship, it's not really workable'. She notes research done by the United Nations where it was discovered that women's ownership of land was a key factor in reducing domestic violence.[47] This was because owning land gave the woman 'consistent authority and status' as opposed to being wholly dependent on the male authority in her life. This affirms my reading of Stark's claim that domestic abuse might be better understood as a human rights violation: it is an attempt to control another person's right to independent existence and autonomy.[48] It was a moment of relief for me when I finally admitted that the violence I endured was not my fault. It was an attack on my rights as a woman, and should have been treated and understood as such.

Yet, this was far from the reality I was faced with. I visited a pastor to ask for help for a 'theoretical' situation of domestic violence. His response was to discover what the wife was doing to provoke her husband. This only affirmed my already lived reality: the blame was always mine, my 'adulterous look', my red lipstick, my 'whoring' ways. My boyfriend's efforts to control me were really 'for my own good'. This story is sadly also mirrored in Hosea

2, which Starr also recognizes. She comments on how seeing marriage as an 'unbreakable covenant' or 'an institution' that 'has to be protected' has at times blinded believers to the realities of domestic violence: partner abuse is understood as a 'workable conflict' rather than 'violence to be separated from'. And how I wish that as a young adult I could have separated from it. However, abusive relationships are often ambivalent and unpredictable, as also depicted in Hosea 2. Violence is often followed by intense wooing, of promises of a better future and, as in my case, extravagant presents, multiple cuddly toys and prophecies and visions from 'God'. However, this 'honeymoon period' is suddenly broken by instances of abuse that do not always follow a predictable pattern. As I recollect, 'even if the guy gives me 50 rules of what not to do, there will be the fifty-first rule that I don't know about'. You may try acting 'properly' with all your might but inevitably there will be something you do wrong. As Starr affirms, this kind of peace is very fragile: it is done on one person's terms and because you don't know all the terms, 'you can never avoid the violence'. And so the cycle continues.

As the dialogue draws to a close, I am exhausted and relieved in equal measure. To be honest, I found the entire experience almost like the therapy I never had. Two days after the interview I wrote: 'I felt that my experience was valued and that I had something to say. My experience with domestic violence ended up being a source of insight, not something shameful I had to hide away.' Such an experience finds echoes in the work of Shelly Rambo, who argues for the power of the witness to remain in 'the middle',[49] that is, to stay with the trauma rather than force a happy ending on the sufferer. It is to witness both the slow trickle of life as well as the depths of darkness and persistently remain with what cannot be fully understood. Thanks to Starr being an empathetic dialogue partner, I felt enabled to bring my experience to the table as something valid to contribute. She helped me to journey through my middle; however, in so doing she also witnessed 'a transformation of the depths themselves'.[50] This was perhaps my biggest gain from the interview: by making myself vulnerable, I had inadvertently made myself strong. In my journey through the middle, I had also created space for life.

Evaluation

As stated during the dialogue, it seemed that both Starr and myself were addressing the same issues from slightly different perspectives. While Starr observed some of the patterns of abuse in the text, I was able to provide real-life examples. This was hardly unexpected given our respective backgrounds. Although Hosea 2 is descriptive of ancient patriarchal society and was hardly written with the contemporary survivor of domestic violence in mind,[51] it was remarkable how some of the patterns of abuse remain recognizable: the threat and/or experience of sexual and physical violence (Hosea

2.3) as well as economic dependency (vv. 8–9, 12) were noted by both of us in the passage.

An example of the above dynamic was our common observation of the woman's survival being wholly dependent upon her relinquishing any form of autonomy and submitting to her husband's authority. Although Starr and I both noticed the pattern, my experience of domestic abuse gave it some depth. My boyfriend's requests for (supposedly biblically based) submission would lead him to surveying my movements and demanding uninhibited access to my innermost thoughts in the name of 'honesty'. Survival meant submission, and was not every good Christian girl supposed to submit to her (future) spouse? Yet at other times I would act out, even if this was merely hiding in a friend's room so that he could not find me. As noted earlier, both submission and acting out were my methods of coping in an unreasonable setting where intimacy could never be achieved. This, I imagine, was even more so for Gomer/Israel, where in a patriarchal culture a total submission to the husband's authority was expected and the termination of the covenant not within her sphere of influence.[52] However, crushing a woman into submission is not the same as gaining her love. As Starr noted, peace gained through such methods is extremely volatile as it is achieved only on one person's terms.

Because of our similar interests, it was perhaps more intriguing to notice where Starr's and my reading differed. As my experience of domestic abuse did not include the control of children or religious activity (Hosea 2.2, 4, 11, 13, 17), I completely glossed over these elements. Research into perceptual processing done by Anke Ehlers and others indicates that trauma survivors with PTSD are much more likely to respond to stimulus that resembles that experienced during a traumatic event.[53] Although the presence or absence of PTSD remains unclear in my case, I would agree that my history with domestic violence has given me a certain lens through which I perceive the text. This lens has made me somewhat negligent regarding some aspects and acutely aware of others. This illustrates the need for multiple readings where one understanding, even when perceived through such a painful experience as domestic violence, cannot possibly include all and invites further research.

Another aspect that both Starr and I focused on was the use of excessive violence in Hosea 2.2–13; however, I picked upon a particular verse that had escaped her attention. This was the description of the husband exposing his wife's 'lewdness' in sight of her lovers in Hosea 2.10. That this would depict the public unveiling of the wife's genitalia and/or even hint at rape is disturbing;[54] however, the humiliating nature of either option evoked memories, some of which only occurred after the dialogue. One of these was my boyfriend treating my sexuality as his property. Although I was never raped, the message from him was clear: my body was his and if previous boyfriends had not insisted on this, they were simply wimps and not real men. The anxiety that arose when I was overpowered or humiliated by my abuser, and the shame that came from longing for love and intimacy with my boyfriend, resulted in huge emotional tension which led to a toxic mix of love, shame and guilt. This same tension I can also see at work in Hosea 2.10. The husband demonstrates his authority over his wife by sexually humiliating her,[55] yet at the end of this episode she is supposed to respond to him as 'in the days of her youth' (2.15), presumably with love and adoration. In short, she must love the man who punished her. This description of the 'honeymoon phase' after punishment made both Starr and me wince. True, periods of abuse are often followed by attempts at wooing[56] but, as in the case of Hosea 2, this 'wooing' is only ever described from the husband's point of view, with imagined joyful responses from the wife. As a survivor of domestic violence I can confirm that this is how the scenario will remain: it is imagined, temporary bliss. It is intimacy that can never occur as long as the same hand that embraces you is also the one holding on to your throat.

The difference in our reading that perhaps surprised me the most was my total lack of observation regarding name-calling in the passage. As noted by Starr, the woman is only ever described from the husband's point of view and her 'whoring'[57] is simply portrayed rather than verified.[58] In a recent article, Holly Morse has addressed a similar phenomenon in Ezekiel 16 and 23 where she treats the explicitly violent and sexual depiction of Samaria and Jerusalem as 'revenge porn' and 'slut-shaming'. In this way the images have the added function of 'a warning to the female population against apostasy, adultery, and sexual interaction with foreign men'.[59] This is similar to the contemporary phenomenon of slut-shaming, where 'sexual images and behavior of women' are perceived in a negative light.[60] That the images slip from the level of a metaphor to 'real life' is observed, among others, in Ezekiel 23.10, 48 where the fates of Samaria and Jerusalem become an example and warning to other women. In this way, the text serves 'to establish an environment in which women police the behavior of other women and are terrified of the punishment that would await them if they breached the boundaries of their ethnic group'.[61]

Similar slippages in identity can also be observed in Hosea 2, where the line between human and divine analogy is not always clear. As Tristanne Connolly has observed, in vv. 2–13a the husband and the wife are not named nor is the symbolic nature of the passage emphasized. Rather, the address by the Lord is only revealed at the very end (v. 13b), by which time the audience has already read the passage (mostly) in light of an actual husband punishing his flesh and blood wife.[62] That the passage could act as a warning to the women of Israel becomes a very real possibility, more so in light of the fact that intimate partner violence as described in the book of Hosea may well have harked back to the lived reality of some of the female audience.

That I had been oblivious to these elements in the text astounded me, not least because Morse's paper was one of the first I read when I started research for this chapter. However, regardless of her insights into the book of Ezekiel, my mind still glossed over similar elements in the book of Hosea. It seems that even years later, part of my mind still hung on to 'the belief system' of my abuser and, most importantly, his view of me.[63] In the days past I had come to believe that I was a crazed sex-object, whose actions, clothing or even make-up needed to be monitored to make sure I did not cross some invisible boundary. It was shocking to me that even now part of my mind did not question this view of events. Some elements of abuse, it seems, are more difficult to uproot than others, and pointing out the obvious is needed time and again to start the process of untangling years of lies. Some need to be named and addressed, or renamed and re-addressed, even years later.

However, in defence of my somewhat selective reading, I would add that the historical realities that underlie Hosea 2 have been of interest to me. That the metaphors used in Hosea 2.2–23 could be read in light of the socio-political climate of the day and/or Ancient Near Eastern treaty curses hardly needs defending, yet the choice of the marriage metaphor to express these truths remains in question. That is, even if the marriage metaphor is in some way 'perfect' to express these elements, the image still firmly holds to a patriarchal notion of marriage where an offended husband can (and should) punish his wanton wife. It is here that I struggle with biblical scholars who emphasize the happy ending of Hosea 2 over its horrific beginnings or embrace the 'message' of the book over its medium.[64] As Julia O'Brien notes, the message and the metaphor are one, and by simply changing the metaphor one has changed the message to something other than what Hosea is preaching.[65] In the book of Hosea, the God of the beginning is also the God of the end and he is also the God of the metaphor.

It is these observations that bring me to biblical trauma studies as raised during the dialogue. Rather than simply being an account of Israel's misdeeds and/or Hosea's prophecies, the book is 'a complex literary response to the massive collapse of social and symbolic structures'.[66] In short, the book of Hosea is trauma and/or survival literature. The book gives witness to untold suffering and makes meaning out of meaninglessness, especially for those who must deal with the consequences of the traumatic event.

In her research into the aftermath of trauma, Judith Herman observed that survivors almost universally felt guilt and inferiority when scrutinizing their actions relating to the trauma.[67] This element of self-blame could be perceived as a survival mechanism: it is an attempt to gain some 'power and control' over the event rather than admit 'utter helplessness'.[68] In Hosea 2, the blame for the trauma is constantly heaped on to the faithless wife and, as noted by Starr, it simultaneously helps the Israelites believe that God is still in control. It is through the act of self-blame that the audience of the book of Hosea regain at least some sense of control over the event while keeping their world view of an invincible God intact. Through his message, the author of Hosea thus addresses the basic needs of the community for survival:[69] he gives them agency in the belief that their behaviour can affect the outcome of the covenant; he also gives them hope, since the God who was so enraged with Israel is also able to restore her fortunes.[70]

However, the following question needs to be addressed: could any amount of good behaviour from the Israelites have averted their fate? As noted by Carole Fontaine, since Israel was located on borderland between rising and falling empires, it is possible that no amount of godly conduct would have saved them.[71] Moreover, even though self-blame might help in restoring agency, it can also result in blaming victims and exonerating human culprits, in this case the invading armies.[72] Although the picture painted in the book of Hosea might be one to give agency and hope, it is also a highly problematic script that empowers victims of war by blaming them and celebrates a God who both hits and heals.

Christopher Frechette has suggested that biblical texts that involve the motif of divine punishment and self-blame could be understood as symbolic representations of the interpretative process of trauma.[73] It is within this concept of processing trauma that I perceive that feminist and trauma studies might have something in common. Reading Hosea 2 and processing it in light of my experience of domestic violence, I was able to see (or be shown) some of the techniques and tactics that had been used by my abuser. This helped me to gain agency rather than remain in a culture of self-blame. In this way, Hosea 2 can be of pastoral and therapeutic use for survivors of domestic violence when perceived through a feminist and trauma-informed reading.[74]

In addition, listening to survivors of trauma might enable researchers to see deeper into the metaphors used and the serious nature of the violence described. Kathleen O'Connor has suggested that similar metaphors in Jeremiah offer a glimpse into the world of 'incipient symbol-making': the rape of the Daughter of Zion in Jeremiah 13.20–27 re-enacts the Babylonian invasion in a way that helps the audience to view the violence they encountered 'at a distance, as if it were happening on a stage to someone else'.[75] To begin the healing process of interpretation, memories of war need to be expressed 'in terms similar enough to the violence to activate the past yet incompatible enough to change it'.[76] This is achieved by bringing the national disaster to the domestic sphere, where the fate of the entire nation is envisaged in the rape of YHWH's wife. Yet the question needs to be asked whether some of Hosea's audience, particularly those with experiences of intimate partner violence, would have been aided in their journey of healing by incorporating the metaphor into the domestic sphere. In fact, Ruth Poser has suggested that some of the symbolic actions portrayed by the prophet Ezekiel, such as going 'on a starvation diet' (Ezekiel 4.9–11) or shaving his head and beard with a sword (5.1), might be understood as resembling actual acts of self-harm committed by victims of trauma.[77] That symbolic actions and/or metaphorical language may contain elements of the lived experience of the target audience obfuscates the realms of 'real' and 'metaphorical' violence. This brings us back to the very real issue of victim re-traumatization, which I myself faced when attempting to do this study based on interviews with victims of intimate partner violence. Whether the Israelite women would have understood the metaphor as traumatizing may be a question to which we can never get a satisfactory answer; however, it should caution us not to be quick to dismiss the violent imagery in the book of Hosea as merely metaphorical: it can be key to understanding the lived experience of trauma survivors.

On another level, Hosea 2 raises questions about the divine portrayed in the passage. As noted earlier, I would have quite happily burned these pages from the Bible. However, rather than simply reject or find a way to minimize the terror, I believe viewing the text through the lens of trauma can help here as well. As survival literature, Hosea 2 is part of a meaning-making process of helping the victims/survivors to cope with an unspeakable tragedy. If we accept that the Hebrew Bible did not simply fall from heaven but is embedded in human understanding and experiences, Hosea 2 might become a text of great value. We can understand the passage as a limited as well as complicated reinterpretation of trauma: it is a glimpse into the process of meaning-making, and thus does not express 'complete or universal truth'.[78] The image portrayed by the author of Hosea is one done by a broken man through a broken lens about a broken world, including men, women and the divine. The statements about the divine thus become, to quote O'Connor, 'momentary glimpses, provisional, partial attempts to say what cannot ever be fully said but which stave off chaos for the moment'.[79] In the midst of catastrophe, having an abusive God might thus become a survival strategy against having no (or at least a weak) God;[80] however, this does not mean we have to hold on to him for ever. Instead, Hosea 2 can become a tool for reflecting on human suffering and the divine in this suffering, without giving us any definite answers about either.

In fact, even in the book of Hosea it is not altogether clear how God should, or even does, respond to his 'rebellious' people. In Hosea 11.8–9, we hear of God pondering about his response, ultimately deciding not to act in anger. Although the passage is encompassed in a metaphor describing God as a parent, which similarly to the husband metaphor raises issues regarding patriarchy and authority,[81] for our purposes it is important that God is seen as acting differently: he is, according to Brueggemann, 'a *recovering agent of violence*', deciding to act with spousal generosity and parental compassion instead of his former anger.[82] Although, *contra* Brueggemann, I am not convinced that the message of the latter part of the book of Hosea overrides the earlier terror, I agree that the Hebrew Bible presents us with a complex image of the deity where his feelings and responses are not neatly catalogued. The Hebrew Bible needs to be read in light of all of its complexity and multiplicity of voices, and celebrated as both divine and human composition. The angry God of Hosea 2 is but one of these compositions, and even he deserves to be heard, even if it is to give him an option to act differently.

This chapter has sought to illuminate Hosea 2.2–23 through various, albeit interlinked, methods: the first was to look at the passage through the eyes of two 'real readers', where one person in the dialogue had experienced domestic violence. The interview was then evaluated in light of feminist biblical and trauma studies, although strands of these methods became evident already during the interview. Some of the outcomes of this project were perhaps expected, while others proved surprising and further illuminated the text as well as the perspective of the reader.

Perhaps the greatest insight from the research was how much the violence and abuse in a text can remain hidden if not subjected to close exegesis. Even experience with violence is not always enough to reveal these depths; rather, what is required is the evaluation and re-evaluation of our experiences, readings as well as meanings created in a given context. An environment where academic rigour and personal experience can be joined to understand violent texts might well be the way for a contemporary reader to find understanding of unsettling passages as well as to give researchers a greater depth on issues we often study on a purely exegetical level.

As this chapter was both an academic and a personal project, I attempted to intertwine these elements cohesively throughout. I sincerely hope that readers will gain both insight and inspiration; however, since much of this paper is based upon my experience and reading, it does not offer, to re-quote Frechette, 'complete or universal truth'.[83] All elements in this paper can benefit from being supported as well as challenged in future projects and need not be excluded from such evaluation due to their delicate content.

As a text produced in the midst of trauma, the book of Hosea remains filled with complexity and contradictions where love is intermingled with domestic violence and hope with hate. It is survival literature, helping us to understand how a people found a way to cope with significant trauma and gain meaning. At the same time, this very process raises questions for contemporary researchers regarding the images and messages used to maintain survival. Can Hosea 2 still bring healing to contemporary survivors of trauma? To this, my tentative answer is yes. It can bring healing as a pastoral and therapeutic tool; however, Hosea 2 is ultimately a representation of that which cannot be uttered. Its message will remain hidden, broken and tentative. It is like a dance where you are always one step behind; but this does not mean it should not be sought.

References

Abma, Richtsje, *Bonds of Love: Methodic Studies of Prophetic Texts with Marriage Imagery (Isaiah 50:1–3 and 54:1–10, Hosea 1–3, Jeremiah 2—3)*, Assen: Van Gorcum, 1999.

Andersen, Francis I. and David Noel Freedman, *Hosea: A New Translation with Introduction and Commentary*, The Anchor Bible 24, New York: Doubleday, 1980.

Bird, Phyllis, '"To Play the Harlot": An Inquiry into an Old Testament Metaphor', in *Gender and Difference in Ancient Israel*, ed. Peggy L. Day, Minneapolis, MN: Fortress Press, 1989, 75–94.

Black, Max, *Models and Metaphors: Studies in Language and Philosophy*, Ithaca, NY: Cornell University Press, 1962.

Brenner, Athalya, 'Pornoprophetics Revisited: Some Additional Reflections', *JSOT* 70 (1996), 63–86.

Brueggemann, Walter, 'The Recovering God of Hosea', *Horizons in Biblical Theology* 30 (2008), 5–20.

Caruth, Cathy, 'Introduction', in *Trauma: Explorations in Memory*, ed. Cathy Caruth, Baltimore, MD: Johns Hopkins University Press, 1995, 151–57.

—— *Unclaimed Experience: Trauma, Narrative, and History*, 20th anniversary edn, Baltimore, MD: Johns Hopkins University Press, 2016.

Connolly, Tristanne J., 'Metaphor and Abuse in Hosea', *Feminist Theology* 6, no. 18 (1998), 55–66.

Day, Peggy L., 'The Bitch had It Coming to Her: Rhetoric and Interpretation in Ezekiel 16', *Biblical Interpretation* 8, no. 3 (2000), 231–54.

Dijk-Hemmes, Fokkelien van, 'The Imagination of Power and the Power of Imagination: An Intertextual Analysis of Two Biblical Love Songs: The Song of Songs and Hosea 2', *JSOT* 44 (1989), 75–88.

Ellis, Carolyn, Christine E. Kiesinger and Lisa M. Tillmann-Healy, 'Interactive Interviewing: Talking about Emotional Experience', in *Reflexivity and Voice*, ed. Rosanna Hertz, London: Sage, 1997, 119–49.

Ellis, Carolyn, Tony E. Adams and Arthur P. Bochner, 'Autoethnography: An Overview', *Forum Qualitative Sozialforschung / Forum: Qualitative Social Research* 12, no. 1, Art. 10 (2010): http://nbn-resolving.de/urn:nbn:de:0114-fqs1101108.

Ellwood, Gracia Fay, *Batter My Heart*, Pendle Hill Pamphlet 282, Wallingford, PA: Pendle Hill Publications [1988] 2017, Kindle edn.

Exum, J. Cheryl, *Plotted, Shot, and Painted: Cultural Representations of Biblical Women*, Sheffield: Sheffield Academic Press, 1996.

Fontaine, Carole R., 'Hosea', in *A Feminist Companion to the Latter Prophets*, ed. Athalya Brenner, Sheffield: Sheffield Academic Press, 1995, 40–59.

Frechette, Christopher G., 'The Old Testament as Controlled Substance: How Insights from Trauma Studies Reveal Healing Capacities in Potentially Harmful Texts', *Interpretation* 69, no. 1 (2015), 20–34.

—— 'Two Biblical Motifs of Divine Violence as Resources for Meaning-Making in Engaging Self-Blame and Rage after Traumatization', *Pastoral Psychology* 66, no. 2 (2017), 239–49.

Fretheim, Terence E., *The Suffering of God: An Old Testament Perspective*, Philadelphia, PA: Fortress Press, 1984.

Galambush, Julie, *Jerusalem in the Book of Ezekiel: The City as Yahweh's Wife*, Atlanta, GA: Scholars Press, 1992.

Gordon, Pamela and Harold C. Washington, 'Rape as a Military Metaphor in the Hebrew Bible', in *A Feminist Companion to the Latter Prophets*, ed. Athalya Brenner, Sheffield: Sheffield Academic Press, 1995, 308–25.

Graetz, Naomi, 'God is to Israel as Husband is to Wife: The Metaphoric Battering of Hosea's Wife', in *A Feminist Companion to the Latter Prophets*, ed. Athalya Brenner, Sheffield: Sheffield Academic Press, 1995, 126–45.

Grung, Anne Hege, *Gender Justice in Muslim–Christian Readings: Christian and*

Muslim Women in Norway Making Meaning of Texts from the Bible, the Koran, and the Hadith, Boston, MA: Brill-Rodopi, 2015.

Hayes-Mackenzie, Shona, 'How Do Young Evangelical Christian Women Interpret the Gender Roles in the Bible?', Master's thesis, University of Chester, 2017.

Heise, Lori L. and Andreas Kotsadam, 'Cross-National and Multilevel Correlates of Partner Violence: An Analysis of Data from Population-Based Surveys', *The Lancet Global Health* 3, no. 6 (2015), 332–40.

Herman, Judith, *Trauma and Recovery: The Aftermath of Violence – From Domestic Abuse to Political Terror*, New York: Basic Books [1992] 2015.

Keefe, Alice A., 'The Female Body, the Body Politic and the Land: A Sociopolitical Reading of Hosea 1-2', in *A Feminist Companion to the Latter Prophets*, ed. Athalya Brenner, Sheffield: Sheffield Academic Press, 1995, 70–100.

—— *Woman's Body and the Social Body in Hosea*, Sheffield: Sheffield Academic Press, 2001.

Kelle, Brad E., *Hosea 2: Metaphor and Rhetoric in Historical Perspective*. Atlanta, GA: SBL Press, 2005.

Kidner, Derek, *Love to the Loveless: The Story and Message of Hosea*, Leicester: IVP, 1981.

Kleim, Birgit, Thomas Ehring and Anke Ehlers, 'Perceptual Processing Advantages for Trauma-Related Visual Cues in Post-Traumatic Stress Disorder', *Psychological Medicine* 42 (2012), 173–81.

Knight, G. A. F., *Hosea: Introduction and Commentary*, London: SCM Press, 1960.

Kruger, Paul A., 'Israel, the Harlot (Hos 2:4–9)', *JNSL* 11 (1983), 107–16.

Lakoff, George and Mark Johnson, 'Conceptual Metaphor in Everyday Language', in *Philosophical Perspectives on Metaphor*, ed. Mark Johnson, Minneapolis, MN: University of Minnesota Press, 1981, 286–328.

Lim, Bo H., 'Hosea 2:2–23 [2:4–25]', in *Hosea*, ed. Bo H. Lim and Daniel Castelo, Grand Rapids: Eerdmans, 2015, 63–78.

Llewellyn, Dawn, *Reading, Feminism, and Spirituality: Troubling the Waves*, Basingstoke: Palgrave Macmillan, 2015.

Macwilliam, Stuart, *Queer Theory and the Prophetic Marriage Metaphor in the Hebrew Bible*, London: Equinox, 2011.

Magdalene, F. Rachel, 'Ancient Near Eastern Treaty-Curses and the Ultimate Texts of Terror: A Study of the Language of Divine Sexual Abuse in the Prophetic Corpus', in *A Feminist Companion to the Latter Prophets*, ed. Athalya Brenner, Sheffield: Sheffield Academic Press, 1995, 326–52.

McFague, Sallie, *Metaphorical Theology: Models of God in Religious Language*, London: SCM Press, 1983.

Michael, Tanja, Anke Ehlers and Sarah L. Halligan, 'Enhanced Priming for Trauma-Related Material in Posttraumatic Stress Disorder', *Emotion* 5, no. 1 (2005), 103–12.

Morse, Holly, '"Judgement was Executed upon Her, and She Became a Byword among Women" (Ezek. 23.10): Divine Revenge Porn, Slut-shaming, Ethnicity, and Exile in Ezekiel 16 and 23', in *Women and Exilic Identity in the Hebrew Bible*, ed. Katherine E. Southwood and Martien A. Halvorson-Taylor, London: T&T Clark, 2018, 129–54.

Moughtin-Mumby, Sharon, *Sexual and Marital Metaphors in Hosea, Jeremiah, Isaiah, and Ezekiel*, Oxford: Oxford University Press, 2008.

Nason-Clark, Nancy, Barbara Fisher-Townsend, Catherine Holtmann and Stephen

McMullin, *Religion and Intimate Partner Violence: Understanding the Challenges and Proposing Solutions*, New York: Oxford University Press, 2018.

O'Brien, Julia M., *Challenging Prophetic Metaphor: Theology and Ideology in the Prophets*, Louisville, KY: Westminster John Knox Press, 2008.

O'Connor, Kathleen M., 'How Trauma Studies can Contribute to Old Testament Studies', in *Trauma and Traumatization in Individual and Collective Dimensions: Insights from Biblical Studies and Beyond*, ed. Eve-Marie Becker, Jan Dochhorn and Else K. Holt, Göttingen: Vandenhoeck and Ruprecht, 2014, 210–22.

—— *Jeremiah: Pain and Promise*, Minneapolis, MN: Fortress Press, 2011.

Office for National Statistics, 'Domestic Abuse in England and Wales – Appendix Tables', released 22 November 2018: www.ons.gov.uk/peoplepopulationand community/crimeandjustice/datasets/domesticabuseinenglandandwalesappendix-tables.

—— 'Domestic Abuse in England and Wales: Year Ending March 2018', released 22 November 2018: www.ons.gov.uk/peoplepopulationandcommunity/crimeand justice/bulletins/domesticabuseinenglandandwales/yearendingmarch2018.

Poser, Ruth, 'No Words: The Book of Ezekiel as Trauma Literature and a Response to Exile', in *Bible Through the Lens of Trauma*, ed. Elizabeth Boase and Christopher G. Frechette, Atlanta, GA: SBL Press, 2016, 27–48.

Rambo, Shelly, *Spirit and Trauma: A Theology of Remaining*, Louisville, KY: Westminster John Knox Press, 2010.

Sakenfeld, Katharine Doob, *Just Wives? Stories of Power and Survival in the Old Testament and Today*, Louisville, KY: Westminster John Knox Press, 2003.

Scolnic, Benjamin Edidin, 'Bible-Battering', *Conservative Judaism* 45, no. 1 (1992), 43–52.

Setel, T. Drorah, 'Prophets and Pornography: Female Sexual Imagery in Hosea', in *Feminist Interpretation of the Bible*, ed. Letty M. Russell, Oxford: Basil Blackwell, 1985, 86–95.

Sherwood, Yvonne, *The Prostitute and the Prophet: Reading Hosea in the Late Twentieth Century*, Sheffield: Sheffield Academic Press, 1996.

Shooter, Susan, 'What on Earth is She Still Thinking of, Still Attending Church?' *Practical Theology* 6, no. 3 (2013), 257–70.

Slee, Nicola, *Women's Faith Development: Patterns and Processes*, Aldershot: Ashgate, 2004.

Smith-Christopher, Daniel L., 'Trauma and the Old Testament: Some Problems and Prospects', in *Trauma and Traumatization in Individual and Collective Dimensions: Insights from Biblical Studies and Beyond*, ed. Eve-Marie Becker, Jan Dochhorn and Else K. Holt, Göttingen: Vandenhoeck and Ruprecht, 2014, 223–43.

Stark, Evan, *Coercive Control: How Men Entrap Women in Personal Life*, Oxford: Oxford University Press, 2007.

Starr, Rachel, *Reimagining Theologies of Marriage in Contexts of Domestic Violence: When Salvation is Survival*, New York: Routledge, 2018.

Stulman, Louis and Hyun Chul Paul Kim, *You are My People: An Introduction to Prophetic Literature*, Nashville, TN: Abingdon Press, 2010.

Stulman, Louis, 'Reading the Bible through the Lens of Trauma and Art', in *Trauma and Traumatization in Individual and Collective Dimensions: Insights from Biblical Studies and Beyond*, ed. Eve-Marie Becker, Jan Dochhorn and Else K. Holt, Göttingen: Vandenhoeck and Ruprecht, 2014, 177–92.

Weems, Renita J., *Battered Love: Marriage, Sex, and Violence in the Hebrew Prophets*, Minneapolis, MN: Fortress Press, 1995.

Yee, Gale A., 'Hosea', in *Women's Bible Commentary*, ed. Carol A. Newsom, Sharon H. Ringe and Jacqueline E. Lapsley, 20th anniversary edn, Louisville, KY: Westminster John Knox Press, 2012, 299–308.

—— *Poor, Banished Children of Eve: Woman as Evil in the Hebrew Bible*, Minneapolis, MN: Fortress Press, 2003.

Notes

1 I recognize the use of gendered language for God in this chapter. This is due to the author of Hosea 2.2–23 using masculine vocabulary and imagery to describe the deity that, in turn, has influenced subsequent interpretations of this passage.

2 See Benjamin Edidin Scolnic, 'Bible-Battering', *Conservative Judaism* 45, no. 1 (1992), 43–52; Derek Kidner, *Love to the Loveless: The Story and Message of Hosea* (Leicester: IVP, 1981); G. A. F. Knight, *Hosea: Introduction and Commentary* (London: SCM Press, 1960).

3 Paul A. Kruger, 'Israel, the Harlot (Hos 2:4–9)', *JNSL* 11 (1983), 107; Gale A. Yee, 'Hosea', in *Women's Bible Commentary*, ed. Carol A. Newsom, Sharon H. Ringe and Jacqueline E. Lapsley, 20th anniversary edn (Louisville, KY: Westminster John Knox Press, 2012), 299.

4 Renita J. Weems, *Battered Love: Marriage, Sex, and Violence in the Hebrew Prophets* (Minneapolis, MN: Fortress Press, 1995), 91.

5 Office for National Statistics, 'Domestic Abuse in England and Wales: Year Ending March 2018', 35, released 22 November 2018, available from www.ons. gov.uk/peoplepopulationandcommunity/crimeandjustice/bulletins/domesticabusein englandandwales/yearendingmarch2018.

6 Office for National Statistics, 'Domestic Abuse in England and Wales – Appendix Tables', table 16, released 22 November 2018, www.ons.gov.uk/ peoplepopulationandcommunity/crimeandjustice/datasets/domesticabuseinengland andwalesappendixtables.

7 Office for National Statistics, 'Domestic Abuse: Year Ending', 35.

8 Nancy Nason-Clark, Barbara Fisher-Townsend, Catherine Holtmann and Stephen McMullin, *Religion and Intimate Partner Violence: Understanding the Challenges and Proposing Solutions* (New York: Oxford University Press, 2018), 8.

9 Nason-Clarke et al., *Religion and Intimate Partner Violence*, 8–9.

10 Louis Stulman and Hyun Chul Paul Kim, *You are My People: An Introduction to Prophetic Literature* (Nashville, TN: Abingdon Press, 2010), 6.

11 Cathy Caruth, *Unclaimed Experience: Trauma, Narrative, and History*, 20th anniversary edn (Baltimore, MD: Johns Hopkins University Press, 2016), 11–12.

12 Kathleen M. O'Connor, 'How Trauma Studies Can Contribute to Old Testament Studies', in *Trauma and Traumatization in Individual and Collective Dimensions: Insights from Biblical Studies and Beyond*, ed. Eve-Marie Becker, Jan Dochhorn and Else K. Holt (Göttingen: Vandenhoeck and Ruprecht, 2014), 212.

13 For issues in comparing contemporary (Western) models of trauma with ancient texts, see Daniel L. Smith-Christopher, 'Trauma and the Old Testament: Some Problems and Prospects', in *Trauma and Traumatization*, ed. Becker et al., 223–43.

14 Weems, *Battered Love*, 110.

15 I will use the term 'marriage metaphor' to indicate the husband–wife relationship between YHWH and Israel as described in the book of Hosea due to the established status of the phrase in academia. However, I acknowledge the complexity and the multifaceted use of this metaphor in the prophetic literature and I do not assume that its use in Hosea is directly transferable to other similar biblical texts. See Sharon Moughtin-Mumby, *Sexual and Marital Metaphors in Hosea, Jeremiah, Isaiah, and Ezekiel* (Oxford: Oxford University Press, 2008).

16 Katharine Doob Sakenfeld, *Just Wives? Stories of Power and Survival in the Old Testament and Today* (Louisville, KY: Westminster John Knox Press, 2003), 105.

17 In fact, threat of physical violence may be as or even more effective than actual violence. See Evan Stark, *Coercive Control: How Men Entrap Women in Personal Life* (Oxford: Oxford University Press, 2007), 251; Judith Herman, *Trauma and Recovery: The Aftermath of Violence – From Domestic Abuse to Political Terror* (New York: Basic Books [1992] 2015), 77. This indicates that even if the violence in Hosea 2 is not meant to be understood as lived reality, it loses none of its efficacy.

18 Richtsje Abma, *Bonds of Love: Methodic Studies of Prophetic Texts with Marriage Imagery (Isaiah 50:1–3 and 54:1–10, Hosea 1–3, Jeremiah 2–3)* (Assen: Van Gorcum, 1999), 7.

19 Abma, *Bonds of Love*.

20 Abma, *Bonds of Love*, 8–10; Stuart Macwilliam, *Queer Theory and the Prophetic Marriage Metaphor in the Hebrew Bible* (London: Equinox, 2011), 65–7; Brad E. Kelle, *Hosea 2: Metaphor and Rhetoric in Historical Perspective* (Atlanta, GA: SBL Press, 2005), 34–8; Moughtin-Mumby, *Sexual and Marital Metaphors*, 1–48.

21 George Caird as quoted by Sallie McFague, *Metaphorical Theology: Models of God in Religious Language* (London: SCM Press, 1983), 149.

22 Max Black, *Models and Metaphors: Studies in Language and Philosophy* (Ithaca, NY: Cornell University Press, 1962), 38–47.

23 Black, *Models and Metaphors*, 40; italics in the original.

24 Shocking elements in Hosea's imagery may have included the feminization of a (mostly) male audience and the husband accepting an adulterous wife back as opposed to insisting on the death penalty (Lev. 20.10; Deut. 22.22). See Yee, 'Hosea', 303.

25 For the use of propaganda, pornography and/or rhetoric in Hosea, see T. Drorah Setel, 'Prophets and Pornography: Female Sexual Imagery in Hosea', in *Feminist Interpretation of the Bible*, ed. Letty M. Russell (Oxford: Basil Blackwell, 1985), 86–95; Athalya Brenner, 'Pornoprophetics Revisited: Some Additional Reflections', *JSOT* 70 (1996), 63–86; Kelle, *Hosea 2*.

26 Moughtin-Mumby, *Sexual and Marital Metaphors*, 4; italics in the original.

27 Pamela Gordon and Harold C. Washington, 'Rape as a Military Metaphor in the Hebrew Bible', in *A Feminist Companion to the Latter Prophets*, ed. Athalya Brenner (Sheffield: Sheffield Academic Press, 1995), 308–25; Bo H. Lim, 'Hosea 2:2–23 [2:4–25]', in *Hosea*, ed. Bo H. Lim and Daniel Castelo (Grand Rapids, MI: Eerdmans, 2015), 63–78; F. Rachel Magdalene, 'Ancient Near Eastern Treaty-Curses and the Ultimate Texts of Terror: A Study of the Language of Divine Sexual Abuse in the Prophetic Corpus', in *Feminist Companion*, ed. Gordon and Washington, 326–52.

28 Yee, 'Hosea', 299–300; *Poor, Banished Children of Eve: Woman as Evil in the Hebrew Bible* (Minneapolis, MN: Fortress Press, 2003), 81–109; Alice A. Keefe, 'The Female Body, The Body Politic and the Land: A Sociopolitical Reading

of Hosea 1—2', in *Feminist Companion*, ed. Gordon and Washington, 70–100; *Woman's Body and the Social Body in Hosea* (Sheffield: Sheffield Academic Press, 2001).

29 Gordon and Washington, 'Rape as a Military Metaphor', 317–25; Magdalene, 'Ancient Near Eastern Treaty-Curses', 335; J. Cheryl Exum, *Plotted, Shot, and Painted: Cultural Representations of Biblical Women* (Sheffield: Sheffield Academic Press, 1996), 120–1.

30 Weems, *Battered Love*, 40–1; Setel, 'Prophets and Pornography', 91–2; Fokkelien van Dijk-Hemmes, 'The Imagination of Power and the Power of Imagination: An Intertextual Analysis of Two Biblical Love Songs: The Song of Songs and Hosea 2', *JSOT* 44 (1989), 76, 78; Exum, *Plotted, Shot, and Painted*, 104–5.

31 See Weems, *Battered Love*, 109–10; Exum, *Plotted, Shot, and Painted*, 105.

32 See George Lakoff and Mark Johnson, 'Conceptual Metaphor in Everyday Language', in *Philosophical Perspectives on Metaphor*, ed. Mark Johnson (Minneapolis, MN: University of Minnesota Press, 1981), 286–328; Julie Galambush, *Jerusalem in the Book of Ezekiel: The City as Yahweh's Wife* (Atlanta, GA: Scholars Press, 1992), 8–9.

33 Rachel Starr, *Reimagining Theologies of Marriage in Contexts of Domestic Violence: When Salvation is Survival* (New York: Routledge, 2018).

34 'Interactive interviewing involves the sharing of personal and social *experiences* of *both* respondents and researchers, who tell (and sometimes write) their stories in the context of a developing relationship' (italics in the original). See Carolyn Ellis, Christine E. Kiesinger and Lisa M. Tillmann-Healy, 'Interactive Interviewing: Talking about Emotional Experience', in *Reflexivity and Voice*, ed. Rosanna Hertz (London: Sage, 1997), 121.

35 Rachel Starr is a biblical studies lecturer at The Queen's Foundation, Birmingham, UK whereas I am the biblical studies lecturer at Cliff College, Calver, UK.

36 Because the focus of this paper is on the experience of domestic violence, as well as the lack of it, some differences between Starr and myself such as nationality (British/Finnish) and denomination (Methodist/Pentecostal) are not emphasized, although might well be of interest for future research projects.

37 Nicola Slee, *Women's Faith Development: Patterns and Processes* (Aldershot: Ashgate, 2004), 46–52.

38 See Susan Shooter, 'What on Earth is She Still Thinking of, Still Attending Church?', *Practical Theology* 6, no. 3 (2013), 262.

39 Shooter, 'What on Earth', 257–70; Anne Hege Grung, *Gender Justice in Muslim-Christian Readings: Christian and Muslim Women in Norway Making Meaning of Texts from the Bible, the Koran, and the Hadith* (Boston, MA: Brill-Rodopi, 2015); Shona Hayes-Mackenzie, 'How Do Young Evangelical Christian Women Interpret the Gender Roles in the Bible?' (master's thesis, University of Chester, 2017). Women's spiritual reading practices have recently been studied in Dawn Llewellyn, *Reading, Feminism, and Spirituality: Troubling the Waves* (Basingstoke: Palgrave Macmillan, 2015).

40 See, for example, Gracia Fay Ellwood, *Batter My Heart* (Pendle Hill Pamphlet 282; Wallingford, PA: Pendle Hill Publications [1988] 2017), Kindle edn; Weems, *Battered Love*; Yee, 'Hosea'; Naomi Graetz, 'God is to Israel as Husband is to Wife: The Metaphoric Battering of Hosea's Wife', in *Feminist Companion*, ed. Gordon and Washington, 126–45.

41 'Real readers' is a reference to 'actual women readers and their experiences

of reading', as opposed to the implied reader (Llewellyn, *Reading, Feminism, and Spirituality*, 14, 193 n. 6). I concede that as both Starr and myself are biblical scholars, the 'real readers' in this paper are ones with formal training. Although this means that the voice of those without such training will not be heard, it also serves to highlight the similarities and differences in our reading.

42 Ellwood, *Batter My Heart*, 29.

43 See Stark, *Coercive Control*, 11.

44 Stark, *Coercive Control*, 339–61. See also Natalie Collin's chapter in this volume on trauma responses as superpowers.

45 Stulman and Kim, *You are My People*, 1.

46 Stark, *Coercive Control*, 209.

47 Lori L. Heise and Andreas Kotsadam, 'Cross-National and Multilevel Correlates of Partner Violence: An Analysis of Data from Population-Based Surveys', *The Lancet Global Health* 3, no. 6 (2015), 332–40.

48 Stark, *Coercive Control*, 219–21.

49 Shelly Rambo, *Spirit and Trauma: A Theology of Remaining* (Louisville, KY: Westminster John Knox Press, 2010), 7–8.

50 Rambo, *Spirit and Trauma*, 172.

51 All comparisons with ancient and contemporary expressions of domestic abuse hence remain conjectural. See Stark, *Coercive Control*, 172ff.

52 Julia M. O'Brien, *Challenging Prophetic Metaphor: Theology and Ideology in the Prophets* (Louisville, KY: Westminster John Knox Press, 2008), 33; Yee, 'Hosea', 301–2; Weems, *Battered Love*, 31–3.

53 Birgit Kleim, Thomas Ehring and Anke Ehlers, 'Perceptual Processing Advantages for Trauma-Related Visual Cues in Post-Traumatic Stress Disorder', *Psychological Medicine* 42 (2012), 173–81; Tanja Michael, Anke Ehlers and Sarah L. Halligan, 'Enhanced Priming for Trauma-Related Material in Posttraumatic Stress Disorder', *Emotion* 5, no. 1 (2005), 103–12.

54 Exum, *Plotted, Shot, and Painted*, 107–9; Yvonne Sherwood, *The Prostitute and the Prophet: Reading Hosea in the Late Twentieth Century* (Sheffield: Sheffield Academic Press, 1996), 303–4. Even if the stripping is understood as an expression of the *lex talionis* as noted by Francis I. Andersen and David Noel Freedman, the troubling nature of the husband's actions as public sexual humiliation remains. See Francis I. Andersen and David Noel Freedman, *Hosea: A New Translation with Introduction and Commentary*, The Anchor Bible 24 (New York: Doubleday, 1980), 248–9.

55 That public stripping of a woman before her lovers was not a standard punishment for adultery. See Peggy L. Day, 'The Bitch had It Coming to Her: Rhetoric and Interpretation in Ezekiel 16', *Biblical Interpretation* 8, no. 3 (2000), 237–41.

56 Herman, *Trauma and Recovery*, 78–9.

57 The description of Gomer as זְנוּנִים אֵשֶׁת (Hos. 1.2) is most likely a reference to extra-marital sexual activity rather than (cultic) prostitution. See Sakenfeld, *Just Wives*, 96–8; Phyllis Bird, '"To Play the Harlot": An Inquiry into an Old Testament Metaphor', in *Gender and Difference in Ancient Israel*, ed. Peggy L. Day (Minneapolis, MN: Fortress Press, 1989), 75–94.

58 Sakenfeld, *Just Wives*, 98–9; Tristanne J. Connolly, 'Metaphor and Abuse in Hosea', *Feminist Theology* 6, no.18 (1998), 57.

59 Holly Morse, '"Judgement was Executed upon Her, and She Became a Byword among Women" (Ezek. 23.10): Divine Revenge Porn, Slut-shaming, Ethnicity, and

Exile in Ezekiel 16 and 23', in *Women and Exilic Identity in the Hebrew Bible*, ed. Katherine E. Southwood and Martien A. Halvorson-Taylor (London: T&T Clark, 2018), 129.

60 Morse, '"Judgement"', 130.

61 Morse, '"Judgement"', 152.

62 Connolly, 'Metaphor and Abuse', 58–9; see also Terence E. Fretheim, *The Suffering of God: An Old Testament Perspective* (Philadelphia, PA: Fortress Press, 1984), 155.

63 Herman, *Trauma and Recovery*, 80–3.

64 For variations on these interpretations, see Yee, 'Hosea', 299, 305, 307; Weems, *Battered Love*, 112–13, 119; Sakenfeld, *Just Wives*, 106; Walter Brueggemann, 'The Recovering God of Hosea', *Horizons in Biblical Theology* 30 (2008), 18; Scolnic, 'Bible-Battering', 43–52.

65 O'Brien, *Challenging*, 45–6.

66 Louis Stulman, 'Reading the Bible through the Lens of Trauma and Art', in *Trauma and Traumatization*, ed. Becker et al., 180.

67 Herman, *Trauma and Recovery*, 53.

68 Herman, *Trauma and Recovery*, 54.

69 Stulman and Kim, *You are My People*, 12–13.

70 O'Connor, 'Trauma Studies', 217; Ruth Poser, 'No Words: The Book of Ezekiel as Trauma Literature and a Response to Exile', in *Bible Through the Lens of Trauma*, ed. Elizabeth Boase and Christopher G. Frechette (Atlanta, GA: SBL Press, 2016), 36–7.

71 Carole R. Fontaine, 'Hosea', in *Feminist Companion*, ed. Gordon and Washington, 42.

72 Stulman and Kim, *You Are My People*, 15.

73 Christopher G. Frechette, 'Two Biblical Motifs of Divine Violence as Resources for Meaning-Making in Engaging Self-Blame and Rage after Traumatization', *Pastoral Psychology* 66, no. 2 (2017), 244–5; 'The Old Testament as Controlled Substance: How Insights from Trauma Studies Reveal Healing Capacities in Potentially Harmful Texts', *Interpretation* 69, no. 1 (2015), 20–34.

74 For further use of biblical passages that contain the motif of self-blame as a therapeutic tool, see Frechette, 'Two Biblical Motifs', 245–6.

75 O'Connor, 'Trauma Studies', 214.

76 O'Connor, *Jeremiah: Pain and Promise* (Minneapolis, MN: Fortress Press, 2011), 48.

77 Poser, 'No Words', 32.

78 Frechette, 'Two Biblical Motifs', 244. See also Cathy Caruth, 'Introduction', in *Trauma: Explorations in Memory*, ed. Cathy Caruth (Baltimore, MD: Johns Hopkins University Press, 1995), 153–4.

79 O'Connor, *Jeremiah*, 56.

80 O'Connor, *Jeremiah*, 55–6.

81 O'Brien, *Challenging*, 77–100.

82 Brueggemann, 'Recovering God', 19; italics in the original.

83 Frechette, 'Two Biblical Motifs', 244.

7

Violating Women in the Name of God: Legacies of Remembered Violence

ROSIE ANDRIOUS

We have learned that trauma is not just an event that took place sometime in the past: it is also the imprint left by that experience on mind, body and brain. This imprint has ongoing consequences ... in the present.[1]

You may think that what happens in Hollywood doesn't affect you. You're wrong ... They are the latest in a long line of myth peddlers, from the men behind the Bible to these modern-day 'content creators'.[2]

Actor Rose McGowan, who triggered the #MeToo 'campaign' and helped to lay bare the brutal realities of male power and privilege in Hollywood, has written a biography of her experiences entitled *Brave*.[3] As a Thecla scholar who takes a particular interest in ancient literature that features eroticized women, I found it impossible, when reading the biography, not to draw a number of analogies between McGowan's description of the 'core concepts' of the complex production machinery of male-dominated Hollywood and how I have read, and continue to read, women in ancient martyrdom texts. This chapter will use her discussion of what occurs in Hollywood today as a stimulus for exploring how men constructed female representations in antiquity and to highlight how many of these constructions continue to this day. Despite huge gains and progress in terms of gender equality, there is still much work to be done. To do this, I discuss the sado-erotic violence women were subjected to in two early Christian texts.

I go on to consider whether the self-inflicted, religiously driven violence acted out in female medieval piety, centuries later, was a haunting legacy of Greco-Roman misogyny and gendered oppression. The provenance of such oppression, beginning with Aristotle, was a philosophy that associated the male with the mind and the female with the body. This philosophy was based on a 'one-sex' model, where the ideal body was deemed to be that of a man, and females were considered to be mere derivatives of males.[4] I want to ask, what were the consequences of this rhetoric for women and girls? In particular, how did masculine sado-erotic representations of women in antiquity inform and shape the identity of women? Is it possible that a legacy of misogyny engendered an existential, psychological and spiritual trauma within women? Ultimately, I want to consider the psychosocial consequences of violent, sexualized and gendered representations in antiquity in an attempt to understand something of the multifaceted impact on women's self-perception and self-expression.

In an endeavour to highlight that a gender stereotyping that has existed for millennia remains deeply entrenched in the societal psyche, I employ the words of McGowan as headings for my discussion on the ancient world, to demonstrate how debates that are happening around the 'culture' of Hollywood today can help us rethink representations of women and conceptions of gender in the ancient world.

Early Martyrdoms: Visualizing Gendered Violence

To the writers who create how we see one another and ourselves: You're responsible. What you write forms the thoughts and self-images of billions of humans.[5]

The critical and commercial success of violent films and computer games, and of sexualized superwomen such as Lara Croft, testifies to the fact that sexuality and violence fascinate.[6] The visual effects that are available today were not available in antiquity. Nevertheless, authors of martyrdoms produced visual effect through narrative. The systematic cruelty and violence that martyrs endured was remembered and recounted in graphic ways. Although martyrdoms were stories about mastery of the self and God's victory over earthly powers, we shall see how female martyrdom accounts depicted the violence women endured as sado-erotic display. Indeed, we shall see at least two accounts told of women who were exposed and sexualized in gladiatorial-type contests: a captivating extravaganza enticing the heterosexual male gaze. Christians, too, participated in this spectacle. This sado-erotic performance had serious religious dimensions to it. However, a summary of the fate of at least two female saints will show that, despite the fact that the saintliness of male and female martyrs required their mutilation and murder, the fate of women required, in addition, their sexual exposure and degradation.

Two early Christian texts that make this phenomenon particularly conspicuous are the *Acts of Paul and Thecla* and the *Martyrdom of Saints Perpetua and Felicitas*.[7] The story of Thecla concerns a young betrothed virgin in Roman Iconium who, upon hearing Paul preach, decides to pursue a chaste Christian life. Spurning her fiancé, and thus rebelling against societal norms, she finds that family, society and city administration contrive to put an end to her life. She is thrown naked into the arena on two occasions, once to be burned and again to face the wild beasts. However, through miraculous interventions, Thecla survives and eventually receives Paul's blessing to go and teach the word of God. Although Thecla survives her martyrdoms and is not officially a martyr, the arena scenes do parallel martyr stories.[8] The story of Perpetua and Felicitas narrates the martyrdom of five Christian converts apprehended in early third-century Carthage. It contains two prison diary accounts alleged to be written by Vibia Perpetua and Saturus. Perpetua was a noblewoman and married mother of a nursing infant. The martyrdom also contains an eyewitness account, by an unnamed editor, of their execution, along with the young pregnant slave Felicitas, and two other men. In drawing analogies between the representations of the women and men in these texts it will become evident that the representations of the women are narrated in stark comparison to those of the men. While the female martyrdom accounts contain elements of pornographic, sexualized torture, the men are represented in a more dignified way.

Of course, what actually constitutes 'pornography' is hugely subjective. Therefore, there exists neither a consensus nor a clear definition of the term; scholarly literature is divided on both its definition and significance.[9] Difficulties tend to focus around feminist and non-feminist debates concerning the separation of 'erotica' from pornography and exactly what constitutes 'sexually explicit' materials.[10] Furthermore, since objectification is a common characteristic of pornography many feminist definitions of pornography go beyond what is often deemed 'sexually explicit' material and include any objectified images of women that may be found in mainstream movies, magazines, television, literature and advertising.[11]

Andrea Dworkin in particular focuses on the objectification of women by men in a hierarchy of domination.[12] Catherine MacKinnon follows Dworkin closely; she argues that pornography turns a woman into a thing to be acquired and used.[13] For MacKinnon, pornography goes beyond its content, it eroticizes hierarchy and sexualizes inequality; it makes dominance and submission into sex. In this way, pornography institutionalizes the sexuality of male supremacy, fusing the eroticization of dominance and submission with the social construction of male and female.[14] Both MacKinnon and Dworkin have been highly influential in the debates surrounding pornography and their definition of pornography, used in drafting the Minneapolis and Indianapolis Ordinances, have extensively influenced much feminist literature.[15] Here, pornography is defined by them as graphic sexually explicit material that subordinates women through pictures or words.[16]

Examples cited by MacKinnon include materials that are not overtly sexual, for example, women hanging from trees without exposing their genitalia and not engaging in sexual acts, and pictures of women's bodies that are scarred or women being hunted down and shot.[17] In this way, MacKinnon broadens the popular definition of the pornographic to include what are primarily representations of violence that are not explicitly sexual, noticing how often these involved a reinforcement of patriarchal institutions. MacKinnon believes that pornography does not work sexually without gender hierarchy. If there is no inequality, no violation, no dominance, no force, there is no sexual arousal.[18] The argument focuses on the specific and 'normalized' ways in which women are objectified and suppressed in a hierarchy of male domination.

In delineating the issue of pornography in this way, Dworkin and MacKinnon have enabled theorists to develop correlations between the pornographic and the process of representation itself. Starting from John Berger's dictum that, 'men look at women: women watch themselves being looked at',[19] feminist scholars question the way in which the spectator is engendered by the experience of watching. They define the gaze, or the process of looking, as male. In this way, the concept of the pornographic provides a paradigm for all representation and comes to refer to much more than the common meaning of the word, thus allowing a broadening of scholarly inquiry into areas such as film, narrative and representational art.[20]

It thus becomes evident that the feminist debate on pornography clearly applies to much more in antiquity than explicitly sexual art and literature.[21] Pornography includes all sexist representation, thus abrogating the necessity to distinguish between pornography and erotica in terms of low or high art, violent or non-violent, or hard or soft content.[22] Broadening the term 'pornography' beyond its much more common usage allows for its application in regard to the scholarly analysis of ancient texts that include representations of women. When applied to ancient texts written by men, such theories help to unveil the underlying ideology contained within.

Having set the stage for the principles at work in discussing pornographic content in ancient textual representations, we begin with an examination of the *Acts of Paul and Thecla*.

Early Martyrdoms: Eroticizing Violence

Why is there no outcry over men telling women's stories?[23]

Let's discuss entertainment as male propaganda, shall we? Questions: Can you imagine if man's history was only depicted, shown, and viewed through a woman's perspective? Do you think there has even been a film where only women were hired to tell a 'man's story'? The answers are No.[24]

The second-century text of the *Acts of Paul and Thecla* (*APTh*) introduces us to the heroine and protagonist Thecla. On hearing the apostle Paul preach, Thecla – an aristocratic woman – becomes entranced and, despite great opposition, renounces her family and fiancé to follow Paul. Thecla is punished for this rebellion by sentence of death and she is thrown into the arena. Once in the arena, the beautiful virgin is stripped naked (*APTh* 22, 33) and forced to 'mount' the pyre (*APTh* 22). Scopophilia and patriarchal norms coalesce. The pleasure in this text is immediately geared towards the heterosexual, patriarchal male, and Thecla, the would-be martyr, doubles up as a pin-up girl. Nevertheless, through miraculous intervention, Thecla is protected by God and survives. She leaves her home town and goes on her way only to be threatened with rape by the high-born man Alexander (*APTh* 26). For resisting the unwanted physical attention of this powerful man, Thecla is condemned to death for a second time. Once again, Thecla is thrown into the arena. However, no matter what they do to this woman, she refuses to die. Alexander, therefore, sadistically informs the Governor that he has two particularly vicious bulls that will undoubtedly ensure this uppity woman is put firmly in her place: read 'trampled well and truly into the ground'. The naked Thecla, a beautiful, desirable young virgin, is thus unceremoniously tied by her feet between two vicious bulls, in an arena full of spectators (*APTh* 35).[25] In adding this gratuitous element, the narrator once again invites the privileged heterosexual male gaze on to the scene to titillate his audience. This is a gaze that carries with it the power of objectification, possession and destruction; a power clearly lacking in the female gaze within this text.[26]

It is important to note at this stage that this is a second-century text. In this period, the bodies of chaste women were concealed. Women and girls of citizen status were rigorously segregated; sexual and social mores were controlled by strict notions of etiquette and propriety, with a sharp distinction between public (for male) and private (for women).[27] Thecla, a high-born woman and virgin, suffers the humiliation and torment usually reserved for shameless women who transgress social, sexual and societal norms.[28] Such exposure deliberately plays on shameful undertones and serves as an instrument of male control of women and their sexuality; a realm designated as women's greatest vulnerability.[29]

It is also difficult to escape the symbolism of the bulls. Jeffrey Henderson notes that in antiquity, bulls represent the phallic.[30] We are told that redhot irons are applied to their underbellies to enrage them (*APTh* 35). Just as the bulls represent the phallic, so too do the red-hot irons that are used to torturously brand them. In all likelihood, this description refers to their sexual parts. Such symbolism brings to mind the male (phallus) inflamed with desire, while Thecla is the passive recipient, suffering what is done to her. The fact that there are two phallic symbols intensifies the lewd pornographic nature of this display. The two bulls are the substitute penises intended to rip her apart. Symbols of the fecundating force of male generative powers come to the fore.

It may well be argued that by present-day standards such scenes are not pornographic. However, if we were viewing this story rather than reading it, perhaps the pornographic elements would become more obvious. In thinking of the imagery in terms of something to be viewed, we can consider the way a scene such as this might be perceived. In his book *Ways of Seeing*, Berger tells us that when someone is naked the focus of perception shifts from eyes, mouth, shoulders and hands to the sexual parts.[31] In this way, the other is reduced to their primary sexual category: male or female. Evoking a visual image of a beautiful, naked, virginal woman tied by the feet between two bulls exposes Thecla's sexuality before our very eyes. Just like the victim in pornography, she is exhibited to those who watch and reduced to a body.

Nancy Sorkin Rabinowitz, in her essay 'Tragedy and the Politics of Containment', which applies feminist theoretical models of the pornographic to Greco-Roman antiquity, notes that we tend to overlook the more brutal aspects of 'Tragedy' simply because we read the plays rather than see them.[32] Imagine, then, a spread-legged image of a naked woman tethered by the legs between two bulls displayed on a screen in front of you. A beautiful naked woman's sexuality is completely exposed before a gathering of fully clothed men and women. How else might we interpret such an image? The would-be female protagonist in the text is de-subjectified and, as the text demonstrates the very real masculine power to terrorize, women gazing on begin to learn their place in society.

Turning to the third-century text of Perpetua and Felicitas, we see the same representational practices come to the fore. Thus we read that the women

> were stripped naked, placed in nets and brought out into the arena. Even the crowd was horrified when they saw that one was a delicate young girl and the other was a woman fresh from childbirth with the milk still dripping from her breasts. (20)

Along with the crowd of spectators who were 'horrified' at the spectacle, we too recoil from the vivid description of the naked young woman who had recently given birth. Like wild animals that have been ensnared, these women are paraded in the most degrading way.

Further, graphic details of Perpetua's experiences in the arena are narrated:

> First the heifer tossed Perpetua and she fell on her back. Then sitting up she pulled down the tunic that was ripped along the side so that it covered her thighs ... Next she asked for a pin to fasten her untidy hair. (20)

We are also informed that, on falling on her back, Perpetua 'was held up by a man' (20), and as she is struck on the bone she screams (21). The account of a vulnerable and powerless woman screaming in agony provides a perverse thrill, and the image of Perpetua with ripped clothing, covering her thighs and rearranging her hair, physically held in the arms of a man, all adds an erotic, sexualized and pornographic tone to the scene.

Perpetua also has a vision where she sees herself as male. However, despite her apparent maleness, the *lanista* (trainer) refers to Perpetua with feminine pronouns and says at the close of the scene, 'Peace be with you, my daughter' (10). Thus, although we are told Perpetua has become *masculus* (male), she is recognized by the authority figure of the dream as female, and, perhaps more importantly, presented to the crowd as a woman. In this way, the narrator seductively toys with Perpetua's body and sexualizes the vision scene as her clothes are stripped off and her 'seconds ... handsome young men' rub her down with oil (10).

As the finale of the martyrdom approaches we are informed that Perpetua guides the sword and 'trembling hand' of the 'young gladiator' to 'her throat' (21). One can hardly miss the nuance of the scene as the sword, a masculine phallic symbol, is consciously and actively directed by Perpetua to her throat. The added description of the young man's 'trembling hand' also heightens the erotic appeal. Such graphic descriptions are highly suggestive and pornographic. Pain, torture and humiliation are made erotic and sensual. Although, guiding the sword to her throat, Perpetua is supposedly demonstrating that she chooses the manner of her death, we cannot escape the sexual symbolism of the scene.

Early Martyrdoms: the Spectacle of Horror

No-one discusses how disconnected people are when they watch horror films ... If you don't think this translates to real-life numbness you're deluding yourself ... it's coming to you through TV and film.[33]

It is not only these two texts that can be argued to present a violent pornographic treatment of women. Although not specifically female martyrdom stories, a number of scenes within the *Apocryphal Acts of the Apostles* describe women who are exposed, sexually debased and treated violently.[34] Even women who are dead do not escape sexualized debasement when within the *Acts of John (AJ)*, Callimachus, unable to win over Drusiana in this life, attempts to exact his revenge by committing necrophilia with her in the tomb, in front of his hapless friend Fortunatus (*AJ* 70). The *Acts of Peter* (128–36) presents Peter's young daughter as an object of voyeurism, as she is watched bathing with her mother. She also becomes the recipient of violence when she is physically debilitated in order not to be a temptation to men. Better a cripple than a source of discomfort to men. In the *Acts of Andrew*, the servant of Maximilla, Eucleia, is persuaded to sleep with Aegeates in her place and at one point we are told Eucleia sets two of her fellow servants at his head while she lies with him. Apart from the fact that the mind boggles at the thought of Aegeates not noticing for some period of time that Eucleia is not his wife, when the deception does eventually come to light Eucleia is punished. Her tongue is cut out, her hands and feet cut off and she becomes fodder for the dogs (*Martyrdom of Andrew* 339–41). Within the *Actus Vercellenses* text of the *Acts of Peter*, Rufina the adulteress is struck down, paralysed and made dumb (*Acts of Peter* 2).

It is clear that these texts all contain violent sexualized debasing representations of women. When set side by side with representations of men in the same texts we begin to see a rather different picture emerges. Thus, within the *Acts of Paul and Thecla* we read that Paul is thrown in prison for disturbing the peace in preaching and promoting sexual continence for women. However, after a brief hearing before the Governor, he is soon granted the freedom to walk away while the judgement delivered to Thecla is harsh, uncompromising and humiliating. When Paul does finally reach the point of martyrdom (within the longer, *Acts of Paul*) he is executed in a relatively honourable way by a straightforward beheading, and lo and behold: when his head is struck off, 'milk spurts out rather than blood'.[35] There is no degradation or humiliation.

So too within the text of Perpetua: in the arena, the Christian men are portrayed with grandeur and glory; they are shown to be 'in control'. Indeed, each of the three men are granted

> the death he had asked for ... (18–19). Saturus ... counted on being killed by one bite of a leopard. Then he was matched with a wild boar; but the gladiator who had tied him to the animal was gored by the boar ... whereas Saturus was only dragged along. Then when he was bound in the stocks awaiting the bear, the animal refused to come out of the cages, so that Saturus was called back once more unhurt. (19)

Eventually we hear Saturus say to a soldier:

> 'It is exactly ... as I foretold and predicted. So far not one animal has touched me. So now you may believe me ... I shall be finished off with one bite of the leopard.' And immediately as the contest was coming to a close a leopard was let loose, and after one bite Saturus was so drenched with blood. (21)

His story does not end there. After he is cast aside unconscious, he manages to regain consciousness and climb the stairway to ensure that he is the first to die (21). Saturus has both the ability to predict the manner of his death and regain consciousness, despite being seriously injured, in order to be the first to climb the stairway to his victorious death. A man, in control, to the end. The narrator spares the audience (and Saturus) any degradation or humiliation on the road to his martyrdom. By contrast, the readers rarely, if ever, receive reassurance that the female martyrs are unhurt, and if they are unhurt, as in the case of Thecla, they are sexually exposed.

The martyrdom of Polycarp and the martyrdom stories of the other male apostles in the *Apocryphal Acts* also convey this idea of glory, dignity and triumph in death.[36] Whereas the spread-legged image of a naked Thecla, the picture of the bare breasted beauties, Felicitas and Perpetua, in bondage are images that violate and demean women and eroticize violence and dominance. They contain representations of women's experience of being vulnerable, exposed and psychologically invaded in a way that men are not.

As argued above, such scenes parallel elements of contemporary pornography in that they reflect unequal social dynamics and portray women as objects of degradation and violence. Bella Zweig notes that such scenes parallel modern pornography in their production in a social environment that condoned and encouraged hostile attitudes and violent actions against women.[37] These scenes also presume a heterosexual male audience, spectator and gaze, which carries with it the power of objectification, possession and destruction. The women within the audience are also made masculine, asked to identify with the male protagonist, and this in turn sets up a pornographic structure of representation; it establishes heterosexual masculine subjectivity.[38] As Berger underscores, the 'ideal' spectator is always assumed to be male.[39]

Graphic violence, of course, regularly accompanies the description of a martyr's death, male and female. However, as Brent Shaw argues, for women, sexual degradation formed part of the spectacle.[40] Clement of Rome comments on how women 'suffered terrible and impious indignities'.[41] Shaw notes that witnessing the public violation and mutilation of otherwise protected and honoured female bodies gave a special edge, a sharper culmination, of the display.[42]

Early Martyrdoms: the Luminous Medium of Desire

> Imagine if your value to the company you work for was measured by how much semen you could extract from anonymous masses of men. 'Cause you know, if strange men masturbate to your movies, you must be of some value.[43]

David Frankfurter argues that female martyrs are put through this sexual display and graphic torture for a 'frankly, prurient gaze'.[44] The spectacle of sado-erotic violence allows the enjoyment of erotic display at the same time as the disavowal of that enjoyment, which is projected on to the violent punitive actions of Roman authorities. For Frankfurter, such legends function both to demonize the 'Other' and to provide that voyeuristic confusion of disgust and arousal. What is important about Frankfurter's insights is his point that spectators got a perverse thrill from this sado-erotic spectacle. No matter how pious Christian spectators claimed to be, they got a 'kick' out of the experience.

However one reads these texts there is little doubt that, while the narratives appear to be advocating the strength and courage of the female martyrs, there is an unhealthy focus on the sexual appeal of these women and their feminine, bodily qualities: a juxtaposing of female *virtus* (power/ gallantry) and its simultaneous containment through sexual disparagement.

Praise and disparagement, acclaim and misogyny co-exist within the same text. The exposed, sexualized, abused female body plays a major role in cementing the female martyr's sanctity.

If we move forward a couple of hundred years from the second-century texts of Thecla and Perpetua and Felicitas to the post-Constantine period, we find further evidence of such sado-erotic representations. Virginia Burrus notes that the lives of male and female saints pick up and continue this theme found in the earlier martyr stories.[45] The writings of Ambrose and the poet Prudentius (c. 348) resonate powerfully with the eroticized rhetoric of gender. Where the 12-year-old virgin martyr Agnes is concerned, she is exposed in the public square and her entire ordeal is read as a sexualized encounter with death. As she prepares to die she says of her executioner, 'This is my lover; a man who pleases me at last, I shall greet his blade's full length.' Agnes welcomes the sword as a deflowering penis and embraces death as marriage to a true man, Christ.[46]

We need to take seriously the androcentrism of ancient Christian discourse. The ways in which women are presented in such texts constitutes, in many ways, a litany of contempt and abuse, and as gender is brought to the centre of analysis a number of questions arise. Most specifically, do representations that violate the female body play a major constitutive role in the production and shaping of female cultural identity and religiosity, and of women's self-identity and self-perception? Although feminist writers have long argued that there is a correlation between violent representation and the violence done to women, in reality the debate about the relationship between real and representational violence continues. There is no consensus whether violent images incite violent actions. However, scholars do agree that societal norms and attitudes influence both life and art and are represented in both. For example, the feminist theorist Susanne Kappeler draws a strong correlation between the process of representation and the process of pornography and argues that representation and representational practices are powerful mechanisms that affect reality.[47] She gives the example of a white Namibian farmer who instigated the torture and death of a young black worker while his friends took pictures. The pictures eventually served as evidence to convict him of the crime of murder. Kappeler argues that the killing and torture done before the camera, that is, the artistic composition or representation itself, was integral to the crime. Her example of the Namibian farmer underscores the fact that representation does not imitate reality but creates reality. For Kappeler, all representation constructs reality in this way. There are strong and permeating mechanisms of power latent within both processes. Images and texts are manifestations of power relationships that affect concepts of gender and culture.

Rape in Art and Real Life

Girls grow up being terrified of rape because it's allowed to happen.[48]

And STOP using rape as a tool for your storytelling: it is damaging and causes trauma.[49]

Other good examples of this correlation between violent representations and the violence done to women in reality are the two iconic ancient images of the Judaea Capta coin and the Imperial relief of Claudius and Britannia from the Sebasteion in Aphrodisias. The Judaea Capta coin (see Figure 1) was first issued by the Roman Emperor Vespasian to commemorate the capture and destruction of Jerusalem around AD 70. Note in particular that Judaea is depicted as a lone, dejected woman seated beneath a palm tree, while the Roman soldier stands over her with a phallic-looking *parazonium* (sword) scabbard set in his groin, thus alluding to the notions of penetration, domination and submission. Turning to the image of Claudius bearing down over Britannia (see Figure 2), we see the heroically naked Claudius pinning his victim down with his knee as he pulls her head up by her hair. Britannia is dressed in a short chiton and alluringly has her (perfectly shaped) right breast exposed. In antiquity a bare breast was a popular motif in depictions of women as violently defeated.[50] The iconography is full of strong innuendo of rape. This relief is one of a number at the Sebasteion in Aphrodisias that depict representations of captured women alongside

Figure 1: 'Judaea Capta' Coin. *c.* AD 70. Issued following the destruction of Jerusalem. Image courtesy of www.romancoins.info, copyright Andreas Pangerl.

Figure 2: Relief of Emperor Claudius over Britannia from the Sebasteion in Aphrodisias. *c.* AD 43. Aphrodisias Excavations, New York University.

victorious Roman emperors. Another representation portrays Nero brutally subduing the nation of Armenia – known as the rape of Armenia. The north portico of the relief at Aphrodisias contains around 50 personified female ἔθνη (nations) featured as life-size single female bodies. Although these examples demonstrate a Roman imperial ideology of hegemony and domination over various nations, depicted as women's bodies, the images signify the very real and frequent violent abuse that women have endured and, indeed, continue to endure, from men who rape and torture in times of war.

Rape and sexual exploitation very much remain weapons of war intended to strike fear into the hearts of women. A 2016 UN Security Council report highlights the link between conflict and trafficking of women and girls for sexual exploitation: an issue identified by the Special Rapporteur of the Human Rights Council in 2018.[51] According to a United States report the most common form of human trafficking (79 pre cent) is sexual exploitation and the victims are predominantly women and girls.[52] More than 200 young women were abducted in 2014 by Boko Haram in Nigeria to be used as sex or labour slaves.[53] The Daesh attack on Sinjar in Iraq in 2014 resulted in the abduction of over 3,200 Yazidi girls and women who would have been subjected to sexual exploitation.[54] Images such as those on the Judaea Capta coin and that of the subdued and exposed Britannia are not created in a vacuum. They tell a story. They are a powerful medium and form a compelling vision to communicate a powerful narrative to all who look upon them. These ancient images continue to communicate what is a lived reality for thousands of women even today.

There are many cases in the history of the Church where the female body has been appropriated to speak for Christianity. We have the ascetic body, the virginal body and the maternal body; each is constructed and valorized in a particular way. Specifically in martyrdoms, so called 'pious' texts, we have the eroticized and sadistically violated female body. What kind of legacy have such representations left for women, and what damage has resulted from this legacy?

Medieval Mystics: Internalized Oppression

> The dying gasps of the Kennedy era and the pervasive requirements of feminine civility and perfection ... The stifled rage must've been a constant for women of that era.[55]

At this point, in an attempt to shed some light on the religious practices of a number of female medieval mystics, I want to take a risk and consider the possible consequences and impact that such representations of sado-erotic violence towards women may have had on the lived reality of some female Christians. In doing so I do, of course, recognize not only that I am making a significant methodological shift but also how difficult, if not impossible, it is to draw a straightforward trajectory from one period to another. This discussion, then, is simply an attempt to engage new ideas, stimulate debate and promote an exploration of the subject.

With that caveat in mind, somewhat methodologically crudely and tentatively, I suggest that such representations as those discussed above should help guide our attempts to understand the later medieval development of female piety some centuries later. This period saw women's devotion characterized by extreme committed penitential asceticism and self-inflicted suffering; a piety that involved abject self-torture in the name of God.[56]

Although the experiencing of pain was a prominent aspect of the spirituality of both late medieval women and men, there is no question that it was more prominent in women's religiosity.[57] Herbert Thurston and Rudolph Bell have provided much evidence of what psychiatrists commonly call 'hysteria' in women's piety.[58] A number of Italian female mystics are said to have drunk pus or scabs from lepers' sores in a bid to physically incorporate disease into their bodies.[59] Alda of Siena slept on a bed of paving stones, whipped herself with chains and wore a crown of thorns.[60] Dorothy of Montau, in imitation of Christ's burial, lay prostrate with the entire weight of her body supported only by toes, nose and forehead.[61] Caroline Walker Bynum highlights the fact that ascetic practices

> commonly reported in these vitae include wearing hair shirts, binding the flesh tightly with twisted ropes, rubbing lice into self-inflicted wounds ... thrusting nettles into one's breasts ... rolling in broken glass, jumping into ovens, hanging from a gibbet ... and even 'lacerating their bodies with all kinds of whips'.[62]

Simone de Beauvoir also refers to women mystics who 'annihilate themselves'.[63] Here de Beauvoir is referring to the propensity of female mystics to torture their flesh and body in conscious acts of self-harm. For example, Marie Alacoque is reported to have cleaned a sick person's vomit with her tongue in disavowal of her body. She describes in her autobiography her happiness when she had filled her mouth with the excrement of a man with diarrhoea.[64] Bell has also identified the manifestation of eating disorders such as anorexia and bulimia among female mystics 400 years before such conditions were first described in medical reports. Bell maintains that the distinctions between holy anorexia and anorexia nervosa may be more a matter of the modifiers than anything else. That is, both conditions are characterized by an unwillingness to eat; however, one is driven by a desire to be 'holy' and the other to be thin.[65]

Thus, deliberate and systematic physical punishment was part of the daily routine for many religious women. Walker Bynum considers these practices as exemplifying 'a profound expression of the doctrine of the Incarnation, a culturally normative understanding of the dominant figuration of Christ's humanity'.[66] Personally, I prefer to ask, 'To what extent can these extreme actions of self-harm be understood as an egregious historic legacy of a gender-based violence towards women through the ages, both representational and actual: an internalization of patriarchal and androcentric misogynistic practices?' Can a correlation be drawn between a female piety – which resulted in extreme bodily self-harm – and representations of female violation, a furthering of societal and social constructs that shaped women's self-perceptions and resulted in self-inflicted violence?

Bearing in mind that the preaching and teaching of medieval theologians was no more respectful of women than the debasing sexualized mistreatment found in the recorded legends of female martyrs, we would do well to consider the endowments of patriarchy over centuries and millennia. For example, medieval theologians regarded sin as a response to an external stimulus for men and yet saw evil and the devil as an internal, domestic parasitic force that easily and naturally inhabited women.[67]

In looking at this idea of a trajectory from the second century through to the medieval period, Barbara Newman has cogently argued that the abundant and direct misogyny found in the writings of the medieval period was directly derived from the Greco-Roman culture and perpetuated by patristic authors, who viewed the female as a sign for all that is weak, carnal and sensual.[68] Spiritual writers drew on this tradition offhandedly as a course of metaphors, regardless of the gender of their audience. She notes that practically the whole patristic and medieval tradition rejected the possibility that women were equally theomorphic. It split the concept of *imago Dei* (image of God) from gender difference. Newman argues that there is a legacy of anti-feminism from the Greco-Roman period, a legacy that was internalized by both men and women in society; a legacy that could not help but influence the Church Fathers who concluded that it was the male who possessed the image of God normatively, whereas women were the image of the body, or the lower creation, which man was given to rule over.[69]

Taking this idea of following a trajectory of violent representations of women further, if we fast forward again from the medieval period to the Victorian era and the painting 'Christian Dirce' by Henry Siemiradzki, dated 1897, once again we see that centuries later this painting visually displays the process of female martyrdom and spectacle begun in the second century.

Figure 3: Christian Dirce, 1897, Henryk Siemiradzki, National Museum in Warsaw (inventory number MP 267 MNW)

The dead, female martyr lies sprawled naked over a dead bull, her arms spread eagled to give a good view of her body. It may seem irrelevant and a world away from our second-century texts, but the painting is a good example of this tradition of erotic spectacle that continued into modern times. The sophisticated, well-dressed spectators look on voyeuristically, with interested yet detached curiosity. They cannot avert their eyes from the naked woman who looks alluring even in death. The early martyr texts have left an imprint that carries through the centuries.

Dimensions of Creative Thinking

Images of violence against women frequently function to support patri-archal hegemonic privilege and women's symbolic oppression, and the sexualized violence of martyrdoms is operating within a certain realistic (and legitimated) mode of representation; the implications for women's piety and their participation in religious life, therefore, require new evaluation. When it comes to sado-erotic violent representations of women, we must bear in mind the possible legacy that such representations left in their wake and what is at stake for women. Although Walker Bynum maintains that the illness and asceticism of female medieval mystics were not an effort to destroy or punish the body but rather an imitation *Christi* – an effort to plumb the depths of Christ's humanity at the moment of his dying[70] – I remain unconvinced by her assertion that these women did not internalize misogyny. The investigation of 170 medieval saints by Bell revealed that half of these women exhibited symptoms of anorexia. Bell has presented these women in both a historical and social psychological context, and his research certainly raises the question of whether holy anorexia was, in part, a response to the patriarchal social structure of medieval Catholicism.[71] Furthermore, as we have seen above, the work of Kappeler, Diana Russell and MacKinnon argues that violent objectification and representation both reflect and create realities; images such as those of the Judaea Capta coin and Britannia and Claudius similarly affirm this view. In which case, can we rule out the possibility that sado-erotic violent representations, which reflect a dominant social and patriarchal ideology, ultimately influence women and their experience of their bodies?

This notion of embodiment, the ways in which societal rules and discourses are assimilated and play out, raises important questions with regard to how women internalize degrading and oppressive messages. Drawing on the phenomenology of French philosopher Maurice Merleau-Ponty, Judith Butler points out that the body is a 'historical idea' rather than a 'natural species'.[72] From this perspective, the body can be understood as being in an active process of embodying certain historical and cultural possibilities: 'the body gains its meaning through a concrete and historically mediated expression in the world'.[73] David Gahnim, writing on gender and violence in the Middle East, argues that the denial of a healthy existence for women forces them to internalize their situation.[74] He quotes Catriona Mackenzie who states, 'oppression structures the psyches and the bodies of women'.[75] Georges Tarabishi, a Syrian writer and translator, expresses this perfectly, when he underscores that woman 'will internalize oppression and end up becoming her own oppressor'.[76] De Beauvoir also argues that oppression becomes naturalized by being internalized.[77] Internalization is the process through which that which is socially constructed appears natural to the individual.[78] As a result, a relationship between representations and self-representations materializes.

Indeed, this idea can be taken further when we consider that there is a growing body of evidence that exposure to negative and violent media may have serious and long-lasting psychological effects upon individuals. The work of British psychologist Graham Davey, specializing in the effects of media violence, suggests that violent media exposure can exacerbate or contribute to the development of stress, anxiety, depression and even post-traumatic stress disorder (PTSD).[79] While the persistent flood of media information today cannot in any way be equated with early martyrdom stories that circulated either through textual means or via word of mouth, perhaps we can begin to think how some women may have internalized negative stimuli in their everyday environments. If exposure to media violence today can affect people's moods and lives, resulting in PTSD, then is it so far-fetched to think that sado-erotic violent representations and a social environment where women have been regarded as bodies and objects of exchange among men, may have had a detrimental psychological impact on women in antiquity? Indeed, Davey notes that the way that anxiety manifests itself has not really changed over the centuries and humanity is still plagued by the same forms of anxiety as our ancient ancestors.[80] Women have been the victims of centuries of oppression and violence: societal, representational and actual. Injury and trauma have been inflicted physically, emotionally, psychologically and spiritually. Such trauma distorts attitudes and beliefs. An area that has received little attention is what role such social norms have played in producing negative perceptions, images and behaviours in women.

I began this chapter with a quote from the psychiatrist Bessel van der Kolk. He poignantly underscores the fact that the imprint of trauma has ongoing consequences for how people manage to survive in the present. His work highlights research from the new disciplines of neuroscience, developmental psychopathology and interpersonal neurobiology, which confirms that the experience of trauma leaves behind an imprint on the mind, body and brain and has ongoing psychological consequences for younger generations, who in turn embody the traumatic experience of their parents or relatives.[81] Although overwhelming experiences, in the form of trauma, fall out of social discourse, the transmission of that unnamed trauma is, nevertheless, communicated to the next generations.[82] Psychic legacies thus continue through unconscious cues and affective messages that flow between adult and child. Oppression leaves scars on the victims, scars that embed themselves on people's psyches and that continue well beyond the actual experience of oppression or trauma. Given that it is now widely acknowledged that trauma is a phenomenon that is carried across generations,[83] as an oppressed group, women have been both the receptors and transmitters of trauma: representational and actual. In thinking about intergenerational trauma, is it possible to link this phenomenon to women's lives as an oppressed group?

Conclusion

As this chapter has made clear, although the saintliness of male and female martyrs required their mutilation and murder, that of the women required in addition their sexual degradation. Female martyrdoms highlight the sanctifying goodness of women, but what a perverse and sadistic way to present a heroine. We need to be mindful that within such texts there is a subtle power operative that demands the sado-erotic torture of women. These female martyrs represent the real violence done to women over the centuries. The fact that the bodies of these women are exposed and tortured should serve as a warning sign to any who might use such texts as positive examples of female subjectivity in antiquity. Always in the grip of some male power, these women are constrained and acted upon by external forces. Their bodies are exposed and tortured by one set of males (Romans) and appropriated by other (Christian) males for their own ends. Just because the violent depictions are set off as the awful actions of the terrible Romans, and for the sake of God and faith, should not make them acceptable.

The medieval female mystics who struggled to express their sense of self by becoming holy did so in a way that reinforced a male interpretation of female psychology and physiology. However, while we may admire the mystics for their determined pursuit of holiness at all costs, just as we admire Thecla, Perpetua, Felicitas and all the other female martyrs, one cannot help wondering whether holiness could have been achieved through less severe forms of asceticism, as indeed it was by many men.

'Naming' is a constructive achievement, an act of defining and authenticating. Naming violence is one of the most powerful ways of confronting violence head on and it is a first step in contesting that violence. Exposing and naming the sado-erotic violation of women in martyrdoms is a first step in the journey of exposing the inherent gendered oppression of women.

References

In citing chapters and fragmentary material of the *Apocryphal Acts of the Apostles* I follow the numbering and usage found in Wilhelm Schneemelcher, ed., *New Testament Apocrypha*, rev. edn, trans. R. McL. Wilson, Cambridge and Louisville, KY: James Clarke and Westminster John Knox Press, 1992.

Aristotle, *Generation of Animals*, in *The Complete Works of Aristotle, Volume 1*, the revised Oxford translation, ed. Johnathan Barnes. Princeton, NJ: Princeton University Press, 1984.

BBC News Boko Haram, *BBC News* report: www.bbc.co.uk/news/world-africa-27342757 (accessed 23 January 2019).

BBC report from 2016 entitled 'Tomb Raider: How Lara Croft Became a Game Changer': www.bbc.co.uk/news/uk-england-derbyshire-37619114 (accessed 11 February 2019). See also www.theguardian.com/stage/2015/sep/21/a-girl-and-a-gun-review-feminist-take-cinema-sexism.

Beauvoir, Simone de, *The Second Sex*, trans. Constance Borde and Sheila Malovany-Chevallier, London: Vintage Books, 2011.

Bell, Rudolph M., *Holy Anorexia*, Chicago and London: University of Chicago Press, 1985.

Berger, John, *Ways of Seeing*, London: British Broadcasting Corporation and Penguin Books, 1972.

Brannigan, Augustine, *The Rise and Fall of Social Psychology: The Use and Misuse of the Experimental Method*, New York: Hawthorne, 2004.

Burrus, Virginia, 'Reading Agnes: The Rhetoric of Gender in Ambrose and Prudentius', *Journal of Early Christian Studies* 3 (1995), 25–46.

Butler, Judith, 'Performative Acts and Gender Constitution: An Essay in Phenomenology and Feminist Theory', in *Writing on the Body: Female Embodiment and Feminist Theory*, ed. Katie Conboy, Nadia Medina and Sarah Stanbury, New York: Columbia University Press, 1997, 401–17.

Carson, Anne, 'Putting Her in Her Place: Woman, Dirt, and Desire', in *Before Sexuality, The Construction of Erotic Experience in the Ancient Greek World*, ed. David M. Halperin, John J. Winkler and Froma I. Zeitlin, New Jersey: Princeton University Press, 1990, 135–70.

Clark, Gillian, 'Bodies and Blood, Late Antique Debate on Martyrdom, Virginity and Resurrection', in *Changing Bodies, Changing Meanings, Studies on the Human Body in Antiquity*, ed. Dominic Montserrat, London, New York: Routledge, 1998, 99–115.

Clement of Rome, *First Epistle to the Corinthians*, in *The Apostolic Fathers*, ed. and trans. Bart D. Ehrman, Cambridge, MA: Harvard University Press, 2014.

Cohen, Beth, 'Divesting the Female Breast of Clothes in Classical Sculpture', in *Naked Truths: Women, Sexuality and Gender in Classical Art and Archaeology*, ed. Ann Olga Kolski-Ostrow and Claire L. Lyons, London, New York: Routledge, 1997, 66–92.

Daesh attack report: Canada, House of Commons report November 2016: www.ourcommons.ca/DocumentViewer/en/42-1/FAAE/report-8/page-33 (accessed 23 January 2019).

Danieli, Yael, *International Handbook of Multigenerational Legacies of Trauma*, New York: Plenum, 1998.

Davey, Graham, *The Anxiety Epidemic: The Causes of our Modern-Day Anxieties*, London: Robinson, 2018.

Dworkin, Andrea and Catharine MacKinnon, *Pornography and Civil Rights: A New Day for Women's Equality*, Minneapolis, MN: Organizing Against Pornography, 1988, distributed by Southern Sisters, Inc., 441 Morris St, Durham, NC 2770.

Dworkin, Andrea, *Pornography: Men Possessing Women*, London: Women's Press, 1981.

Dworkin, Ronald, 'Is There a Right to Pornography?', *Oxford Journal of Legal Studies* 1 (1981), 177–212.

Easton, Susan M., *The Problem of Pornography, Regulation and the Right to Free Speech*, London and New York: Routledge, 1994.

Fossion, P., M. Rejas, L. Servais, I. Pelc and S. Hirsch, 'Family Approach with Grandchildren of Holocaust Survivors', *American Journal of Psychotherapy* 57, no. 4 (2003), 519–27.

Frankfurter, David, 'Martyrology and the Prurient Gaze', *Journal of Early Christian Studies* 17 (2009), 215–45.

Ghanim, David, *Gender and Violence in the Middle East*, Westport, CT: Praeger, 2009.

Hanson, Ann Ellis, 'The Medical Writers' Woman', in *Before Sexuality, The Construction of Erotic Experience in the Ancient Greek World*, ed. David M. Halperin, John J. Winkler and Froma I. Zeitlin, New Jersey: Princeton University Press, 1990, 309–38.

Henderson, Jeffrey, *The Maculate Muse: Obscene Language in Attic Comedy*, New Haven, CT, and London: Yale University Press, 1991.

Kaplan, E. Ann, 'Is the Gaze Male?', in *Powers of Desire, The Politics of Sexuality*, ed. Ann Snitow, Christine Stansell and Sharon Thompson, New York: Monthly Review Press, 1983, 309–27.

Kappeler, Susanne, *The Pornography of Representation*, Minneapolis, MN: University of Minnesota Press, 1986.

Laquer, Thomas, *Making Sex: Body and Gender from the Greeks to Freud*, Cambridge, MA: Harvard University Press, 1990.

Lipsius, Richard Adelbert and Maximillianus Bonnet,. *Acta Apostolorum Apocrypha, Post Constantinum*, Leipzig: Hermann Mendelssohn, 1891–1903; reprint, Hildenscheim: G. Olms Verlagsbuchhandlung, 1959.

MacDonald, Margaret Y., *Early Christian Women and Pagan Opinion: The Power of the Hysterical Woman*, Cambridge: Cambridge University Press, 1996.

MacKinnon, Catharine A., 'Feminism, Marxism, and the State: An Agenda for Theory', in *Signs Reader: Women, Gender and Scholarship*, ed. Elizabeth Abel and Emily Abel, Chicago, IL: University of Chicago Press, 1983, 227–56.

—— *Feminism Unmodified, Discourses on Life and Law*, Cambridge, MA: Harvard University Press, 1987.

—— *Toward a Feminist Theory of the State*, Cambridge, MA: Harvard University Press, 1991.

Musurillo, Herbert, *The Acts of the Christian Martyrs, Introduction Texts and Translation*, Oxford: Clarendon Press, 1972.

Plato, *Timaeus*, in *Plato, Complete Works*, ed. John M Cooper, Indianapolis, IN/ Cambridge, MA: Hackett Publishing, 1997.

Prager, Jeffrey, 'Lost Childhood, Lost Generations: The Intergenerational Transmission of Trauma', *Journal of Human Rights* 2, no. 2 (2003), 173–81.

Rabinowitz, Nancy Sorkin, 'Tragedy and the Politics of Containment', in *Pornography and Representation in Greece and Rome*, ed. Amy Richlin, Oxford: Oxford University Press, 1992, 36–52.

Richlin, Amy, ed., *Pornography and Representation in Greece and Rome*, Oxford: Oxford University Press, 1992.

Russell, Diana E. H., ed., *Making Violence Sexy: Feminist Views on Pornography*, Buckingham: Open University Press, 1993.

Schmidt, Carl and Wilhelm Schubart, Πραξεις Παυλου: *Acta Pauli nach dem Papyrus der Hamburger*, Glückstadt, Hamburg: Staatsund Universitäts-Bibliothek, 1936.

Schneemelcher, Wilhelm, ed., *New Testament Apocrypha II*, trans. R. McL. Wilson, rev. edn, Cambridge and Louisville, KY: James Clarke and Westminster John Knox Press, 1992.

Schwab, Gabriele, *Haunting Legacies: Violent Histories and Transgenerational Trauma*, New York: Columbia University Press, 2010.

Shaw, Brent, 'The Passion of Perpetua', *Past and Present* 139 (1993), 3–45.

Spittler, Janet E., *Animals in the Apocryphal Acts of the Apostles*, Tübingen: Mohr Seibeck, 2008.

The Apostolic Fathers, Greek Texts and English Translations, 3rd edn, ed. and trans. Michael W. Holmes, Michigan: Baker Academic, 2007.

United Nations Report of the Special Rapporteur on trafficking in persons, especially women and children: A/HRC/38/45, 18 June–6 July 2018: https://reliefweb. int/report/world/report-special-rapporteur-trafficking-persons-especially-women-and-children-ahrc3845 (accessed 23 January 2019).

United States of Office of Drugs and Crime report: www.unodc.org/unodc/en/ human-trafficking/global-report-on-trafficking-in-persons.html (accessed 23 January 2019).

van der Kolk, Bessel, *The Body Keeps the Score: Mind, Brain and Body in the Transformation of Trauma*, New York: Penguin, 2014.

Walker Bynum, Caroline, *Fragmentation and Redemption: Essays on Gender and the Human Body in Medieval Religion*, New York: Zone Books, 1991.

Weinstein, Donald and Rudolph M. Bell, *Saints and Society: The Two Worlds of Western Christendom, 1000–1700*, Chicago, IL: University of Chicago Press, 1982.

Zweig, Bella. 'The Mute Nude Female Characters in Aristophanes' Plays', in *Pornography and Representation in Greece and Rome*, ed. Amy Richlin, Oxford: Oxford University Press, 1992, 73–89.

Notes

1 Bessel van der Kolk, *The Body Keeps the Score, Mind, Brain and Body in the Transformation of Trauma* (New York: Penguin, 2014), 21.

2 Rose McGowan, *Brave* (London: HarperCollins, 2018), 2.

3 It should be noted that Tarana Burke, an African-American activist for women of colour, initially founded the 'Me Too' campaign to raise awareness of the pervasiveness of sexual abuse in society. Some years later Rose McGowan made use of 'MeToo' as a hashtag following the Harvey Weinstein scandal.

4 Aristotle, *Generation of Animals*, in *The Complete Works of Aristotle, Volume 1*, ed. Jonathan Barnes (Princeton, NJ: Princeton University Press, 1991), 728a18–20; 737a25–35; 775a10–15; Plato, *Timaeus*, in *Plato: Complete Works*, ed., John M. Cooper (Indianapolis, IN/Cambridge, MA: Hackett Publishing, 1997), 69c–81c. See also Thomas Laquer, *Making Sex: Body and Gender from the Greeks to Freud* (Cambridge, MA: Harvard University Press, 1990); Anne Carson, 'Putting Her in Her Place: Woman, Dirt, and Desire', in *Before Sexuality: The Construction of Erotic Experience in the Ancient Greek World*, ed. David M. Halperin, John J. Winkler and Froma I. Zeitlin (Princeton, NJ: Princeton University Press, 1990), 135–70; Ann Ellis Hanson, 'The Medical Writers' Woman', in *Before Sexuality*, ed. Halperin et al., 309–38.

5 McGowan, *Brave*, 234.

6 An online BBC report from 2016, entitled 'Tomb Raider: How Lara Croft Became a Game Changer' perhaps most clearly highlights the impact of the sexualized superwoman. It describes how her character has been seen as a 'feminist icon, a virtual blow-up doll, the sixth Spice Girl, a cyberbabe, an ambassador for Britain, or a distorted male fantasy', www.bbc.co.uk/news/uk-england-derbyshire-37619114 (accessed 23 January 2019). See also Lyn Gardner, 'A Girl and a Gun Review – A Feminist Take on Cinema and Sexism', *Guardian*, 21 September 2015, www.theguardian.com/stage/2015/sep/21/a-girl-and-a-gun-review-feminist-take-cinema-sexism.

7 Text and translation in Herbert Musurillo, *The Martyrdom of Saints Perpetua and Felicitas, The Acts of the Christian Martyrs: Introduction Texts and Translation* (Oxford: Clarendon Press, 1972), 106–31. Musurillo places the dating of the text in the first decade of the third century.

8 *The Acts of Paul and Thecla* (*APTh*) is found within the longer apocryphal *Acts of Paul*. The standard edition for the text is Richard Adelbert Lipsius and Maximillianus Bonnet, *Acta Apostolorum Apocrypha, Post Constantinum* (Leipzig: Hermann Mendelssohn, 1891–1903; reprint, Hildenscheim: G. Olms Verlagsbuchhandlung, 1959). Translation in Wilhelm Schneemelcher, ed., *New Testament Apocrypha II*, trans. R. McL. Wilson, rev. edn (Cambridge and Louisville, KY: James Clarke and Westminster John Knox Press, 1992). Most scholars subscribe to a second-century date (AD 185–200), see Schneemelcher, *New Testament Apocrypha* (*NTA*), 235.

9 It should be noted that legal usage does not conform to everyday language or

to dictionary definitions. Susan M. Easton, *The Problem of Pornography, Regulation and the Right to Free Speech* (London and New York: Routledge, 1994), xii.

10 Diana E. H. Russell, ed., *Making Violence Sexy: Feminist Views on Pornography* (Buckingham: Open University Press, 1993), 5. For a discussion on pornography and erotica, see Susanne Kappeler, *The Pornography of Representation* (Minneapolis, MN: University of Minnesota Press, 1986), 35–48; see also Amy Richlin, ed., *Pornography and Representation in Greece and Rome* (Oxford: Oxford University Press, 1992), 35–48. There is great disagreement among feminists on the issue of pornography. The anti-pornography movement produced a backlash within feminism, as some feminists argued in defence of pornography. See Richlin, *Pornography and Representation*, xiv–xv.

11 Russell, *Making Violence Sexy*, 5–6.

12 Andrea Dworkin, *Pornography: Men Possessing Women* (London: The Women's Press, 1981), 14–15, 24, 80–106, 200–1.

13 Catharine A. MacKinnon, *Toward a Feminist Theory of the State* (Cambridge, MA: Harvard University Press, 1991), 199.

14 Catharine A. MacKinnon, *Feminism Unmodified: Discourses on Life and Law* (Cambridge, MA: Harvard University Press, 1987), 172.

15 In 1983 and 1984, Minneapolis and Indianapolis passed municipal ordinances to prohibit the selling of pornography. See E. R. Shipp, 'A Feminist Offensive against Exploitation', *The New York Times*, 10 June 1984, www.nytimes.com/1984/06/10/weekinreview/a-feminist-offensive-against-exploitation.html.

16 Andrea Dworkin and Catharine MacKinnon, *Pornography and Civil Rights: A New Day for Women's Equality* (Minneapolis, MN: Organizing against Pornography, 1988; distributed by Southern Sisters, Inc., 441 Morris St., Durham, NC 2770), 36.

17 Cited in Susan M. Easton, *The Problem of Pornography: Regulation and the Right to Free Speech* (London and New York: Routledge, 1994), xii.

18 MacKinnon, *Toward a Feminist Theory*, 211.

19 John Berger, *Ways of Seeing* (London: British Broadcasting Corporation and Penguin Books, 1972), 47.

20 Richlin, *Pornography and Representation*, xiv.

21 Richlin, *Pornography and Representation*, xvii.

22 Kappeler, *Pornography of Representation*, 2–3.

23 McGowan, *Brave*, 162.

24 McGowan, *Brave*, 223.

25 It should be noted that the text makes reference to a 'fire' that surrounds Thecla. However, it is unlikely that this fire could have veiled Thecla's nakedness from sight. Had Thecla permanently been surrounded by a cloud of fire it is difficult to understand how anyone managed to tie her to the bulls in the first place. The flame may be associated with the scorching irons used to goad the bulls. Janet E. Spittler, *Animals in the Apocryphal Acts of the Apostles* (Tübingen: Mohr Seibeck, 2008), 177–8. This confusion over the source of the flames/fire also manifests itself in both the Greek and Latin texts, which reveal extensive textual variation.

26 For a similar interpretation of the gaze, see E. Ann Kaplan, 'Is the Gaze Male?', in *Powers of Desire: The Politics of Sexuality*, ed. Ann Snitow, Christine Stansell and Sharon Thompson (New York: Monthly Review Press, 1983), 311.

27 See for example, Margaret Y. MacDonald, *Early Christian Women and Pagan Opinion: The Power of the Hysterical Woman* (Cambridge: Cambridge University

Press, 1996), 27–40; Jeffrey Henderson, *The Maculate Muse: Obscene Language in Attic Comedy* (New Haven, CT, and London: Yale University Press, 1991), 32.

28 Margaret MacDonald, *Early Christian Women*, 176; Gillian Clark, 'Bodies and Blood: Late Antique Debate on Martyrdom, Virginity and Resurrection', in *Changing Bodies, Changing Meanings: Studies on the Human Body in Antiquity*, ed. Dominic Montserrat (London and New York: Routledge, 1998), 103.

29 See Bella Zweig, 'The Mute Nude Female Characters in Aristophanes' Plays', in *Pornography and Representation*, ed. Richlin, 84–5, who makes this point in relation to Aristophanes' plays.

30 Henderson, *Maculate Muse*, 127.

31 Berger, *Ways of Seeing*, 59.

32 Nancy Sorkin Rabinowitz, 'Tragedy and the Politics of Containment', in *Pornography and Representation*, ed. Richlin, 38.

33 McGowan, *Brave*, 109.

34 Translation of these texts may be found in Schneemelcher *NTA*.

35 See *Acts of Paul, Martyrdom of the Holy Apostle Paul*, 5.

36 Text and translation of the Martyrdom of Polycarp in *The Apostolic Fathers: Greek Texts and English Translations*, ed. and trans. Michael W. Holmes, 3rd edn (Michigan: Baker Academic, 2007), 306–3. See also the martyrdom stories of the apostles in Wilhelm Schneemelcher, *NTA: Acts of Andrew (348–35); Acts of John (111–15); Acts of Paul (4–7); Acts of Peter (35–40); Acts of Thomas (165–70)*.

37 Zweig, 'Mute Nude Female', 88.

38 See Rabinowitz, 'Tragedy', 51.

39 Berger, *Ways of Seeing*, 64.

40 Brent Shaw, 'The Passion of Perpetua', *Past and Present* 139, no. 1 (1993), 3–45, 10.

41 Clement of Rome, *First Epistle to the Corinthians*, ch. 6, 1–2.

42 Shaw, 'Passion of Perpetua', 18.

43 McGowan, *Brave*, 8.

44 David Frankfurter, 'Martyrology and the Prurient Gaze', *Journal of Early Christian Studies* 17 (2009), 215–45.

45 Virginia Burrus, 'Reading Agnes: The Rhetoric of Gender in Ambrose and Prudentius', *Journal of Early Christian Studies* 3 (1995), 25–46, 27.

46 Burrus, 'Reading Agnes', 34–37.

47 Kappeler, *Pornography of Representation*, 2–8.

48 McGowan, *Brave*, 128.

49 McGowan, *Brave*, 235.

50 Beth Cohen, 'Divesting the Female Breast of Clothes in Classical Sculpture', in *Naked Truths: Women, Sexuality and Gender in Classical Art and Archaeology*, ed. Ann Olga Koloski-Ostrow and Claire L. Lyons (London and New York: Routledge, 1997), 66–92, 72, 74, 77.

51 United Nations Report of the Special Rapporteur on trafficking in persons, especially women and children: A/HRC/38/45, 18 June–6 July 2018, https://relief web.int/report/world/report-special-rapporteur-trafficking-persons-especially-women-and-children-ahrc3845 (accessed 23 January 2019).

52 See United States of Office of Drugs and Crime report, www.unodc.org/unodc/en/human-trafficking/global-report-on-trafficking-in-persons.html (accessed 23 January 2019).

53 See BBC news report, 'Nigeria Abductions: Timeline of events', *BBC News*, www.bbc.co.uk/news/world-africa-27342757 (accessed 23 January 2019).

54 See the Canada, House of Commons report November 2016, www.our commons.ca/DocumentViewer/en/42-1/FAAE/report-8/page-33 (accessed 23 January 2019).

55 McGowan, *Brave*, 29.

56 Caroline Walker Bynum, *Holy Feast and Holy Fast, The Religious Significance of Food to Medieval Women* (Los Angeles and London: University of California Press, 1987); Rudolph M. Bell, *Holy Anorexia* (Chicago, IL and London: University of Chicago Press, 1985).

57 Bynum, *Holy Feast*, 209.

58 Cited in Caroline Walker Bynum, *Fragmentation and Redemption: Essays on Gender and the Human Body in Medieval Religion* (New York: Zone Books, 1991), 55–6, n.7.

59 Bynum, *Holy Feast*, 209–10.

60 Bynum, *Holy Feast*.

61 Bynum, *Holy Feast*, 210.

62 Bynum, *Holy Feast*, 210.

63 Simone de Beauvoir, *The Second Sex*, trans. Constance Borde and Sheila Malovany-Chevallier (London: Vintage Books, 2011), 731.

64 Beauvoir, *The Second Sex*, 732.

65 Bell, *Holy Anorexia*, 20–1. William N. Davis, a clinical psychologist, writes an Epilogue to Bell's book in an endeavour to bridge the gap between 'holy' anorexia and anorexia nervosa. He similarly argues that a main marker of anorexia nervosa is a dread of fatness and a self-conscious, unremitting pursuit of thinness. See Bell, *Holy Anorexia*, 180–1. However, it should be borne in mind that characterizing anorexia as simply a 'desire to be thin' is perhaps an oversimplification of a mental illness that is affected by a combination of biological, psychological and environmental factors.

66 Bynum, *Holy Feast*, 294.

67 See Bell, *Holy Anorexia*, 16. See also Donald Weinstein and Rudolph M. Bell, *Saints and Society: The Two Worlds of Western Christendom, 1000–1700* (Chicago, IL: University of Chicago Press, 1982), 227–8.

68 Barbara Newman, *From Virile Woman to Woman Christ, Studies in Medieval Religion and Literature* (Philadelphia, PA: University of Pennsylvania Press, 1995).

69 Newman, *From Virile Woman*, 2, 3, 22.

70 Bynum, *Holy Feast*, 294–6.

71 Bell, *Holy Anorexia*; see in particular 16–21. See also Weinstein and Bell, *Saints and Society*, 86–99, which paints a dismal picture of women's place in a society where they had little control over their lives and bodies.

72 Judith Butler, 'Performative Acts and Gender Constitution: An essay in Phenomenology and Feminist Theory', *Writing on the Body: Female Embodiment and Feminist Theory*, ed. Katie Conboy, Nadia Medina, Sarah Stanbury (New York: Columbia University Press, 1997), 403.

73 Butler, 'Performative Acts', 403.

74 David Ghanim, *Gender and Violence in the Middle East* (Westport, CT: Praeger, 2009), 76.

75 Quoted in Ghanim, *Gender and Violence*, 76 n.25.

76 Quoted in Ghanim, *Gender and Violence.*

77 Beauvoir, *The Second Sex*, 610, 773.

78 Ghanim, *Gender and Violence*, 76.

79 Graham Davey, *The Anxiety Epidemic: The Causes of Our Modern-Day Anxieties* (London: Robinson, 2018).

80 Davey, *Anxiety Epidemic*, i.

81 See van der Kolk, *Body*, in particular 44, 51–73.

82 van der Kolk, *Body*, 43, 54.

83 In addition to van der Kolk, see also Jeffrey Prager, 'Lost Childhood, Lost Generations: The Intergenerational Transmission of Trauma', *Journal of Human Rights* 2, no. 2 (2003), 173–81; P. Fossion, M. Rejas, L. Servais, I. Pelc and S. Hirsch, 'Family Approach with Grandchildren of Holocaust Survivors', *American Journal of Psychotherapy* 57, no. 4 (2003), 519–27; Gabriele Schwab, *Haunting Legacies: Violent Histories and Transgenerational Trauma* (New York: Columbia University Press, 2010); Yael Danieli, *International Handbook of Multigenerational Legacies of Trauma* (New York: Plenum, 1998).

PART 3

Feminist Trauma Theologies: Christian Communities and Trauma

8

Women in the Pulpit:
A History of Oppression and Perseverance

LEAH ROBINSON

Just bear in mind that you have to be ten times 'better' in every respect than a man going for ordination and it would be very helpful if you were submissive, motherly, and not overly educated and can accept decisions with which you don't agree quietly and without retort ... Don't refer to God as She and make it very clear that you are heterosexual and if you're not, say so apologetically ... women have fought a long battle, but they have had to play the slow game.[1]

Introduction

There is a young girl who is about 13 years old standing in front of a minister's office in a traditional Southern Baptist church in a small town in Georgia, USA. The girl nervously plays with the hem of her sleeve and tries to straighten her wild hair that refuses to sit right. She isn't someone who is usually at the front door of an office. She doesn't tend to get into trouble at school, so this direct interaction with authority is something that is new and terrifying to her. The girl is ushered in, and she sits in a chair that is about two sizes too big for her tiny frame. She stares at the books on the shelf in amazement. The minister asks her why she is here. The girl responds that she feels as though she has been called by God into the ministry. Specifically, the girl states, 'I want to be a preacher.' The minister sits for a moment, shakes his head, and says, 'You can't be a preacher.' The girl stares back in shock and confusion. She had felt that pull in her heart towards this. She had felt God telling her that this was her future in no uncertain terms. She knew she had the skills and the ability to be great at it. 'Why?' the girl asks. 'Because women can't be ministers. God tells us so in the Bible,' replies the minister. Invoking the Bible to a Southern Baptist is as powerful as a Southern grandma's stare when you are acting up in church. It is the law. The final say. The girl leaves the office, head down. She must have been wrong, she thinks. If God says so, then she must have been wrong.

It is probably not a stretch of the imagination to learn that this young girl was the author of this chapter. This interaction happened when I was a young woman, and it stayed with me throughout my ordination, into my ministry, and to this day. Although significant to me at the time (it changed the course of my life plan), this interaction did not seem significant enough to be worth anything to the academy. That being said, this chapter came about, like most of my academic work, through a desire to discuss in a theological manner the issues that are of vital importance to the world in which we live today. As a card-carrying practical theologian, I have always had a desire to see what is going on theologically in the here and now. My desire to offer a platform for the voices to the voiceless is an overwhelming theme in my research. Whether it is peace-building, violence, theological oppression, or now trauma and feminist theology, it has always been of the utmost concern that I try and keep my eyes open to theology in all the nooks and crannies of the world in which we live.

This collection is one such opportunity. When I first began thinking about the idea of trauma and feminist theology, the possibilities in our contemporary world are – unfortunately – endless. In my contemplations, I began to speak with the wonderful women in theology whom I feel very lucky to know. As these conversations progressed, it became increasingly clear that the process of ordination served as an extremely high and also an extremely low experience for many women. As I enquired deeper into this topic, the stories that began to emerge were seemingly endless. Although ordination of women is accepted across a wide swath of global, Christian denominations, I began to realize that the trauma that can occur throughout the process of ordination is very present with many women. In other words, there is lifelong trauma that occurs when women feel called into ordination but experience negative events prior to, during and after their ordination. And these experiences have consequential influence on women's understanding of themselves in relation to God, in relation to their own bodies, and in relation to their calling as ministers.

At first I thought I would write this piece as autoethnography: a chapter along the lines of Natalie Wigg-Stevenson's fantastic article, 'You Don't Look Like a Baptist Minister'.[2] But, as I spoke to more and more women ministers, I began to realize that this was not just my story to own. I sent out a call via social media for women to tell me about their stories of trauma and ordination, and the emails flooded in (and continue to do so). I was so eager to write this chapter because it became increasingly clear that I had put a finger on the pulse of something very real, and very present in the lives of these women. I was both excited to research and gravely disappointed that the data was so overwhelming for this particular type of trauma.

As I reflected on my own experience of ordination, I realized that this is a topic that had been weighing on my own mind for a very long time. My own experience growing up Southern Baptist in a rural town in north Georgia where I was rejected as a minister was a deeply traumatic theological mismatch to me. And I was not alone. I am not under the impression I am the first to tell this story, but these narratives need to be repeated until change occurs. The first-hand account of the pain and suffering within our community should be highlighted until this experience of trauma is seen as being a problem that demands attention.

As a side note, I should state the fact that I am deeply appreciative of the women and men who came before me to pave the way for the ordination of women to even be possible. I applaud their bravery, their hermeneutical intelligence, and their voices that were loud enough to stir the hearts of the most ardent rejecters of female ministry. We have come a long way. But this story is not about that, though there are many volumes that can be read that praise the journey to equality that women in ministry have undertaken. This chapter takes a different approach. It acknowledges this important history of women breaking through the stained-glass ceiling of the clergy, but it asks the question, 'What comes next?'

This chapter offers a mixed methodology to answer this question. It includes both literature engagement as well as qualitative research via surveys with women in the UK and the USA. In regards to the literature, I will look briefly at the history of feminist theological engagement with women's ordination, as well as offer a brief introduction to trauma theology. I will then look at three areas that hold particularly traumatic events for women in the ordination process: denial of ordination, rejection in ordination, and being ordained. This chapter will examine these particular time periods for women within the ordination process. It will contain stories of traumatic moments women have suffered in these time periods, as well as the emotions that were closely associated with these events.

A question that could arise from the study is: are these women's experiences really traumatic? According to Shelly Rambo's groundbreaking text on trauma theology, trauma is 'an event that continues, that persists in the present. Trauma is what does not go away. It persists in symptoms that live on in the body, in the intrusive fragments of memories that return.'[3] Much like the young girl in North Georgia who continues to carry the weight of feeling inadequate in the face of her rejection from the Southern Baptist Church, the women who speak in this chapter also associate their own experiences with this understanding of trauma. As a result, they have self-identified their experiences as traumatic, and their understandings of these events as traumatic will be honoured in this text.

My overall question for this chapter is: in what ways does trauma theology speak to the experiences of women who have suffered during the ordination process? Based on the stories that have emerged in this research, serious consideration needs to be placed on the ordination process for women. The seeming freedom of women to become ordained does not mean equal treatment under the law. And it often seems as though women take their freedom of ordination as a signal of equality while simultaneously bearing the burdens of trauma as they navigate this new 'accepted' status. I argue that we do this because of feelings of inadequacy, shame and imposter syndrome that continue to be enacted upon women clergy in order to make them feel as though their status within the Church is precarious at best, and a gift from their male counterparts at worst.

I will begin an exploration of this question by looking at the ways that women were portrayed throughout two key points in Christian history: the patristic period and the Reformation. These periods solidified the view of women as second-class humans within the context of Christianity. I will then show responses by feminist theologians as they pertain to this history.

The Role of Women in the Christian Church: Duelling Perspectives

When did women begin to be systematically removed from the overall narrative of Christian history? When did they start to be seen as something other than able carriers of the good news of Jesus? This development can be traced to the first hundred years of the Christian Church. The early Church Fathers (theologians who lived during the patristic period roughly AD 100–400) solidified the theological belief that women were second-class creations. Tertullian, writing 'On the Apparel of Women', states that women are the 'devil's gateway', as well as the very reason that 'the Son of God had to die'.[4] Origen, another early Church Father, adds that men should not bother sitting and listening to a woman because there is no point in doing so. He says, 'if she says admirable things or even saintly things, this is of little consequence because it came out of the mouth of a woman'.[5] These are but two examples during this period that could be discussed in relation to men's misuse of theology as misogyny, but there are many more. The early Church Fathers were pivotal in crafting theological stereotypes of women that have lasted until our present day. They are also the foundation upon which the contemporary Church (and its theology) sits. As a result, their writings of women and women's place in the Church and in society are of incredible consequence.

The Reformers of the sixteenth and seventeenth centuries, despite their desire to create a new way of understanding the Christian Church, still adhered to a theology that placed women as second class to males in the divine order. Martin Luther writes that women had a 'weaker mind'[6] than men, and that women 'did not equal the glory of the male creature'.[7] The ever-cheery Scottish Reformer John Knox writes in his book, *The First Blast of the Trumpet against the Monstrous Regiment of Women*: 'Nature, I say, paints women further to be weak, frail, impatient, feeble and foolish, and experience has declared them to be inconstant, variable, cruel and lacking the spirit of counsel and regiment [or leadership].'[8]

Portraying women as being either too weak or too emotional for ministry is something that will painfully ring true in the ears of women who have gone through the ordination process and it is a common criticism of women in ministry. A fear of our ability to be able to handle tough situations within the context of leadership without completely breaking down is also not a new criticism. The Reformers, despite their desire to create a bold new world within the context of the Christian Church, were still held back by archaic and immature caricatures of women.

Dismantling these caricatures represents some of the first tasks tackled by feminist theologians in the 1960s and 1970s. A further area of study for these scholars related to examining the exclusion of women from the narrative of Christian history and the misuse of Paul's writings to circumvent women's calling into ministry. In her text *In Memory of Her*,[9] Elisabeth Schüssler Fiorenza breaks down a particular argument that has long kept women out of the pulpit. She argues that the idea that there is one way to organize the Church, and that Jesus himself dictated this particular way, is not historically or biblically sound:

> This biblicist-historicist understanding of early Christian beginnings still prevails in many textbooks and in the consciousness of many Christians and theologians. According to this understanding, Jesus instituted the church, ordained the twelve, and determined the institutional forms of the church. The apostles continued the mission and work of Jesus, and their message in turn is codified in the New Testament as Holy Scripture.[10]

The understanding of Jesus as creating the institution of the Church, and that no later developments deviated from that creation, is dangerous and false according to Schüssler Fiorenza. She argues:

> such an ideological construct of early Christian beginnings is no longer scientifically acceptable and *is theologically destructive of the self-identity of Christian women* who, according to this portrayal of early Christian development, were members but not leaders within the church.[11]

Susan Ross, a feminist theologian who is interested in feminist expressions of worship, traces the developments of the systematic removal of women from the narrative of leadership of the early Church. She argues that church history portrays women's roles in the ministries of both Jesus and Paul as being casual at best, non-existent at worst. Ross argues that this understanding is a result of Christianity becoming the official religion of the Roman Empire in the fourth century. During this time period, women's roles within the context of house churches were drastically reduced. As Christianity became a public religion, women were forced out of their leadership roles.[12] With the development of Christianity as an official religion of the Empire, there was a move towards a systematic, legalistic turn for the grass-roots religion. The Church became powerful, and with this power – much like other forms of discrimination – came oppression of certain groups. This resulted in a removal of women from the formal church structure.

Another prominent feminist theologian, Rosemary Radford Ruether, argues for the inclusion of women in ministry and explores the systems that meant women were seen as being less-than by the Church throughout history. She is not surprised by the exclusion of women from the office of ministry, and says that it is par for the course of the history of patriarchy within Christianity (and any system of power).[13] Ruether argues that female exclusion from the ministry is not related to the nature of the position, but instead its place within societal leadership.

> The arguments for women's exclusion from ministry are application of the general theology of headship and female subordination. This sub-ordination, while attributed to women's physiological role in procreation, extends to an inferiority of mind and soul as well.[14]

Ruether also addresses the recent developments of the acceptance of women in ministry in the contemporary setting. While this development of seeming equality is helpful for women to some degree, it is still, Ruether argues, inviting women to a world that has largely been shaped and created by and for men. Adopting the same clothing, stances, voices and actions as male counterparts means that women 'play the ministerial role by endlessly proving that they can think, feel, and act like "one of the boys"'.[15] This play-acting is key, according to Reuther, because women who are being admitted into the ministry are doing so under the rules of a system that was not created with them in mind.

Within this idea of the male-created role of the ordained minister, and indeed the Church itself, is the understanding of the role of femininity within the context of female ministers. A constant argument against female ordi-nation is that women should use their feminine attributes to lead ministries that do not include men. So, ministries like children, youth and women's groups are acceptable, but not senior minister of a church. If women do become leaders of churches, they have seemingly done so in token numbers. According to Benjamin Knoll and Camme Jo Bolin's recent study of wom-en's ordination, three out of five US denominations allow women to serve in a leading ministerial role. Despite this, women are senior ministers in only 11 per cent of congregations (as of 2015).[16]

Feminist theology speaks to this trend by highlighting the difficulties that women experience in the pastorate (even if their denominations are sup-portive of their ordination). While 'allowing' female ordination in certain churches, the churches do not address the unjust systems that have caused women to be excluded from this realm for centuries. Churches also do not address the historical stereotypes that follow women into the pulpit. Accord-ing to Wigg-Stevenson, 'the church and the world become co-conspirators in injustice, with the church somewhat ironically losing its distinctiveness and potential prophetic voice'.[17]

Asking women to bear the burden of a world and a church that is bent on silencing the voices of women in leadership positions is a mighty task. The Church has historically wrestled with its own view of women in ministry:

on the one hand acknowledging the need for a more inclusive vision, but on the other denying the calls of those who do not 'embody identity markers which much social privilege already accrues (e.g. white, heterosexual, able-bodied, male, cis-gender)'.[18] The result, however, is that women are often called to ordination and denied, enter the ordination process and are rejected, or become ordained and suffer once they are in their positions of authority. These are traumatic events that showcase the emotional, psychological and spiritual trauma that women carry as they attempt to fulfil a divine calling. According to Wigg-Stevenson, this weighted-down state cannot be maintained:

> A feminist theological vision cannot rest satisfied with a woman's body bearing the burden of liberative change ... transformative judgment requires that my body be objectified, excluded, made anxious, and feel dissonance between its various locations of belonging ... this interpretation feeds the myth of redemptive suffering that feminist theologians have long been resisting.[19]

This redemptive suffering that women take on as a result of actualizing their own calling can result in serious trauma. While many might scoff at the idea of suffering within ordination as trauma, there is an incredible spiritual crisis that can occur when one feels called to do something by the God one worships. At the same time, women are told that they cannot do such a thing because of their physiology. Not only that, but the historic theology that implies that physiology in some way limits the ability of females to be intelligent, capable, spiritual beings means that women are left feeling as though they are less-than in divine creation. This often results in the following emotions: feelings of inadequacy in relation to our own bodies, as our bodies are linked to the inability to live out our call fully; shame that comes when we are held to a different standard during ordination processes because of our bodies; and the feeling of being an imposter once we do reach ordained status – because of our inability to change our bodies to fit what is considered normative.

These are the traumatic emotions that can and do occur with women who are brave enough to follow their calling. As Ruether puts it:

> Women in ministry, like all women trying to function in public roles under male rules, find themselves in a double bind. They are allowed success only by being better than men at the games of masculinity, while at the same time they are rebuked for having lost their femininity. In such a system it is not possible for women to be equal, but only to survive in a token and marginal way at tremendous physical and psychological cost.[20]

What is this 'tremendous physical and psychological cost' that Ruether is referring to? This cost manifests itself in areas of emotions like shame, guilt and inadequacy, which can lead to feelings of trauma by way of depression, despair and disconnect with their own bodies, their own religion, their own call and their own God. We will move now to a discussion about what this might look like in relation to the area of trauma, and specifically trauma theology.

A Brief Discussion of Trauma

Trauma studies, and specifically trauma theology, is a relatively new area of theological enquiry. That being said, major texts are being written in this area as people begin to examine the toll that trauma can take on the day-to-day existence of those who have experienced it. Undoubtedly the most comprehensive book to come out of the theological study of trauma in recent times is Shelly Rambo's monograph, *Spirit and Trauma: A Theology of Remaining*.[21] Rambo's text offers insights into the understanding of trauma as an ongoing state. Trauma lives on after the initial traumatic event occurs, and it is with this idea that Rambo frames her text. What happens when we are left with the memories of a traumatic event, especially when that memory is relived throughout our entire lives? Trauma, according to Rambo, 'is an event that continues, that persists in the present. Trauma is what does not go away. It persists in symptoms that live in the body, in the intrusive fragments of memories that return.'[22]

From a theological perspective, Rambo envisions that trauma is like the death and resurrection of Jesus. The suffering of Jesus is a traumatic series of moments. Jesus is ridiculed, abused and shamed in the crucifixion event. Despite this traumatic event, the crucifixion is a central event in Christian theology because of what follows – the resurrection. With the death of Jesus on the cross, new life is ushered in and is available for humanity. Jesus overcomes death and lives eternally. While this narrative can provide hope for many, it can also gloss over the 'remaining' period that exists between the death and resurrection. The in-between time or, put simply, life after the traumatic event and before the eternal life of the resurrection.

This in-between time of living is key to understanding those who have experienced trauma, according to Rambo. Those who have experienced traumatic events reside in this time. They feel a disconnect with the reality that surrounds them after the trauma. There are emotions of shame, guilt and loss in relation to the world around them. There is also a disconnect with their physical self, as if their bodies are not their own. It is in this in-between place where those who have experienced trauma often relive their traumatic events. The memories of these events stay with those who have suffered throughout this remaining phase, even if it looks on the outside as if the one who has suffered trauma has 'recovered'. So the focus of Rambo's work is this remaining time – those who are living and dealing with the in-between of death (trauma) and resurrection (a return to life).

Another text that deals with the idea of trauma as a theological idea is Deborah van Deusen Hunsinger, *Bearing the Unbearable: Trauma, Gospel, and Pastoral Care*.[23] Van Deusen Hunsinger's text is more in the realm of pastoral care to those who have experienced trauma, and while this chapter does not attempt to enter into this field, it is worth noting that this text is a worthy companion to those who are entering into a ministry where they might be dealing with people who have experienced traumatic events. Van Deusen Hunsinger shares with Rambo many of the same concepts about trauma. She speaks about the idea of trauma being unique because it limits people's ability to adapt to ordinary life after the traumatic event occurs. This echos Rambo's understanding of the status of 'remaining'. Remaining is what is left after the ability to return to a normalized life is impossible under the memories of the traumatic circumstances.

Another area where both authors are in agreement is the importance of witness by/for those who have experienced trauma. Van Deusen Hunsinger states, 'time and again one hears people minimizing or discounting the anguish of others, essentially encouraging them to "get over it"'.[24] Van Deusen Hunsinger's answer to this is that space must be given to those who have experienced trauma to tell their stories. They need a listener they trust to bear witness to their pain, and they need to be offered time to bring their story together in a way that makes sense to them (even if it does not make sense to others).[25] Bearing witness to trauma and being witnessed by others is a key aspect of those who are stuck in this 'remaining' status.

Rambo likewise highlights the importance of witness within the context of trauma. According to Rambo,

> although the suffering is present, it is often not given voice in order to keep a certain understanding of the world in place. Though it is marked in the text, it is not vocalized, because the pattern of things is smoother when it is not spoken.[26]

Witness, in this context, encourages those who have experienced trauma to speak out about their pain. It also encourages those who are around people who have experienced trauma to listen and learn. Likewise, by its nature, it confronts those who have silenced, ignored or even exacerbated the trauma of an oppressed group. Christianity has silenced the voices of women throughout history. The institution has mocked women and their status. Some of the 'greats' of Christian history are overwhelmingly misogynistic. And while women are able to be ordained in some denominations through-out the world, we can often turn a blind eye to the witness of the continuing 'holy' discrimination that occurs.

What does this type of witness in the 'remaining' look like? The following sections offer insights into the lives of those who have suffered trauma in the processes of ordination, and who stand in their positions between the death of trauma and the fullness of life in order to tell their stories.

Denial of Ordination: Inadequacy

The women I have surveyed for this project have all either attempted ordination or are currently ordained. Despite this, many of the women whom I have spoken to have stories relating to the difficulties that they faced when attempting to realize their call in a concrete way. Much like my own difficulties in the Southern Baptist Church, some of the women surveyed faced feelings of inadequacy over their own calling. Often these feelings were a result of denominational theology that made them feel as though they were not able to perform the role of minister because of their gender.

One surveyed ordained minister, Miriam, offers insights into her ordination into the Baptist Church where she had feelings of inadequacy caused by the members of the denominational body. In this particular case, Miriam felt the call into ministry while she was pursuing her master of divinity degree. She was already serving as an intern at her local Baptist church, and so she decided to put forward a request to the church to ordain her into the ministry. She recounts what happened next:

> Immediately the Chair of the Deacons at the time came to my home to inform me that he could not support that request, nothing personal he says, because I am a woman. I specifically remember him asking me that he might be able to support it if I promise him that I won't ever use that ordination for anything besides teaching in a college setting. I told him that I didn't know what the future held for me so I couldn't make that promise. He agreed to send the request to the local association of churches that typically handle these requests. Within a week, every member of that local association resigned from the committee.[27]

Eventually, Miriam was able to go through with her ordination. She credits the women in her congregation for supporting her through this time. Her church claimed that Baptists have autonomy when it comes to matters such as these, and as a result they proceeded with the ordination at a local level. These actions by the authorities within the church are telling, however. Based completely on their own bias against her physiology, these men were not willing to listen or discuss her call to ministry. They also removed themselves from their positions as a result of her attempting to pursue this call.

This sense of inadequacy also transcends denominational bureaucracy. Many of those who pursue ordination in non-supportive denominations find that their family and friends (who might also be a part of these denominations) are not sympathetic to their endeavours. Miriam experienced this as she went through her ordination in the Baptist Church.

> [At my ordination service] My husband's parents came for the occasion. And though my entire family attended the ordination service for my brother who was ordained into the ministry a couple of years earlier, no

family member attended mine. For me, the lack of family support was the most traumatic part of the whole thing. My father had argued with me on the issue, basically saying that God's desire is peace, not contention. So if my ordination is causing problems, then it must not be of God.[28]

The pull between pursuing God's call and not having the support of your close family in pursuing this call can create a traumatic disconnect between what you feel you are supposed to be doing as a vocation and the importance of having your loved ones support your decision. In Miriam's case her call was denied by those she loved the most. She was made to feel as though her call was not from God because it challenged the historic oppression of women in ministry. She continued on with her ordination despite these traumatic events, but the feelings of inadequacy that resulted in this lack of support followed her throughout her ministry.

Across an ocean, in the UK, Ruth wrestled with her own sense of calling in the ministry. She was within a 'conservative evangelical fellowship' when she felt her first call to ministry. However, according to Ruth, because of her denomination's beliefs, she 'did not have the theology to back that up'.[29] As a result, Ruth tried to explore the idea of women in leadership on her own. She knew that she had felt the call, and she wanted to further understand why women were denied this type of position in her denomination:

> I sensed that I was called into a ministry of leadership and so found evidence of women leaders in the Bible: Lydia, Priscilla, as well as Old Testament characters. Eventually I discovered Junia and the shameful cover up of her role in Church leadership. I reasoned that God would not have given me the gifts and the call if it was contrary to His word.[30]

Ruth's actions of digging deeper into Christian history are not unusual for those women who feel called to ordination. There is a desire from women in this position to find examples within the biblical text or Christian history that provide confirmation of their own call. As we have discussed, however, the early Church systematically removed these figures from the narrative of Christian history. Theologians used selective and misogynistic hermeneutics to justify oppression of women in their texts.

Despite the attempts to silence the women of the biblical text/early Church, their stories have slowly started to be collected by scholars who wish to highlight the figures who paved the way for women in ministry today. The importance of lifting these figures up to shine in the context of the heritage of Christianity is of vital importance.[31] Much like Ruth, I began my own research after I was rejected from starting the process of ordination in the Southern Baptist Church. What I found was a hidden history that offered examples of the wonderful leadership that women offered throughout Christian history. Finding the stories of these women helped to confirm my call within the context of ministry. It also lifted the feelings of inadequacy that I (and others) feel as a result of the removal of role models that we can look up to in regards to our own calling. As research continues, these women's stories link up to our own, and the result is a divinely inspired lineage that we can hold on to in the midst of trauma. It historically grounds us in a world where we can often feel like strangers.

Rejection in Ordination: Shame

There are several forms of rejection that can happen when someone is in the ordination process. One example of this type of rejection occurs within the process of ordination. These events can cause those who are training to be ministers to question their own calling. Ruth experienced this second type of rejection as a result of conversations with friends about her husband, who is also a minister. As Ruth was training to be a minister, a friend began to discuss her ministry courses with her:

> My husband is also a minister and a friend, on asking what I was going to do when I was finished training, said: 'You've done this course [as if it was a night class or a hobby], but you have to remember that your husband's call comes first!' I should add this is not how my husband saw it! Another (male) friend said, 'Are you going to work with your husband when you are finished? I'm just wondering about the authority!'[32]

We see here the idea that even with Ruth's ordination being accepted, her call is seen as being less important than that of her husband's. Her friend accepts that Ruth has a calling, but there is rejection in regards to the equality of that call to her husband's. This is often the case with women in ministry, especially in denominations where women's ordination is accepted. Women are told they can become ordained, and that they should follow their call, but that call is seen as being less important than their male counterparts' call.

Within the process of ordination there are those who begin to follow their call but are rejected once they begin. Deborah lives in the UK, and felt called to pursue ordination. She began a path to ordination that seemed like an obstacle course involving meetings, projects and a great deal of financial investment. Eventually, Deborah was told that she could meet with an official panel that would decide her ordination status. During this time period, Deborah's husband of 27 years was discovered to be having an affair and said he wanted to leave their marriage. Deborah was assured this would not influence her application. The panel did suggest that Deborah take some time to reflect, which she did. She followed all the guidelines of the panel, but she was told after a year that she was not going to be ordained. The reasoning behind the rejection in the ordination process was as follows: 'It is because I have had three marital relationships and that is not the image that the [denomination] wants portrayed by the priests. There is no discussion or enquiry into these relationships.'[33] Deborah was told she had the option to meet with another representative of the church in a year's time, but that it probably will not make a difference to the decision not to ordain her. Since then, Deborah's name has been officially removed from the mailing list of her regional church group. 'I now feel officially rejected,'[34] she said.

Deborah reflects on this rejection of her calling – a rejection based on theological interpretation concerning what is moral and immoral – in the following comment: 'I feel rejected and second class ... I feel I'm not a good person. I do not meet the standards of morality required by my church, a church that has been in my bones since I was a young child.'[35] The Church rejected Deborah's ordination because of a situation that was not in her control. As a result, she carries the residual effects of this by way of shame about her status. Her further removal from mailing lists reflects a wider rejection by the Church at large. Rejection, either by questioning the importance of one's call or by complete rejection of one's ordination status based on moral interpretations of the few, highlights the level at which women have to 'perform' in order to be seen as being equal to their male counterparts in the midst of the process of ordination.

I will conclude with a final thought from Deborah, who expresses what this rejection and trauma feels like in a personal way:

> [As] horrible as it sounds, it is like having to give birth to a stillborn child. I have to go through it but unlike my peers, it will have no life. You may find this a flippant and insensitive use of a simile but I can assure you that this is the nearest I can get to the feeling of loss for something I have nurtured over six years but to which I cannot give life.[36]

Being Ordained: Imposter Syndrome

I am at the American Academy of Religion's annual conference in Denver, 2018. I am sitting with a colleague and a collection of my colleague's friends at a dinner that I was graciously invited to. The group is comprised of male theologians and ministers from across the USA. I am the only woman. We exchange pleasantries throughout the meal until the subject of women's ordination comes up. I explain that I am an ordained minister. The man beside me says that he does not agree with ordaining women. He states that he sees no biblical texts that suggest women should be ordained. His friend across the table jokes and says that he probably should have started our conversation with that admission: 'She probably wouldn't have been so nice to you the whole evening if you had told her what you thought!' They both laugh. All of a sudden, I am 13 again and back in my minister's office where I'm sitting in the seat that is too large. He is telling me that I cannot be a minister because God said so. I am not good enough. Twenty-plus years after this event in that office I am an ordained minister. I have a PhD in theology from a world-renowned university. I teach theological studies to students in the United Kingdom and the United States, but at this table, with these men, my position and my titles mean nothing. I am an imposter. Just like that, in an instant, the trauma returns.

The feeling of being an imposter follows women even after they are ordained. Whether a woman comes from a supportive denomination or one that allows for congregational autonomy, ordained women are not only held to a different standard but are often made to feel as though their status is not as important as their male counterparts. This can often manifest in belittling female ministers. Wigg-Stevenson explores this in her article, 'You Don't Look Like a Baptist Minister'.[37] Throughout this article, she encounters members of her own denomination who tell her that she does not look or sound like a typical minister in the Baptist tradition. She believes that this is intended as a compliment, but it is difficult for her to hear, because the idea of being an imposter, or somehow 'getting away with something' in her ordination, is ever-present.

An example of this occurs at her ordination service. During the service, Wigg-Stevenson preaches. After the sermon, a man comes up to her and says that one of the 'pillars' of the church approved of her sermon. The man says, 'When I asked [the member] what he thought of your sermon, do you know what he said? He laughs. "Couldn't hear a word she said, but I sure enjoyed watching her say it."'[38]

Ruth experienced an almost identical scenario in her ministry.

> Generally when I led services I was well received, although one gentleman told me he couldn't hear a word I said, despite the very excellent sound system and the fact that the most common compliment that I would receive at the door was how clearly I spoke.[39]

There is a commonality in these stories, despite taking place on two different continents. It is a simple criticism, that one cannot be heard, but it symbolizes something much greater. Much like the women in Christian history whose voices were silenced by men who were in power, so this practice continues even when women are speaking from the pulpit. The idea here of not being able to hear someone who is speaking clearly and loudly possibly reflects a desire by some not to hear what is being said, and specifically not to hear what is being said by those they think should not be speaking. Ruth believes that the issue here is a 'blindness',[40] that some people have a blindness that

> prevents them from seeing the truth in any arguments other than their own. Somewhere in the psyche of some people there is something, possibly a result of upbringing I think, which cannot dare to admit that they may be wrong, or that a different point of view has merit.[41]

With congregations that have historically rejected women in ministry there is difficulty adjusting to a new reality of women in the pulpit. A common reaction to this development is to belittle or reject women who serve as minsters; alternatively, as is present in these examples, to be deaf to the words of those who are speaking.

The consequence of this 'deafness' is that those who are ordained feel as though they are imposters. Despite going through discerning a call, training for ministry and finally ordination, women are still made to feel as though they are not doing what they should be doing in the context of the Church. Miriam says:

> The feeling of inadequacy or being an imposter is the most prevalent for me. When I tell people that I am ordained, I often feel as if I'm admitting something I should be ashamed of ... Though I've gotten more comfortable with it, I still feel like a failure in some ways. I never talk about that part of who I am around my family still. Whenever I refer to my experiences in the church, when I'm in class or just a conversation, I feel like a fraud. Like I'm a wannabe who never could have actually been a minister.[42]

Even when women have moved past what they see as the major hurdles in their ordination process, they are still faced with defending their status against those who wish to make them feel as though they are a fraud. These recurring acts of belittlement mean that we are constantly reminded of our feelings of inadequacy, despite our accomplishments or our abilities as ministers. It is a method of control, and it can be deeply traumatic for those who are made to feel as though they have somehow 'gotten away with something' simply by following their call from God.

Conclusion

> The student of trauma is one who bears witness to a phenomenon that continually escapes comprehension and that, as a result, is continually contested, forgotten and covered over in public discourse. A student of trauma works to uncover and excavate what does not come into light.[43]

The hope for this chapter is that the trauma experienced by the women whose voices you have witnessed here will not be forgotten. Not only will their stories not be forgotten, but also their stories can provide a window into the continued suffering of those who attempt to pursue their calling from God. As we listen to the stories of women who have suffered trauma in the midst of their ordination, we are reminded of their witness and why their witness is important.

Trauma is fundamentally something that we want to prevent people from having to experience. We hear stories of trauma and we are called to action to try and offer some form of sympathy, empathy and justice for whatever situation has occurred. We do not want those who suffer to continue to suffer. But what do we do if there is a trauma that is so deep, so entrenched in Christian community, that women continue to experience it for 2,000 years?

The incredible harm that is taking place against women who are brave enough to step forward and follow their God-given call into ministry is increasingly clear. Even in denominations where women are affirmed in their call, there is still belittling that takes place to increase feelings of inadequacy. Following the call to ministry means that women are often scrutinized to a much higher degree than their male counterparts. This can lead to rejection, and the shame that comes with this rejection can be immense. Alongside this scrutiny about the actuality of a call from God are the ever-present questions about women's feminine roles if they go through with their ordination. Even upon ordination, some women carry around a feeling of being an imposter, or a fraud. They have realized their call, but these memories of trauma continue to follow them. Women in ministry, who have suffered during and after ordination, remain with the traumatic memories of being not quite good enough in the eyes of their peers, loved ones and the Church as a whole.

Rambo uses examples from New Orleans in the United States to illustrate her points about the idea of remaining in the midst of suffering. She speaks to a minister who explains that, after Hurricane Katrina devastated the city, there was increasing pressure for people to move on as quickly as possible. The minister rejects this pressure. Rambo embraces this imagery of the storm:

> The story of trauma is a story about the storm that does not go away. It is a story of remaining ... The narrative of a triumphant resurrection can often operate in such a way as to promise a radically new beginning to those who have experienced a devastating event ... This way of reading can, at its best, provide a sense of hope and promise for the future. But it can also gloss over the realities of pain and loss, glorify suffering and justify violence.[44]

These women's stories are not unique. While we celebrate the fact that women are increasingly accepted in ministry, we do not acknowledge the trauma that they experienced on the journey to the pulpit. These are but some of the witnesses that have come forward to speak about their time in the process of accepting their call to ministry. And the traumatic events that include feelings of inadequacy, shame and the feeling of being an impostor stay with those who continue to minister in this context.

The brilliant acceptance of women as ministers at a denominational level cannot be understated. But the traumatic events that are associated with this inclusion can often be more than a human can bear. Our moves within the Christian Church towards inclusion continue as denominations around the world move their gaze to the ordination of LGBTQI members. I fear that the overt rejection of the call of women in ministry by certain members of the Church is but one story of what will continue to be a difficult journey for those who wish to hold ordination status. Moving forward, we must continue to bear witness to our traumas as women in ministry. We must not allow the stories of women in Christianity today to end up like the women in the early Church. As we are rejected by our peers and denominations, held to higher standards than our male counterparts, and made to feel as imposters, we must remember that we are fulfilling our calling from God. If those in the congregations have gone deaf to our words, then we must speak louder and with more frequency. We will offer a bold reality that says, 'If you want to reside in the pews, you will see our faces in the pulpit.' We do this not only for ourselves, but for all those who have suffered trauma as a result of what the Church has told them about their bodies, their colour, their sexuality or any identifying aspects of what makes a person a brilliant creation of God. What is important about this story is that it is ongoing – as the Church attempts to move itself towards a prophetic and justice-based witness, and away from misogyny, racism and homophobia – the story will continue. There will be more witnesses that come forward. While this time of change sounds like it will be filled with trauma and pain – there is hope. The hope lies in the fact that as we continue to push against ancient structures – we will remain called to God's divine plan. The Church, as a painfully human structure, cannot take that away from us. For, as Wigg-Stevenson states, despite events that have occurred in her ordination process which have caused her to question everything about herself in regards to her abilities to be a minister, she *is* a minister. And no one can take that away from her.

> But each time it happens, each time that potential opens us as someone declares you don't look like a Baptist minister, I wonder how possible it might be for those words to carry a message of healing and accept-ance rather than the judgment ... Not looking like a Baptist minister is exhausting when I'm simply trying to be the Baptist minister that I already, in fact, am.[45]

References

Clark, Elizabeth, *Women in the Early Church*, Wilmington, NC: Michael Glazier, 1983.

Fiorenza, Elisabeth Schüssler, *In Memory of Her: A Feminist Theological Recon-struction of Christian Origins*, New York: Crossroad, 1984.

Knoll, Benjamin R. and Cammie Jo Bolin, *She Preached the Word: Women's Ordin-ation in Modern America*, Oxford: Oxford University Press, 2018.

Knox, John, *First Blast of the Trumpet Against the Monstrous Regiment of Women*: www.gutenberg.org/files/9660/9660-h/9660-h.htm.

Luther, Martin, 'Commentary on Genesis': www.gutenberg.org/ebooks/48193?msg=welcome_stranger.

Macy, Gary, *The Hidden History of Women's Ordination*, Oxford: Oxford University Press, 2007.

Origen, *Fragments on 1 Corinthians*: www.newadvent.org/cathen/11306b.htm.

Rambo, Shelly, *Spirit and Trauma: A Theology of Remaining*, Louisville, KY: Westminster John Knox Press, 2010.

Ross, Susan A., 'Church and Sacrament – Community and Worship', in *The Cambridge Companion to Feminist Theology*, ed. Susan Frank Parsons, Cambridge: Cambridge University Press, 2008, 224–42.

Ruether, Rosemary Radford, *Sexism and God-Talk: Towards a Feminist Theology*, Boston, MA: Beacon Press, 1983.

Tertullian, 'On the Apparel of Women': www.newadvent.org/fathers/0402.htm.

Trible, Phyllis, *Texts of Terror: Literary-Feminist Readings of Biblical Narratives*, Grand Rapids, MI: Fortress Press, 1984.

van Deusen Hunsinger, Deborah, *Bearing the Unbearable: Trauma, Gospel, and Pastoral Care*, Grand Rapids, MI: Eerdmans, 2015.

Wigg-Stevenson, Natalie, 'You Don't Look Like a Baptist Minister: An Autoethnographic Retrieval of "Women's Experience" as an Analytic Category for Feminist Theology', *Feminist Theology* 25, no. 2 (2017), 182–196.

Notes

1 All surveys with women have been anonymized. Pseudonyms are in place. Survey with Deborah.

2 Natalie Wigg-Stevenson, 'You Don't Look Like a Baptist Minister: An Autoethnographic Retrieval of "Women's Experience" as an Analytic Category for Feminist Theology', *Feminist Theology* 25, no. 2 (2017), 182–96.

3 Shelly Rambo, *Spirit and Trauma: A Theology of Remaining* (Louisville, KY: Westminster John Knox Press, 2010), 2.

4 Tertullian, 'On the Apparel of Women', www.newadvent.org/fathers/0402.htm (accessed 9 February 2019).

5 Origen, *Fragments on 1 Corinthians*, www.newadvent.org/cathen/11306b.htm (accessed 9 February 2019).

6 Martin Luther, 'Commentary on Genesis', www.gutenberg.org/ebooks/48193?msg=welcome_stranger (accessed 9 February 2019).

7 Luther, 'Commentary on Genesis'.

8 John Knox, *First Blast of the Trumpet against the Monstrous Regiment of Women*, www.gutenberg.org/files/9660/9660-h/9660-h.htm (accessed 9 February).

9 Elisabeth Schüssler Fiorenza, *In Memory of Her: A Feminist Theological Reconstruction of Christian Origins* (New York: Crossroad, 1984).

10 Schüssler Fiorenza, *In Memory of Her*, 68–9.

11 Schüssler Fiorenza, *In Memory of Her*, 69.

12 Susan A. Ross, 'Church and Sacrament – Community and Worship', in *The Cambridge Companion to Feminist Theology*, ed. Susan Frank Parsons (Cambridge: Cambridge University Press, 2008), 227.

13 Rosemary Radford Ruether, *Sexism and God-Talk: Towards a Feminist Theology* (Boston, MA: Beacon Press, 1983), 194.

14 Ruether, *Sexism and God-Talk*, 195.

15 Ruether, *Sexism and God-Talk*, 200.

16 Benjamin R. Knoll and Cammie Jo Bolin, *She Preached the Word: Women's Ordination in Modern America* (Oxford: Oxford University Press, 2018), 10.

17 Wigg-Stevenson, 'You Don't Look Like a Baptist Minister', 193.

18 Wigg-Stevenson, 'You Don't Look Like a Baptist Minister', 193.

19 Wigg-Stevenson, 'You Don't Look Like a Baptist Minister', 193–4.

20 Ruether, *Sexism and God-Talk*, 201.

21 Rambo, *Spirit and Trauma*.

22 Rambo, *Spirit and Trauma*, 2.

23 Deborah van Deusen Hunsinger, *Bearing the Unbearable: Trauma, Gospel, and Pastoral Care* (Grand Rapids, MI: Eerdmans, 2015).

24 van Deusen Hunsinger, *Bearing the Unbearable*, 5.

25 van Deusen Hunsinger, *Bearing the Unbearable*, 11.

26 Rambo, *Spirit and Trauma*, 42.

27 Survey with Miriam.

28 Survey with Miriam.

29 Survey with Ruth.

30 Survey with Ruth.

31 For examples of these collections, see: Elizabeth Clark, *Women in the Early Church* (Wilmington, NC: Michael Glazier, 1983); Gary Macy, *The Hidden History of Women's Ordination* (Oxford: Oxford University Press, 2007); Phyllis Trible, *Texts of Terror: Literary-Feminist Readings of Biblical Narratives* (Grand Rapids, MI: Fortress Press, 1984).

32 Survey with Ruth.

33 Survey with Deborah.

34 Survey with Deborah.

35 Survey with Deborah.

36 Survey with Deborah.

37 Wigg-Stevenson, 'You Don't Look Like a Baptist Minister'.

38 Wigg-Stevenson, 'You Don't Look Like a Baptist Minister', 188.

39 Survey with Ruth.

40 Survey with Ruth.

41 Survey with Ruth.

42 Survey with Miriam.

43 Rambo, *Spirit and Trauma*, 25.

44 Rambo, *Spirit and Trauma*, 4.

45 Wigg-Stevenson, 'You Don't Look Like a Baptist Minister', 190.

9

The Precarious Position of Indian Christian Women in Cinema and Everyday Life

SONIA SOANS

Outside the west door of Westminster Abbey stands the statue of Esther John, a Pakistani Christian. The demure figure of Esther wrapped up in a sari is a familiar figure to me. Esther represents a long line of Christian martyrs, but specifically she reminds me of Christian women I have seen growing up. While she and I are separated by time and place, she seems familiar. Esther John was a nurse killed for her faith in 1960. Esther's case is not unusual or unheard of in Christian history. Similar to the saints before her, Esther's conversion caused her family and community to regard her decision with suspicion, an act that brought family dishonour. Commonly termed an 'honour-based crime', Esther's death must not be written off through such shorthand descriptions of crime against women within non-Western societies. Esther John's martyrdom points to the precarious position Asian women occupy with regard to their gender, faith and ethnicity. Each of these markers of identity renders women more vulnerable to oppression. Caste, class, religious and ethnic identities make women more vulnerable in their own unique way.

Violence against women is a significant problem around the world. While it is a universal problem, it also needs to be understood in its local context. Violence against Christian women has existed for as long as the faith has existed. Most of these women martyred for their faith have been immortalized as saints. In order to prevent such incidents from becoming mere footnotes in Christian history it is essential to understand the context in which they occur.

Christianity in South Asia

Christianity has existed in India since the first century, with many Christians tracing their origins back to the earliest missions of the first century brought by the apostle Thomas. This century also saw the arrival of the Jewish community in India.[1] 'St Thomas Christians', as they are called, make up a large part of the Christian population in Kerala, in South India. By the sixteenth century, the faith had grown and spread across the country during

Mughal rule, due to the work of Portuguese, German and British missions.[2] Historical accounts from that era show a cross-cultural exchange of ideas that led to the development of a distinctive art form that adapted Christian iconography into the existing Mughal style.[3]

During the colonial era, missionaries from Britain, Germany, Portugal, America and other Western countries helped set up churches, hospitals and schools. Their mission work included women and men alike. Missionary work included cultural changes and adjustments in how the Bible was transmitted. In an attempt to foster and tame native women's god-talk, women missionaries founded a seminary for Telugu women in 1922, introducing the Bible and teaching them literacy for their continued reading of the biblical texts.[4]

Currently, India has several Christian denominations, some dating back to the early centuries and some more recent. Where permitted, women contribute to and are ordained within the Church. Many continue to advocate for changes within their respective denominations. Yet, despite this longstanding history, the faith is often associated with foreign missionaries and colonialism, and used to vilify the community and question its allegiance to the state. These strains of thought have been found in the discourse of both ultra-nationalists and postcolonial thinkers who seek 'authentic' cultural heritage and communities. For example, the writing of Ashis Nandy,[5] which reclaims the loss of identity under colonial rule, uses similar metaphors of invoking that pride back through an idealized pre-colonial past. His writing is not dissimilar to the propaganda used by right-wing groups that discredit minorities and their allegiance to the Indian state.

Cultural amnesia surrounds origins of Christianity in India and the contributions of Christians in the nation. Cultural amnesia combined with political propaganda have rendered Christians and Christian history in India invisible. This has led to the community being construed as a product of colonization and coercion by missionaries. This lack of agency ascribed to the Christian community has often led to reconversion drives. In recent times the ghar wapsi (return home) movement, undertaken by right-wing vigilante forces, has attempted to return Christian converts to their original religion.[6] Similarly, the defence and reinvention of upper-caste traditions have become a source of violence against Dalit and non-Hindu women.[7]

Christianity is constructed as a foreign religion and one that has erased pre-existing pre-colonial culture. The loss of culture and tradition that is attributed to colonization is a deeply gendered process. Partha Chatterjee points out that this loss of culture was bifurcated and attributed to male and female spheres of life. Reclaiming one's identity, modernizing and maintaining tradition under colonialism became a gendered process. Science and industrialization were male spheres; this was an area in which Indian men were allowed to exert their power and learn from the colonist. Domesticity and rearing children was relegated to women who could claim this untouched space and raise a family. Nationalists in the late nineteenth century made a distinction between Western women (also assumed to be universally Christian) and Indian women, who were cautioned against imitating them. Those distinctions then continue to influence how the Indian state has constructed itself. Conflating the West with Christianity has left an indelible mark on the Indian psyche, which continues to attribute westernization to Christianity and vice versa.

Violence against Christian women in India and South Asia is not a recent phenomenon; it has been building up for decades and is often sublimated into the mundane. Research has shown that India is the fourth most dangerous country for women to live in; Afghanistan is ranked first on the list, followed by Congo and Pakistan.[8] This violence manifests itself through female foeticide, acid attacks, daily harassment, rape, honour-based violence, caste-based violence and domestic violence. Violence against women in India affects women of all ages and classes; however, its manifestations and justifications vary.

The Role of Cinema

Cinema is a powerful medium for transmitting ideas. In India, it has often been a primary source for learning,[9] especially when it comes to issues around sexuality. Steve Derné and Lisa Jadwin point out that in the absence of sex education, cinema often becomes the primary means of learning about heterosexual relationships, with many viewers gaining scopophilic gratification from unusual sources such as medical films.[10]

The portrayal of women in Indian cinema is deeply controversial. Challenged by feminists, the representation of women has been contested on grounds of sexism, stereotyping and violence. The primary focus of this chapter is Bollywood cinema, which is a part of Indian cinema. Bollywood is the most widely known of all the branches of Indian cinema based in Mumbai (formerly known as Bombay). Cinema was the primary means of entertainment until the advent of cable television in the 1990s.[11] Television in India was limited to a single state-owned channel – Doordarshan – introduced as an experimental telecast starting in Delhi on 15 September 1959. As a state-run network, the government has used Doordarshan for spreading propaganda, especially during the Emergency Era. The state of emergency lasted for 21 months, between 1975 until 1977. During this time, Prime Minister Indira Gandhi allowed for the imprisonment of political opponents, censored the press, conducted mass sterilizations, postponed elections and changed laws.[12]

However, television did not become a part of the 'fabric of Indian everyday life' until much later in the mid-1980s.[13] Currently, Indian cinema competes with cable television, Netflix and other digital and internet-based sources as an entertainment provider. Despite this, its popularity has not waned. Over the decades there has been a change in content; the distinction between art and mainstream cinema is gradually narrowing. Influenced by popular social movements and conversations about representation, Bollywood cinema is beginning to incorporate those narratives within plot lines. While this self-aware cinema is trying to provide socially aware content, it remains firmly entrenched in patriarchal and sexist structures.

Cinematic Representations

The origins of Indian cinema lie in pre-independence India. Released on 18 May 1912, *Shree Pundalik*[14] was India's first silent film. Indian films have found a place in the international market, a trend that began in the late 1940s shortly after independence in 1947. Indian cinema has found a market in countries where Hollywood films have been perceived as too Western and vulgar. Soviet Russia, Nigeria and Turkey are a few of the countries where Bollywood films were routinely screened. For instance, in Turkey, the 1951 film *Awaara*[15] (vagabond) was voted the best movie of 1955, beating Hollywood films such as *Roman Holiday*[16] and *Limelight*[17].[18] The film had similar impact in the Soviet Union. Bollywood movies have also been adapted and adopted by other nations with colonial histories, having similar cultural reference points such as Nigeria.[19] Currently, the Bollywood film industry is a major employer and an influential industry that is growing economically and providing employment to several thousands of people.[20]

Although Bollywood has been known for portraying 'traditional values', it also manages to portray sexuality in its own veiled manner, through subversive means that can simultaneously be read as conservative yet provocative. Characters from minority communities often fill these roles that are too racy or controversial to be played by a Hindu character.[21] These messages are culturally and cinematically coded in such a way that the viewer is titillated while giving the illusion of decency. While the films may not overtly depict nudity or scenes of a sexual nature, they manage to do so in a subversive manner. The wet sari is one of the common tropes employed – a mode of dress that at the same time both conceals and exposes the body, it is a dress that is simultaneously read as sexual and Indian. It is this paradox and others that allow Bollywood to create sexual content that is passed through the censor board. Sexuality is mostly portrayed through characters deemed as others. Westernized/Anglicized women provide the space for conveying sexuality on screen while simultaneously being used to convey the message of superior Indian morality, which is embodied by the heroine. This form of faux morality can be observed through most popular cinema.

Westernized women on screen have traditionally occupied the space of the vamp. A common trope in films of the 1960s right through to the 1970s, the vamp provided a stark moral contrast to the heroine of the film.[22] Between the moral authority of the state's censor board and preoccupation with women's bodies through strategic camera angles and movement is the gratification and scopophilic pleasure that filmed bodies, especially those of the vamp, offer to both male and female viewers. The vamp is presented as the sexualized woman, craving men and their attention by inviting their gaze upon herself, her body, her eroticized gestures and movements. This exhibitionism, pleasurable to the audience, is simultaneously condemned as immodest, prurient and 'bad'. Thus one can enjoy the visual pleasure, the spectacular and erotic dance numbers, while keeping intact a sense of moral indignation by condemning the woman in unison with the narrative.[23]

The vamp invariably had a Western/Christian name; she worked in night-clubs as a dancer, and was often associated with the villain of the film. Her promiscuity and collusion with the negative characters of the film added to the punishment she would face later in the film. Film critic Jerry Pinto writes about the function of the vamp that followed a formulaic pattern. In almost everything that has been written about vamps in Hindi cinema, there has been a tendency to reduce the figure of the bad girl to a caricature. Her story is seen as the Progress of the Harlot: she fell, she smoked, she drank, she danced, she snuggled, she smuggled, she died.[24]

What sets the vamp apart from the heroine is that, despite her charms, the hero does not succumb to her. Her eventual death, like that of the villain, is the triumph of good over evil. This simplistic formula is what made Bollywood cinema appealing to audiences. However, her ethnicity and religion also distinguished the vamp from the chaste heroine. The vamps who dominated the screen for the longest time – Helen Ann Richardson, Cuckoo Moray and Florence Ezekiel Nadira – were of mixed race. Helen was of Franco, Bur-mese and Spanish origin; she arrived in India from Burma during the Second World War. Cuckoo Moray was an Anglo-Indian. Nadira was of Baghdadi Jewish origin, who invariably played as an Anglo-Indian or a Christian on screen. Both Helen and Cuckoo dominated the screens for decades. Their mixed ethnicity allowed them to be objectified in a way in which the upper-caste heroine was not. Tatiana Szurlej locates the popularity of these actresses in terms of their whiteness or their status as a 'memsahib', which was in living memory of the Indian audience.[25] Memsahibs were white or Anglo-Indian women of high social status, living in India especially. These women were both exotic and unattainable. They were shrouded in mystery, and strict rules governed their conduct. Seen as fascinating and as forbid-den, they were treated with awe and derision. Anxieties of racial mixing were of great concern in the colonial era.[26] While some of these anxieties decreased in the post-independence era, they did not diminish.

While these actresses were never white, their mixed-race status made them outsiders. These women did not fit with the stereotype of the trad-itional upper-caste/upper-class Hindu woman, who had been idealized for over two centuries. Memsahib is a slur (one among many) that Anglo-Indians and Christians have to contend with still today.[27] While much has been written about the taboos around interracial relationships in the colo-nial era, the Indian male gaze is rarely analysed when it comes to interracial relationships. As such, white or mixed-race women like Helen and Cuckoo could be objectified in a manner that was normalized on screen.

While the Anglo-Indian and Christian communities are often conflated, they are separate. However, many Anglo-Indians are Christian, either practising or lapsed. A minority and neglected community during colonial rule, they remained similarly neglected after independence.[28] The Anglo-Indian community has been treated as an exotic other. Negative stereotypes of the community have persisted despite evidence to the contrary.

It is a widely held belief that in order to compensate for their marginalization, Anglo-Indians have sought solace in the dissolute trappings of Western culture. Consequently, they have traditionally been represented as a people corrupted by alcoholism, sexual promiscuity, indolence and lax morality. Shifty, untrustworthy and gormless, the Anglo-Indian can, nevertheless, dance.[29]

Anglo-Indian, and by extension Christian, women fall into this category of 'promiscuous people'. This stereotype has affected women more adversely than men. On screen and off screen, women's morality has been measured by their purity and adherence to Indian values. Anglo-Indian and Christian women by virtue of their identity as Western and followers of a foreign religion have been categorized as less moral. This grading of women on screen has played into the social imagination of many Indians who view westernized women as sexually available. As noted by Geetanjali Gangoli, cinema often actively legitimizes ideas about identity. She writes: 'however, cinema does more than reflect existing vales in society. It also plays a vital role in creating, legitimizing and entrenching identities.'[30]

This process of legitimizing identities of the Anglo-Indian and Christian women through cinema has had its consequences. Portrayed as a vamp, she dazzled on screen. Despite this, the vamp invariably became a victim of violence, and she was either raped, killed by the hero or the villain. However, even when she repented of her villainy it was often too late and she would die as punishment. In the 1966 film *Teesri Manzil* (English: *Third Floor*), the vamps are victims of their promiscuity.[31] Helen, who plays a cabaret dancer, dies while protecting the hero she was pursuing in an unrequited romance. Similarly, the mysterious mistress of the wealthy hotel owner, the real villain of the story dies, but not before confessing her crimes. This trope has played itself out in so many ways in films, with a few variations, but always pointing to the eventual demise of the vamp.

In films where there were no vamps, the heroine embodied the flaws of the vamp. Released in 1971, films such as *Purab Aur Paschim* (English: *East and West*)[32] and *Hare Rama Hare Krishna*[33] rely on the heroine to fulfil the role of the vamp. Preeti, the heroine of *Purab Aur Paschim*, is oblivious about her Indian culture and knows next to nothing about her Hindu religion. When we first see her, the camera focuses on her bare legs and eventually her face. She is interested in living a fast-paced life in England, drinking, smoking and partying. From her appearance one can tell she is trying to look like an Englishwoman; her mannerisms are indicative of a dissolute life. Her brash and bold behaviour makes her the object of the villain's lust who attempts to rape her. Towards the end of the film, she realizes how far she has strayed from her roots and so-called 'normal' feminine roles. In the last scene of the film, she puts on a red bridal sari and is seen in a temple. Preeti is redeemed through embracing Indian/Hindu culture and femininity, and this allows her to live in the film.

Hare Rama Hare Krishna tells a similar cautionary tale through a dysfunctional family living in Canada. The parent's infidelity causes the children to develop behaviour problems to the point where their daughter Jasbir steals money and runs away to Nepal with her hippie friends. While in Nepal, she takes on the name Janice and lives with her boyfriend. However, her addiction to drugs begins to destroy her and she eventually dies.

In both films, the West becomes a site of moral corruption, where Indian values are lost. However, the ill effects of the West seem to harm women differently and more significantly than men. Taking on Western identities makes the heroines vulnerable and erodes their moral character. Male characters, however, seem stoic and unchanged by such cultural exchanges. While all the male characters wear Western dress or live and study in the West, they are less susceptible to its dangers. This distinction goes back to the colonial era when nationalists demarcated the boundaries of the East and the West and gendered its functions.[34] The heroes of these and other films are merely taking in the cultural advances of the West to use in their motherland, whereas the women are actively erasing their identity and taking in the cultural aspects of the West.

While the heroine's descent into corruption is being denounced on screen, it is also depicted in a titillating manner. For the audience, this is a moment imbued with scopophilic pleasure. The strategic nature of these scenes cannot be underestimated as they allow the viewer to subversively find pleasure while decrying the female character on screen.[35] Her transformation into that of a vamp in Western dress is important as it sets her apart from the stereotypical heroine and the idealized Indian woman. This on-screen alienation allows for the film to create an easy binary between good and bad women.

Deepa Mehta's film *Fire*,[36] which portrayed a homosexual relationship between two women, was attacked by protesters on its release, on the basis that it would spoil Indian culture.[37] The lead actresses portrayed married women in a middle-class family. Protestors claimed that they found it offensive that ordinary, Indian, Hindu women had been portrayed this way. Previous films by Deepa Mehta were met with riots and death threats from Hindu fundamentalists who claimed her films depicted Indian culture in a poor light and eroded Indian values. Bose would term the film *Fire* (made in 1996) as an act of feminist resistance, subverting gender expectations against the backdrop of the traditional Hindu middle-class family.[38] However, to the audience, issues of sexuality, alcohol and drug consumption can only be understood if the subject is not Hindu or Indianized.

Transforming Silence

The constant objectification of Christian women and their sexuality has led to crimes being committed against them. Most of these crimes are not written about seriously, or dismissed as inevitable given the moral position they are ascribed. In the collective imagination of the nation, violence against Christian women often goes unnoticed or is never considered to be of significance.

In the early hours of 6 February 2012, a victim of gang rape picked up her wounded body from the side of the road where her attackers dumped her, and got home. This victim would go on to register a police case against her attackers and make headlines across the country. While she got some support from a few sections of the media and citizenry, she was also widely criticized. The police and other authorities to whom she reported this case were unsupportive and unprofessional at best.[39]

In 2013, Suzette Jordan, then known only as the Park Street rape victim, waived her right to anonymity. Under Indian law, the identity of a victim of rape cannot be revealed without the individual's permission. When Suzette chose to come out publicly, she did so to raise awareness of what had happened to her. Her actions were met with a backlash. The chief minister of West Bengal, Mamata Banerjee, went on to denounce her as a liar and called her actions subversive to the ruling government.[40] Other ministers from the state government similarly called Suzette's character into question.

Unfortunately, Suzette's case is neither an aberration nor an isolated case in India, which has seen a lot of national and international attention in recent years. While the other rape cases have gained national and international sympathy, in Suzette's case her identity as a single Anglo-Indian mother was weaponized against her. Relegated as a minority within a minority, her clothing, divorce, drinking, smoking and clubbing were used to question the validity of her claims. The narrative that followed made her seem complicit in the crime. Similarly, the police used the same arguments to dismiss her claims while simultaneously harassing her. In many ways, Suzette's case played out like the tropes of a Bollywood film.

While the West has similar problems in reporting sexual violence, in India those same arguments are used to dismiss victims on the ground of their westernization, which is entwined with Christianity. Chandra Mallampalli argues that Christians in the colonial era were not privileged, as their race excluded them from white spaces.[41] Post-independence Christians were seen as apostates of the Hindu religion who embraced westernization: 'the prevailing tendency of existing scholarship has been to attribute this isolation to essential features of the Christian religion or to Western cultural values of foreign missionaries'.[42]

In her paper titled 'The Erotics of the Wet Sari in Hindi Films', Rachel Dwyer writes about the way in which the sari is constructed as both an Indian and sexualized dress. In her analysis, she ascribes ethnic norms to the dress. Christian women, she claims, do not wear the sari.[43] Within popular imagination and cinematic representation, this stereotype has been perpetuated in order to emphasize the foreign origins and nature of the Christian community, especially its women. This construction has appealed to nationalistic propaganda, which has created neat categories of East and West, morality and decadence.

This constant othering has meant that Christian/Anglo-Indian women are rarely written about or studied as a category worthy of scholarship. Persistent threats based on several facets of marginalized identities (race, gender and faith in this instance) make it difficult to negotiate daily life and access public spaces. While not all of these threats materialize into acts of violence, persistent threats, or witnessing these acts, is enough to cause lasting trauma. However, the threat of violence does not always lie outside the community, but also within. For Christian women in India the threat of violence comes from both outside the community and within the community. In both instances, women's voices are silenced through narratives invoking forgiveness.

The Consequences of Speaking Up

Since the revelations that came out of the #MeToo movement the issue of sexual harassment and abuse has been gaining momentum. In 2018, India saw a similar wave of activism where women from all walks of life came out and spoke up against their perpetrators. Conversations about abuse and its implications are being discussed widely, in the public sphere. Hashtags such as #ChurchToo and #MosqueToo have opened up conversations about abuse in religious institutions. In light of the #MeToo movement and its religious counterpart #ChurchToo, it is essential to look at the abuse Christian women face within their own communities and in society at large.

A similar wave of revelation and protest followed in churches across India. A Catholic nun spoke of being raped several times by the Bishop of Jalandhar (North India). This incident became known when the #MeToo movement was at its height; the prevailing attitude in the country was different at this time. Protests and conversations about sexual abuse were frequent. The nun got support from across the nation. However, there were many in powerful positions who were sceptical of her claims. Legislator P. C. George began to question the nun's morality, claiming that her silence meant she was a willing participant.[44]

By September 2018, the #VaayaMoodal campaign gripped India. Started by activist Aysha Mahmood, the campaign urged people to send duct tape to the minister to shut his mouth. Social media and new sources began talking about a nun who was raped by a bishop and subsequently maligned by her diocese and chief minister. Kerala, where the nun, bishop and minster lived, saw protests that took place around the state. While nuns, lay people and non-Christian people supported the campaign, it has been met with a back-lash within the Church, fearing these claims will play into anti-Christian narratives, which would legitimize violence against the community. Silence from the Church on the issue of abuse is not new, neither is the silencing of women from oppressed groups. Audre Lorde notes a similar phenomenon in the black community, where black women speaking about black male violence feared playing into racist narratives.[45]

Given the proliferation of social media in activism in the past five years, these cases have gained significant attention. Yet, this has not been so for the numerous attacks on Christian women, most of which are largely unreported and never make headlines.[46] The rise of right-wing vigilantes in India has meant that people who are perceived as deviant are attacked violently. This aggression takes on a gendered form, while male victims are beaten up or killed, women are often gang raped. Choosing to violate the bodies of women is a deliberate act of sexualized violence, fuelled by propa-ganda. Constructing the bodies of non-upper-caste/caste Hindu women as easy to violate is a way shaming the entire community. In a deeply patriar-chal society such as India, male aggression often uses women as a means of making a statement against an entire clan or community. The public nature of these crimes makes them a cautionary means of control.

Women's victimhood is often decided on external factors such as dress, morality and other markers, which are weaponized against their innocence. When these layers of blame are peeled away, sexual violence can be under-stood for the crime it is.

Christian women have faced violence since the beginning of the faith. Violence against women is a part of many biblical texts; the horror of these actions has been interpreted in various ways, either to blame women or to make a case against patriarchy within religion.[47] In our everyday lives as Christian women, we face the threat of violence and harassment not only from outside our community but also within our communities. In the wake of the #MeToo and #ChurchToo movements, the imperative of speaking up and taking action against perpetrators has intensified. Dismantling the structures that allow perpetrators to commit such crimes and be shielded afterwards has been normalized. However, this is not an easy task. For Christian women who speak up, the consequences have been severe. The nuns who have spoken up have been dismissed, been denounced as liars and have received no support from the Church.

The constant othering of Christians, especially Christian and westernized women in India, has meant that violence against them has become justified on grounds of morality. This violence is wrongly attributed to our alleged promiscuity in order to justify the perpetrators' actions. While violence committed against Christian women in India is no different to violence committed against other women, it is important to deconstruct the narra-tives and explanations that attempt to minimize the impact of these crimes.

The statue of Esther John should not become a tool of perfunctory remembrance; instead the violence that she (and other women like her) suffered during their lives should be addressed. The process of articulating and acknowledging these crimes is a long-needed measure. Christian women's trauma is often negated through arguments for forgiveness and martyrdom. While celebrating the resistance of modern saints like Esther John and others before and after her, the violence they have been subjected to has to be at the forefront. In India and South Asia, the culture of honour and misogyny that exists subsumes crimes against Christian women as part of crimes against the community. While understanding these crimes through a Christian lens is important, the gendered nature of these crimes should not go unnoticed.

References

Adamu, Abdalla Uba, 'The Muse's Journey: Transcultural Translators and the Domestication of Hindi Music in Hausa Popular Culture', *Journal of African Cultural Studies* 22, no. 1 (2010), 41–56.

Anand, Dev, *Hare Rama Hare Krishna*, 1971.

Anand, Vijay, *Teesri Manzil*, 1966.

Anon, 'Hashtag Drive to Shut up PC George', *Deccan Chronicle*, 11 September 2018. www.deccanchronicle.com/nation/current-affairs/110918/hashtag-drive-to-shut-up-pc-george.html.

Bailey, Gauvin Alexander, *Art on the Jesuit Missions in Asia and Latin America, 1542–1773*, Toronto: University of Toronto Press, 2001.

Bauman, Chad M., 'Pentecostals, Proselytization and Anti-Christian Violence in Contemporary India', *Journal for the Study of Religion* 28, no. 2 (2015), 220–2.

Blunt, Alison, 'Land of Our Mothers: Home, Identity, and Nationality for Anglo-Indians in British India, 1919–1947', *History Workshop Journal: HWJ* 54, no. 1 (2002), 49–59.

Bose, Brinda, 'The Desiring Subject: Female Pleasures and Feminist Resistance in Deepa Mehta's *Fire*', *Bulletin (Centre for Women's Development Studies)* 7, no. 2 (2000), 249–62.

Chaplin, Charlie, *Limelight*, 1952.

Chatterjee, Partha, 'Colonialism, Nationalism, and Colonialized Women: The Contest in India', *American Ethnologist* (April 1989), 622–33.

Cressey, Paul Frederick, 'The Anglo-Indians: A Disorganized Marginal Group', *Social Forces* 14, no. 2 (1935), 263.

D'Cruz, Glenn, 'Anglo-Indians in Hollywood, Bollywood and Arthouse Cinema', *Journal of Intercultural Studies* 28, no. 1 (2007), 55–68.

Derne, Steve and Lisa Jadwin, 'Male Hindi Filmgoers' Gaze: An Ethnographic Interpretation', *Contributions to Indian Sociology* 34, no. 2 (2000), 243–69.

Dwyer, Rachel, *Bollywood and the World*, University of Rhode Island, 2009: www.youtube.com/watch?v=7vdJ9KA68Wo.

—— 'Bollywood's India: Hindi Cinema as a Guide to Modern India', *Asian Affairs* 41, no. 3 (2010), 381–98.

—— 'The Erotics of the Wet Sari in Hindi Films', *South Asia: Journal of South Asian Studies* 23, no. 2 (1 December 2000), 143–60: https://doi.org/10.1080/00856400008723418.

Frykenberg, Robert Eric, *Christians and Missionaries in India: Cross-Cultural Communication since 1500*, Grand Rapids, MI, and London: Eerdmans and RoutledgeCurzon, 2003.

Gangoli, Geetanjali, '"Sexuality, Sensuality and Belonging: Representations of the 'Anglo-Indian' and the 'Western' Woman in Hindi Cinema." Bollyworld: Popular Indian Cinema through a Transnational Lens', in *Bollywood: Popular Indian Cinema through a Transnational Lens*, ed. Raminder Kaur and Ajay J. Sinha, New Delhi, California, and London: Sage Publications, 2005, 143–62.

Gurata, Ahmet, '"The Road to Vagrancy": Translation and Reception of Indian Cinema in Turkey', *BioScope: South Asian Screen Studies* 1, no. 1 (2010), 67–90.

Kapoor, Raj, *Awaara*, 1951.

Kim, Heewon, 'Understanding Modi and Minorities: The BJP-Led NDA Government in India and Religious Minorities', *India Review* 16, no. 4 (2017), 357–76.

Kumar, Manoj, *Purab Aur Paschim*, 1970.

Lorde, Audre, *Sister Outsider: Essays and Speeches*, Berkeley, CA: Crossing Press, 1984.

Lorenzen, Mark and Florian Arun Täube, 'Breakout from Bollywood? The Roles of Social Networks and Regulation in the Evolution of Indian Film Industry', *Journal of International Management* 14, no. 3 (2008), 286–99.

Mallampalli, Chandra, *Christians and Public Life in Colonial South India, 1863–1937: Contending with Marginality*, London: RoutledgeCurzon, 2004.

Mankekar, Purnima, 'Dangerous Desires: Television and Erotics in Late Twentieth-Century India', *The Journal of Asian Studies* 63, no. 2 (2004), 403–31.

Mazzarella, William, '"Reality Must Improve": The Perversity of Expertise and the Belatedness of Indian Development Television', *Global Media and Communication* 8, no. 3 (2012), 215–41.

McClintock, Anne, Aamir Mufti and Ella Shohat, eds, *Dangerous Liaisons: Gender, Nation, and Postcolonial Perspectives*, vol. 11, Minneapolis, MN: University of Minnesota Press, 1997.

Mehta, Deepa, *Fire*, 1996.

Mohan, Shriya, 'How do You Survive Being Named "The Park Street Rape Victim"?', *The Ladies Finger* (blog), 3 July 2015: http://theladiesfinger.com/how-do-you-survive-being-named-the-park-street-rape-victim/.

Monideepa, Banerjie, 'Not Park Street Rape Survivor, I am Suzette Jordan, She Said', NDTV, 13 March 2015, www.ndtv.com/blog/not-park-street-rape-survivor-i-am-suzette-jordan-she-said-746447.

Mulvey, Laura, *Visual and Other Pleasures*, Basingstoke and New York: Palgrave Macmillan, 1989.

Neill, Stephen, *A History of Christianity in India: The Beginnings to AD 1707*, vol. 1, Cambridge: Cambridge University Press, 2004.

Obiaya, Ikechukwu, 'A Break with the Past: The Nigerian Video-Film Industry in the Context of Colonial Filmmaking', *Film History: An International Journal* 23, no. 2 (2011), 129–46.

Pinto, Jerry, *Helen: The Life and Times of an H-Bomb*, Mumbai: Penguin Books India, 2006.

Rajgarhia, Manoj, '39 Years on: 7 Things You Need to Know about Emergency Imposed by Indira Gandhi', *DNA Now* (blog): www.dnaindia.com/india/report-39-years-on-7-things-you-need-to-know-about-emergency-imposed-by-indira-gandhi-1997782 (accessed 20 January 2015).

Rekhari, Suneeti, 'Sugar and Spice', in *Bollywood and Its Other(s): Towards New Configurations*, ed. V. Kishore, A. Sarwal and P. Patra, London: Palgrave Macmillan, 2014, 133–45.

Sahu, Gopal Krushna and Sameera Khan Rehmani, 'Representation of Minorities in Popular Hindi Cinema', *Media Watch* 1, no. 1 (2010), 27–32.

Sharma, Hari P., '"National Emergency" in India', *Journal of Contemporary Asia* 5, no. 4 (1975), 462–70.

Storkey, Elaine, *Scars across Humanity: Understanding and Overcoming Violence against Women*, London: SPCK, 2018.

Szurlej, Tatiana, 'Item Girls and Objects of Dreams: Why Indian Censors Agree to Bold Scenes in Bollywood Films', *Kervan. International Journal of Afro-Asiatic Studies* 21 (2018).

Taneti, J., *Caste, Gender, and Christianity in Colonial India: Telugu Women in Mission*, New York: Palgrave Macmillan, 2013.

Torne, Dadasaheb, *Shree Pundalik*, 1912.

TrustLaw. 'FACTSHEET – The World's Most Dangerous Countries for Women', London, New York and Mumbai: Thomson Reuters Foundations, 2011: www.trust.org/trustlaw/news/factsheet-the-worlds-most-dangerous-countries-for-women.

Virdi, Jyotika, *The Cinematic ImagiNation: Indian Popular Films as Social History*, New York: Rutgers University Press, 2003.

Williams Örberg, Elizabeth, 'The "Paradox" of Being Young in New Delhi: Urban Middle Class Youth Negotiations with Popular Indian Film', Lund: Lund University, 2007, https://lup.lub.lu.se/student-papers/search/publication/1325066.

Wyler, William, *Roman Holiday*, 1953.

Notes

1 Stephen Neill, *A History of Christianity in India: The Beginnings to* AD *1707*, vol. 1 (Cambridge: Cambridge University Press, 2004), 24.

2 Robert Eric Frykenberg, *Christians and Missionaries in India: Cross-Cultural Communication since 1500* (Grand Rapids, MI, and London: Eerdmans and RoutledgeCurzon, 2003), 63.

3 Gauvin Alexander Bailey, *Art on the Jesuit Missions in Asia and Latin America, 1542–1773* (Toronto: University of Toronto Press, 2001), 45.

4 J. Taneti, *Caste, Gender, and Christianity in Colonial India: Telugu Women in Mission* (California: Springer, 2013), 85.

5 Nandy, Ashis, *Intimate Enemy* (Oxford: Oxford University Press, 1989).

6 Heewon Kim, 'Understanding Modi and Minorities: The BJP-Led NDA Government in India and Religious Minorities', *India Review* 16, no. 4 (2017), 357–76, 60.

7 Partha Chatterjee, 'Colonialism, Nationalism, and Colonialized Women: The Contest in India', *American Ethnologist* (April 1989), 622–33, 623.

8 TrustLaw, 'FACTSHEET – The World's Most Dangerous Countries for Women' (London, New York and Mumbai: Thomson Reuters Foundations, 2011), www.trust.org/trustlaw/news/factsheet-the-worlds-most-dangerous-countries-for-women.

9 Rachel Dwyer, *Bollywood and the World* (University of Rhode Island, 2009), www.youtube.com/watch?v=7vdJ9KA68W0; Rachel Dwyer, 'Bollywood's India: Hindi Cinema as a Guide to Modern India', *Asian Affairs* 41, no. 3 (2010), 381–98.

10 Steve Derne and Lisa Jadwin, 'Male Hindi Filmgoers' Gaze: An Ethnographic Interpretation', *Contributions to Indian Sociology* 34, no. 2 (2000), 243–69, 250.

11 Purnima Mankekar, 'Dangerous Desires: Television and Erotics in Late Twentieth-Century India', *The Journal of Asian Studies* 63, no. 2 (2004), 403–31, 416. Elizabeth Williams Örberg, 'The "Paradox" of Being Young in New Delhi: Urban Middle Class Youth Negotiations with Popular Indian Film' (Lund: Lund University, 2007), https://lup.lub.lu.se/student-papers/search/publication/1325066, 3.

12 Hari P. Sharma, '"National Emergency" in India', *Journal of Contemporary Asia* 5, no. 4 (1975), 462–70, 462. Manoj Rajgarhia, '39 Years on: 7 Things You Need to Know about Emergency Imposed by Indira Gandhi', *DNA Now* (blog), www.dnaindia.com/india/report-39-years-on-7-things-you-need-to-know-about-emergency-imposed-by-indira-gandhi-1997782 (accessed 20 January 2015).

13 William Mazzarella, '"Reality Must Improve": The Perversity of Expertise and the Belatedness of Indian Development Television', *Global Media and Communication* 8, no. 3 (2012), 215–41, 216.

14 Dadasaheb Torne, *Shree Pundalik*, 1912.

15 Raj Kapoor, *Awaara*, 1951.

16 William Wyler, *Roman Holiday*, 1953.

17 Charlie Chaplin, *Limelight*, 1952.

18 Ahmet Gurata, '"The Road to Vagrancy": Translation and Reception of Indian Cinema in Turkey', *BioScope: South Asian Screen Studies* 1, no. 1 (2010), 67–90.

19 Abdalla Uba Adamu, 'The Muse's Journey: Transcultural Translators and the Domestication of Hindi Music in Hausa Popular Culture', *Journal of African Cultural Studies* 22, no. 1 (2010), 41–56, 43. Ikechukwu Obiaya, 'A Break with the Past: The Nigerian Video-Film Industry in the Context of Colonial Filmmaking', *Film History: An International Journal* 23, no. 2 (2011), 129–46, 134.

20 Mark Lorenzen and Florian Arun Täube, 'Breakout from Bollywood? The Roles of Social Networks and Regulation in the Evolution of Indian Film Industry', *Journal of International Management* 14, no. 3 (2008), 286–99.

21 Gopal Krushna Sahu and Sameera Khan Rehmani, 'Representation of Minorities in Popular Hindi Cinema', *Media Watch* 1, no. 1 (2010), 27–32, 29.

22 Suneeti Rekhari, 'Sugar and Spice', in *Bollywood and Its Other(s): Towards New Configurations*, ed. V. Kishore, A. Sarwal and P. Patra (London: Palgrave Macmillan, 2014), 133–45, 135.

23 Jyotika Virdi, *The Cinematic ImagiNation: Indian Popular Films as Social History* (New York: Rutgers University Press, 2003), 25–6.

24 Jerry Pinto, *Helen: The Life and Times of an H-Bomb* (Mumbai: Penguin Books India, 2006), 52.

25 Tatiana Szurlej, 'Item Girls and Objects of Dreams: Why Indian Censors Agree to Bold Scenes in Bollywood Films', *Kervan. International Journal of Afro-Asiatic Studies* 21 (2018), 124.

26 Anne McClintock, Aamir Mufti and Ella Shohat, eds, *Dangerous Liaisons: Gender, Nation, and Postcolonial Perspectives*, vol. 11 (Minneapolis, MN: University of Minnesota Press, 1997), 93.

27 Alison Blunt, 'Land of Our Mothers: Home, Identity, and Nationality for Anglo-Indians in British India, 1919–1947', *History Workshop Journal: HWJ* 54, no. 1 (2002), 49–59, 51.

28 Paul Frederick Cressey, 'The Anglo-Indians: A Disorganized Marginal Group', *Social Forces* 14 (1935), 263–64.

29 Glenn D'Cruz, 'My Two Left Feet: The Problem of Anglo-Indian Stereotypes in Post-Independence Indo-English Fiction', *The Journal of Commonwealth Literature* 38, no. 2 (2003), 105–23, 106.

30 Geetanjali Gangoli, '"Sexuality, Sensuality and Belonging: Representations of the 'Anglo-Indian' and the 'Western' Woman in Hindi Cinema." Bollyworld: Popular Indian Cinema through a Transnational Lens', in *Bollywood: Popular Indian Cinema through a Transnational Lens*, ed. Raminder Kaur and Ajay J. Sinha (New Delhi, California and London: Sage Publications, 2005), 143–62, 145.

31 Vijay Anand, *Teesri Manzil*, 1966.

32 Manoj Kumar, *Purab Aur Paschim*, 1970.

33 Dev Anand, *Hare Rama Hare Krishna*, 1971.

34 Chatterjee, 'Colonialism, Nationalism, and Colonialized Women', 624.

35 Laura Mulvey, *Visual and Other Pleasures* (Basingstoke and New York: Palgrave Macmillan, 1989), 21.

36 Deepa Mehta, *Fire*, 1996.

37 Mankekar, 'Dangerous Desires', 416.

38 Brinda Bose, 'The Desiring Subject: Female Pleasures and Feminist Resistance in Deepa Mehta's *Fire*', *Bulletin (Centre for Women's Development Studies)* 7, no. 2 (2000), 249–62, 250.

39 Shriya Mohan, 'How Do You Survive Being Named "The Park Street Rape Victim"?', *The Ladies Finger* (blog), 3 July 2015, http://theladiesfinger.com/how-do-you-survive-being-named-the-park-street-rape-victim/.

40 Monideepa, Banerjie, 'Not Park Street Rape Survivor, I am Suzette Jordan, She Said', *NDTV*, 13 March 2015, www.ndtv.com/blog/not-park-street-rape-survivor-i-am-suzette-jordan-she-said-746447.

41 Chandra Mallampalli, *Christians and Public Life in Colonial South India, 1863–1937: Contending with Marginality* (London: RoutledgeCurzon, 2004), 9.

42 Mallampalli, *Christians and Public Life*.

43 Rachel Dwyer, 'The Erotics of the Wet Sari in Hindi Films', *South Asia: Journal of South Asian Studies* 23, no. 2 (1 December 2000), 143–60, 146.

44 Anon., 'Hashtag Drive to Shut up PC George', *Deccan Chronicle*, 11 September 2018, www.deccanchronicle.com/nation/current-affairs/110918/hashtag-drive-to-shut-up-pc-george.html.

45 Audre Lorde, *Sister Outsider: Essays and Speeches* (Berkeley, CA: Crossing Press, 1984), 84.

46 Chad M. Bauman, 'Pentecostals, Proselytization and Anti-Christian Violence in Contemporary India', *Journal for the Study of Religion* 28, no. 2 (2015), 220–22, 221.

47 Elaine Storkey, *Scars across Humanity: Understanding and Overcoming Violence against Women* (London: SPCK, 2018), 185.

10

Broken or Superpowered? Traumatized People, Toxic Doublethink and the Healing Potential of Evangelical Christian Communities

NATALIE COLLINS

Introduction

During a long phone call with my dear friend who is filled with insight that only comes with age, she declared that 'feminism is when any woman, anywhere, realizes that women are disadvantaged due to their sex'. The trouble with feminism is that there are as many feminisms as there are women who are feminists. My feminism was forged in the crucible of male violence as I, an evangelical Christian, recovered from my ex-husband's abuse of me and my children. I approach trauma from this vantage point; as such, my method includes autoethnography, which Heather Walton describes as 'a way of using personal experience to investigate a particular issue or concern that has wider cultural or religious significance'.[1] This method allows my 'embedded theological convictions' to become 'primary theology itself'.[2] For me, trauma responses (which are often used to evidence the brokenness of traumatized people) are 'superpowers': strengths that helped me to survive and protect my children. Without romanticizing or valorizing these responses, and acknowledging that they can interfere with life once a traumatic threat is ended, I argue that they are seen fundamentally as strengths and not weaknesses.

Jesus saved my life, and feminism made sense of my life; but, in general, the evangelical community in which I find myself remains ambiguously helpful to traumatized people. Some resources within Christian tradition contribute to the healing of trauma, such as love, witnessing, testimony, creative prayer and community belonging. However, simultaneously, communities (particularly evangelical ones) may hold beliefs that make them unsafe for women subjected to abuse by a partner. Using George Orwell's concept of *doublethink*, as it appears in the novel *Nineteen Eighty-Four* to make sense of this contradiction,[3] I will examine the toxic elements of evangelical Christian culture through autobiographical account, trauma theory, analysis of evangelical rhetoric and the British Psychological Society's 'Power Threat Meaning Framework'. What emerges is a complex picture with no easy solutions, as we examine how the healing resources of evangelical Christian cultures are intertwined with toxic elements that undermine these resources.

My Story

I was born in the north of England into 1980s evangelical Christianity, and I loved it.[4] Church was a large extended family with regular quiche-laden bring-and-share meals binding us together. I learned to pray with the acronym 'STOP': sorry, thank you, others, please. I fell asleep before ever praying for myself. With primary and secondary education in faith schools, my closest friends were Christians. At 16, I began a childcare course. My working-class parents insisted that my education could earn me a living. I proudly declared my virginal status to my sexually active 'heathen' college friends. I had internalized implicit evangelical messages that my virginity marked my 'set apartness' for Jesus. After a classroom discussion about abortion, I brought in leaflets of dead foetuses. I was living the dream; so I thought.

I was 17 when a mutual friend introduced me to Craig,[5] who had recently become a Christian. What more did I need to know? He was washed in Jesus' blood, ticking the only box that mattered. And so began the worst years of my life. I told him I was committed to sexual abstinence; within 12 days, he had coerced me into sex. I knew then that I would have to marry him; sex is basically marriage anyway, isn't it? Nobody had told me about consent, so I attributed my intense anxiety at being sexually abused to having betrayed Jesus. Within six months, I was pregnant as Craig refused to use contraception and my Catholic education hadn't taught birth-control methods. Craig isolated, humiliated and controlled me, lied to me and cheated on me. I was pregnant and working three jobs. I believed my love, forgiveness and compliance would enable Jesus to save Craig. Then everything would be wonderful. But it wasn't.

I was 18 when my daughter was born in 2003. I married Craig soon after.

Within a year, Craig had been convicted of sex offences against a teenage girl. In 2005, I was 21 and six months pregnant with my second child. Craig raped me and, a week later, my son was born three months premature. My 2lb 6oz baby was immediately transferred to a hospital over an hour from our home. This forced separation enabled me finally to leave Craig.

After a month of sitting beside my tiny son's incubator, watching him unable to breathe without a ventilator, I reported Craig to the police for raping me. He was charged. Before the court date, he manipulated me into sex, which led to the court finding him not guilty. I was dealing with the needs of a premature baby and a traumatized toddler, living in a new town, coping with a court case (and the aftermath of a not-guilty verdict). This is where I would say that I met Jesus for real. Living in hospital after moving out of the home I had shared with Craig, there was no church I could join; my son's regularly deteriorating health meant that he had to be transferred to whichever hospital had paediatric intensive care available. I was totally alone, highly traumatized, with two children dependent on me. At the end of everything, I believe I found the God Who Is. This God, I believe, told me to stop praying for my son to live, but instead to confidently love him, whether my son lived or died – to pray for God's will to be done and not my own. I had lived in a kind of hell for four years and I became convinced that life with this God was of greater value than anything else. It was the pearl of great price. In a hospital with no hope, I chose the God who hadn't offered any hope other than his presence.

Trauma and Recovery

My son did survive and my daughter did recover. God called us to move to the south of England and we became part of a charismatic Free Church where I miraculously ended up married to Baggy, a long-time friend. Baggy was a safe person, dedicated mainly to loving me. I fell apart. I had no name for this collapse, but with hindsight it could have been diagnosed as Post-Traumatic Stress Disorder.[6] I would lose the ability to move and speak, going floppy or rigid as my mind shut down. Becoming hysterical or totally numb, I was compelled to cut myself in order to feel something. My body would feel like it didn't belong to me; holding my hand close to my face, I would be convinced it belonged to someone else. Looking in the mirror, I would wonder whose face looked out at me. Dissociation, depersonalization and derealization are the official names for these disturbing experiences.[7] Staring at every face in a crowd, I would be paranoid that one of them would be Craig. This is known as hypervigilance. I was petrified that if I saw Craig I would not be able to stop myself doing whatever he wanted me to; this is variously known as Stockholm Syndrome, trauma bonding, the betrayal bond, and traumatic attachment.[8] I blamed myself for everything Craig had done to me; I was so bad that I had made him hurt me.

Judith Herman explains that 'traumatic events overwhelm the ordinary systems of care that give people a sense of control, connection and meaning'.[9] Bessel van der Kolk clarifies that

> trauma is not just an event that took place sometime in the past; it is also the imprint left by that experience on mind, brain and body ... It changes not only how we think and what we think about, but also our very capacity to think.[10]

Car accidents, cancer, natural disasters, reproductive loss and the death of a relative or close friend are all examples of circumstances that can overwhelm our normal systems of care and leave a traumatic imprint. A similar traumatic imprint is created, for instance, when someone is forcibly held down to save their life (e.g. intubating them) as when they are held down to hurt them (e.g. during rape).[11] That said, as Jennifer Erin Beste asserts, trauma will generally be greater when it is caused by someone deliberately hurting us.[12]

Trauma Response as a Superpower

Within trauma theology, dissociation, depersonalization, derealization, hypervigilance, traumatic attachment and self-blame are often seen as dysfunctional; trauma theologian Shelly Rambo exemplifies this idea of dysfunction by referring to 'the pathology of trauma'.[13] Responses to threat evidence the brokenness of traumatized people, and trauma theologians seek an important corrective to a theology that makes no space for the reality of trauma.[14] Yet in doing so, trauma theologians often see a lack of ability. Instead, I will argue, there is *capability*. Hypervigilance gave me the capacity to think extremely fast while living with someone who was dangerously unpredictable. When Peter Parker is bitten by a spider and becomes Spiderman, his capacity for hypervigilance is celebrated as a superpower.[15] Why not think the same about the changes in me? Craig constantly guilted and manipulated me into sexual acts that were humiliating, painful and unwanted; dissociation enabled me to disappear, no longer required to tolerate the unbearable, like time travel or invisibility. Human beings are designed for attachment;[16] when we are threatened our primary biological need is to maintain this attachment. Craig isolated me from friends and family and so when he hurt or threatened me, the only person I could attach to was him. The attachment imperative cannot distinguish between safe and unsafe people. Even when I felt compelled to stay with Craig, these behaviours were my body keeping me safe. Self-blame is entirely understandable when I was powerless in a situation where the person I loved the most was hurting me so badly; my train of thought was that if it's my fault then I can change it, if I make him abusive then I must be powerful. If he hurt me because of my badness, then his unbearable behaviour makes sense and keeps me from despair. These 'superpowers' developed in a dysfunctional situation so I could cope with what Craig was doing to me and survive it.

Using Karl Rahner's work, Beste argues that trauma could prevent someone from accessing the fundamental option of God's grace; that dissociation, depersonalization, self-harm, hypervigilance, self-hatred and self-blame could destroy someone's capacity for free will. She explains that abuse can 'gravely, and perhaps entirely, debilitate the process of realizing the freedom to accept God's grace'.[17]

In doing so, Beste challenges Christians to support traumatized people more adequately. Traumatized people may encounter God primarily through contact with Christians; she thus emphasizes the responsibility Christians have for mediating God's grace.[18] While her intentions are positive, my suggestion is that trauma is only dysfunctional when we lose sight of the purpose of trauma responses. When we remember what has been done to someone, instead of seeing trauma in isolation from its cause, we could instead see these responses as manifestations of grace in the darkest of places. This is no easy matter, but is the capacity to dissociate and fly free while a man rapes us actually grace infused into the human body enabling survival? What is the shutting down of feelings if not grace to survive when our partner humiliates us? Could we even ask, what is self-harm in the midst of that numbness if not a creative gift that makes survival possible? What is the possibility of escape by suicide except the grace to feel some power in powerlessness? Psychologist Paul Joeffe's two decades of suicide prevention work with students led him to criticize the 'distress model of suicide'.[19] He explains:

> while suicidal students might or might not feel distressed about conditions in their lives, they generally don't feel distressed about being suicidal. Many will openly admit that being suicidal is one of the few, if not the only, bright spots in their lives ... Many are proud, if not proudly defiant, of their power to control their own fate.[20]

Trauma responses emerge to survive evil, that is to say, they are not to be romanticized or glorified, but rather contextualized as gifts of survival. Beste comments: 'it is conceivable that the presence of grace has sustained incest victims in ways they are unaware of and has enabled them to survive the human cruelty and abuse they have been subjected to.'[21] Regardless of whether the traumatized person recognizes it or not, their responses to trauma – hypervigilance, dissociation, derealization (which I have described as superpowers) – could be understood as the 'presence of grace' that enables survival.

If a woman escapes the abuser, these 'superpowers' become defunct – but how does she switch them off? In a scene from Sam Raimi's *Spiderman*,[22] Peter Parker's web grabs a bully's lunch tray, causing mayhem as he learns to control his newly gained superpowers.[23] In the same way, when our 'superpowered' trauma responses are no longer needed to keep us safe, relinquishing those powers is going to take time, awareness and conscious effort. They kept us functioning during danger, but leave us dysfunctional once we escape the abuser. The hypervigilance that kept us alert when threatened now makes us jump at the slightest noise. The dissociation that enabled our mind to fly free while our body was violated leaves us feeling spaced out and frozen. Our brain's useful compartmentalization of the traumatic memories becomes horrifying as flashbacks violently interrupt life. If trauma literacy shifts from a disability model to a capability framework, traumatized individuals are empowered to see their responses to trauma as strengths that kept them safe, but that can now be deactivated.

In 2018, the British Psychological Society published just such a capability framework in their *Power Threat Meaning Framework*. It asserts:

> unless there is strong evidence to the contrary, our behaviour and experience can be seen as intelligible responses to our current circumstances, history, belief systems, culture and bodily capacities, although the links amongst these may not always be obvious or straightforward.[24]

It problematizes psychiatric diagnosis of trauma, locating these within the philosophical framework of positivism, and presenting medical models as pathologizing human distress. [25] The framework asserts that humans are 'active, purposeful agents, creating meaning and making choices in their lives, while at the same time subject to very real enabling and limiting factors, bodily, material, social and ideological'.[26] The framework views the vast majority of mental and emotional difficulty as resulting from a negative operation of power (that is, having power taken from us), broadly defining power as 'biological/embodied; coercive; legal; economic/material; ideological; social/cultural; and interpersonal'.[27] Exploring 'the central role of meaning (as produced within social and cultural discourses, and primed by evolved and acquired bodily responses) in shaping the operation, experience and expression of power, threat and our responses to threat',[28] the framework traces what is threatened when power is lost. It examines an individual's responses to threats, ranging 'from largely automatic physiological reactions to linguistically-based or consciously selected actions and responses'.[29] The elements of power, threat, meaning and threat response are explored through asking four questions:

1 *Power.* What happened to you?
2 *Threat.* How did it affect you?
3 *Meaning.* What sense did you make of it?
4 *Threat response.* What did you have to do to survive?

Through the framework, traumatized people are encouraged to integrate their answers to these four questions into an 'evolving story', which includes identifying their strengths.[30] Dissociation and self-harm can be pointed to as strengths that are (hopefully!) no longer needed: 'It's amazing that your body gave you an escape route and helped you survive, but now that you're safe could we work with your other resources to help you stay present?' 'Self-harm was a creative way to survive; however, you've said that it's now become a compulsion. Shall we honour the way it has helped you, but explore new ways of breaking out of the numbness?'

This strengths-based capability model is rooted in contemporary research on successful trauma recovery. Feminist trauma theorist Judith Herman's crucial book *Trauma and Recovery* offers a three-part meta-structure for recovery: (1) establishing safety; (2) reconstructing the trauma story; and (3) restoring the connection between survivors and their community.[31] Bessel van der Kolk's influential book *The Body Keeps the Score* builds literacy about the physiology of trauma, though leaves much to be desired on the feminist front (with him describing the perpetration of domestic abuse as couples 'engaging in physical violence', and minimal engagement with the endemic nature of patriarchy).[32] Presenting his pioneering neurosequential approach, Bruce Perry's invaluable book *The Boy Who was Raised as a Dog* identifies key elements needed to help children recover from abuse and neglect.[33] Pat Ogden's book *Sensorimotor Psychotherapy* focuses particularly on the body's somatic recovery resources. All these researchers recognize that trauma responses are normal responses to an abnormal situation, which is something with which theologians could benefit from engaging.

Trauma theologians Shelly Rambo and Serene Jones both use Judith Herman's and Bessel van der Kolk's work. For Rambo, trauma theory '[constitutes] the hermeneutical lens through which an alternative theological vision of healing and redemption emerges'.[34] Rambo establishes alternative ways of seeing key aspects of Christian theology with a 'theology of the middle',[35] in which Holy Saturday becomes a space for challenging the surety of the Christian redemptive narrative, which is often more tentative and less realized for traumatized people. While there has been partial engagement with trauma theory, there is still so much potential to be tapped. By using trauma as a lens for theological study, there is a risk that the purpose of trauma responses is separated from what has been done to someone, leaving the response to be perceived as pathological rather than logical.

The Healing in Christianity

The resources of trauma theory can offer a new perspective not simply as a 'lens' for theology, but because they can be argued to evidence, first, God's intention for the recovery of traumatized people through creation, and second, the potential Christian communities have to contribute to the healing of traumatized people. In van der Kolk's work, it becomes clear that many trauma therapies have parallels in the Christian tradition. Bruce Perry's assertion that positive relationships are 'the true vehicle for all therapeutic change'[36] allows God's commandment to love God and neighbour to stand vindicated, in stark contrast to a neo-liberal Western culture that demands the prioritization of individual productivity and disintegrates relationships. The power of testimony within the Christian tradition is validated within Judith Herman's second stage of reconstructing the trauma story. The importance of the body in Pat Ogden's work struck me, as she asserts that 'the body's language itself is richly nuanced, mysterious, and multifaceted. It interfaces with a multitude of systems that together comprise the complex moment-to-moment process of making meaning and forecasting the future'.[37] This understanding of the body as shaping human experience and meaning-making could be considered even more profound in light of the belief that God created our bodies with these capacities; that perhaps trauma responses are created and gifted to humans, by God.

While evangelical Christianity has often devalued the body, theologian Paula Gooder points out:

> Paul's theology provides us with ample threads from which we might weave a beautiful theology of the body ... a theology that sees an integration of all aspects of who we are as the source of true beauty; a theology that recognizes the importance of relationship and the role our bodies play in relationship as contributing to our sense of self.[38]

There is a perfectly sound non-religious admiration for these kinds of responses on the biological level, but thinking of them in theological and faith terms gives them a deeper spiritual resonance, with God giving humankind somatic resources to survive and thrive no matter what people do to us.

The impact of trauma can be depicted fatalistically within trauma theology. Serene Jones visualizes the imagined meeting between her fictional character Rachel and Jesus' mother. Rachel, the mother of a child murdered 32 years previously in the slaughter of the innocents, encounters Mary at the crucifixion. Jones describes Rachel:

> She has begun to think she is too old to create again, having lost the most beautiful creation of her life, her child, to a calculated act of state-sanctioned violence, a military sword, in the land we now call the Middle East. She is the fractured creative spirit of many; wounded, unable to bear forth the glory of God that is in her.[39]

Distilled into trauma, Rachel is one-dimensional. The creative resources (what I would term her 'superpowers') that ensured her over 30 years of survival are not mentioned; instead, she is presented as irrevocably broken. It should also be noted that Rachel's trauma response is to a one-off traumatic event, not the ongoing trauma of someone with an abusive partner. The psalmist tells us that

> The heavens declare the glory of God;
>   the skies proclaim the work of his hands.
> Day after day they pour forth speech;
>   night after night they reveal knowledge.[40]

Within this theological view, inanimate objects can declare God's glory but, for Jones, this traumatized woman cannot. However, the damage is not so great that she is no longer *imago Dei*. My experience as a traumatized person, and over a decade of working with traumatized people, is that we are some of the most able to know God and show God to others; indeed, Jesus stated that blessed are those who mourn.[41]

Rambo explains that 'the central problem of trauma is that an experience repeats'.[42] Repetition is an aspect of trauma, but it need not be a fixed element. It is important that the physiological processes that take place during trauma inform theological and pastoral responses. Trauma repeats because of the body's inbuilt threat response system. The prefrontal lobe is the most developed part of the brain, dealing with language, imagination, reasoning and rational thinking.[43] The limbic system processes emotions, memories, habits and decisions.[44] The brain stem responds to threats and deals with autopilot processes. Threats need the immediate response of the brain stem rather than the slower, rational capacity of the prefrontal lobe. After screaming in fear at the spider in the kitchen, a split-second later we feel stupid as we realize it was just a tomato stalk. The prefrontal lobe deems it a false alarm after the brain stem's threat response has prepared our body for a potential threat.

In threat response mode, the brain has five options: fight, flight, freeze, flop and friend (the five Fs).[45] Fight, flight and friend are active responses, while flop and freeze are passive. Wild animal threat response systems operate in the same way; if Albert Antelope is caught by Laura Lioness, his brain stem chooses whichever response from the five Fs has the highest probability of survival. If Albert Antelope's brain stem chooses a passive response of flop or freeze, he plays dead. When Laura Lioness is distracted, Albert suddenly leaps up and runs away, whistling the *Born Free* soundtrack. As he escapes, his body shakes and judders, which is the visible element of a process called 'self-paced termination',[46] and allows Albert to discharge the adrenaline and cortisol that his body released in case his brain chose fight or flight.[47] Humans and domestic animals do not naturally experience self-paced termination to release these hormones. Trauma repeats when passive responses to trauma and a lack of self-paced termination leave the trauma 'stuck' in the brain stem.[48] The trauma can't be discharged, so the brain thinks it is ongoing. Life continues, but part of the brain is in permanent threat response mode – hence the repetition of trauma with ongoing hypervigilance, hypersensitivity and dissociation.

One process that enables the trauma to discharge is the Rewind Technique, which was fine-tuned by Human Givens therapists Joe Griffin and Ivan Tyrrell. The traumatized person (whom we will refer to here as Doris) is encouraged into a relaxed state by a trained therapist (we'll call him Derek). Derek calmly delivers a relaxation script: Doris is walking along a beach, she can hear seagulls, the waves are gently swishing to and fro. When Doris is relaxed, Derek encourages her to imagine a TV screen in front of her; she is to visualize herself coming out of her own body and observing herself. When she is ready, she watches herself viewing the trauma as it plays on the television. She views it in rewind, fast-forward and fast-rewind. Afterwards, Derek gently brings Doris out of the relaxed state. This guided engagement allows the trauma to be processed and stored as a memory, and it no longer repeats.[49] Griffin explains that through this technique

> a new message is put into memory and, while still in this state of low arousal, the neocortex can be engaged in reinforcing the new learning, by drawing further distinctions between the traumatic (but now non-emotionally arousing) event and present-day life.[50]

Other trauma therapies that use similar theories are Eye Movement Desensitization Reprocessing (EMDR) and Tapping, both of which involve a therapist asking a client to notice what memories and emotions emerge as they either follow the therapist's moving finger with their eyes (EMDE) or as the therapist taps the client's pressure points.[51] If the key to overcoming the repeating nature of trauma is to remain relaxed while recalling trauma, could this offer an explanation for how prayer can be effective in trauma recovery? If, during prayer ministry, a person believes they experience God's peace descending on them as they recall trauma, could this produce a similar (or even more effective) calm than the Rewind Technique's relaxation script?

Another method for treating trauma is Boyden-Pesso System Psychomotor (BPSP) therapy, developed by Albert and Diane Boyden Pesso.[52] The traumatized person is described as the protagonist, and other members of group therapy (or inanimate objects) play significant people from a historic traumatic incident.[53] Van der Kolk explains:

> protagonists became the directors of their own plays, creating around them the past they never had, and they clearly experienced profound physical and mental relief after these imaginary scenarios. Could this technique instil imprints of safety and comfort alongside those of terror and abandonment, decades after the original shaping of the mind and brain?[54]

On reading about this technique, the similarities became clear for healing prayer practices in which Jesus is visualized as present during a historic traumatic situation.

More general elements of trauma recovery present within certain Christian traditions include meaningful relationships, breathing and meditation, belonging to a community, safe touch (through the laying on of hands during prayer), mindfulness, telling our story, being listened to, rhythmic activities (drumming, singing, playing an instrument, choir). Other elements that could easily be incorporated into pastoral care include physical exercise (running, swimming, cycling) and bilateral movement (knitting, crochet, running, walking, clapping).[55]

There is the potential for healing within the Christian tradition, and although trauma theologians acknowledge trauma can repeat, it is also possible to stop that repeating. Trauma can also be recovered from. Shelly Rambo cites Hurricane Katrina victim Deacon Julius Lee in her book: 'the storm is gone, but "after the storm" is always here.'[56] He is right, male violence and other threats cannot be erased; there is only 'after the storm' and, to some degree, the trauma (the storm) becomes the reference point of life. Yet Rambo paints a rather bleak picture of trauma: 'it is a place of alienation, confusion and godforsakenness. But it is also a place that is continually covered over, dismissed, rendered unintelligible, and therefore subsumed under operative narratives of the progression from death to life.'[57] Rambo is right that the pain and brutality of trauma is covered over. A corrective is needed to open up this space that is bleak and terrible. However, traumatized people need not stay there for ever. There may only be 'after the storm', but could after the storm perhaps include rebuilding and recovering, by accessing therapies or ministries that acknowledge God's grace in creating human beings with the capacity to recover?

The Harm in Christianity

Although I am advocating for the potential of Christian community to be a place of recovery for traumatized people, my enthusiasm is severely squashed (and occasionally almost entirely suffocated) by harmful aspects of some Christian theologies and practices. I stayed with an abusive man for years believing that God wanted me to forgive him, submit to him and love him sacrificially. The evangelical culture I had grown up in left me vulnerable to manipulation and ill-equipped to deal with intimate relationships. If we are all sinners, I thought I must be just as bad as Craig. Though I grew up in a church with female (and male) priests, I absorbed an understanding that men were in charge and women served God through marriage and children. As a teenage mother, I was asked at a Christian youth event to stop breastfeeding my baby; apparently it would arouse the teenage boys who were present. A culture that blames girls for male sexual desire compounded my self-blame. Even as trauma theory gives hope for Christianity's capacity to care for traumatized people, certain Christian cultures, theologies and practices raise concerns. Can this capacity be realized, and can the evangelical church ever truly be a safe place for traumatized people, particularly those traumatized by intimate partner violence?

It could be argued that my experiences are atypical, that abuse is rare, that churches are generally safe places for traumatized people, and that I am entirely biased and jaded by my experiences. However, having spent a decade working to address domestic abuse, both within Christian communities and more broadly, my professional experience echoes the Office for National Statistics, who have found that, 27 per cent of women in England and Wales will be subjected to abuse by a partner.[58] What is more, only around two in seven churchgoers consider their church able to deal with domestic abuse.[59] Domestic abuse is a shorthand way of articulating the many ways someone may terrorize and torture their partner. Sociologist Evan Stark's work on coercive control has informed public policy in the UK, and is defined as follows:

> Coercive behaviour is an act or a pattern of acts of assault, threats, humiliation and intimidation or other abuse that is used to harm, punish, or frighten their victim. Controlling behaviour is a range of acts designed to make a person subordinate and/or dependent by isolating them from sources of support, exploiting their resources and capacities for personal gain, depriving them of the means needed for independence, resistance and escape and regulating their everyday behaviour.[60]

Stark, along with many other theorists (such as Liz Kelly, Marilynn French and Judith Herman), presents a feminist analysis of domestic abuse,[61] acknowledging that the majority of perpetrators are men (2018 data from the Office for National Statistics found that 92 per cent of defendants in domestic abuse-related crime were men).[62] While men, boys and transgender people can be subjected to abuse, as feminist philosopher Marilyn French points out 'it cannot be an accident that everywhere on the globe one sex harms the other so massively that one questions the sanity of those waging the campaign: can a species survive when half of it systematically preys on the other?'[63]

Using the Power Threat Meaning Framework as a basis for an examination of how some evangelicals approach domestic abuse, I have experienced that evangelicalism normalizes power differentials, minimizes threats, legitimizes toxic meaning-making, and then either demonizes or pathologizes threat responses. Am I unique in experiencing this? I will now examine evangelical Christian culture, to see whether there are examples that point to broader issues.

Normalizing Power Differentials

Complementarian theology is a theological position that views men and women as equal in value, but called to different roles.[64] It has had a significant influence on evangelicalism and is based on normalizing power differences between men and women. In responding to a question about whether women can be police officers, complementarian figurehead John Piper asserts:

If a woman's job involves a good deal of directives toward men, they will need to be non-personal in general. If they don't, men and women won't flourish in the long run in that relationship without compromising profound biblical and psychological issues ... My own view is that there are some roles in society that will strain godly manhood and womanhood to the breaking point. But I leave women and men in those roles to sort that out. I have never tried to make that list.[65]

John Piper may not have made that list, but Wayne Grudem has! In an article for the Council for Biblical Manhood and Womanhood, Grudem lists 80 'leadership' roles and invites (male) church elders to decide whether women should be allowed to do them. His list includes voting in church meetings, counselling women, singing hymns within the congregation, reading Scripture aloud in a meeting, editing a church newsletter and welcoming people into church.[66] We may even go as far as to suggest that questioning whether women can welcome people in church (or sing!) creates a context in which women's credibility or value is doubted.

If trauma results from the negative operation of power in someone's life, and we are particularly considering domestic abuse, does evangelical Christian culture ever normalize an abuser's abuse of power? At a conference in 2000, Paige Patterson, then President of the Southern Baptist Convention, was asked whether women should leave their abusive husbands. After telling the audience that no woman should ever divorce an abusive husband, he shared the following:

> I had a woman who was in a church that I served in. *She was being subject to some abuse, and I told her, I said, 'Alright, I want you to do this, every evening, I want you to get down by your bed just as he goes to sleep. Get down by the bed, and when you think he's just about asleep, you just pray and ask God to intervene. Out loud, quietly.' But I said, 'You just pray there,' and I said, 'Get ready because he may get a little more violent, you know, when he discovers this.'*
>
> And sure enough, he did. *She came to church one morning with both eyes black. And she was angry at me – and at God in the world for that matter. And she said, 'I hope you're happy.' And I said, 'Yes ma'am, I am.' And what she didn't know when we sat in church that morning was her husband had come and was standing at the back – the first time he ever came.* And when I gave the invitation that morning, he was the first one down to the front. And his heart was broken. He said, 'My wife's praying for me and I can't believe what I did to her.' And he said, 'Do you think God can forgive somebody like me?' And he's a great husband today. And it all came about because she sought God on a regular basis.
>
> Remember: When nobody else can help, God can. And *in the meantime, you have to do what you can at home to be submissive in every way that you can and to elevate him.*[67]

An influential figure in conservative Christian culture, Patterson's example shows just how normalized the negative operation of power is. He doesn't intervene, call the police or advise the woman to seek safety, instead, his advice places her in greater danger from the abuser. The woman in his story remains powerless until God intervenes. Her suffering is irrelevant; she is merely a prop to show God's power.

Minimizing Threat

In sending a woman back to a violent husband and encouraging her to antagonize him, Patterson clearly minimizes the threat abusive men pose. Patterson is not alone. In a blog post, fundamentalist pastor Mike Pearl declares, 'an angry husband cannot defeat a Spirit-filled wife, nor can he take satisfaction in her silent suffering, for she stands straight and unapologetic as she looks him in the eye with a knowing that pierces to his innermost being'.[68] In 2017, 50,000 women globally were murdered by a partner or family member;[69] no amount of a woman looking her abusive partner in the eye is going to stop him killing her.

Published in 1997, Stormie Omartian's book *The Power of the Praying Wife* continues to be a bestseller.[70] She recommends that when men are uninterested in sex, the couple should seek sex therapy. For women uninterested in sex, rather than suggest professional help, she advises:

> When your husband communicates to you what he has in mind, as only a husband can do, don't roll your eyes and sigh deeply. Instead say, 'Okay give me fifteen minutes' ... During that time do something to make yourself feel attractive ... Comb your hair. Wash your face and prepare it with products that make your skin look dewy and fresh. Put on lip gloss and blush. Slip into lingerie you know he finds irresistible ... Whilst you're doing this, pray for God to give you renewed energy, strength, vitality, and a good attitude. Hopefully when you're ready, your husband will find you were worth the wait. You'll be surprised at how much better a sex partner you are when you feel good about yourself. He'll be happier and you'll both sleep better.[71]

Given that 90 per cent of rapists are known to their victim,[72] the majority of rapists will likely violate their partner. As 30 per cent of women are subjected to abuse by a partner, up to a third of Omartian's readership might take her advice into their relationship with an abuser. A woman's husband may already be coercing or forcing her into sexual activity, and Omartian's advice perpetuates the abuser's view that he is entitled to sex from his wife. In responding to a blog post by Pastor Reggie Osborne that a woman's 'yes' on the wedding night is the only time she need consent to sex for the rest of her marriage,[73] Valerie Hobbs remarks:

Christians ... have inherited and been influenced by a ... destructive long-standing theological tradition. From the early church through the Reformation and beyond, theologians (almost always male) have interpreted biblical narratives about sexual violence in ways which 'reinforce patterns of subjugation, silencing, and violence against women'.[74]

Omartian's blindness to the possibility of abuse is not new. Christianity has historically failed to even acknowledge the potential of male violence. In such a context, active support for women and challenging of abusive men remains an impossibility.

The immediate and ongoing threats from an abuser include physical violence, isolation, exhaustion, humiliation, degradation and violation. If a woman (and any children she has) escape the abuser, these threats continue in his post-separation abuse. None of these threats concern Patterson, Pearl and Omartian. They minimize them or are unmoved by them. For Pearl and Patterson, the marriage covenant is more sacred than women's lives. For Omartian and Osbourne, the abuser's threat remains outside their frame of reference.

Legitimizing Toxic Meaning-Making

The Power Threat Meaning Framework describes meaning-making as an 'attempt to construct meaning in our lives, including experiences of distress – our own or other people's'. This meaning is developed as 'we "choose" narratives from those that are culturally available'.[75] While I was with Craig, I sought meaning through believing I was to blame, that I drove him to abuse me. After leaving him, I was able to reject this toxic meaning-making by developing a feminist understanding of abuse, in which I began to understand Craig's behaviour as a choice, designed to control, due to his belief he owned me. Placing his behaviour within a wider patriarchal framework enable me to make sense of it, without taking on false responsibility and blame for it.

For many Christian women, the available narratives are dominated by woman-blaming: from the Church Fathers' view of woman as the devil's gateway,[76] she who is 'defective and misbegotten',[77] to contemporary websites like www.secretkeepergirl.com who offer 'Truth or Dare' modesty tests to help girls assess whether their clothing could arouse male desire. They make suggestions such as:

take the tips of your fingers and press into your shirt, right where your ribs come together in the 'valley' in the middle of your chest. When you take your fingers away, does your shirt immediately spring back like a small Smurf trampoline? If so, your shirt is too tight![78]

Toxic meaning-making starts early in evangelicalism!

Mike Pearl's exhortation to a woman that her pure heart will save her husband is an example of the legitimization of toxic meaning-making, as is Patterson's assertion that a woman praying for her husband and enduring his abuse will make him change. Pearl is quoted in his wife's book *Created to be His Helpmeet*:

> Just as we are to obey government in every ordinance, and servants are to obey their masters, even the ones who are abusive and surly, 'likewise, ye wives, be in subjection to your own husbands' ... You can freely call your husband 'lord' when you know that you are addressing the one who put him in charge and asked you to suffer at your husband's hands just as our Lord suffered at the hands of unjust authorities ... When you endure evil and railing without returning it, you receive a blessing, not just as a martyr, but as one who worships God.[79]

The toxic meaning-making of self-blame and self-sacrifice that women use to survive are both legitimized and encouraged by Pearl. Though toxic meaning-making is a survival tactic, recovery is only possible when this harmful narrative is rejected in favour of the 're-storying'[80] of life 'in a way that allows [traumatized people] to understand the origins, meanings, and significance of [their] present difficulties and to do so in a way that makes change conceivable and attainable'.[81] This is much more difficult to achieve in a culture that demeans and blames women and legitimizes toxicity.

Demonizing or Pathologizing Threat Responses

After normalizing the power differentials, minimizing the threat abusive men pose, and then legitimizing toxic meaning-making, is it any wonder that evangelical women who have been subjected to abuse are highly traumatized? Are women cared for as they physiologically respond to existing or past trauma through dissociation, self-harm, hypervigilance, paranoia, anxiety, eating disorders, drug or alcohol use, becoming hypersexualized, developing autoimmune or digestive issues,[82] or when they lose hope and become suicidal? Sadly, it seems not.

Two dominant responses to traumatized women can be detected in evangelical culture: demonization and pathologization. Matthew Stanford found that negative reactions from Christians about mental health included 'equating mental illness with the work of demons, and suggesting that the mental disorder was the result of personal sin'.[83] For centuries, the Roman Catholic Church taught that those who died by suicide could not have a Christian burial, for they had committed a mortal sin.[84] Although this prohibition no longer stands, the stigma and religious judgement of suicide continues in many faith communities.

In the UK, the Christian organization Mind and Soul works to support the Church in more effectively responding to mental health issues. They suggest evangelical Christian culture has shifted from viewing mental health issues as demon-possession to an 'informed-hybrid' of this position, with mental ill-health now seen as a result of not trusting God, of self-indulgence, or of the devil undermining God's mission.[85] The demonization of mental health issues continues, albeit in a more palatable way.

Ironically, Mind and Soul pathologize trauma and so offer solutions that are problematic for different reasons. As an organization addressing mental health, they use a medical model to understand human responses to threat; their 'Mental Health Access Pack' provides information on common mental health diagnoses, but does not cover abuse or trauma.[86] In the pack's explanation of therapy types, there is no mention of specialist trauma therapies.[87] Their website explains: 'With one in four people experiencing a mental health issue at some point in their lifetime, this is an important issue for the church to engage with effectively.' For them, mental health is isolated from the experiences that led to the distress. The Power Threat Meaning Framework explains the danger of this dissociation:

> The medicalization of emotional and psychological distress is deeply entrenched within existing systems ... it is impossible to separate out the emergence and experience of mental distress from wider society and culture and associated forms of power. Replacing the diagnostic model with a non-diagnostic understanding of emotional and psychological distress and troubled or troubling behaviour will inevitably force us to face up to some of the complexities that diagnosis has obscured. This, as Bessel van der Kolk has noted, will be challenging. 'Academic laboratories are funded to study particular disorders ... If you say that your disorder is part of a larger picture, which includes elements from several other diagnoses, then you'd have to rearrange your lab, your concepts, your funding, and your rating scales.'[88]

When Christians reject approaches that demonize threat responses, they often replace them with a medicalized approach that pathologizes the individual as sick and in need of treatment. The development of the mental health conversation in many parts of Christian culture remains divorced from conversations about abuse, violence, inequality, racism, sexism and misogyny.

Understandably, when the cause of mental health issues is a binary choice of either 'blame or brain'[89] (blaming the person for a moral failure or seeing the cause as physical and out of their control), blaming chemical imbalances in their brain appears preferable. However, this is a false dichotomy. Perhaps it is neither their fault nor their brain's fault. Instead, could it be an abuser's fault? Or the fault of a society that has perpetrated systemic oppression towards people of colour, women, disabled people or LGBT people? It is convenient that within the dominant binary, the problem remains within the individual; society is absolved when it is either their moral failing or their brain's failing. This is not to deny that there are indeed complex physiological factors involved in mental health, but these factors cannot be divorced from the wider contexts.

Christian Doublethink

Therefore, we find ourselves in an interesting space. Christian communities have much to commend themselves to traumatized people. Long before trauma theory existed, Christian communities provided key elements of trauma therapy: places of testimony and being witnessed to, safe touch, belonging, meaningful relationships, and the facility to re-story life with the continuing presence of Jesus' love, rhythm and song, meditation and more. Yet these communities are often unsafe for traumatized women. Power differentials are normalized, threats to women are minimized, toxic meaning-making is legitimized and threat responses are demonized or pathologized. George Orwell, in his novel *1984*, offers us a framework to understand this conflict: 'Doublethink means the power of holding two contradictory beliefs in one's mind simultaneously, and accepting both of them.'[90] While William Empson, a vocal critic against Christianity, used Orwell's concept of doublethink to assert that various Christian doctrines were 'a double-talk by which Christians hide from themselves the insane wickedness of their God',[91] my suggestion is that Christian doublethink is closer to Judith Herman's application of doublethink to traumatized people. She suggests they operate in a state of 'altered-consciousness',[92] which 'through the practice of dissociation, voluntary thought suppression, minimization and sometimes outright denial, they learn to alter an unbearable reality'.[93]

A form of 'collective disassociation' occurs within evangelical Christianity in response to traumatized people. Evangelical Christians are dependent on a world that is ordered towards God's goodness; marriage is a metaphor for God's relationship with humanity; those who confess Jesus as Lord are sanctified and transformed. They believe their faith community is safe and holds the hope for the whole world. When a woman discloses that her Christian husband is abusing her, they must deal with a seemingly unbearable reality that their world view is flawed, that marriage can be toxic, that those who profess to be Christians can in fact be dangerous, violent and controlling. So they employ doublethink to set the world straight: instead of accepting the woman's version of events, which will turn their world upside down, they instead reshape the narrative through their (false) world view: abuse is wrong – *but* our community is safe – *therefore* this disclosure can't be abuse. Abuse is wrong – *but* I like this man and he's a good worship leader – *therefore* his wife's disclosure can't be accurate. Abuse is wrong – *but* marriage is for life – *therefore* she should work at her marriage even though he tried to kill her. Abuse is wrong – *but* this woman is strong and reminds me of my daughter – *therefore* she is not the sort to be abused and she must be mistaken when she said her husband is controlling her. Abuse is wrong – *but* children need a father – *therefore* she should stay with the abuser for the sake of the children.

When the '*but*' element remains implicit, no amount of education or information will enable evangelical Christians to respond appropriately to women traumatized by abusive partners, because they don't even realize that they are engaging in doublethink.

One of these '*buts*' is the Christian redemptive narrative, which tells us that death always gives way to life. For Christians pastorally support-ing women subjected to abuse, this narrative may motivate them to advise women to reconcile with abusive husbands, because 'this time he really seems to have changed'. The pastoral supporter's yearning for life to become ordered around goodness may cause them to ignore evidence of the abuser's badness. Rambo suggests that, 'theology must account for the excess, or remainder, of death in life that is central to trauma'.[94] This accounting, says Rambo, should 'operate alongside' (rather than supersede) the redemptive narrative.[95] In the same way, the theology that leads to Christian double-think about domestic abuse is rarely entirely wrong, but instead must sit alongside a much more well-informed understanding of the reality and danger of abusive men, otherwise it will remain dangerous and harmful to women and children subjected to abuse.

Making Sense of the Contradiction

Can we access the healing and recovery offered by the Christian tradition when it is so tainted by doublethink, normalization, minimization, legiti-mization, demonization and pathologization? I did; but I managed it only because circumstances enabled me to escape the abuser, and my relation-ship with God deepened (through great suffering) to such a degree that my dependence on a faith community was at all points superseded by being in relationship with a God whom I had experienced as entirely loving and liberating. Being raised in evangelical Christian culture contributed hugely to my inability to identify the negative power operating in my relationship with Craig, and I minimized the threat he posed to me. I had been taught to overvalue marriage and devalue myself, and this planted the seed of toxic meaning-making, which kept me with Craig and left my responses to threat pathologized. Yet, being raised Christian increased my sensitivity to the God who I believe truly saved my life and in whom I live and move and have my being. While the Christian communities I have been part of since leaving Craig have continued to be problematic, they also provided a space where recovery became my reality. Perhaps Rambo's theology of remaining can be applied here too? Rambo explains:

This transformation, this redemption in the abyss of hell, is not about deliverance from the depths, but instead, a way of being in the depths, a practice of witnessing that senses life arising amid what remains. The middle story is not a story of rising out of the depths, but a transformation in the depths themselves.[96]

While I am not suggesting evangelical communities are the 'abyss of hell', there is pain in being a traumatized woman in a space that feels as if it should be safe yet is not. Nevertheless, in the midst of that pain, for those who believe in God, there is a Being who can heal, transform and love. This is not straightforward. It is messy, and there is no definitive path to healing and wholeness. For some, leaving evangelical Christianity has been the only way to access healing, evidenced by the emergence of 'exvangelical' communities oriented around healing from trauma;[97] while for myself and others, the healing resources within evangelical Christianity outlined in this chapter have been important in our recovery from trauma.

We must not idealistically advocate that evangelical Christianity has the potential to aid traumatized people's recovery without acknowledging that toxic doublethink informs much of Christian theology and pastoral practice. But we cannot deny the healing potential within evangelicalism. Who are we to refuse people access to that which might be the key to their recovery? The twin potentials for healing and for harm must be held in tension, in a posture of remaining, seeking out transformation while also being vigilant to the threats posed by the depths and the doublethink.

References

Amazon, 'Amazon Best Sellers': www.amazon.com/Best-Sellers-Books-Christian-Prayer/zgbs/books/12470 (accessed 29 January 2019).

Archive, 'Paige Patterson (SBC) Advice to Victims of Domestic Violence': archive.org/details/PaigePattersonsbcAdviceToVictimsOfDomesticViolence (accessed 17 June 2019).

Arnsten, Amy, 'Stress Signalling Pathways that Impair Prefrontal Cortex Structure and Function', *Nature Reviews Neuroscience*, 10, no. 6 (2009), 410–22.

Aune, Kristin and Rebecca Barnes, *In Churches Too: Church Responses to Domestic Abuse – A Case Study of Cumbria*, Coventry and Leicester: Coventry University and and University of Leicester, 2018.

Beste, Jennifer Erin, *God and the Victim; Traumatic Intrusions on Grace and Freedom*, New York: Oxford University Press, 2007.

Bowlby, John, *Attachment and Loss; Volume I, Attachment*, New York: Basic Books, 1982.

Carnes, Patrick, *The Betrayal Bond: Breaking Free of Exploitative Relationships*, Deerfield Beach, FL: Health Communications, 1998.

Collins, Natalie, *Out of Control: Couples, Conflict and the Capacity for Change*, London: SPCK, 2019.

Crown Prosecution Service, 'Controlling or Coercive Behaviour in an Intimate or Family Relationship', 30 June 2019: www.cps.gov.uk/legal-guidance/controlling-or-coercive-behaviour-intimate-or-family-relationship.

DC and Marvel, 'Spider-Man; The First-Day of Being an Extraordinary Man', You-Tube, 21 August 2016: www.youtube.com/watch?v=7B2-AM7fUsQ.

French, Marilyn, *The War against Women*, St Ives: Hamish Hamilton Ltd, 1992.

Gooder, Paula, *Body: Biblical Spirituality for the Whole Person*, London: SPCK, 2016.

Graham, Dee, Edna Rawlings and Nelly Rimini, 'Survivors of Terror: Battered Women, Hostages, and the Stockholm Syndrome', in K. Yllö and M. Bograd, eds, *Feminist Perspectives on Wife Abuse*, Newbury Park, CA: Sage Publications, 1988, 217–33.

Griffin, Joe, 'PTSD', Human Givens Institute: www.hgi.org.uk/resources/delve-our-extensive-library/anxiety-ptsd-and-trauma/ptsd-why-some-techniques-treating-it (accessed 29 January 2019).

Grudem, Wayne, 'But What Should Women Do in Church?', *CBMW News*: http://cbmw.org/wp-content/uploads/2013/05/1-2.pdf (accessed 29 January 2019).

Haffenden, John, *William Empson: Volume II, Against the Christians*, Oxford: Oxford University Press, 2006.

Herman, Judith, *Trauma and Recovery: The Aftermath of Violence – From Domestic Abuse to Political Terror*, New York: Basic Books, 1992.

Hobbs, Valerie, 'Rape Culture in the Bible', Shiloh Project, 19 June 2017: https://shiloh-project.group.shef.ac.uk/rape-culture-in-the-christian-church/.

James, Aaron, 'Tony Campolo: I Refuse to Call Myself an Evangelical Anymore', Premier Christianity: www.premierchristianity.com/News/World/Tony-Campolo-I-refuse-to-call-myself-an-Evangelical-anymore (accessed 29 January 2019).

Joffe, Paul, 'An Empirically Supported Program to Prevent Suicide in a College Student Population', *Suicide and Life-Threatening Behavior* 38, no. 1 (March 2008), 87–103.

Johnstone, Lucy and Mary Boyle with John Cromby, Jacqui Dillon, David Harper, Peter Kinderman, Eleanor Longden, David Pilgrim and John Read, *The Power Threat Meaning Framework: Towards the identification of patterns in emotional distress, unusual experiences and troubled or troubling behaviour, as an alternative to functional psychiatric diagnosis*, Leicester: British Psychological Society, 2018.

Jones, Serene, *Trauma and Grace; Theology in a Ruptured World*, Louisville, KY: Westminster John Knox Press, 2009.

Levine, Peter, 'Healing Trauma' Daily OM: www.dailyom.com/cgi-bin/display/librarydisplay.cgi?lid=2018 (accessed 29 January 2019).

Lodrick, Zoe, 'Psychological Trauma': www.zoelodrick.co.uk/training/article-1 (accessed 29 January 2019).

Lyons, Shoshanah, 'The Repair of Early Trauma: A "Bottom Up" Approach', *Beacon House*: https://beaconhouse.org.uk/developmental-trauma/the-repair-of-early-trauma-a-bottom-up-approach/ (accessed 29 January 2019).

Mental Health Access Pack, 'Download the Whole Pack': www.mentalhealthaccess-pack.org/download-the-whole-pack/ (accessed 29 January 2019).

—— 'Forms of Counselling': www.mentalhealthaccesspack.org/install/wp-content/uploads/2018/06/Cards_Pratical-Tips_Counselling_May-2018.pdf (accessed 29 January 2019).

Merritt, Jonathan, 'Defining "Evangelical"', *The Atlantic*, 7 December: www.the atlantic.com/politics/archive/2015/12/evangelical-christian/418236/ (accessed 29 January 2019).

Mind and Soul, '6 Christian Mental Health Conversations': www.mindandsoul foundation.org/Articles/515149/Mind_and_Soul/Articles/6_Christian_Mental. aspx (accessed 29 January 2019).

Ministry of Justice, 'An Overview of Sexual Offending in England and Wales', 10 January 2013: https://assets.publishing.service.gov.uk/government/uploads/system/ uploads/attachment_data/file/214970/sexual-offending-overview-jan-2013.pdf.

Nagoski, Emily, *Come As You Are; The Surprising New Science that will Transform Your Sex Life*, Victoria: Scribe, 2015, Kindle edn.

Office for National Statistics, 'Domestic Abuse in England and Wales: Year Ending March 2018', 22 November 2019: www.ons.gov.uk/peoplepopulationand community/crimeandjustice/bulletins/domesticabuseinenglandandwales/year endingmarch2018.

—— 'Intimate Partner Violence and Partner Abuse', 11 February 2016: www.ons. gov.uk/peoplepopulationandcommunity/crimeandjustice/compendium/focuson violentcrimeandsexualoffences/yearendingmarch2015/chapter4intimatepersonal violenceandpartnerabuse.

Ogden, Pat, *Sensorimotor Psychotherapy: Interventions for Trauma and Attachment*, Norton Series on Interpersonal Neurobiology, New York: W.W. Norton and Company, 2015, Kindle edn.

Omartian, Stormie, *The Power of a Praying Wife*, Eugene, OR: Harvest House, 2014.

Onishi, Bradley, 'The "Exvangelical" Movement will Continue to Grow', *Religion News Service*, 20 December 2018: https://religionnews.com/2018/12/20/bradley-onishi-the-exvangelical-movement-will-continue-to-grow/.

Orwell, George, *Nineteen Eighty-Four*, London: Penguin Books, 2004.

Osborne, Reggie, 'She Only Said "Yes" Once', For Every Mom, 5 April 2016: http:// foreverymom.com/mom-gold/she-only-said-yes-once/.

Pearl, Michael, 'The Devil's Hug', No Greater Joy, 15 June 2017: https://nogreater joy.org/articles/39260/.

Perry, Phillip, 'Been Traumatized? Here's How PTSD Rewires the Brain', Big Think, 7 April 2019: https://bigthink.com/philip-perry/been-traumatized-here-is-how-ptsd-rewires-the-brain.

Perry, Bruce and Maia Szalatvitz, *The Boy Who was Raised as a Dog; And Other Stories from a Child Psychiatrist's Notebook*, New York: Basic Books, 2006.

Pesso Boyden System Psychomotor, 'About BPSP': https://pbsp.com (accessed 17 June 2019).

Piper, John, 'Should Women be Police Officers?', Desiring God, 13 August 2015: www.desiringgod.org/interviews/should-women-be-police-officers.

Piper, John and Wayne Grudem, *Recovering Biblical Manhood and Womanhood; A Response to Evangelical Feminism*, Wheaton, IL: Crossway Books, 1992.

Raimi, Sam, *Spiderman*, Columbia Pictures, Marvel Enterprises, Laura Ziskin Productions, 2002.

Rambo, Shelly, *Spirit and Trauma; A Theology of Remaining*, Louisville, KY: Westminster John Knox Press, 2010.

Reid, Joan, Rachael Haskell, Christina Dillahunt-Aspillaga and Jennifer Thor, 'Trauma Bonding and Interpersonal Violence', *Faculty Publications*, 2013.

Secret Keeper Girl, 'Truth or Bare Fashion Test': http://secretkeepergirl.com/truth-or-bare-fashion-test/ (accessed 29 January 2019). This original link has now gone, but details of the tests I mentioned can be found on the blog at https://friendly atheist.patheos.com/2012/06/27/the-ugly-side-of-modesty/.

Sommer-Rotenberg, Doris, 'Suicide and Language', *Canadian Medical Association Journal* 159, no. 3 (August 1998), 239–40.

Stanford, Matthew, 'Demon or Disorder: A Survey of Attitudes toward Mental Illness in the Christian Church', *Mental Health, Religion and Culture* 10, no. 5 (August 2007), 445–9.

Tertullian, 'On the Apparel of Women': www.newadvent.org/fathers/0402.htm (accessed 1 August 2019).

Thomas Aquinas, *Summa Theologiae*: www.newadvent.org/summa/1092.htm (accessed 1 August 2019).

United Nations Office on Drugs and Crime, *Global Study on Homicide*: www.un odc.org/documents/data-and-analysis/GSH2018/GSH18_Gender-related_killing_ of_women_and_girls.pdf (accessed 29 January 2019).

University of Queensland, 'The Limbic System': https://qbi.uq.edu.au/brain/ brain-anatomy/limbic-system (accessed 29 January 2019).

US Department of Veteran Affairs, 'PTSD Basics': www.ptsd.va.gov/understand/ what/ptsd_basics.asp (accessed 17 June 2019).

van der Kolk, Bessel, *The Body Keeps the Score; Mind, Brain and Body in the Transformation of Trauma*, New York: Penguin, 2014, Kindle edn.

Walton, Heather, *Writing Methods in Theological Reflection*, London: SCM Press, 2014.

Wigg-Stevenson, Natalie, *Ethnographic Theology*, New York: Palgrave MacMillan, 2014.

Willis, Alicia, 'Created to be His Helpmeet': http://aliciaannewillis.blogspot. com/2017/07/created-to-be-his-helpmeet-discovering.html (accessed 29 January 2019).

Yuan, Teri, 'Episode 2', *En(gender)ed*, 28 May 2018, https://engendered.us/episode-2-evan-stark-on-coercive-control/.

Notes

1 Heather Walton, *Writing Methods in Theological Reflection* (London: SCM Press, 2014), xxxi–xxxii.

2 Natalie Wigg-Stevenson, *Ethnographic Theology* (New York: Palgrave Mac-Millan, 2014), 167.

3 George Orwell, *Nineteen Eighty-Four* (London: Penguin Books, 1984).

4 Bebbington viewed evangelicals as having four main qualities: biblicism, crucicentrism, conversionism and activism (Merritt, 'Defining Evangelical'). In more recent years, evangelicalism (particularly in the USA) has become synonymous with capital punishment, being pro-war, homophobic and misogynistic (James, 'Tony Campolo').

5 His name has been changed to protect his anonymity.

6 US Department of Veteran Affairs, 'PTSD Basics', 17 June 2019, www.ptsd. va.gov/understand/what/ptsd_basics.asp.

7 Bessel van der Kolk, *The Body Keeps the Score; Mind, Brain and Body in the Transformation of Trauma* (London: Penguin, 2014), Kindle edn, 7593.

8 Dee Graham, Edna Rawlings and Nelly Rimini, 'Survivors of Terror: Battered Women, Hostages, and the Stockholm Syndrome', in *Feminist Perspectives on Wife Abuse*, ed. Kersti Yllö and Michele Bograd (Newbury Park, CA: Sage Publications, 1988), 217–33. Joan Reid, Rachael Haskell, Christina Dillahunt-Aspillaga and Jennifer Thor, 'Trauma Bonding and Interpersonal Violence' (*Faculty Publications*, 2013), 198. Patrick Carnes, *The Betrayal Bond; Breaking Free of Exploitative Relationships* (Deerfield Beach, FL: Health Communications, 1998). Natalie Collins, *Out of Control* (London: SPCK, 2019), 114–18.

9 Judith Herman, *Trauma and Recovery; The Aftermath of Violence – From Domestic Abuse to Political Terror* (New York: Basic Books, 1992), 33.

10 van der Kolk, *The Body Keeps the Score*, 390.

11 Peter Levine, 'Healing Trauma', Daily OM, www.dailyom.com/cgi-bin/display/librarydisplay.cgi?lid=2018 (accessed 29 January 2019).

12 Jennifer Erin Beste, *God and the Victim; Traumatic Intrusions on Grace and Freedom* (New York: Oxford University Press, 2007), 38.

13 Shelly Rambo, *Spirit and Trauma: A Theology of Remaining* (Louisville, KY: Westminster John Knox Press, 2010), 35.

14 Rambo, *Spirit and Trauma*, 17.

15 Sam Raimi, *Spiderman* (Columbia Pictures, Marvel Enterprises, Laura Ziskin Productions, 2002).

16 John Bowlby, *Attachment and Loss: Volume I, Attachment* (New York, Basic Books, 1982).

17 Beste, *God and the Victim*, 106.

18 Beste, *God and the Victim*, 112.

19 Paul Joeffe, 'An Empirically Supported Program to Prevent Suicide in a College Student Population', *Suicide and Life-Threatening Behavior* 38, no.1 (March 2008), 6.

20 Joeffe, 'An Empirically Supported Program', 6–7.

21 Beste, *God and the Victim*, 110.

22 Sam Raimi, *Spiderman*.

23 DC and Marvel, 'Spider-man: The First-Day of Being an Extraordinary Man', YouTube, 21 August 2016, www.youtube.com/watch?v=7B2-AM7fUsQ.

24 Lucy Johnstone and Mary Boyle, *The Power Threat Meaning Framework* (Leicester: British Psychological Society, 2018), 8.

25 Johnstone and Boyle, *Framework* , 5.

26 Johnstone and Boyle, *Framework*, 6.

27 Johnstone and Boyle, *Framework*, 9. The framework is partly informed by Foucault's work on disciplinary power.

28 Johnstone and Boyle, *Framework*, 9.

29 Johnstone and Boyle, *Framework*, 9.

30 Johnstone and Boyle, *Framework*, 77.

31 Herman, *Trauma and Recovery*, 3.

32 van der Kolk, *The Body Keeps the Score*, 54.

33 Bruce Perry and Maia Szalatvitz, *The Boy Who was Raised as a Dog: And Other Stories from a Child Psychiatrist's Notebook* (New York: BasicBooks, 2006), 125.

34 Rambo, *Spirit and Trauma*, 11.

35 Rambo, *Spirit and Trauma*, 7.

36 Perry and Szalatvitz, *The Boy Who was Raised as a Dog*, 126.

37 Pat Ogden, *Sensorimotor Psychotherapy; Interventions for Trauma and Attachment*, Norton Series on Interpersonal Neurobiology (New York: W.W. Norton and Company, 2015), Kindle edn, 31.

38 Paula Gooder, *Body: Biblical Spirituality for the Whole Person* (London: SPCK, 2016), 131.

39 Serene Jones, *Trauma and Grace; Theology in a Ruptured World* (Louisville, KY: Westminster John Knox Press, 2009), 10–11.

40 Psalm 19.1–2, NIV.

41 Matthew 5.4.

42 Rambo, *Spirit and Trauma*, 127.

43 Amy Arnsten, 'Stress signalling Pathways that Impair Prefrontal Cortex Structure and Function', *Nature Reviews Neuroscience* 10, no. 6 (June 2009), 410–22.

44 University of Queensland, 'The Limbic System', https://qbi.uq.edu.au/brain/brain-anatomy/limbic-system (accessed 29 January).

45 Zoe Lodrick, 'Psychological Trauma', www.zoelodrick.co.uk/training/article-1 (accessed 29 January 2019).

46 Emily Nagoski, *Come As You Are; The Surprising New Science that will Transform Your Sex Life* (Victoria: Scribe, 2015), Kindle edn, 2038.

47 Nagoski, *Come As You Are*, 2017.

48 Shoshana Lyons, 'The Repair of Early Trauma: A "Bottom Up" Approach', Beacon House, https://beaconhouse.org.uk/developmental-trauma/the-repair-of-early-trauma-a-bottom-up-approach/ (accessed 29 January 2019).

49 Phillip Perry, 'Been Traumatized? Here's how PTSD Rewires the Brain', Big Think, https://bigthink.com/philip-perry/been-traumatized-here-is-how-ptsd-rewires-the-brain.

50 Joe Griffin, 'PTSD', Human Givens Institute, www.hgi.org.uk/resources/delve-our-extensive-library/anxiety-ptsd-and-trauma/ptsd-why-some-techniques-treating-it (accessed 29 January 2019).

51 van der Kolk, *The Body Keeps the Score*, 3927, 2309.

52 Pesso Boyden System Psychomotor, 'About BPSP', https://pbsp.com (accessed 17 June 2019).

53 van der Kolk, *The Body Keeps the Score*, 5405.

54 van der Kolk, *The Body Keeps the Score*, 5405.

55 Nagoski, *Come As You Are*, 2121–61.

56 Rambo, *Spirit and Trauma*, 1.

57 Rambo, *Spirit and Trauma*, 138.

58 Office for National Statistics, 'Intimate Partner Violence and Partner Abuse', 11 February 2016, www.ons.gov.uk/peoplepopulationandcommunity/crimeandjustice/compendium/focusonviolentcrimeandsexualoffences/yearendingmarch2015/chapter4intimatepersonalviolenceandpartnerabuse.

59 Kristin Aune and Rebecca Barnes, *In Churches Too: Church Responses to Domestic Abuse – A Case Study of Cumbria* (Coventry and Leicester: Coventry University and University of Leicester, 2018), 24.

60 Crown Prosecution Service, 'Controlling or Coercive Behaviour in an Intimate or Family Relationship', 30 June 2019, www.cps.gov.uk/legal-guidance/controlling-or-coercive-behaviour-intimate-or-family-relationship.

61 Teri Yuan, 'Episode 2', *En(gender)ed*, 28 May 2018, https://engendered.us/episode-2-evan-stark-on-coercive-control/.

62 Office for National Statistics, 'Domestic Abuse in England and Wales: Year Ending March 2018', 22 November 2019, www.ons.gov.uk/peoplepopulationand community/crimeandjustice/bulletins/domesticabuseinenglandandwales/yearending march2018.

63 French, *The War against Women* (St Ives: Hamish Hamilton Ltd, 1992), 18.

64 John Piper and Wayne Grudem, *Recovering Biblical Manhood and Womanhood; A Response to Evangelical Feminism* (Wheaton, IL: Crossway Books, 1992).

65 Piper, 'Should Women Be Police Officers?', Desiring God, 13 August 2015, www.desiringgod.org/interviews/should-women-be-police-officers.

66 Grudem, 'But What Should Women Do In Church?', *CBMW News*, http://cbmw.org/wp-content/uploads/2013/05/1-2.pdf, 3 (accessed 29 January 2019).

67 Archive, 'Paige Patterson (SBC) Advice to Victims of Domestic Violence', https://archive.org/details/PaigePattersonsbcAdviceToVictimsOfDomesticViolence (accessed 17 June 2019). Italics added for emphasis.

68 Michael Pearl, 'The Devil's Hug', No Greater Joy, 15 June 2017, https://nogreaterjoy.org/articles/39260/.

69 United Nations Office on Drugs and Crime, *Global Study on Homicide*, www.unodc.org/documents/data-and-analysis/GSH2018/GSH18_Gender-related_killing_of_women_and_girls.pdf, 10 (accessed 29 January 2019).

70 Amazon, 'Amazon Best Sellers', www.amazon.com/Best-Sellers-Books-Christian-Prayer/zgbs/books/12470 (accessed 29 January 2019).

71 Stormie Omartian, *The Power of a Praying Wife* (Eugene, OR: Harvest House, 2014), 63.

72 Ministry of Justice, 'An Overview of Sexual Offending in England and Wales', 10 January 2013, https://assets.publishing.service.gov.uk/government/uploads/system/uploads/attachment_data/file/214970/sexual-offending-overview-jan-2013.pdf, 6.

73 Reggie Osborne, 'She only said "Yes" Once', For Every Mom, 5 April 2016, http://foreverymom.com/mom-gold/she-only-said-yes-once/.

74 Valerie Hobbs, 'Rape Culture in the Bible', Shiloh Project, 19 June 2017, https://shiloh-project.group.shef.ac.uk/rape-culture-in-the-christian-church/.

75 Johnstone and Boyle, *Framework*, 80.

76 Tertullian, 'On the Apparel of Women', www.newadvent.org/fathers/0402.htm (accessed 1 August 2019).

77 Thomas Aquinas, *Summa Theologiae*, www.newadvent.org/summa/1092.htm (acccessed 1 August 2019).

78 Secret Keeper Girl, 'Truth or Bare Fashion Test', *Secret Keeper Girl*, http://secretkeepergirl.com/truth-or-bare-fashion-test/ (accessed 29 January 2019).

79 Pearl cited by Alicia Willis, 'Created to be His Helpmeet', *Alicia A. Willis*, http://aliciaannewillis.blogspot.com/2017/07/created-to-be-his-helpmeet-discovering. html (accessed 29 January 2019).

80 Johnstone and Boyle, *Framework*, 89.

81 Johnstone and Boyle, *Framework*, 89.

82 During threats, the body shuts down immune and digestive function, which can cause long-term damage. Emily Nagoski, *Come As You Are*, 2006.

83 Matthew Stanford, 'Demon or disorder: A Survey of Attitudes Toward Mental Illness in the Christian Church', *Mental Health, Religion and Culture* 10, no.5 (August 2007), 2.

84 Doris Sommer-Rotenberg, 'Suicide and Language', *Canadian Medical Association journal* 159, no. 3 (August 1998), 239–40.

85 Mind and Soul, '6 Christian Mental Health Conversations', www.mindandsoulfoundation.org/Articles/515149/Mind_and_Soul/Articles/6_Christian_Mental.aspx (accessed 29 January 2019).

86 Mental Health Access Pack, 'Download the Whole Pack', www.mentalhealthaccesspack.org/download-the-whole-pack/ (accessed 29 January 2019).

87 Mental Health Access Pack, 'Forms of Counselling', www.mentalhealthaccess-pack.org/install/wp-content/uploads/2018/06/Cards_Pratical-Tips_Counselling_May-2018.pdf (accessed 29 January 2019).

88 Johnstone and Boyle, *Framework*, 263–4.

89 Johnstone and Boyle, *Framework*, 24.

90 Orwell, *Nineteen Eighty-Four*.

91 John Haffenden, *William Empson: Volume II, Against the Christians* (Oxford: Oxford University Press, 2006), 269.

92 Herman, *Trauma and Recovery*, 87.

93 Herman, *Trauma and Recovery*, 87.

94 Rambo, *Spirit and Trauma*, 6.

95 Rambo, *Spirit and Trauma*, 164.

96 Rambo, *Spirit and Trauma*, 172.

97 Bradley Onishi, 'The "Exvangelical" Movement will Continue to Grow', *Religion News Service*, 20 December 2018, https://religionnews.com/2018/12/20/bradley-onishi-the-exvangelical-movement-will-continue-to-grow/.

PART 4

Feminist Trauma Theologies: Post-Traumatic Remaking

11

The Changing Self: Forming and Reforming the *Imago Dei* in Survivors of Domestic Abuse

ALLY MODER

Introduction

One in three women experience abuse from a male intimate partner in their lifetime.[1] This prolific reality for women around the world represents one of the most traumatizing and profoundly dehumanizing experiences.[2] Domestic abuse can be defined as a pattern of abusive behaviour that is used by one partner to gain or maintain power and control over another intimate partner.[3] This deeply personal form of trauma often results in a shattering of one's sense of self,[4] rooting survivors' identity in the core experience of shame that many women struggle to recover from. In this chapter, I seek to reclaim women's full personhood after their experience of domestic abuse by ultimately proposing a model of prayer that restores their *imago Dei*. Towards this aim, I utilize fellow feminist pastoral theologian Carrie Doehring's critical-correlational method rooted in the praxis of pastoral care that integrates cross-disciplinary conversations among theology and the social sciences.[5] My primary conversation partners are Julian of Norwich from medieval Christian mysticism, and contemporary systematic feminist theologian Elizabeth Johnson. In their writing, both women explore the concept of self as formed within the *imago Dei*, with a particular emphasis on God imaged as a female Trinity. This provides a robust feminist theological foundation on which I will build, utilizing my next conversation partner in trauma theory and psychology, primarily through the work of Judith Herman and her work in understanding women's personhood and domestic abuse. Finally, I present my own feminist pastoral theological model of Inner Healing Prayer as a praxis that empowers Christian women survivors to reform their sense of self as the beloved *imago Dei* in relationship with the loving, compassionate God who liberates women from the oppression and violence of men who abuse.

The *Imago Dei* and Feminist Theology: The Self and the Female Trinity

Feminist theology is centred on the principle that women are created by God as equals with men in the *imago Dei*.[6] This egalitarian position says that women are created by God as full equals in God's image, both ontologically and functionally, while also recognizing that women and men are different. The doctrine of the Trinity has long been a tool theologians engage with in order to understand what human personhood is – particularly how the self forms within the context of a threefold relationship of self, God and others. While there are many ways to engage this field of theological anthropology,[7] I have chosen for the purposes of this chapter to focus on the following three characteristics of the Trinity imaged in the self: that of the self as loved, formed of multiple parts and created for and within relationship. Tracing these elements through the work of feminist theologians Julian of Norwich and Elizabeth Johnson, we will discover a divine female Trinity that invites women to embrace their identity as fully *imago Dei*.

The feminist spiritual theology of Christian mystic Julian of Norwich

The primary question for medieval Christian mystics concerning the self can be articulated by the following paradox: 'Can we know God without knowing our self?' and 'Can we know our self without knowing God?' The self and God are inseparable for the mystics. Indeed, a central theme among the Christian mystics is that the self – or soul, as many referred to it – is an immortal part of our being. Embracing a Neoplatonic-Augustinian dualism of body and soul, the mystics often see the self as separate from the body that God created, while highlighting another dualism within our spiritual self.[8] From their powerful mystical experiences with God, many mystics picked up on this idea of a separation of an earthly self and a heavenly self – or an outer and inner self – with only the latter being the eternal part of our *imago Dei* that ultimately is fully reunited with God. I have chosen to explore this concept in the writings of Julian of Norwich, who not only proposed an integrated theory of multiple selfhood that demonstrates this intriguing multiplicity of personhood within the *imago Dei*, but also because of her remarkable feminist imaging of God as Mother.

The self in relation to God

In the midst of the rise of mysticism and contemplative spirituality in fourteenth- and fifteenth-century Western Europe, the voice of Englishwoman Julian of Norwich emerged (c. 1343–1416). A mystic and theologian, as well as the first known woman to write a book in English, Julian is best known for her writings she originally called *Showings*. This work consists of 16 visions God showed Julian at the age of 30 while she was extremely ill, and which revealed to her the immense love of God as she meditated on a crucifix.[9] Following this, she was cloistered in a small brick room as an anchoress in the Church of St Julian. Here she meditated for over 20 years on her visions, eventually writing her manuscripts that today we call *Revelations of Divine Love*.[10] As with the earlier Church Fathers and many of the Christian mystics of her time, Julian develops a binary anthropology of the soul, articulating human nature as comprising 'the Substance' and 'the Sensuality'. The Substance is our higher self that is created, but made of the same substance of God, thus connecting us to God eternally, according to theologian Grace Jantzen. She explicates the way Julian refers to the lower self as the Sensuality – which she envisions as our entire earthly existence that is fundamentally good, because all of God's creation is good, although it suffers due to sin and evil in the world. Importantly, the two elements of the self are unique and distinct from each other, Jantzen concludes, but these parts together make up the whole self. For Julian, it is sin – which she envisions as wandering away from God – that distances us from God and our higher self. To bridge this divide between our two parts, Julian asserts that our faith in God and the work of the Holy Spirit enables our substance to reach down to our sensuality because of Christ.[11] This knitting together of the two parts of the soul, or self, includes both male and female who equally are recipients of the deep love of God.[12]

For women who experience domestic abuse from a male partner, Julian's equality of the sexes not only reaffirms their personhood as made equally in the image of God, but wraps up their shattered self into the loving embrace of a compassionate God with the promise that one day 'all will be well, and all will be well, and every kind of thing will be well'.[13] Survivors, then, can have confidence in Julian's theology of love that their unique personhood is created in God's image, and is lovingly received in the midst of their broken, abused self. While Julian does not address the systemic or social sins of patriarchy so vital to contemporary feminist theologians, we might reinterpret her understanding of individual sin through a feminist lens to include the sin of domestic abuse as that which mars the *imago Dei* in women. In broadening Julian's concept of sin from a personal distancing from God to include the injustice men perpetrate against women as sin inflicted on survivors, we importantly recognize that domestic abuse often tears at survivors' relationship with God. Julian's response to this breaking of the *imago Dei* and relationship with God in abuse is her depiction of God as an unconditional loving Mother who will not be separated from her beloved children by sin. As she writes, through 'this experience of ... falling we shall have a great and marvellous knowledge of love in God without end; for enduring and marvellous is that love which cannot and will not be broken because of offences'.[14] All persons are created in the image of this loving God for Julian, and our personhood is inseparable from relationship with the triune Mother, even in the most traumatic experiences of abuse.

God as mother

Julian's revelations reveal a gospel of love articulated through the mother-hood of God as depicted in Christ's passion. Though this may seem revolutionary today, her spiritual theology was built on an established theological tradition of viewing God as mother. What is unique for her time is that her use of feminine imagery and language depicts God's nature as *equally* male and female.[15] Julian's remarkable theological contribution stems from her images of the Trinity primarily as a mother, characterized by compassion and love. She writes:

> As truly as God is our Father, so truly is God our Mother ... I understand three ways of contemplating motherhood in God. The first is the foundation of our nature's creation; the second is his taking of our nature, where the motherhood of grace begins; the third is the motherhood at work. And in that, by the same grace, everything is penetrated, in length and in breadth, in height and in depth without end; and it is all one love.[16]

While the Bible portrays both male and female imagery of God, Scripture predominantly refers to God as Father or Son, and we see this emphasis on the maleness of God in the images and speech of the Trinity throughout church history and still today. In Julian's time the language for God highlighted God's roles as lord, king, ruler, master and judge – all roles that would have made sense within the structure of medieval European society, especially in view of the hierarchical positions filled by men who ruled over both state and church. Julian reinterprets her contemporary theologians' view of a wrathful, powerful judge who demands satisfaction for our sins, in her visions of God as a comforting, nourishing, and loving Mother revealed in feminine imagery and language. She articulates this female Trinity in her sixteenth revelation:

> This fair lovely word 'mother' is so sweet and kind in itself that it cannot truly be said of anyone or to anyone except of him and to him who is the true Mother of life and of all things. To the property of motherhood belong nature, love, wisdom and knowledge, and this is God.[17]

The maternal act of our creation, even our very nature joined in the womb of God, is encapsulated in Julian's writing: 'And so Jesus is our true Mother by nature at our first creation, and he is our true mother in grace by taking on our created nature.'[18]

Julian's language highlights that our very nature is one with God in Christ, just as an infant is with its mother. Similarly, the nature of God is not just *like* a mother, but God is Mother, although importantly she seeks not to replace God as Father, but rather to highlight God's love as a compassion-ate mother enfolding her beloved children rather than a stern patriarchal judge to be feared. While she highlights this difference, Julian also seeks to unite the Trinitarian God as one characterized by intimacy and love:

> Our great Father ... in his most wonderful deep love, by the prescient eternal counsel of all the blessed Trinity, he wanted the second Person to become our Mother, our brother, and our saviour. From this it follows that as truly as God is our Father, so truly is God our Mother. Our Father wills, our Mother works, our good Lord the Holy Spirit confirms.[19]

Holding the tension of the wrathful God often portrayed by the medieval Church with contrasting maternal images of the motherhood of grace depicted for Julian by Christ in her revelations, all of humanity is nourished and sustained in the bosom of Christ through the Eucharist:

> Our precious Mother Jesus can feed us with himself, and does, most courteously and most tenderly, with the blessed sacraments, which is the precious food of true life; and with all the sweet sacrament he sustains us most mercifully and graciously.[20]

Christ our Mother is loving and tender, near and true to us in creating and sustaining her children, but also in his work of love suffering on the cross just as a mother bears birth pangs to give forth life.[21] As one who suffers with and for us, Julian's image of Christ our Mother emphasizes womb imagery as well as the comforting maternal embrace:

> I saw that he is to us everything which is good and comforting for our help. He is our clothing, who wraps and enfolds us for love, embraces us and shelters us, surrounds us for his love, which is so tender that he may never desert us.[22]

Julian's work, then, illustrates a most intimate relationship of love between God and humans, where separation is not possible. We are to run to God our Mother in time of sin and suffering, and because of Christ's incarnation, passion and resurrection, which embodies God's motherly love for us, we find our self safe at home in her embrace. For survivors of domestic abuse, this image of God as Mother may be profoundly helpful in reimaging God from a distant, punishing male figure who allowed their trauma, towards a feminine concept of a God who embraces their shattered self without judgement, inviting them into safety and healing in the divine Mother's love.

The systematic feminist theology of Elizabeth Johnson

Our second feminist theological conversation partner in reflecting on the personhood of domestic abuse survivors is Catholic feminist theologian

Elizabeth Johnson. A contemporary writer in systematic theology, Johnson focuses much of her work on female imaging and discourse of God, which she ultimately limns in a female Sophia-Trinity Johnson refers to as 'She Who Is'. In her innovative book of the same name, Johnson aims to reclaim the full personhood of women who have long been denied their right to full status as the *imago Dei* in the history of Christianity. She is particularly concerned with reclaiming the Trinity from its patriarchal, androcentric images and language that she – and many feminist theologians – view as subordinating women to oppression by men. While Johnson's work is less centred on the individual self than Julian's writing, she does helpfully broaden our understanding of women's sense of self as equal image-bearers through her focus on the vast injustices men inflict on women, and the way in which women resist the loss of self in their suffering and move towards flourishing as the full *imago Dei*.

Women as full image bearers

Johnson's envisioning of the God-, Christ- and Spirit-*Sophia*, drawing on the female personification of God (based on the Greek word throughout the Bible) as 'wisdom', is a Trinity that embodies a self-giving and empowering love. Similar to Julian, women's selfhood in Johnson's writing is equal to men as made fully in God's image, and also firmly rooted and developed in relationship to God's love.[23] This inclusive stance is empowering for survivors who are welcomed into abundant life – and freedom from violence – by the grand and mysterious love of God who, Johnson says, is revealed throughout the Bible 'in imaginative parables, compassionate healings, startling exorcisms, and festive meals ... he spells out the reality of the gracious goodness and renewing power of Sophia-God drawing near'.[24] Selfhood forms and re-forms from the violence of sexism and abuse as 'self-in-relation' to God and others based on the feminist principles of mutuality and equality in relationships.[25] For Johnson, it is the incredible mystery of God that draws us into just such loving relationship that frees us to know ourselves as truly loved:

> Being related is at the very heart of divine being. God's being is not an enclosed, egocentric self-regard but is identical with an act of free communion, always going forth and receiving in. At the deepest core of reality is a mystery of personal connectedness that constitutes the very livingness of God. The category of relation thus serves as a heuristic tool for bringing to light not just the mutuality of trinitarian persons but the very nature of the holy mystery of God herself. Divine unity exists as an intrinsic *koinonia* of love, of love freely blazing forth, love not just as divine attitude, affect, or property but as God's very nature: 'God is Love' (1 John 4:16).[26]

Additionally, Johnson's feminist methodology of Sophia relies heavily on the multiplicity of God as a foundation component of personhood. In contrast to the dualism and binary self of the early Church Fathers and many mystics such as Julian, Johnson's feminist theology understands the three persons of the Trinity as much-needed corrective to women's selfhood that invites the wide variety of women's experiences – and their oppression – to be included in loving, restorative relationship with God. Essential to her writing is the belief that the divine multiplicity is also revealed in the Bible in multiple female images that illustrate that God is not male. This enables Johnson to push back against the gender dualism of selfhood in Christian theology that historically has separated women from their bodies, symbolized females as evil, and subordinated women to men – and thus perpetuated experiences of oppression and abuse.[27] Johnson's feminist envisioning of Sophia thus sees:

> a reflection on God and all things in the light of God that stands consciously in the company of all the world's women, explicitly prizing their genuine humanity while uncovering and criticizing its persistent violation in sexism, itself an omnipresent paradigm of unjust relationships.[28]

She Who Is, then, invites women to resist the sin of abusive men that diminishes women's personhood, and name their own reality and God, who restores their 'human dignity and value' as *imago Dei*.[29] This is good news for survivors in their painful journey of recovering from the shattering trauma of domestic abuse.

God as Sophia

Unlike most systematic theologians, Johnson begins not with God the Father, but with Spirit-Sophia, then Jesus-Sophia, then Mother-Sophia:

> Moving from speaking about God-with-us to the immanent trinity, we remember that here language is stretched to the breaking point, for God's inner life remains a mystery, strictly speaking, even including the meaning of the word 'inner'. Speaking from a perspective that prizes the equal humanity of women as imago Dei, imago Christi, imago Spiritui, we can enlist female metaphors in the task of speaking the unspeakable.[30]

Addressing the fundamental question, 'What is the right way to speak about God?', Elizabeth Johnson sets out in *She Who Is* to tackle the patriarchal interpretation of the Christian God as male.[31] With a view to facilitating the flourishing of women as ontologically equal to men as the *imago Dei*, Johnson aims to emancipate speech about God from androcentric theology that frames the divine as male, leading to domination and oppression of females.[32] Her primary premise is that speaking of God in male terms has dehumanized women and we must, therefore, move beyond scriptural terms for God to feminine language that more adequately images the biblical divine being who creatively and compassionately suffers with and renews God's creation with liberative care.[33]

Johnson's image of God as Mother-Sophia begins with God as 'Spirit-Sophia' – the Spirit that is ontologically God in her presence throughout Scripture in the creation, incarnation, resurrection and beyond.[34] This emphasis on Spirit is intended to contrast the early church debate of hierarchy in the Trinity, reversing the traditional order of God as the monarchical source of Jesus and the Spirit. Sophia is Johnson's attempt to reimagine a relational Trinitarian theology characterized by a pneumatological, rather than the Christological approach of most classical theologians. Framing a triune Spirit-, Jesus- and Mother-Sophia, Johnson is careful to acknowledge that using the metaphor of motherhood presents the historical challenge of women's value being extolled in their role as mothers and their rightful place as in the home.[35] Still, the gift of motherhood as witnessed in Mother-Sophia illustrates God's commitment to justice and right relationships. Jesus-Sophia draws our awareness to Mother-Sophia in his life, ministry, death and resurrection, revealing a Trinitarian God who suffers with us, fights for justice and actively works towards the flourishing of humanity, particularly the most vulnerable. As Johnson writes:

> Such a symbol of the triune God, Holy Wisdom as *imago feminae*, signifies for women the call to grow into the abundance of their human powers, and for the community of women and men together to be creative and loving in ways that address human brokenness, violence, and the destruction of the earth. The triune God exists as a communion of radically equal, mutual relations.[36]

For Johnson, the maternal love of Mother-Sophia is illustrated in creation, and in Jesus-Sophia as redeemer, and Spirit-Sophia as sustainer.[37] Together, the Trinity of Sophia actively engages in the work of social justice, liberating women from the oppression of patriarchy and its violent breaking of women's *imago Dei*. An essential part of Johnson's thesis is that reclaiming women's selfhood from the grips of patriarchy requires not only renaming God as female, but also including in our speech the life-giving female images of *She Who Is*. There are many to draw on, as Johnson enthusiastically recounts:

> from the biblical portrayal of God in maternal images: pregnant, crying out in labor, nursing, carrying on her shoulders, comforting, never abandoning; to the great figure of Holy Wisdom (Sophia), the intensely female personification of Israel's God's who leads the people across the Red Sea, and against whom evil does not prevail; from the great Spirit ruah, to Jesus' image of God the Redeemer as a woman looking for her lost coin,

to glimpses of God as midwife, teacher, female beloved, hostess, justly angry prophet, sister, female friend, in a word: Creator, Redeemer, and Sanctifier, the Holy One of Blessing, Blessed be She.[38]

Johnson's feminist theology empowers women to reclaim their sense of self as fully created in the *imago Dei* in the divine love of the Sophia-Trinity who seeks to liberate them from their suffering under patriarchy. Survivors of domestic abuse may particularly resonate with the freedom offered by female images of God that are nurturing, compassionate and powerful, to overcome the injustice of their experiences of abuse by their male partner. The loving, relational, multiplicity of *She Who Is* powerfully invites survivors to bring the broken pieces of their self into intimate relationship with the compassionate God who restores their *imago Dei* in divine love.

The Broken Image: Domestic Abuse and the Self

The concepts of *imago Dei* and the divine feminine Trinity as we explored in the feminist theologies of Julian of Norwich and Elizabeth Johnson revealed that the essential personhood of all humans is formed in God as self that is loved, multiple and relational. Both Julian and Johnson propose an egalitarian view of self that includes women as fully *imago Dei*, while also recognizing that brokenness in humanity caused by sin or evil malforms the self. Domestic abuse is a particularly egregious evil that deeply tears at the *imago Dei* in the abusive destruction of loving relationship that breaks women's self in the overwhelming experience of trauma. Indeed, many women describe the trauma of domestic abuse as a profound loss of self, as though their personhood shattered into multiple fragments in the painful ongoing abuse of their partner.

Moving from feminist theology to trauma theory with the goal of deepening our understanding of women's self as malformed by domestic abuse, we can see that the aspects of loving relationality and multiplicity of self are also key elements to healing in the field of psychology and trauma. In her groundbreaking book on trauma theory entitled *Trauma and Recovery*, psychiatrist and researcher Judith Herman elucidates that trauma experiences represent a profound threat to an individual's identity, which many survivors experience as a threat to one's very existence.[39] The natural defence reaction against trauma is multiplicity of the mind, or what can also be described as a fragmented self that cannot coherently weave together the broken pieces of a person's abused self with other parts of their personhood.[40] This leaves survivors with an incoherent, disorganized sense of self that is stuck in repeated experiences of the abuse trauma memories, often long after they have left the abuser.[41] As Herman outlines, healing from domestic abuse necessarily requires an integration of the multiple parts of self – from before, during and after the abuse – into a new, whole self.

According to trauma theory, healing can take place when all of a survivor's experiences are compassionately held in the loving presence of others.[42] This again affirms our feminist understanding of the *imago Dei* as formed in loving relationship that embraces the multiplicity of our experiences; for survivors, this importantly includes the abused self as well as the self made fully in the image of God and perfectly loved by the divine feminine Trinity. From a feminist Christian perspective, then, we can also look to the compassionate, loving God as the ultimate source of healing presence for survivors of domestic abuse, as we shall explore in the final section of this chapter.

For now, we turn to the core experience of domestic abuse as a loss of self for women, which is perhaps best characterized by a deep feeling of shame.[43] Domestic abuse, as we have previously said, is a violation of personhood and the primordial *imago Dei*. Given that the perpetrator is not a stranger but rather one's boyfriend or husband, this breaking of what should be the most intimate human relationship of love is particularly damaging to a woman's sense of self, leading to overwhelming feelings of shame.[44]

Shame and the Self in Domestic Abuse

Domestic abuse is essentially about one person exerting power and control over their partner. This dominance over another in an intimate relationship dehumanizes women and frequently yields a deep feeling of guilt that they are to blame for the abuse, rather than the perpetrator, limns Herman.[45] In her view, guilt enables victims to reclaim a sense of power and control over their life as they imagine how they could disrupt or end the abuse through their own intervention. In reality, abuse is solely the choice of the perpetrator, but acknowledging this may foster feelings of helplessness in victims, so guilt frequently becomes a coping technique in the face of the overwhelming terror of abuse.[46] Inevitably, the abuse dehumanizes a victim, imbuing their sense of self with shame. Sociologist and shame researcher Brené Brown makes an important distinction from Herman's use of the term guilt, which she defines as 'I did something bad', whereas shame is 'I am bad'.[47] As intimate partner violence is beyond the control of its victims, the resulting identity damage is that of shame; victims end up carrying a deeply held belief that they are unworthy of love due to their partner's abuse.

Intimate partner violence leaves a survivor deeply shamed in her identity – her sense of self – as the abuse carries on over time. As she continues to experience the erratic, irrational, and frightening choices of her partner, the survivor becomes deeply confused and often enmeshed with his abusive behaviour as she diligently strives to understand how she can stop these painful incidents. This is the crux of shame in an abusive relationship: the victim internalizes the shame of her partner's abuse, believing that her very being is worthless and unlovable. This leads us back to Brown's conceptualization of shame: the belief that one's very self – or being – is ultimately bad. It is important to note that guilt – the feeling of having done something wrong – is actually a healthy part of one's self-concept, but in this case should be experienced by the perpetrator of abuse. Such acknowledgement of abuse is extraordinarily rare by the abuser, leaving the victim's sense of self embedded in the 'intensely painful feeling [of shame that she is] unworthy of love and belonging'.[48] The shame of intimate partner violence, thus, undermines the greatest human need: to be loved. Research shows that the shame of abuse is experienced in a lack of self-worth and self-esteem, an increase in self-doubt in their decisions and abilities, a lack of a sense of agency to make changes or improve their situation, and self-blame for staying in the abusive relationship or failing to make the relationship work.[49] Shame, then, leaves women feeling not only unloved and unlovable, but also profoundly powerless and incapacitated.

Reconstructing the self

Thus far we have talked of recovery and healing as an integrated self. It is a process of pulling together the fragmented pieces of identity from before, during and after the abuse, into a new sense of self that allows these multiple parts to embrace the complex, multi-storied meanings of abuse and survivor. The terrifying, problematic, ambivalent, uncertain and fragmented memories must be held within a compassionate space that empowers the survivor not only to tell their trauma stories as the author of their own experience but to make sense of the abuse in ways that ultimately don't control the survivor's personhood. The fields of psychology and trauma theory inform us that common signs of healing and well-being for survivors of domestic abuse are a sense of self as lovable, agentic and powerful in their own lives and the world, and increased resilience to cope with the ongoing challenges of life. I will now explore these concepts.

The self as lovable

If we understand that humans are created from the triune relationship of the Godhead, for intimate relationships of equality, mutuality and flourishing – as the Christian mystics image for us – then it makes sense that a whole or healthy self would be epitomized by love. God made humans in the *imago Dei*, and thus we are created for loving relational mutuality. Domestic violence, then, is not only antithetical but abhorrent to the development of self and, as we have seen, results in a deeply embedded shame-based sense of self. As Brown says, love is the antidote to shame:

We cultivate love when we allow our most vulnerable powerful selves to be deeply seen and known, and when we honor the *spiritual connection* that grows from that offering with *trust, respect, kindness*, and *affection*. Love is not something we give or get; it is something that we *nurture and grow*, a connection can only be cultivated between two people when it exists within each one of them – we can only love others as much as we love ourselves. Shame, blame, disrespect, betrayal, and the withholding of affection damage the roots from which love grows. Love can only survive these injuries if they are acknowledged, healed, and rare.[50]

As Christians we recognize that the ultimate source of love is God, and thus God is also the true source of healing the trauma of domestic abuse. Recovery, then, must involve survivors experiencing their broken selves as compassionately loved by God, who reforms their identity as the beloved *imago Dei*.

The self as agentic

As this project primarily centres on women who have left their abusive partner and are seeking healing, we can recognize that these women have already demonstrated extraordinary agency in their lives.[51] Intimate partner violence, as we have seen, is an ongoing experience of one partner maintaining power and control over the other through a wide variety of abusive behaviours. In order to reform her identity as the *imago Dei*, then, I propose that God calls a woman towards a full personhood that resists abuse and stands up for her rights as a victim of injustice. The metanarrative of Scripture reveals that God's love is profoundly rooted in pursuing the justice and shalom of the Kingdom of God in the midst of harrowing experiences, as witnessed in the stories of Hagar, Moses, Tamar, Deborah, Ruth, Jesus, Mary (of sisters, Martha and Mary), the disciples, Pontius Pilate's wife, and others.

Psychological research confirms that developing agency is an essential component of healing, and is marked by increased self-esteem and feelings of control and empowerment – primarily influenced by compassionate, supportive others.[52] Rediscovering and developing new strengths, coping skills and power to rebuild their lives after abuse is critical in the journey of recovery for survivors. Agency, then, is necessary to counteract or reform the disempowering sense of shame and guilt that malforms survivors' identity in the experience of domestic abuse.

The self as resilient

While there are many ways to conceptualize healing for survivors of domestic abuse, the term 'resilience' is often employed; this multi-layered concept, I argue, is utilized to envision the many ways women not only survive the terror of abuse, but also cope and recover from their trauma. These strategies of developing resiliency are varied, from fostering authentic, loving relationships with friends, family and others as they seek help to recover, to sharing their stories of abuse, to reconstructing a new, hopeful sense of self and rebuilding their life apart from the abuser.[53] The Church can play a vital role in this by nurturing safe spaces for women to share their stories, be compassionately listened to and believed. Additionally, pastoral care-giving that reframes God as a loving, powerful being that suffers with and enables survivors to heal from abuse can empower women to re-tell their stories within a new, loving framework. Spiritual practices can be particularly beneficial in empowering this resiliency in survivors as they are equipped to heal in the loving, embodied presence of God.

Healing in relationship with God

Given this chapter's thesis that women are created fully in the image of God and that the re-formation of the *imago Dei* is vital in the process of healing for survivors of domestic abuse, the frequent question of Christian feminist theologians as to whether women can heal in relationship with the God who is predominantly depicted in patriarchal, androcentric terms is deeply important to our quest. In our earlier discussion of the divine feminine Trinity I believe Julian of Norwich and Elizabeth Johnson provide a robust foundation for reclaiming God from patriarchy in liberative images of the female God that lovingly embraces the trauma of female survivors of domestic abuse and empowers them towards healing and flourishing. Nonetheless, we must be cognizant of the reality that the majority of survivors today do not attend churches, which recognize or promote such a God. Most usually women hear only patriarchal theology in their churches that frequently perpetuates their experience of domestic abuse through such teachings as male hierarchy in the *imago Dei*, women's submission to men, divorce as sinful, forgiveness as requiring women to stay with abusive men, and women's suffering as redemptive.[54] These beliefs communicated by the Church often translate to women feeling distant from God or fearing that God will condemn them if they separate from or divorce their abusive partner. Despite this, women overwhelmingly look to God for support, and highly report that their relationship with God is fundamental for their re-formation of self after domestic abuse.[55]

A growing body of research on the essential role of spirituality in the recovery of trauma has been developing in neuroscience, psychology and religion. This exciting new field of study reminds us of the vital role of spiritual practices in recovery for Christian women survivors. Going back to Herman's treatise on trauma, a fundamental impact of intimate partner violence is the shattering of self: the loss of safety in the world, their framework for meaning-making, as well as trust in God and others. As Herman describes:

> Traumatized people feel utterly abandoned, utterly alone, cast out of human and divine systems of care and protection that sustained life. Thereafter, a sense of alienation, of disconnection, pervades every relationship, from the most intimate familial bonds to the most abstract affiliations of community and religion ... A secure sense of connection with caring people is the foundation of [personhood]. When this connection is shattered, the traumatized person loses her basic sense of self.[56]

Fundamental to care and counsel for abused Christian women, then, is nurturing a loving relationship with God. As feminist theologians Julian of Norwich and Elizabeth Johnson have articulated – in addition to many of the global voices of feminist theologians – reclaiming the feminine imagery, symbols and language for God used throughout the Bible can be powerful for women to reform their sense of self in relationship with God.[57] It follows that a feminist framing of Christian practices of spirituality can thus empower women to reconstruct their concepts of God through inclusive, multiple images of the divine that support survivors' healing[58] from domestic abuse, from a self rooted in shame, to her rightful identity as the beloved *imago Dei*.

Restoring the *Imago Dei*: A Feminist Pastoral Praxis of Healing Prayer

Throughout the history of Christianity is the journey of spiritual formation of the self in relationship with God, which this chapter has framed within a feminist conceptualization of the *imago Dei* in loving communion with the divine feminine Trinity. As prayer is at the heart of Christian spirituality, it is also my feminist praxis of re-forming the *imago Dei* in faith-based female survivors of domestic abuse. As a feminist pastoral theologian, I recognize the vital role that clergy play in women's experience, particularly in light of research that demonstrates 'many religious women seek help first from their faith community when violence strikes at home'.[59] While clergy are of utmost importance in the Church's response to women who experience domestic abuse, survivors often rate their effectiveness lower than other forms of support, such as trained counsellors. I suggest that this is strongly linked to the substantial lack of clergy training on this critical issue facing so many women.[60] As a response to this need for clergy and lay leaders to be equipped to respond helpfully to survivors, I developed a model of prayer in my doctoral research[61] that utilizes contemporary research on contemplative and meditative prayer practices associated with healing from trauma. My model of Inner Healing Prayer is an integration and adaptation based on the contemporary writings of Leanne Payne,[62] Rick Richardson[63] and Brad Jersak,[64] with the goal of healing the trauma of abuse memories through God's compassionate interaction with them. My research involved using Inner Healing Prayer in a weekly meeting with Christian female survivors. The results indicated a strong correlation between the use of this form of prayer as a spiritual practice that helped the women move towards an integrated self, or the *imago Dei* as lovable, agentic and resilient – the three elements of healing we previously explored in this chapter. It is my hope that pastoral care-givers will embrace their essential role in a survivor's journey of healing by incorporating my model of Inner Healing Prayer into their praxis of care-giving to empower women to be free to heal from abuse.

Inner Healing Prayer

As we have seen throughout this chapter, women's sense of self is continually being formed and malformed within their multivariate experiences of relationship and is particularly damaged in the trauma of domestic abuse. A feminist theological reframing of God and women's identity as fully *imago Dei* in loving relationship with the divine female Trinity has been articulated as part of the healing journey for survivors. I propose that my model of Inner Healing Prayer empowers Christian female survivors to be restored as the *imago Dei* as they experience the healing presence of God's love suffering with them in their experiences of trauma. Inner Healing Prayer (IHP) is a contemporary Christian spiritual practice that is based on the concept that humans can connect personally with God by means of their imaginal capacity, and then together go back into the person's painful memories where Jesus facilitates transformation of wounds and trauma.[65] IHP thus involves reprocessing the trauma memories – utilizing the techniques of visualization and listening – to address particular emotions and memories connected to historical trauma experiences. In this way, IHP's concept of the self can be understood as the primordial good *imago Dei* that is also present in multiplicity from a chronological or historiological viewpoint; the self imaginatively goes back in time with Jesus to any number of memories to interact with their past selves in the midst of their traumatic history. Just as in our earlier discussion of the multiplicity of selfhood, IHP can be interpreted to resonate with this dichotomy of a whole essential self and a wounded self caused by the sin of domestic abuse; however, this framework understands multiplicity of self as the innumerable historical past selves based on memory. In plain terms, a survivor post-abuse can go back into her memories, imaginatively viewing her former self in an experience of abuse. Here she can not only witness any number of past selves in trauma from the viewpoint of her present, more resilient self, but she can also imaginatively interact with them through the healing power of Jesus transforming her past abuse memories. I will now briefly describe this practice in three stages to provide a sense of my overall model of IHP as a practitioner might implement it, although I refer you to my doctoral thesis for much-needed additional details.

Stage one

The practitioner first grounds the survivor in safety and security in her body through breathing exercises, and then invites her to imagine in her mind a place where she is fully safe and at peace. This place can be real or imagined; what matters most is that the survivor can as vividly as possible colour in this safe place and attach securely to it in her emotions and body. It may be helpful for the practitioner – who functions as a facilitator in the practice of Inner Healing Prayer – to provide calm, gentle support through-out the experience by offering suggestions that help the survivor activate her imaginal capacity. This could involve phrasing such as:

> Perhaps you are in a beautiful wood cabin in the woods, curled up by a warm fire with a hot cup of tea. Or maybe you are at the ocean, watching the waves gently roll into the shore as the warm sun shines upon you. However your safe place appears to you is perfectly fine.

In this way, the practitioner helps activate the creative parts of the survivor's mind that may have been blocked by the trauma of her abuse, while also acting agentically to empower her to choose her imaginal experience.

Stage two

Once the survivor has been grounded in both the safety of her body and her safe, peaceful place in her mind, the practitioner can invite her to imagine God or Jesus to be present with her in her safe place. In accordance with our earlier discussion of the importance for women and survivors of domestic abuse to have access to female images and language of God, the practitioner would be wise to have a conversation – prior to initially beginning the IHP practice – about how the survivor understands and conceptualizes God, and creatively explore together safe and peaceful God images. Ultimately, it is important that the survivor has complete control over how God appears to her and how close she is to God in her safe place. Again, the practi-tioner might encourage the survivor with different suggestions of how God might look. 'Perhaps God comes to you as a beautiful butterfly, or a golden retriever, or maybe like Aslan from Narnia, or a beautiful Asian woman like Sarayu in *The Shack*. However God appears to you is perfectly fine.'

If the survivor is unable to verbalize any positive, affirming God images she might use in IHP, the care-giver should stop the practice and return to safe-place practice and/or grounding breathing exercises, until the survivor feels ready or able to conceptualize God in love and safety – which may take weeks or even months, depending on the individual. The hope is that through ongoing practices of Inner Healing Prayer survivors will develop the capacity to feel secure within themselves to imagine God as loving and compassionate. As the aim is to foster secure relationship with the triune God/Christ/Spirit, only after secure attachment with a positive God image should the practitioner move onwards in the prayer model towards healing trauma memories.

Stage three

From a therapeutic stance in terms of working with female survivors of intimate partner violence, the goal of Inner Healing Prayer is to 'heal' memories of the abuse so the survivor can be free from the ongoing trauma of the abuse. The premise of my model is that as Jesus compassionately interacts with the abuse experiences, the survivor is enabled to reconstruct new, hopeful meanings of the abuse within the broader context of God's love and her whole self, in order to re-form her sense of self as the beloved *imago Dei*. In stage three, then, the practitioner carefully facilitates the survivor re-entering her memories of abuse from a witnessing stance – in order to avoid re-traumatization – and invites Jesus, God, Sophia, or whatever language for God the survivor chooses – to interact with memories of the abuse. Once the survivor has grounded herself in safety through breathing exercises and her imaginative safe place in her mind with the loving presence of God, the practitioner may invite the woman either to choose a memory of the abuse she wants to encounter with God or ask God to bring to mind a particular memory. Following her lead, the practitioner listens as the woman describes the trauma memory from the witnessing stance of her present self who is free from the abuse. As she observes the memory, the practitioner can invite her to view God in the past experience of abuse and ask God for a renewed understanding of her trauma. Often survivors will have profound experiences of God telling her that the abuse was the perpetrator's fault and not hers, and that God was not only compassionately holding her in the midst of the trauma, but also condemning the actions of her abuser. In this embodied practice of IHP, then, a survivor can experientially encounter the loving, compassionate God who suffers with her, stands in solidarity that the perpetrator was to blame, and acts with and for her to resist the evil of abuse. In my research results, survivors were able to move towards a more integrated sense of self through the regular, ongoing practice of IHP with a trained practitioner.

Conclusion

Recovering from the trauma of domestic abuse is a long, complicated and painful journey, but it is not one without hope. We have discovered through our feminist theological approach that the fragmented self of survivors rooted in shame can be restored in the loving embrace of the divine female Trinity that liberates women from the abuse of men. Towards the goal of empowering survivors of domestic abuse to heal from their trauma, I offer my model of Inner Healing Prayer for trauma-informed practitioners to employ as one of the practices Christian women can engage in towards their re-formation of their self as fully *imago Dei*.

References

Beck, Richard and Angie McDonald, 'Attachment to God: The Attachment to God Inventory, Tests of Working Model Correspondence, and an Exploration of Faith Group Differences', *Journal of Psychology and Theology* 32, no. 2 (2004), 92–103.

Brown, Brené, *I Thought It Was Just Me (But It Isn't): Telling the Truth about Perfectionism, Inadequacy, and Power*, New York: Gotham Books, 2007.

—— *The Gifts of Imperfection: Let Go of Who You Think You're Supposed to Be and Embrace Who You Are*, Center City, MN: Hazelden, 2010.

Cooper-White, Pamela, *Braided Selves: Collected Essays on Multiplicity, God, and Persons*, Eugene, OR: Wipf and Stock, 2011.

Crawford, Emma, Helen Liebling-Kalifani and Vicki Hill, 'Women's Understanding of the Effects of Domestic Abuse: The Impact on Their Identity, Sense of Self and Resilience. A Grounded Theory Approach', *Journal of International Women's Studies* 11, no. 2 (2009), 63–82.

Doehring, Carrie, 'A Method of Feminist Pastoral Theology', in *Feminist and Womanist Pastoral Theology*, ed. Bonnie J. Miller-McLemore and Brita L. Gill-Austern, Nashville: Abingdon Press, 1999, 95–111.

Drumm, René, Marciana Popescu, Laurie Cooper, Shannon Trecartin, Marge Seifert, Tricia Foster and Carole Kilcher, 'God Just Brought Me through It: Spiritual Coping Strategies for Resilience among Intimate Partner Violence Survivors', *Clinical Social Work Journal* 42, no. 4 (December 2013), 385–94.

Fowler, Dawnovise N. and Michele A. Rountree, 'Exploring the Meaning and Role of Spirituality for Women Survivors of Intimate Partner Abuse', *Journal of Pastoral Care and Counseling* 64, no. 2 (Summer 2010), 1–13.

Garzon, Fernando, 'Cognitive Restructuring through Contemplative Inner Healing Prayer: Clinical Demonstration and Current Research', in *VISTAS: Perspectives on Counseling 2004*, ed. Garry Walz and Richard Yep, Alexandria, VA: American Counseling Association Press, 2004.

Gonzalez, Michelle A., *Created in God's Image: An Introduction to Feminist Theological Anthropology*, Maryknoll, NY: Orbis Books, 2007.

Graff, Ann O., ed., *In the Embrace of God: Feminist Approaches to Theological Anthropology*, Eugene, OR: Wipf and Stock, 2005.

Herman, Judith, *Trauma and Recovery: The Aftermath of Violence – From Domestic Abuse to Political Terror*, New York: Basic Books, 1997.

Isasi-Diaz, Ada Maria, *Mujerista Theology: A Theology for the Twenty-First Century*, New York: Orbis Books, 1996.

Jantzen, Grace, M., *Julian of Norwich: Mystic and Theologian*, London: The Cromwell Press, 2000.

Jersak, Brad, *Can You Hear Me?: Tuning in to the God Who Speaks*, Abbotsford, BC: Fresh Wind Press, 2012.

Johnson, Elizabeth A., *She Who Is: The Mystery of God in Feminist Theological Discourse*, 10th anniversary edn, New York: Crossroad, 2002.

—— 'Female Symbols for God: The Apophatic Tradition and Social Justice', *International Journal of Orthodox Theology* 1, no. 2 (2010), 40–57.

Jones, Serene, *Trauma and Grace: Theology in a Ruptured World*, Louisville, KY: Westminster John Knox Press, 2009.

Julian of Norwich, *Showings*, trans. Edmund Colledge and James Walsh, New York: Paulist Press, 1978.

Katerndahl, David, Sandra Burge, Robert Ferrer, Johanna Becho and R. Wood, 'Effects of Religious and Spiritual Variables on Outcomes in Violent Relationships', *The International Journal of Psychiatry in Medicine* 49, no. 4 (2015), 249–63.

McCullough, Eleanor, 'Julian of Norwich: The Inclusive Christian', in *Sources of the Christian Self: A Cultural History of Christian Identity*, ed. James M. Houston and Jens Zimmerman, Grand Rapids, MI: Eerdmans, 2018.

McGinn, Bernard, ed., *The Essential Writings of Christian Mysticism*, New York: Random House, 2006.

Moder, Ally, 'Free to Heal: Towards a Feminist Pastoral Theology and Praxis of Recovery for Christian Survivors of Intimate Partner Violence', PhD dissertation, Claremont School of Theology, 2019.

Moriarty, Glendon and Louis Hoffman, eds, *God Image Handbook for Spiritual Counseling and Psychotherapy: Research, Theory, and Practice*, New York: Routledge, 2013.

Nason-Clark, Nancy, Barbara Fisher-Townsend, Catherine Holtmann and Stephen McMullin, *Religion and Intimate Partner Violence: Understanding the Challenges and Proposing Solutions*, New York: Oxford University Press, 2017.

Nordling, Cherith Fee, *Knowing God by Name: A Conversation between Elizabeth A. Johnson and Karl Barth*, New York: Peter Lang, 2010.

Oduyoye, Mercy Amba, *Introducing African Women's Theology*, Sheffield: Sheffield Academic Press, 2001.

Payne, Leanne, *Restoring the Christian Soul: Overcoming Barriers to Completion in Christ Through Healing Prayer*, Grand Rapids, MI: Baker Publishing Group, 1991.

—— *Listening Prayer: Learning to Hear God's Voice and Keep a Prayer Journal*, Grand Rapids, MI: Baker Publishing Group, 1994.

—— *The Healing Presence: Curing the Soul Through Union with Christ*, Grand Rapids, MI: Hamewith Books, 1995.

Pui-lan, Kowk, *Introducing Asian Feminist Theology*, Cleveland, OH: The Pilgrim Press, 2000.

Rakoczy, Susan, 'The Theological Vision of Elizabeth Johnson', in *Scriptura* 98 (2008), 137–55.

Richardson, Rick, *Experiencing Healing Prayer: How God Turns Our Hurts into Wholeness*, Downers Grove, IL: InterVarsity Press, 2005.

Rizzutto, Ana-Marie, *The Birth of the Living God: A Psychoanalytic Study*, Chicago, IL: The University of Chicago Press, 1979.

Ruether, Rosemary R., *Sexism and God-Talk: Toward a Feminist Theology*, Boston: Beacon Press, 1993.

Solomon, Marion and Daniel Siegel, *Healing Trauma: Attachment, Mind, Body, and Brain*, New York: W. W. Norton and Company, Inc., 2003.

Tan, Siang-Yang, 'Use of Prayer and Scripture in Cognitive-Behavioral Therapy', *Journal of Psychology and Christianity* 26, no. 2 (2007), 101–11.

van der Kolk, Bessel A., *The Body Keeps the Score: Brain, Mind, and Body in the Healing of Trauma*, New York: Penguin Books, 2014.

United Nations Women, 'Facts and Figures: Ending Violence against Women', New York, 2013: www.unwomen.org/en/what-we-do/ending-violence-against-women/facts-and-figures.

Williams, Delores S., *Sisters in the Wilderness: The Challenge of Womanist God-Talk*, Maryknoll, NY: Orbis Books, 2003.

Notes

1 UN Women, 'Facts and Figures: Ending Violence against Women', New York, 2013: www.unwomen.org/en/what-we-do/ending-violence-against-women/facts-and-figures (accessed 22 May 2019).

2 It is important to note here that men are also victims of domestic abuse, and this truth necessitates further research and advocacy work. However, the vast majority of victims are women abused by their male partners and thus this remains the focus of my research and this chapter.

3 While academically the term 'intimate partner violence' is commonly employed to differentiate between experiences of abuse in teen or adult intimate relationships from that of violence experienced by children in their homes, I have chosen to utilize the phrase 'domestic abuse' in this chapter as this is more widely understood in society. For further information on the highly complex experience of domestic abuse, I have provided free resources on the topic at my website, www.allymoder.com.

4 Serene Jones, *Trauma and Grace: Theology in a Ruptured World* (Louisville, KY: Westminster John Knox Press, 2009), 12–13.

5 Carrie Doehring, 'A Method of Feminist Pastoral Theology', in *Feminist and Womanist Pastoral Theology*, ed. Bonnie Miller-McLemore and Brita Gill-Austern (Nashville, TN: Abingdon Press, 1999), 95–111.

6 Cherith Fee Nordling, *Knowing God by Name: A Conversation between Elizabeth A. Johnson and Karl Barth* (New York: Peter, 2010), 37–9.

7 Two sources for feminist theological anthropology can be found in: Ann O. Graff, ed., *In the Embrace of God: Feminist Approaches to Theological Anthropology* (Eugene, OR: Wipf and Stock, 2005), and Michelle A. Gonzalez, *Created in God's Image: An Introduction to Feminist Theological Anthropology* (Maryknoll, NY: Orbis Books, 2007). Additionally, feminist pastoral theologian Pamela Cooper-White presents a robust psychologically informed theological anthropology particularly related to multiplicity in her book, *Braided Selves: Collected Essays on Multiplicity, God, and Persons* (Eugene, OR: Wipf and Stock, 2011).

8 Bernard McGinn, ed., *The Essential Writings of Christian Mysticism* (New York: Random House, 2006), 483.

9 Eleanor McCullough, 'Julian of Norwich: The Inclusive Christian', in *Sources of the Christian Self: A Cultural History of Christian Identity*, ed. James M. Houston and Jens Zimmerman (Grand Rapids, MI: Eerdmans, 2018), 341.

10 Grace M. Jantzen, *Julian of Norwich: Mystic and Theologian* (London: The Cromwell Press, 2000), 142.

11 Jantzen, *Julian of Norwich*, 89, 121.

12 McCullough, 'Julian of Norwich', 347.

13 Julian of Norwich, *Showings*, trans. Edmund Colledge and James Walsh (New York: Paulist Press, 1978), 225. Hereafter referred to as Julian, *Showings*, followed by the page number.

14 Julian of Norwich, *Showings*, 300.

15 McCullough, 'Julian of Norwich', 348.

16 Julian of Norwich, *Showings*, 296–7.

17 Julian of Norwich, *Showings*, 298–9.

18 Julian of Norwich, *Showings*, 296.

19 Julian, *Showings*, 296.

20 Julian, *Showings*, 298.

21 Julian, *Showings*, 298.

22 Julian, *Showings*, 183.

23 Nordling, *Knowing God by Name*, 39–40.

24 Elizabeth A. Johnson, *She Who Is: The Mystery of God in Feminist Theological Discourse*, 10th anniversary edn (New York: Crossroad, 2002), 157.

25 Nordling, *Knowing God by Name*, 40.

26 Johnson, *She Who Is*, 192.

27 Johnson, *She Who Is*, 70–1.

28 Johnson, *She Who Is*, 8.

29 Johnson, *She Who Is*, 71, 244.

30 Elizabeth A. Johnson, 'Female Symbols for God: The Apophatic Tradition and Social Justice', *International Journal of Orthodox Theology* 1, no. 2 (2010), 55.

31 Johnson, *She Who Is*, 3.

32 Johnson, *She Who Is*, 13, 38.

33 Johnson, *She Who Is*, 7, 152.

34 Johnson, *She Who Is*, 156.

35 Susan Rakoczy, 'The Theological Vision of Elizabeth Johnson', in *Scriptura* 98 (2008), 145.

36 Johnson, 'Female Symbols for God', 56.

37 Rakoczy, 'The Theological Vision of Elizabeth Johnson', 144.

38 Johnson, 'Female Symbols for God', 42.

39 Herman, *Trauma and Recovery*, 33.

40 A great deal of research in the past couple of decades in the fields of psychology and neuroscience explains this fragmentation of mind for survivors of domestic abuse and its impact on their sense of self. I put forward much of this research within a feminist pastoral theological framework of healing for female survivors in my recent doctoral thesis, Ally Moder, 'Free to Heal: Towards a Feminist Pastoral Theology and Praxis of Recovery for Christian Survivors of Intimate Partner Violence' (PhD diss., Claremont School of Theology, 2019).

41 Herman, *Trauma and Recovery*, 45, 89.

42 Recent research in this field can be found in: Marion Solomon and Daniel Siegel, *Healing Trauma: Attachment, Mind, Body, and Brain* (New York: W. W. Norton and Company, Inc., 2003), and Bessel van der Kolk, *The Body Keeps the Score: Brain, Mind, and Body in the Healing of Trauma* (New York: Penguin Books, 2014).

43 As this chapter is focused only on women's sense of self in relation to their experience of domestic abuse, it is beyond our scope to delve into the many other complex and multifaceted effects of this type of trauma. However, it is important to note that survivors' identity malformation and recovery is also complicated by the numerous psychological and physiological impacts of trauma, such as anxiety, depression, problems sleeping, eating disorders, emotional numbness or dissociation, PTSD, neurobiological disorders, gastrointestinal and gynaecological disorders, and more.

44 Emma Crawford, Helen Liebling-Kalifani and Vicki Hill, 'Women's Understanding of the Effects of Domestic Abuse: The Impact on Their Identity, Sense of Self and Resilience. A Grounded Theory Approach', *Journal of International Women's Studies* 11, no. 2 (2009), 65.

45 Herman, *Trauma and Recovery*, 53.

46 Herman, *Trauma and Recovery*, 53–4.

47 Brené Brown, *I Thought It Was Just Me (But It Isn't): Telling the Truth about Perfectionism, Inadequacy, and Power* (New York: Gotham Books, 2007), 13.

48 Brown, *I Thought It Was Just Me*, 5.

49 Crawford, 'Women's Understanding of the Effects of Domestic Abuse', 63–82.

50 Brené Brown, *The Gifts of Imperfection: Let Go of Who You Think You're Supposed to Be and Embrace Who You Are* (Center City, MN: Hazelden, 2010), 23. Italics in original text.

51 Crawford et al., 'Women's Understanding of the Effects of Domestic Abuse', 78.

52 Crawford et al., 'Women's Understanding of the Effects of Domestic Abuse', 64–5.

53 Crawford et al., 'Women's Understanding of the Effects of Domestic Abuse', 76.

54 Canadian sociologist Nancy Nason-Clark is largely responsible for the significant volume of research on women's experience of domestic abuse as it relates to the Christian Church in North America. Along with other sociological researchers, she explains the multiple ways that the Church both negatively and positively impacts Christian women as they suffer from domestic abuse in her recent book, Nancy Nason-Clark, Barbara Fisher-Townsend, Catherine Holtmann and Stephen McMullin, *Religion and Intimate Partner Violence: Understanding the Challenges and Proposing Solutions* (New York: Oxford University Press, 2017).

55 Research on the role of spirituality and relationship with God as helpful for recovery from abuse can be found in: René Drumm et al., 'God Just Brought Me through It: Spiritual Coping Strategies for Resilience Among Intimate Partner Violence Survivors', *Clinical Social Work Journal* 42, no. 4 (December 2013), 385–94; David Katerndahl et al., 'Effects of Religious and Spiritual Variables on Outcomes in Violent Relationships', *The International Journal of Psychiatry in Medicine* 49, no. 4 (2015), 249–63; Dawnovise Fowler and Michele Rountree, 'Exploring the Meaning and Role of Spirituality for Women Survivors of Intimate Partner Abuse', *Journal of Pastoral Care and Counseling* 64, no. 2 (Summer 2010), 1–13; and

Richard Beck and Angie McDonald, 'Attachment to God: The Attachment to God Inventory, Tests of Working Model Correspondence, and an Exploration of Faith Group Differences', *Journal of Psychology and Theology* 32, no. 2 (2004), 92–103.

56 Herman, *Trauma and Recovery*, 52.

57 Although it is beyond the scope of this chapter to dive into the richness of global feminist theologies, such a journey would certainly enrich the broader discussion of women's personhood and the many injustices they face around the world. As both of my primary conversation partners are Western Caucasian women, it is critical to acknowledge that the larger conversation of feminist theology must include the vital work from women theologians of colour, such as: Delores S. Williams, *Sisters in the Wilderness: The Challenge of Womanist God-Talk* (Maryknoll, NY: Orbis Books, 2003); Kwok Pui-lan, *Introducing Asian Feminist Theology* (Cleveland, OH: The Pilgrim Press, 2000); Ada Maria Isasi-Diaz, *Mujerista Theology: A Theology for the Twenty-First Century* (New York: Orbis Books, 1996); and Mercy Amba Oduyoye, *Introducing African Women's Theology* (Sheffield: Sheffield Academic Press, 2001).

58 Glendon Moriarty and Louis Hoffman, eds, *God Image Handbook for Spiritual Counseling and Psychotherapy: Research, Theory, and Practice* (New York: Routledge, 2013), 1–12.

59 Nason-Clark et al., *Religion and Intimate Partner Violence*, 30.

60 Nason-Clark et al., *Religion and Intimate Partner Violence*, 68.

61 It is critical to note that I encourage only trained trauma-informed therapists, clergy and lay leaders to implement my model of Inner Healing Prayer with survivors of domestic abuse as working with trauma survivors is incredibly complex and can easily go from a space of healing to re-traumatization, despite one's best efforts and intentions. I refer you again to my doctoral research in Ally Moder, 'Free to Heal', 2019 for further details.

62 Leanne Payne, *Restoring the Christian Soul: Overcoming Barriers to Completion in Christ through Healing Prayer* (Grand Rapids, MI: Baker Publishing Group, 1991); Leanne Payne, *Listening Prayer: Learning to Hear God's Voice and Keep a Prayer Journal* (Grand Rapids, MI: Baker Publishing Group, 1994); Leanne Payne, *The Healing Presence: Curing the Soul Through Union with Christ* (Grand Rapids, MI: Hamewith Books, 1995).

63 Richardson, *Experiencing Healing Prayer*.

64 Jersak, *Can You Hear Me?*

65 Payne, *Restoring the Christian Soul*, 67–80; Fernando Garzon and Lori Burkett, 'Healing of Memories: Models, Research, Future Directions', *Journal of Psychology and Christianity* 21, no. 1 (2002), 42–9; Richardson, *Experiencing Healing Prayer*, 149–60; Tan, 'Use of Prayer and Scripture in Cognitive-Behavioral Therapy', 103–4; Jersak, *Can You Hear Me?*, 231–59.

12

Losing a Child:
A Father's Methodological Plight

SANTIAGO PIÑÓN

Many fathers turn to the Bible for comfort and guidance following the death of their child. Some will arbitrarily choose biblical narratives that seemingly exemplify how a father ought to respond to his child's death. Second Samuel 12.19–20 presents David as a faithful servant of God, which often becomes a source for how fathers ought to deal with loss of their child:

> 'Is the child dead?' he asked. 'Yes,' they replied, 'he is dead.' Then David got up from the ground. After he had washed, put on lotions and changed his clothes, he went into the house of the LORD and worshipped. Then he went into his own house, and at his request they served him food, and he ate.[1]

The text becomes problematic because it fails to deal with grief in a realistic way. Frequently, Christians use this biblical text as a template for how to respond to bereaved parents. And those parents, because they are often unable to act like King David, will feel profound guilt, a guilt that only compounds their loss.

Certainly some bereaved parents try to emulate David's action by vocalizing their faith and trust in God. Eventually, however, the weight and impact of the trauma is too great for them to bear, and it manifests in addictive behaviours,[2] divorce,[3] depression,[4] and various other mental illnesses.[5]

Among men, the trauma often manifests physically – as hypertension, stroke, reduced life expectancy, and so on.[6] At other times, the traumatic experience of losing a child may result in men becoming depressed. Such depression can take many forms, some that may not be particularly obvious externally.

Many men follow King David's pattern when dealing with the experience of losing a child. Like David, they approach their child's death through a rationalistic lens in a way that becomes almost robotic: death occurred. Arrangements must be made. My spouse is hurting. I must be strong. I must comfort and support my wife who has just experienced this terrible and tremendous loss of the child who was growing inside her.

Of course, parenting can take many forms, not just heteronormative ones. Single parents, same-sex couples and even a larger group such as extended family may take on the role of parent, as do foster parents, adoptive parents, parents of *hijos de crianza*,[7] and so on. And they each bear the trauma of their child's death in different ways. My focus in this chapter is fathers of all kinds – gay, bisexual, homosexual, transgender, cisgender, etc. – and my point is that they are all often neglected, forgotten and left on their own to deal with the trauma of losing a child, and furthermore that for all of them leaving this trauma unaddressed can have severe negative consequences. So what is different about a father's grief? And why has it not been taken seriously?

When a father joins his spouse in the grieving process, he does this as a partner. If the spouse is a woman, and particularly if she has borne the child, then the mother's grief is considered superior, not just different. The mother grieves because she has experienced the trauma of losing the child that was a part of her body. If the father or partner grieves, his experience is often considered merely an addendum to the traumatic experience. A case in point is the well-known trauma theology of Serene Jones, who focuses on women who are unable to have children.[8] What is disturbing to me is her justification for focusing on women. She writes:

> There are, however, differences in men's and women's embodied relation to this kind of loss and hence differences in their texture of grief; my selective focus on women allows me to highlight the features of their grief particular to their embodied reality.[9]

If Jones' focus on women is based on the fact that they are able to get pregnant and give birth to a child, then how are we to think of those women who are unable to get pregnant? Or those who do not carry their pregnancy to full term? Are these women in some way defective as women? While Jones argues for a feminist theology of trauma, it seems that she has fully embraced the Western-imposed gender distinction. By focusing on the differences in how men and women grieve, Jones focuses on the very thing that feminism seeks to deconstruct – imposed gender roles. Feminism, as I teach it in the classroom, try to practise it in my relationships, and help my children to embrace, sees the other person as a fellow human being who deserves to be treated with respect and, more importantly, with kindness, regardless of their genitalia, gender or sexual orientation.

Is it even possible to consider the grief that men experience without assimilating Western notions of gender roles? Or are we destined to accept the male/female dichotomy, as Serene Jones has appeared to do? A possible solution, I suggest, can be found in the writings of Gloria Anzaldúa, the Chicana feminist who developed a *mestiza* consciousness. This new way of being provides a framework by which men are able to break free from the gender roles that Western society has imposed on all men and women.

Moreover, this *conciencia mestiza* contributes to a trauma theology that acknowledges the depth of pain associated with the death of a child and, thereby, resists a triumphalist theology that tends to dismiss trauma in order to justify the presence of a divine being who is ever present.

Conciencia mestiza as a New Way of Being

In *Borderlands/La Frontera*, published in 1987, Anzaldúa describes her life as being in constant ambiguity due to who she is as a person. There is an established way of being that is advocated by the dominant culture that excludes all other ways of being. For Anzaldúa, there are two dominant cultures that are constantly demanding that she acquiesce to their forms of being. On the one hand, white culture insists that Anzaldúa tone down or even jettison her Chicanoness so that she can assimilate into the American ideal (of whiteness). This struggle is made obvious when Anzaldúa describes the rejection of Chicana literature as a legitimate object of study. The mounting pressure of white culture is portrayed when she describes Anglo[10] kids using the term 'tortilleros' – a reference to a kind of food that some Mexicans eat – to insult one another.[11] This and other forms of insult, invoked simply on the basis of one's skin and one's culture, eventually convinces some to believe that being white is better than other ways of being.[12] Arnoldo de Leon rightly summarizes dominant Anglo sentiments when he argues that many Anglos perceive Mexicans as indolent, immoral, uneducated and subversive.[13] Anglo men sexually objectify Latinas by erotically describing how Latinas seductively swing their hair or their hips in a particularly provocative way. Foundational to these insults and descriptions is the assumption that Mexicans/Latinas can never measure up to the Anglo culture.

Mexican culture, on the other hand, also pressured Anzaldúa into a specific form of being. Especially prevalent is the patriarchal society's expectations that individuals fulfil their gender roles. Anzaldúa describes how she rejected compliance with this system by 'being a tomboy and wearing boots, being unafraid of snakes or knives, showing my contempt for women's roles, leaving home to go to college, not settling down and getting married, being a *política*, siding with the Farmworkers'.[14]

In addition to such patriarchal expectations of both men and women, there is another fundamental expectation that gets at the essence of what it means to be Mexican/Latina: language. 'So, if you want to really hurt me, talk badly about my language,'[15] says Anzaldúa. For her, as for many Latino/as, language is fundamental to who she is as a person. Given that she is a writer, this should be no surprise. Yet it is language that fuels exclusion and ridicule. Anglos expect and even require Chicanas to erase their Spanish accents. Even more upsetting is when one's own culture ridicules one's language due to either over-emphasizing English and forgetting Spanish or speaking with a regional accent. Anzaldúa is accused of being a '*pocho*,[16] cultural traitor, you're ruining the Spanish language'.[17] The accusation is more than just about language. It is about one's very being. It is about belonging. As a *pocho*, such accusers insist that Anzaldúa no longer belongs to the culture of her childhood and upbringing. Neither can she belong to the culture that rejects her. But she has devised a solution: rather than becoming an individual with no land, no setting and no culture, she says she belongs to a place that she calls *La Frontera*.

To illuminate the notion of *Frontera*, Anzaldúa refers to a particular place in the south-west of the United States. *La Frontera* is a geographical location that includes both Mexico and the USA. It is a place where ambiguity exists because there is no clear distinction between the two nations. When crossing from the USA into Mexico, one must use the Santa Fe bridge in El Paso, TX and Juarez, Chihuahua. Right in the very middle of the bridge is a placard that states, 'Limite de los Estados Unidos Mexicanos'. Immediately next to this statement is another that reads, 'Boundary of the United States of America'. Between both statements is a very thin line that one can straddle while crossing the border. Such straddling is ironic; after all, the border is meant to keep people out. Yet by straddling the border one demonstrates the ability to be in two places at once, with one foot in the USA and another foot in Mexico. This line, or rather border, was created after the Mexican–American war (1846–48) via the Guadalupe Hidalgo Treaty, in order to distinguish between those who belong in the USA and those who belong in Mexico. The difficulty with this distinction is that the Guadalupe Hidalgo Treaty guaranteed that the people living in what was Mexico, but is now the USA, are given USA citizenship and should enjoy all the benefits and rights thereof. Yet, the inhabitants of *La Frontera*, which exists in both nations, never experienced a sense of belonging because they are 'the prohibited and forbidden'.[18] As a Chicana who inhabits *La Frontera*, Anzaldúa never really belongs because she is deemed to be an alien, a wetback, illegal. The last adjective is especially interesting: based on the Guadalupe Hidalgo Treaty and birthright citizenship as found in the Constitution of the USA, legally a Chicana should be treated as a citizen, but instead is treated as an invading foreigner. There is, then, an ambiguity of being. For, in the midst of simultaneous belonging and not belonging, she finds a third space.

In trying to make sense of belonging to the ambiguity of *La Frontera*, Anzaldúa writes, 'in attempting to work out a synthesis, the self has added a third element which is greater than the sum of its severed parts'.[19] It is especially important to understand there is a shift from the geographical to an existential understanding of *La Frontera*. In the midst of belonging neither to the white dominant culture nor the Mexican culture, Anzaldúa claims a space to belong. More importantly, she claims a sense of being that affects her psyche. She writes:

> The third element is a new consciousness – a mestiza consciousness – and though it is a source of intense pain, its energy comes from continual

creative motion that keeps breaking down the unitary aspects of each new paradigm.[20]

Rather than remaining in a state of self-loathing, she unlearns the identity and insult of being the '*pocho*', the 'wetback', the 'alien' and the 'illegal', and so finds a sense of belonging. Anzaldúa states, 'as a mestiza, I have no country, my homeland cast me out'. She continues, 'yet all countries are mine because I am every woman's sister or potential lover. (As a lesbian I have no race, my own people disclaim me; but I am all races because there is the queer of me in all races).'[21] This 'new consciousness' is ambiguous because the dualism of belonging and not belonging is overcome by remaking who she is; 'She learns to transform the small "I" into the total Self. *Se hace moldeadora de su alma. Segun la concepcion que tiene de sí misma, así sera.*'[22] The one who was unaccepted and unacceptable suddenly exercises her own agency to become who she wants. Using religious language, Anzaldúa describes this new creation, this new consciousness, like this: 'la mestiza has gone from being the sacrificial goat to becoming the officiating princess at the crossroads'.[23] By accepting the ambiguity of being and non-acceptance, Anzaldúa is able to become an individual who breaks down the dichotomy of belonging to neither this nor that nation. Through this third way of being, she opens the doors of possibilities that are inclusive of those who were previously excluded, even if by their own choice. Anzaldúa states:

> I am participating in the creation of yet another culture, a new story to explain the world and our participating in it, a new value system with images and symbols that connect us to each other and to the planet.[24]

The creation of this new way of being is concrete and situated within the historical.

Key to my constructive move of using Anzaldúa for a trauma theology is my strict stance against any idealistic or utopian notion of being. Any trauma theology must consider life in its fullest sense, which includes the good and the bad. A triumphalist theology or, rather, a theology of glory, attempts to reach God by avoiding the cross. As understood by Martin Luther, a theology of glory allows human beings to rely on their own understanding and their ability to accomplish what is needed, that is, salvation.[25] A theology of the cross, however, considers the messiness of life; in Lutheran terms, the cross deals with sin. Understood this way, bigotry, racism, misogyny and so on are not human flaws, but the result of sin or separation from God. For Luther, the only way to reconcile human beings to God, and humans to humans, especially as one is moved to do living works through mercy, is found in and through the suffering and horrendous act of the cross.[26] To completely grasp, or be grasped by, the power of the cross is to recognize and acknowledge the dreadful and hideous nature of the cross. To do otherwise is to adopt a theology of glory.

For Anzaldúa, the *new mestiza consciousness* does exactly as Luther's theology of the cross, in that it recognizes and names the appalling and ghastly experience of being rejected by two cultures. This new consciousness recognizes and embraces the pain even while it is creating a new way of being. Expanding upon the notion of the mestiza consciousness, Anzaldúa writes: 'though it is a source of intense pain, its energy comes from continual creative motion that keeps breaking down the unitary aspect of each new paradigm'.[27] Like Anzaldúa, a trauma theology faces the trauma that was experienced, embraces it and creates something new. To be certain, the embrace of the trauma is not sadistic, but rather recognizes that one's pain belongs to oneself. It is this pain, and through this pain, that a new possibility becomes actual. By identifying the pain or trauma, one is able to move beyond the circumstances that led to the trauma. Again, moving beyond the circumstances does not entail forgetting or dismissing. Instead, this new consciousness breaks forth in the form of a new being and new consciousness by rupturing the dualism of the rejecting cultures.

One aspect of the dualism that Anzaldúa has in mind includes the male/female dichotomy. She writes: 'The answer to the problem between the white race and the colored, between males and females, lies in healing the split that originates in the very foundation of our lives, our culture, our languages, our thoughts.'[28] Before healing can become a possibility it is necessary to acknowledge the pain that was caused by the male/female dualism.

A New Way of Being a Man

Thus, in *Que no se nos olviden los hombres*,[29] Anzaldúa focuses on the prevailing male chauvinism that exists within the Latino community. For Latinos, to be macho is always juxtaposed to the idea of woman, considered a defect. In an attempt to achieve superiority, the Latino continuously feels the need to '*chingar mujeres*'.[30] The Latino need to 'fuck the women' stems from an 'adaptation to oppression and poverty and low self-esteem'.[31] The conveyed machismo is primarily developed from his relation to the Anglo male. According to Anzaldúa, the Anglo male feels inadequate and inferior and powerless. Unable to manage his feeling of inferiority, the Anglo male transfers these to the Latino male, who then transfers the self-effacement to the woman. (Interestingly, the Anglo male labels the Latino as *machista* when the Latino abuses and oppresses a Latina, but will never turn his critical eye on himself.) To break free from the stranglehold of the Anglo male, the Latino male must listen to Latina women who are demanding to be treated with respect, kindness and tenderness. However, this can only be done through the liberation of the Chicana.

The struggle against men who abuse women is a struggle upon which both men and women must embark. Anzaldúa writes, 'the struggle of the mestiza is above all a feminist one'.[32] As Anzaldúa understands it, to continue the abusive relations between men and women is detrimental to the psyches of both. Healing is possible only through the liberation of both men and women. The woman struggles against the man by breaking the bondage of misogyny. The man struggles against himself by seeking to break free from the imposed gender roles that the male feels he must uphold. As Anzaldúa argues, 'men, even more than women, are fettered to gender roles'.[33] Without gender, the man is no longer man, a terrifying prospect as he has been identified and defined solely in relation to woman. He is man because he is not woman. Without the superimposed gender roles, he is no longer man – an existential dilemma that shakes him to the very core. Yet, throwing off the shackles of misogyny and male superiority is crucial to the survival of the woman. After all, she is the one who is raped, abused, insulted, forced to bear children and killed by men. Yet, while feminism liberates the woman, it also liberates man from himself. No longer does he have to succumb to the gendered expectations of the male/female dichotomy. He is free to express himself as a human being who takes into himself all that it means to be human. For Anzaldúa, this new consciousness is a 'new masculinity' that is able to express vulnerability and tenderness.[34] This new masculinity is perhaps best expressed in the life of the homosexual who is able to express both vulnerability and tenderness. Unfortunately, Anzaldúa succumbs to a stereotype of homosexuality that is based on the socially constructed notion of *machismo*/male chauvinism.

The Man Who Binds

Besides such gender constructions, among the many influences that determine a father's response to trauma is media. A quick glance at movies and TV shows demonstrates what a man ought to be and what he ought to avoid. Lynnette S. Moran argues that film often portrays men as being stoic and rationalistic in relation to trauma.[35] Often, films portray men as 'isolated from family and friends in their attempts to cope with grief'.[36] This isolation can have both physical and relational effects on men. Physically, men who lack adequate outlets for their grief may, as I noted earlier, experience a reduction in life expectancy, hypertension, heart attack, depression and addictive behaviours, and relational issues that can end in divorce.[37] Clearly, men face many challenges when they experience the trauma of a child's death. Yet, there are few outlets for men to express their experience, and even fewer theologians and ethicists who try to address this need.

To engage the trauma that men experience it is necessary to be clear what we mean when we speak of man as the object of our study. There are two ideas that seem to be prevalent in this discussion. First, there is the idea of man who is the social construct based on gender roles and expectations. This man remains within the realm of the intellect as there is nothing essential about this idea. The idea becomes concrete only when one accepts the notion of man and allows it to embody one's being. As an idea, however, it can be removed or ignored, although to do so is difficult. The second idea of man is historically situated. This man lives and breathes, hopes, desires, loves and is loved. This man experiences life in its fullness, which includes both death and life. Man, is this sense, is a paradox.

Here, it can be helpful to consider the thought of Miguel de Unamuno, the Spanish philosopher who wrote *The Tragic Sense of Life* in 1913. We desire life, but the reality of death is always before us. Unamuno attempts to make sense of this paradox by reminding his readers that 'The man we have to do with is the man of flesh and blood.'[38] The paradox only becomes comprehensible as one understands that the I who understands is rooted in the concreteness of life and death. Yet, the man who is situated in this concreteness is sexual. This notion of man is in contrast to the rationalists who envision man as a mere idea, thus as one who has no sex. While Unamuno understands man as having sex, he fails to inform the reader about what is entailed in being a sexual being. Is Unamuno's notion of man based on gender constructs that define clear roles that women and men are to fulfil?

A key moment in Unamuno's life provides insight into how he understands this man of flesh and bone. He wakes from a dream in which he was falling into nothingness. The dream is prompted by the fact that his infant son developed an infection that led to meningitis, which left his child both physically and mentally disabled. Sobbing because of his dream of falling into nothingness, Unamuno's wife comforts him by calling out, 'My child.' Unamuno would later describe this experience:

> In a moment of supreme, of abysmal anguish, wracked with superhuman weeping, when she saw me in the claws of the Angel of Nothingness, she cried out to me from the depths of her maternal being, superhuman and divine, 'My child!' I discovered then all that God had done for me in this woman, the mother of my children, my own virgin mother ... my mirror of holy, divine unconsciousness and eternity.[39]

In the midst of his tragedy and despair he relies on the comfort of his wife, who takes on the role of mother. Similar to how Rebekah becomes the comforter after the death of Isaac's mother (Genesis 24.67), so Unamuno's wife becomes the comforting mother. To be certain, there is nothing wrong with adults comforting one another. But note that both Isaac and Unamuno take on the roles of the gender constructs, which places the woman at the service of the man. Unamuno, in reflecting on the tragedy of his son's illness and the despair associated with the Angel of Nothingness, embraces the male/female dichotomy, which Anzaldúa describes as *chingando las mujeres*. Even in the midst of trauma, the misogynistic power and influence become obvious.

Anzaldúa suggests how this male/female dichotomy may be overcome when she writes, 'Chicanos need to acknowledge the political and artistic contribution of their queer. People, listen to what your *joteria*[40] is saying.'[41] As understood by Anzaldúa, the homosexual becomes the key to finding a new masculinity because the gay person is unafraid to express tenderness and demonstrate vulnerability. Yet, even this suggestion is problematic as it relies on specific stereotypes of gay men and ignores that violence and domestic abuse exist in same-sex relationships.[42]

In one of her best-known statements, Simone de Beauvoir opens volume two of *The Second Sex* by saying, 'one is not born, but rather becomes a woman'. Gender, and the assigned roles, are social constructs. Yet, this construction is developed over and against the identity of man. A woman becomes a woman because she is not a man. Even contemporary identities such as transgender, cisgender and so on, are understood in relation to man. A person is gay because he is a different kind of man – a man attracted to men. Regardless of how one defines these identities, the primary identity remains intact: man is man; all others are not.

When grieving for a child, others are always coercing (even if gently!) the father to accept the established gender construct that clearly defines the roles of men and women (Be a man! Support your wife! Don't cry!). Yet, the traumatic experience of losing a child is itself an ambiguity, for it embraces both life and death. To break free from the male/female dichotomy it is necessary to be explicit about what we are trying to overcome. Miriam J. Abelson considers the categories of 'thugs, rednecks and faggy men' as possible identities for trans men.[43] Yet, like Unamuno's man and Anzaldúa's gay, these identities can only be understood in relation to an ideal masculinity. Is it possible to break totally free from the grasp of male superiority and misogyny?

Following Anzaldúa's lead, I initially thought that the *muxe* could overcome the male/female dichotomy. The *muxe* may be found in Juchitán, Oaxaca, which some consider to be a 'gay paradise'.[44] Here, one finds the *muxe* who is a traditionally identified male according to the genitalia, but who rejects the role laid out for men. Instead, the *muxe* adopts a different way of being. Antonio Prieto Stambaugh describes Lukas Avendaño, a Mexican artist who identifies as a *muxe*, as 'unos de los pocos artistas mexicanos de performance que trabajan la con ausencia de género y etnicidad'.[45] By resisting both gender and ethnicity, Avendaño breaks free from the Western-imposed gender roles, even as Alfredo Mirandé imposes this system in the description of the *muxe* by describing them as a gender hybridity. Yet, when one listens to Avendaño in *A Lifestyle Distinct* documentary, he argues that a *muxe* does not want to be or to replace a woman.[46] A *muxe* transcends the male/female categories as 'people perceive them as having the physical bodies of men but different aesthetic, work, and social skills from most men'.[47] Though the *muxe* has male genitalia, those genitalia do not determine the role that he plays in society.

I was first attracted to the notion of the *muxe* because it transcends the male/female dichotomy and resists the gender roles that society constructs for all people. In the *muxe* I believed there was a way for both men and women to break from gender roles. However, being a *muxe* is a male privilege; women are unable to adopt a similar role for themselves. A new masculinity must transcend all gender roles, and not only those roles that bind men. If women are expected to stay within their gendered roles, but are able to break from the expected genders, then it is liberating for neither the male nor the female. A theology of trauma must be applicable to both men and women.

The Stories that Shape Us: Autoethnography

A father's trauma of losing a child can best be grasped through storytelling. While it is entirely possible to consider the death of a child from a purely rationalistic perspective, this approach would do injustice to the father who experiences this pain to the very core of his being. Yet, the question remains as to how an academic theologian can talk about such a death through storytelling without coming across as either simplistic or unacademic. A viable possibility is through the use of autoethnography.

Norman K. Denzin defines autoethnography as 'a critical, performative practice, a practice that begins with the biography of the writer and moves outward to culture, discourse, history, and ideology'.[48] Like biography, autoethnography incorporates a turn to the self. But, unlike biography, it turns to the self for the sake of the other because 'we write as an Other, and for an Other'.[49] Autoethnography is an invitation 'into the lived experience of a presumed Other, and to experience it viscerally'.[50] The stories that are told express the encounter that human beings have with one another. They also express the common bond that we have with one another, even when those bonds are broken.

When one's gaze is turned to the Other it is not as an object of our study. Instead, we turn to the Other because we recognize that the Other and I, as Other, have something in common. Denzin describes this process as 'turning of the ethnographic gaze inward on the self (auto), while maintaining the outward gaze of ethnography, looking at the larger context wherein self-experiences occur'.[51] Autoethnography encompasses an emphatic stance of reflexivity, which has at least two components. First, 'the researcher needs to actively engage with her story, reflect her affects, physical experiences, mental states, anxieties, joy, and excitement, and work on their textual or performative representation'.[52] In terms familiar to Anzaldúa, autoethnography takes into itself all the pain and emotions involved, and includes these within the academic endeavour. The second element involves the readers and the recipients of one's work by creating a 'potential to connect with the stories of the recipients and evoke reflexive moments in their minds and bodies'.[53] The reader engages the autoethnography with the intellect and reason, but also with the emotions and body. To use Tillich's language, an autoethnography is a centred act as it encompasses the person as a whole, including the conscious/unconscious, the ego/superego and the cognitive/emotions.[54] By embracing the person as a whole, one is able to acknowledge the *sachzwang* – the force of the circumstances – being considered.[55] The *sachzwang* that interests me is the force of losing a child who was born too early to survive.

On 10 November 2009, Amelia and Alexander were born at 22 weeks' gestation, too early to survive outside the womb. As I held them in my hands, I whispered to them, 'You are not alone. Your daddy loves you and will see you again on another day.' This moment became my *sachzwang* as the hopes and dreams that I had had about being a father were shattered.[56] I suffered because I myself experienced the trauma of losing a child – not simply because I experienced my wife's suffering. The reality of this trauma is sometimes difficult to comprehend because of the overwhelming notions of what it means to be a man.

Most fathers dream big dreams about their children. We dream about brushing hair, singing songs, watching plays, playing with cars, robots, dolls and tea sets. We look forward to hearing the four most powerful words we know, 'I love you, Daddy.' When we hear that children will be joining our family, we dream that our sons will be kind, respectful, and we dream that our daughters will be strong and independent. When these dreams are ripped out of our lives due to the death of our child or children, we are devastated. Often, our trauma knows only one outlet – and that is anger. Yet, we resist lashing out at our partner as they are already experiencing an overwhelming traumatic experience and we do not wish to add to that pain. So, we turn our attention to the only being who is able to handle our anger in the midst of this devastating experience: God.

The Divine

I chose to focus on David's story at the beginning of this chapter because many Christians use it as a template to deal with the loss of a child. In that story, David pleads with God after the child had fallen ill. David refuses to eat while the child is ill, asks God to show mercy to the child, and undergoes self-inflected penance by lying on the ground while the child still lived. As soon as the child dies, David gets up, washes himself, worships and goes home to be with his wife. What is sometimes overlooked is the beginning of the narrative, which states, 'The LORD struck the child that Uriah's wife bore to David, and it became very ill.' Whether the illness came about as punishment for David's adultery or for murdering Uriah, it is disturbing that God would strike down a child who had done nothing to merit such a punishment. Some justify this act as being aligned with the exilic teaching that God will punish 'the children for the sin of the parents to the third and fourth generation' (Exodus 20.5). Even if this is true, what kind of divine being is reflected in such teaching? One's so-called theological insights are often simply anthropological reflection.

In *Cur Deus Homo?* Anselm, Archbishop of Canterbury (1033–1109), develops his theological insight into the need for the cross and the death of Christ to achieve atonement.[57] To clarify the point he is making, Anselm tells a story of a master who sends his servant on a quest. The master warns the servant to avoid falling into a pit from which there is no escape. Anselm continues with the story by describing the servant: 'he despises the command and the warning of his master and, of his own free will, throws himself into the pit that has been shown him, so that he is unable to carry out his assigned task'.[58] Anselm continues by emphasizing the servant's inability to get out of the pit, as well as the inability to perform his task, as being due to his own choices. The consequences of his actions are based on his complete disregard for the command and his scornfulness towards the master. Anselm demonstrates how redemption is achieved through the atonement of the cross. Humanity's relationship with God is restored because the Christ has died an unwarranted death on the cross and is then able to pass his reward on to the disobedient and undeserving servants of God. For Anselm, God is portrayed as righteous. God must do what justice demands, and justice demands that sinners be punished because this is what righteousness demands. In spite of the overwhelming influence of Anselm's theology in the eleventh century, as well as contemporary times, there are individuals who resisted emphasizing righteousness as the primary characteristic of God.

Julian of Norwich (1342–1416), author of *Revelations of Divine Love*, the earliest surviving English text written by a woman, writes in stark contrast to Anselm's rational and scholastic reflection of the divine. To highlight this distinction, I will focus on the story of the servant that Julian contrasts to Anselm's story. Similar to Anselm's, her story begins with a servant who is willing and ready to do the master's will. She writes, 'the Lord looks at his servant lovingly and kindly, and he greatly sends him to a certain place to do his will'.[59] The divine is presented as being both loving and kind rather than a righteous Being who expects disobedience. Julian continues the story by emphasizing that the servant is willing and runs quickly to do what the master has asked. However, in his rush to serve the master, the servant falls into a pit and is severely hurt. The greatest fault of the servant is that he is unable to see 'his loving lord, who was very close to him, and who is the source of all help'.[60] For Julian, God is loving and caring, always ready to assist the weak and hurting servant. Clearly, the contrast with Anselm is both anthropological and theological. Theologically, a comforting and loving God is more sustainable for a trauma theology as the victims are often in despair, remembering again and again the death of their child(ren). But perhaps even more important is how these two theologians view the human being.

Anselm presents human beings as willing to despise the commands issued by God because that is who they are. Human beings, for Julian, are willing to do the master's will, and want to do it quickly, but take missteps in their haste. Julian's anthropological view is similar to that of Irenaeus of Lyons, who describes human beings as infants who need milk for nourishment.[61] It is interesting that he refers to a mother's care of a child to describe how God interacts with human beings. Irenaeus did not fall into the trap of categorizing God according to male characteristics, but is able to recognize that God, in God's fullness, is able to demonstrate qualities that are often attributed to both males and females.

This view of God transcends the male/female dichotomy that Anzaldúa seeks to overcome. It is also the dichotomy that binds both men and women to conform to expected gender roles. Rather than a God who brings about redemption through the atonement of the cross, for those experiencing the trauma of losing a child, the divine needs to be portrayed as a loving and comforting presence.

Before concluding, out of my own experience I find it necessary to address the dark night of the soul (St John of the Cross), the depth of the abyss (Unamuno), the pain of ambiguity (Anzaldúa), or the silence of the cross. When Jesus was on the cross, he let out what is commonly known as the cry of dereliction, 'Eloi, Eloi, lema sabachthani' (Mark 15.13–39). Mark described the moment of death in apocalyptic terms. This scene is analogous to the traumatic experience fathers face when their child dies. The death of a child cannot be explained or adequately described. In the blink of an eye, one's world collapses, overturns, and comes to a catastrophic end. In desperation, like Jesus, we fathers cry out to the heavens for some kind of comfort, response or answer. And, like Jesus, we hear nothing but silence.

In this silence, the depths of death, we experience the absence of God. Like Jesus, we pray, but there is no response. Grieving fathers typically face death on their own; often, they are ill-equipped, lack an appropriate theological framework by which to make sense of the loss and, due to the gender role they are expected to inhabit, are limited in how they can respond emotionally.

Yet fathers, similar to feminists like Anzaldúa, do have the capacity to embrace the ambiguity of pain. Through the pain, fathers acknowledge the traumatic experience of losing a child. We feel the loss and are overwhelmed by the burden of sadness. A theology of trauma cannot hope to overcome this pain. Instead, it must embrace the pain as part of who we are as fathers who have experienced the loss of a child. For even if we wanted to, the reality is that we can never forget that pain.

Conclusion

I began this chapter with a reference to David's reaction to his child's death because, regardless of how much I want to, I can never react as he did. As a father who held his twins, Amelia and Alexander, in his hands until they stopped living, I cannot get past the fact that I should be stressed out by the thought of two additional children who would have been ten years old in 2019. I want to mourn their loss, but more importantly I want to remember. This, however, is impossible, as society's expectations of what it means to be a man do not include such expressions of grief. Such an understanding of masculinity can and does prevent fathers from accepting the loss of their children, instead pressuring them to 'be a man', to get over the loss, and to turn their attention to being a supportive partner to their wives.

I have suggested that Gloria Anzaldúa, a Latina feminist, has tools that could assist men in overcoming the male/female dichotomy that often constrains fathers to act in ways that are aligned to a perceived notion of what it means to be a man. I identified in Anzaldúa's *Frontera* and *mestiza conciencia* an ambiguity that allows fathers to accept the pain of death with a direction to the future. This future is not a triumphalist notion that overcomes in the sense of forgetting the past. Instead, it entails that as fathers who have experienced trauma we look forward to a new kind of being that embraces both the pain of death and the hope for something new – a paradox – or, in the words of Anzaldúa, an ambiguity. In this ambiguity, we find a divine being who is ready to comfort those who have gone through the traumatic experience. The ambiguity is found in the fact that this divine being who comforts is often perceived as absent or silent.

We tell the stories of the death of our children so that others may see that they are not alone in their trauma. The ethnographical approach seeks to bring together those with similar experience, but it is an effort to become something more, something new. We tell the stories of our children who have died so that others can change, but we also tell the stories of death so that we can be changed. The stories take us deep into the abyss of despair, dereliction, and nothingness. But it is precisely in this darkness that we find a new way of being that is able to move out of the darkness, even if only momentarily.

References

Abelson, Miriam J., *Men in Place: Trans Masculinity, Race, and Sexuality in America*, Minneapolis, MN: University of Minnesota Press, 2019.
—— *A Lifestyle Distinct: The Muxe of Mexico*, New York: New York Times Company, 2008.
Anzaldúa, Gloria, *Borderlands: La Frontera*, vol. 3, San Francisco: Aunt Lute, 1987.
—— *The Gloria Anzaldúa Reader*, Durham, NC: Duke University Press, 2009.

Boylorn, Robin M. and Mark P. Orbe, eds, *Critical autoethnography: Intersecting Cultural Identities in Everyday Life*, vol. 13, New York: Routledge, 2016.

De León, Arnoldo, *They Called Them Greasers: Anglo Attitudes Toward Mexicans in Texas, 1821–1900*, Austin, TX: University of Texas Press, 2010.

Denzin, Norman K., *Interpretive Ethnography: Ethnographic Practices for the 21st Century*, Thousand Oaks, CA: Sage, 1997.

—— *Performance Ethnography: Critical Pedagogy and the Politics of Culture*, Thousand Oaks, CA: Sage, 2003.

de Unamuno, Miguel, *Selected Works of Miguel de Unamuno, Volume 2: The Private World*, Princeton, NJ: Princeton University Press, 2017.

—— *Tragic Sense of Life*, trans. J. E. Crawford Flitch, New York: Dover Publications, 1954.

Dillon, John J., *St. Irenaeus of Lyons Against the Heresies*, vol. 1, New York: Newman Press, 1992.

Ellis, Carolyn, Tony E. Adams and Arthur P. Bochner, 'Autoethnografie', in *Handbuch qualitative forschung in der psychologie*, Wiesbaden: VS Verlag für Sozialwissenschaften, 2010, 345–57.

Fairweather, Eugene Rathbone, ed., *A Scholastic Miscellany: Anselm to Ockham*, vol. 10, Louisville, KY: Westminster John Knox Press, 1956.

Ford, Julian D., Andres R. Schneeberger, Irina Komarovskaya, Kristina Muenzenmaier, Dorothy Castille, Lewis A. Opler and Bruce Link, 'The Symptoms of Trauma Scale (SOTS): Psychometric Evaluation and Gender Differences with Adults Diagnosed with Serious Mental Illness', *Journal of Trauma and Dissociation* 18, no. 4 (2017), 559–74.

Jones, Serene, *Trauma and Grace: Theology in a Ruptured World*, Louisville, KY: Westminster John Knox Press, 2019.

Juan, Mary Joyce D., Sarah E. Nunnink, Ebony O. Butler and Carolyn B. Allard, 'Gender Role Stress Mediates Depression among Veteran Men with Military Sexual Trauma', *Psychology of Men and Masculinity* 18, no. 3 (2017), 243.

Julian of Norwich, *Revelations of Divine Love*, London: Penguin, 1998.

Luther, Martin, 'Heidelberg Disputation', *Luther's Works*, vol. 31, ed. H. J. Grimm, Philadelphia, PA: Fortress Press, 1957, 39–70.

Mirandé, Alfredo, *Behind the Mask: Gender Hybridity in a Zapotec Community*, Tucson, AZ: University of Arizona Press, 2017.

Piñón, S., '"The Box" and the Dark Night of the Soul: An Autoethnography from the Force of Losing a Child in the Delivery Room', *Online Journal of Health Ethics*, 12, no. 1 (2016): http://dx.doi.org/10.18785/ojhe.1201.06.

Ploder, Andrea and Johanna Stadlbauer, 'Strong Reflexivity and Its Critics: Responses to Autoethnography in the German-speaking Cultural and Social Sciences', *Qualitative Inquiry* 22, no. 9 (2016), 753–65.

Rogers, Catherine H., Frank J. Floyd, Marsha Mailick Seltzer, Jan Greenberg and Jinkuk Hong, 'Long-term Effects of the Death of a Child on Parents' Adjustment in Midlife', *Journal of Family Psychology* 22, no. 2 (2008), 203.

Slanbekova, Gulnara K., Man C. Chung, Aliya A. Tolegenova and Satibaldy M. Jakupov, 'Theoretical Analyze of Relationships between Psychological Trauma and Divorce', *Education and Science without Borders* 5, no. 9 (2014).

Sorenson, Susan B. and Kristie A. Thomas, 'Views of Intimate Partner Violence in Same- and Opposite-Sex Relationships', *Journal of Marriage and Family* 71, no. 2 (2009), 337–52. www.jstor.org/stable/40262883.

Stambaugh, Antonio Prieto, '"RepresentaXión" de un muxe: la identidad performática de Lukas Avendaño', *Latin American Theatre Review* 48, no. 1 (2014), 31–53.

Stephen, Lynn, 'Sexualities and Genders in Zapotec Oaxaca', *Latin American Perspectives* 29, no. 2 (2002), 41–59.

Thege, Barna Konkolÿ, Lewis Horwood, Linda Slater, Maria C. Tan, David C. Hodgins and T. Cameron Wild, 'Relationship between Interpersonal Trauma Exposure and Addictive Behaviors: A Systematic Review', *BMC Psychiatry* 17, no. 1 (2017): https://doi.org/10.1186/s12888-017-1323-1.

Tillich, Paul, *Dynamics of Faith*, vol. 42, Grand Rapids, MI: Zondervan, 2001.

Notes

1 All biblical quotations are from the New International Version.

2 B. K. Thege, L. Horwaood, L. Slater, M. C. Tan, D. V. Hodgins and T. C. Wild, 'Relationship between Interpersonal Trauma Exposure and Addictive Behaviors: A Systematic Review', *BMC Psychiatry* 17, no. 1 (2017), 164–17.

3 Guinara K. Slanbekova, Man C. Chung, Aliya A. Tolegenova and Satibaldly M. Jakupos, 'Theoretical Analyze of Relationships between Psychological Trauma and Divorce', *Education and Science without Borders* 5, no. 9 (2014), 140.

4 M. J. D. Juan, S. E. Nunnink, E. O. Butler and C. B. Allard, 'Gender Role Stress Mediates Depression among Veteran Men with Military Sexual Trauma', *Psychology of Men and Masculinity* 18, no. 3 (2017), 243–50.

5 Julian D. Ford, Andres R. Schneeberger, Irina Komarovskaya, Kristina Muernzenmaier, Dorothy Castille, Lewis A. Opler and Bruce Link, 'The Symptoms of Trauma Scale (SOTS): Psychometric Evaluation and Gender Differences with Adults Diagnosed with Serious Mental Illness', *Journal of Trauma and Dissociation* 18, no. 4 (2017), 559–74.

6 C. H. Rogers, F. J. Floyd, M. M. Seltzer, J. Greenberg and J. Hong, 'Long-term Effects of the Death of a Child on Parents' Adjustment in Midlife', *Journal of Family Psychology* 22, no. 2 (2008), 203–11.

7 *Hijos de crianza* are individuals who are taken in by a family who is not biologically related to them.

8 Serene Jones, *Trauma and Grace: Theology in a Ruptured World* (Louisville, KY: Westminster John Knox Press, 2009), 130.

9 Jones, *Trauma and Grace*, 131.

10 This term is used by Anzaldúa to describe white European Americans not of Latin American descent. I have consistently used this term with Anzaldúa's understanding.

11 Gloria Anzaldúa, 'La Prieta', in *The Gloria Anzaldúa Reader*, ed. AnaLouise Keating (Durham, NC and London: Duke University Press, 2009), 42.

12 Anzaldúa, 'La Prieta', 43.

13 Arnoldo de Leon, *They Called Them Greasers: Anglo Attitudes toward Mexicans in Texas, 1821–1900* (Austin, TX: University of Texas Press, 1983).

14 Anzaldúa, 'La Prieta', 43.

15 Gloria Anzaldúa, *Borderlands: La Frontera*, vol. 3 (San Francisco: Aunt Lute, 1987), 81.

16 *Pocho* is a derogatory term used by Mexicans to designate Mexican Ameri-

cans or Mexicans in the USA who speak English and are unable to speak Spanish fluently.

17 Anzaldúa, *Borderlands*, 77.

18 Anzaldúa, *Borderlands*, 25.

19 Anzaldúa, *Borderlands*, 102.

20 Anzaldúa, *Borderlands*, 102.

21 Anzaldúa, *Borderlands*, 102.

22 Anzaldúa, *Borderlands*, 105; 'She becomes the shaper of her own soul. According to her own conception, that is who she will be' (translation mine).

23 Anzaldúa, *Borderlands*, 102.

24 Anzaldúa, *Borderlands*, 103.

25 Martin Luther, 'Heidelberg Disputation', *Luther's Works*, vol. 31, ed. H. J. Grimm (Philadelphia, PA: Fortress Press, 1957), 39–70.

26 Luther, 'Heidelberg Disputation'.

27 Anzaldúa, *Borderlands*, 102.

28 Anzaldúa, *Borderlands*, 102.

29 Anzaldúa, *Borderlands*, 105; 'Let's not forget the men' (translation mine).

30 Anzaldúa, *Borderlands*, 106; 'Fuck the women' (translation mine).

31 Anzaldúa, *Borderlands*, 104.

32 Anzaldúa, *Borderlands*, 106.

33 Anzaldúa, *Borderlands*, 106.

34 Anzaldúa, *Borderlands*, 106.

35 Lynette S. Moran, 'Men in Mourning: Depictions of Masculinity in Young and Older Widowers in Contemporary Film', *Men and Masculinities* 19, no. 1 (2016), 96.

36 Moran, 'Men in Mourning', 96.

37 Rogers et al., 'Long-term Effects', 203–11.

38 Miguel de Unamuno, *Tragic Sense of Life in Men and Nations*, vol. 85 (Princeton, NJ: Princeton University Pres, 1972), 1.

39 Miguel de Unamuno, *Selected Works of Miguel de Unamuno, Volume 2: The Private World* (Princeton, NJ: Princeton University Press, 2017), xiv.

40 Reference to people who are marginalized because they belong to the LGBTQ community.

41 Anzaldúa, *Borderlands*, 107.

42 Susan B. Sorenson and Kristie A. Thomas, 'Views of Intimate Partner Violence in Same- and Opposite-Sex Relationships', *Journal of Marriage and Family* 71, no. 2 (2009), 338.

43 Miriam J. Abelson, 'Masculinities in Space: Thugs, Rednecks, and Faggy Men', in *Men in Place: Trans Masculinity, Race, and Sexuality in America* (Minneapolis, MN: University of Minnesota, 2019).

44 Alfredo Mirandé, *Behind the Mask: Gender Hybridity in a Zapotec Community* (Tucson, AZ: University of Arizona Press, 2017), 10

45 Antonio Prieto Stambaugh, 'RepresentaXión de un muxe: la identidad performática de Lukas Avendaño', *Latin American Theatre Reviews* 48, no. 1 (Fall 2014), 45; 'One of the few Mexican performance artists who works without reference to gender or ethnicity' (translation mine).

46 *A Lifestyle Distinct: The Muxe of Mexico* (New York: The New York Times Company, 2008).

47 Stephen, Lynn, 'Sexualities and Genders in Zapotec Oaxaca', *Latin American Perspectives* 29, no. 2 (March 2002), 44.

48 Norman K. Denzin, *Performance Ethnography: Critical Pedagogy and the Politics of Culture* (Thousand Oaks, CA: Sage, 2003), x.

49 Robin M. Boylorn and Mark P. Orbe, eds, *Critical Autoethnography: Intersecting Cultural Identities in Everyday Life*, vol. 13 (New York: Routledge, 2016), 15.

50 Boylorn and Orbe, *Critical Autoethnography*.

51 Norman K. Denzin, *Interpretive Ethnography: Ethnographic Practices for the 21st Century* (Thousand Oaks, CA: Sage, 1997), 227.

52 Andrea Ploder and Johanna Stadlbauer, 'Strong Reflexivity and Its Critics: Responses to Autoethnography in the German-speaking Cultural and Social Science', *Qualitative Inquiry* 22 (2016), 753–65, 754.

53 Ploder and Stadlbauer, 'Strong Reflexivity', 754.

54 Paul Tillich, *Dynamics of Faith* (Grand Rapids, MI: Zondervan, 2001).

55 C. Ellis, T. E. Adams, and A. P. Boehner, 'Autoethnografie', in *Handbuch qualitative forschung in der psychologies* (2010), 345–57. See my article, S. Piñón, '"The Box" and the Dark Night of the Soul: An Autoethnography from the Force of Losing a Child in the Delivery Room', *Online Journal of Health Ethics* 12, no. 1 (2016), http://dx.dol.org/10.18785/ojhe.1201.06, for a fuller consideration of the impact of the *sachwang*.

56 I am completing a manuscript that considers the death of a child from a father's perspective, *A Father's Shattered Dreams*.

57 Eugene Rathbone Fairweather, ed., *A Scholastic Miscellany: Anselm to Ockham* (Louisville, KY: Westminster John Knox Press, Ichthus Edition, 1956).

58 Fairweather, *Scholastic Miscellany*, 142.

59 Julian of Norwich, *Revelations of Divine Love*, Long Text, 51.

60 Julian of Norwich, *Revelations*, 51.

61 Irenaeus of Lyons, *Against Heresies* IV.38.

13

The Trauma of Mothers: Motherhood, Violent Crime and the Christian Motif of Forgiveness

ESTHER MCINTOSH

Where Forgiveness Begins? Early Trauma and the Lessons We Teach Children

'I remember you fondly by the soil./ I vow I will never forget';[1] these words are the last two lines of a poem translated from the Welsh language. Originally written in 1984, the poem commemorates two of the poet's close friends, John and Rhoda, a husband and wife who had died in a fatal traffic accident eight years earlier. At the time of their death, the couple were in their early thirties and, perhaps, the fact that their untimely death occurred around the same age as the Christian tradition believes that Jesus was crucified in an act of humility and for the purpose of redeeming others, gave the bereaved some sense of special significance, maybe even of hope.

Prior to the aforementioned tragedy, the couple in question had dedicated their adult lives to pursuing missionary work in the field. In 1968, John, a mathematics teacher from Wales, and Rhoda, a midwife from Scotland, completed their missionary training in separate locations (John at a Bible college in Switzerland and Rhoda at Faith Mission in Edinburgh) before setting sail for the Congo under the auspices of the Regions Beyond Missionary Union (RBMU). On arrival in the Congo, several weeks after embarkation, both spent time learning Lomongo, the local tribal language, and adjusting to working environments with a scarcity of staff and basic resources. Rhoda worked in the hospital at the RBMU's Baringa station, while John cared for and taught Maths and Science to the 150 pupils, mostly boys, at the Maringa Christian Institute French-speaking boarding school. On 3 June 1969, the couple's marriage was recorded by the Civil Registrar at Basankusu, and later certified by the British Embassy in Kinshasa. Although not due for furlough until 1973, the couple returned to the UK early, following illness (probably malaria) and a miscarriage; they settled into church and civil life in South Wales, where Rhoda gave birth to their first daughter in 1971 and their second in 1973.

Unexpectedly, on 24 February 1976, returning home from visiting relatives, the family car – a Wartburg known to have challenging steering – careered out of control, veered across the road, turned on to its side and slid into the path of an oncoming double-decker bus. In the aftermath of the accident, news reports referred to the location of the accident, the A48 between Newport and Cardiff, as a crash blackspot. Both adults died before they reached hospital; their daughters, however, survived, albeit as orphans and with multiple injuries, some serious. Those presiding over the funeral service in the huge Heath Evangelical Church, which at that time had over 600 members, chose quotations such as 'to be with Christ, which is far better' and 'except a corn of wheat fall into the ground and die, it abideth alone: but if it die, it bringeth forth much fruit'; the congregation tried their best to convince themselves that there is meaning in death as they sang the rousing and forward-looking hymns 'Love divine', 'Great is thy faithfulness' and 'Thine be the glory'. Similarly, Rhoda's parents chose the following inscriptions for the gravestone: 'in death they were not divided'; 'they that turn many to righteousness shall shine as the stars for ever and ever' and 'severed only till he come'. Deep-seated Christian beliefs were clearly evident on both the Welsh and Scottish sides of their extended families regarding the inherent goodness of missionary work, the acceptance of death as God's will in a plan that mere mortals cannot begin to understand, and an unshakeable trust in an afterlife with the promise of reuniting with previously departed loved ones. For the surviving children, released from hospital into the care of relatives sometime after the double funeral of their parents, the reiteration of these messages of faith eased the pain of some of the darkest days, until education and a changing world led to the questioning of former missionary endeavours and a realization that childhood beliefs in reunion are not equivalent to the meaning intended by such phraseology when employed by adults.

What remained with me, though, for I was the younger of the two children, was a memory of a Welsh Presbyterian relative asking me if I forgave God. When he posed the question, I was confused; it did not make any sense to me at that time. I mulled over the phrase in my mind: 'Did I forgive God?' Up to this point, it had not occurred to me that forgiveness had anything to do with my grief, my parentless situation, my injuries. I started to ponder the meaning of the question: what was my relative asking? What did he think I needed to forgive God for: for taking my parents, for allowing them to die, for causing or not stopping the accident? As a young child, I was not preoccupied with such thoughts; I was grief-stricken and traumatized, but I was not angry with God. In fact, despite longing for the reunion in heaven that the adults talked about, I did not think God had anything to do with the crash. I suspect that my parents' devout friends, my grandparents, my uncles and aunts were angry with God, and so they assumed that we, the orphans, felt the same.

I have since often wondered about the wisdom of asking children to forgive God. Support for childhood bereavement and a nuanced psychological understanding of childhood trauma and spirituality has grown significantly since the 1970s. Charities offering bereavement camps for children began to appear in the 1980s, growing in prevalence in the 1990s and 2000s, including Comfort Zone camp in the USA, the National Centre for Childhood Grief in Australia, Winston's Wish and Child Bereavement UK (the latter of which now claims HRH Duke of Cambridge, Prince William, as a patron, given his experience of the death of his mother, Diana Princess of Wales, in 1997 when he was 15 years old). Such camps are now held to be an effective means of assisting children in processing their grief,[2] but academic studies into the impact of bereavement and trauma on childhood spirituality are few and far between (outnumbered by psychological studies examining the spirituality of parents and the loss of a child),[3] even though, according to Sir Al Aynsley-Green, President of the British Medical Association, 'a child loses a parent through death every 20 minutes'.[4] In one such study, James Garbarino and Claire Bedard note that 'trauma represents an enormous challenge to any individual's understanding of the meaning and purpose of life, the metaphysical and spiritual dimensions, and that this crisis is particularly difficult for children'.[5] Evidence for this claim comes from Bessel van der Kolk, who asked his psychiatric patients whether they had 'given up all hope of finding meaning in … life'.[6] His statistical analysis in relation to young children is stark: 'Among those who experience major trauma prior to age 5, 74 per cent answer "yes"'; whereas, 'among those who experience trauma after the age of 20, the figure is "only" 10 percent' and among older adults the figure drops to 'about 1 percent'.[7]

Hence, while trauma at any age represents a potential threat to the spiritual beliefs of the traumatized, the lived experience and cognitive development that comes with age is a significant factor in the ability to construct and reconstruct meaning. For a child reared in a household that professes belief in God as a benevolent protector, following trauma that child is left 'literally looking for God in a world in which God has disappeared'.[8] Consequently, Garbarino and Bedard argue that effective psychological intervention for the traumatized should 'recognise the need to deal with the metaphysical wounds that arise from … the eclipse of God'.[9] Moreover, due to a child's susceptibility to taking beliefs literally, the notion of spirits can be a source of further anxiety as much as a comfort; thus, adults need to be conscious of the potential harm done to children by proffering spiritual interpretations of traumatic events.[10] Whether or not the promotion of forgiveness is appropriate here or in any way aids healing is not discussed by Garbarino and Bedard. For my part, since having children of my own and becoming a feminist theologian, I have found myself querying not only the appropriateness of asking traumatized children to forgive but, equally, the appropriateness of asking traumatized women to forgive both in situations of domestic violence and in the event of the traumatic loss of a child.

The Motif of Forgiveness: Required, Therapeutic or Dangerous?

Forgiveness is the bedrock of the Christian tradition; it is at the centre of the Christian story. As he is crucified, according to the Gospel of Luke in the famous words heard, recited and repeated by Catholic and Protestant congregations around the world every Holy Week, 'Jesus said, "Father, forgive them; for they do not know what they are doing"' (Luke 23.34).[11] Previous to this, in Matthew's retelling, at the final Passover meal before his crucifixion, Jesus connects his death with forgiveness: 'Then he took a cup, and after giving thanks he gave it to them, saying, "Drink from it, all of you; for this is my blood of the covenant, which is poured out for many for the forgiveness of sins"' (Matthew 26.27–28). If the biblical canon is read chronologically, this ultimate act of forgiveness occurs after numerous reports in the Hebrew Scriptures of familial forgiveness, of atonement sacrifices required to obtain divine forgiveness and of the Lord forgiving the Israelites' iniquity (see, for example, Genesis 50; Leviticus 5; Numbers 14). Furthermore, the crucifixion narrative in Matthew's Gospel is preceded by several accounts of Jesus promoting forgiveness. In Matthew 6, Jesus teaches the disciples to pray 'Our father … forgive us our debts', on the grounds that 'if you forgive others … your heavenly Father will also forgive you'. Then, after foretelling his death and resurrection, Peter asks Jesus: '"Lord, if another member of the church sins against me, how often should I forgive? As many as seven times?"'; Jesus replies '"Not seven times, but, I tell you, seventy-seven times"' (Matthew 18.21–22).

   Given the above, and the numerous other narratives of forgiveness in the Scriptures, it is not surprising that countless theological works and sermons focus on forgiveness. In particular, forgiveness in the face of the brutality of Nazi Germany stands as an extreme illustration of the possibility of forgiving even the most heinous of crimes. Among theologians and pastors, the life and works of Dietrich Bonhoeffer stand as a testament to the strength of a Christian faith that takes an ethical stand against a destructive populist narrative. Forgiveness is a central theme in Bonhoeffer's writings, even when incarcerated in Tegel prison in Berlin during the Second World War.[12] Importantly, however, Bonhoeffer speaks out against 'cheap grace', which he defines as 'the preaching of forgiveness without requiring repentance'.[13] For Bonhoeffer, the assertion that grace is costly entailed denying the special status of Christianity, experiencing suffering, opposing anti-Semitism and, therefore, accepting execution as the consequence of resisting the Nazi regime. Decades later, in 1995, on the fiftieth anniversary of the liberation of Auschwitz, Eva Mozes Kor, a survivor of Josef Mengele's human experimentation on twins, publicly forgave Hans Munch, a doctor who worked alongside Mengele. Kor insists that forgiveness is liberating and that the power to forgive remains with the victim even in the absence of repentance from the perpetrator.[14] Twenty years later, in 2015, Kor angered co-plaintiffs in the trial of former SS officer Oskar Gröning for again offering public forgiveness without securing legal guilt and justice.[15]

Kor's actions have been defended by Marina Cantacuzino, founder of the Forgiveness Project.[16] Cantacuzino notes that 'Forgiveness is hotly contested territory – contentious, risky messy, misunderstood and potentially divisive'; yet, she also claims that forgiveness 'is most certainly a transformative and powerful route to healing'.[17] Her perspective has high-profile support from Desmond Tutu who, along with Nelson Mandela and the Truth and Reconciliation Commission in South Africa, advocated forgiveness as the means to repair race relations and move forwards following decades of brutal apartheid.[18]

Not only is forgiveness frequently assumed to be therapeutic for those who have been harmed by others, church documents and media reports tend to create the impression that those who forgive perpetrators of violence are extraordinary and inspirational human beings, morally superior to those who cannot or do not forgive. Conversely, the feminist critique of Christian forgiveness and engagement with trauma reaches a different conclusion. In 2006, the Church of England's publication *Responding to Domestic Abuse* represented an overdue acknowledgement of its inability 'to address the processes that lead to domestic abuse', in conjunction with a long-awaited recognition that church teaching and practice 'reinforced abuse, failed to challenge abusers and intensified the suffering of survivors'.[19] In particular, the document recognized that 'a theology of humility has often been misapplied to women'[20] and that 'the example of Christ's sacrificial self-giving has ... encouraged compliant and passive responses by women'.[21] Nevertheless, I argued that the document had not gone far enough, since it still claimed that 'genuine self-denial ... is a gateway to abundant life and a means of bringing good out of evil'.[22] It is precisely this connection between suffering and redemption that encourages women to repeatedly forgive an abuser and to remain in an abusive relationship in the hope that the abusive partner will eventually be transformed as a result of their forbearance of suffering.

Given my critique, the 2017 update of the Church of England document ushers in a welcome emphasis on responding *well*, which includes raising awareness of the statistics on domestic abuse and the variety of types of abuse – from intimate partner violence to coercive control, from same-sex abuse to elder abuse, from financial to spiritual abuse – and foregrounds the importance of believing victims.[23] In addition, it advocates safeguarding procedures, promotes clergy training and stresses the value of supporting victims with a multi-agency approach in responding to accusations of abuse. Accordingly, on the subject of suffering, this amended version counters the perception that 'suffering is an opportunity to grow' and suggests instead that 'abused women should be safe and protected'.[24] Positively, then, the updated publication includes alternative interpretations of biblical passages that have been construed so as to encourage female submission and legitimize male dominance and, hence, have operated as divine sanction for male partners to punish women who do not obey. Nevertheless, while the document promotes 'mutual submission' and suggests that God's plan for humanity is one of equality, it also states that 'a consequence of sin is that a man will rule over his wife'; such a statement appears to be in direct contrast with the aforementioned mutual submission.[25] Moreover, on the subject of forgiveness, the document constructively opposes the assumption that 'forgiving someone should mean disregarding what they have done and maintaining the same relationship with them regardless of whether they change'; yet, rather than emphasizing an abused woman's prerogative not to forgive, the document's alternative interpretation states that 'Women should not have to stay in an abusive situation in order to forgive their partner.'[26] Disturbingly, even when the repentance of the abuser is required, or escape from an abusive relationship is deemed necessary for survival, the Church of England still seems to maintain an assumption that women should forgive their abusers. Additionally, both the diocesan and parish statements contained within the publication refer to 'valuing, listening to and respecting both survivors and alleged or known perpetrators of domestic abuse';[27] it is not at all clear how the Church intends to value perpetrators, while providing a safe space for survivors nor, indeed, whether the latter is compatible with the former.

Untold damage has been done to the abused in church settings, which has only recently started to come to light through the hashtag #ChurchToo.[28] As an offshoot of the #MeToo movement,[29] #ChurchToo, pioneered by Hannah Paasch and Emily Joy, enables women to voice their anger and hurt following experiences of abuse in churches, perpetrated by partners, fellow congregants and clergy and, further, to expose the ensuing pressure not to report to external authorities or to sustain marriage at all costs. Women have been told to remain with abusive partners; they have been victim-shamed, rebuked for their sinful sexual conduct; or dismissed and silenced as the church hierarchy defensively protected ordained men.[30] What is abundantly clear from the stories shared via the hashtag is not only that predatory sexual behaviour is prevalent among churches; equally, the response of church leaders has been woefully inadequate. In short, theologies of submission and forgiveness have not served women well. Ethnographic research carried out by Kristin Aune and Rebecca Barnes in Cumbria confirms that churches are naively less aware of abuse within their congregations than in wider society and that church support for survivors includes 'examples of dangerous practice and disclosures of domestic abuse being minimised or silenced'.[31] Consequently, among their recommendations, Aune and Barnes insist that church teaching 'that implies that male control and abuse could be divinely-mandated' should be challenged via 'alternative theological interpretations of concepts such as forgiveness'.[32]

Knives, Bombs and the Traumatic Loss of a Child[33]

Alongside the survivors of domestic abuse, we find more vocal opponents and advocates of forgiveness, especially mothers whose lives have been shattered by violent crime; their visibility is not necessarily intentional, but they may find themselves thrust into the media spotlight when journalists decide to home in on their reaction to the loss of a child through violent crime. Since 1993, when her 18-year-old son Stephen Lawrence was stabbed to death in a racist attack, Doreen Lawrence has been an active campaigner for justice against a backdrop of institutional racism. On the approach to the twenty-fifth anniversary of Stephen's murder, his father, Neville Lawrence, stated that he would spend the day in church, 'embracing his Christian faith' which, for him, meant making the incredibly hard decision to forgive the young men who killed his son.[34] He explained that forgiving had improved his quality of life.[35] However, Doreen, also a churchgoing Christian, has continued to maintain that she cannot forgive the men who killed her son, because 'you can only forgive somebody when they have shown remorse and accepted what they have done – and they haven't'.[36] Her lack of forgiveness first made news headlines in 2012, when two of the killers were finally convicted, nearly 20 years after the crime was committed; her stance was reiterated in 2018, 25 years after Stephen's unlawful killing. Diverging from Neville's decision to forgive, Doreen reaffirmed her stance that she cannot forgive in the absence of an admission of guilt from the murderers.[37] She has been the more visible and vocal campaigner of Stephen's parents, clarifying, during the course of the public inquiry into the 2017 fire at the Grenfell Tower block in North Kensington, that she identifies with the pain and anger of the relatives of the 72 residents who died. In her lengthy fight for justice and in the face of similar 'institutional indifference', classism and racism, she asserts: 'My anger became my motivation; it kept me driving forwards for years.'[38]

In a racist attack similar to the one perpetrated against Stephen Lawrence, Gee Walker's son, 18-year-old Anthony Walker, was killed in Huyton, Merseyside, in 2005, by two young men armed with an ice axe. Public attention was trained on the case: Anthony's funeral was broadcast live on television; media coverage of the arrest and trial of the perpetrators was widespread. Additionally, Anthony's mother's attitude towards the perpetrators was highlighted by journalists. Gee, a gospel singer in an evangelical church, announced that she would emulate Jesus' example by forgiving her son's killers, saying: 'At the point of death, Jesus said, "I forgive them for they know not what they do." I have got to forgive them.'[39] On the tenth anniversary of Anthony's murder, Gee reiterated her commitment to forgiveness, stating: 'The moment it happened I knew forgiveness was the right thing to do', further insisting that, despite the unanswered prayers for Anthony's recovery at the time, it is her Christian faith that has enabled her to endure the grief and trauma.[40] Unlike the Stephen Lawrence case, subsequent to Anthony Walker's murder, police action was swift and effective; justice as understood in law was served, while the killer who delivered the fatal blow admitted guilt and expressed remorse for his actions.[41] Even though it might seem that punishment and repentance would be significant in enabling the traumatized mother to forgive, Gee's explanation places love at the centre of her motivation: 'I don't have the capacity or capability to balance bitterness and hate with the love I had for my son.'[42]

A similar contrast to, and press interest in, the reactions of Doreen Lawrence and Gee Walker towards the racist murders of their teenage sons is found in the responses of mothers Julie Nicholson and Marie Fatayi-Williams. Julie's 24-year-old daughter Jennifer and Marie's 26-year-old son Anthony were killed on their journeys to work in the 7/7 (July 2005) bombings in London, along with 56 others (including the suicide bombers). Several days after the bombings, Anthony's Catholic mother captured the attention of the press and public when, standing not far from the wreckage of the bus at Tavistock Square where she suspected her son had died, she delivered an impassioned plea for information and for an end to hatred and violence.[43] Less than a fortnight after that speech, at Anthony's funeral in Westminster Cathedral, Marie declared her intention to avoid anger by forgiving the bombers, avowing: 'I am distraught, but I'm not angry. I could be very angry, but if I was angry what would that do? Anger begets hatred, begets more violence, so let's forgive.'[44]

Julie Nicholson also subsisted for an agonizing five days before the death of her daughter Jennifer, who was killed at Edgware Road in one of the three explosions on the London underground, was confirmed; it was several more days before Jenny's body was released to her family. In keeping with her occupation as an ordained priest, Julie was determined to anoint her daughter's body. Once she was finally able to do so on 16 July, it confirmed her priestly vocation; recounting the anointing, she writes: 'I believe it was for this moment I was ordained a priest.'[45] As the police start to piece together the events that led up to the bombings, and the media publish images of the bombers, Julie records attempting not to hate, despite being filled with loathing for the man responsible for her daughter's death.[46] Scrutinizing the tunnel where the Circle Line train transporting her daughter exploded, she depicts her wrath rising to the surface:

> I thought there was no room in my heart for anger because I was too full of sadness. Yet, standing here, looking into the tunnel, the shadowy face of a stranger intrudes. A stranger who has come into our lives and did not know or did not care what beauty he was killing. And I am angry.[47]

Sympathy cards arrive in droves, but Julie finds that she is irritated by Christian platitudes that are intended to be comforting. She does not feel blessed by God; if the dead are being held by God, why, she questions, does God not hold the dead while they are still alive?[48] She is unable to find passages in the Bible to ease her pain; likewise, the ample supply of texts on grief on her bookshelves employ phrases such as 'acceptance' and 'moving on' that are simplistic and ineffective now.[49]

During the planning of Jenny's funeral, Julie discovers that she cannot relate to the usual Christian funereal phrases referring to resurrection and light; she has 'not arrived at a point of comfort', rather, she is 'still at the crucifixion'.[50] She is, however, able to identify with Rachel's lament for her children (Matthew 2.18), as well as with artistic renditions of Mary holding Jesus' crucified body. She states: 'The image I hold in my heart ... is the Pietà, the suffering mother whose heart has been pierced, the image of Mary cradling the broken and lifeless body of her son, Jesus.'[51] Most of all, rather than any theological teaching, Bible verse, prayer or liturgy, Julie is preserved through her traumatic loss by poetry, music and unexpected acts of human kindness, leading her to the recognition that 'Even through the bleakness and horror – or maybe in spite of it – there has been the best of humanity.'[52]

Two particularly significant examples occur one week after the bombings, on 14 July 2005, the date on which there is to be a vigil in Trafalgar Square, preceded by a national two minutes' silence at St Paul's Cathedral. At the cathedral, Julie encounters an elderly priest who refrains from offering shallow words of comfort, sensitive enough to spend time with Julie in near silence and to promise to hold Jenny and Julie in his daily prayers for as long as he shall live.[53] Later that day, Julie is overwhelmed by a panic attack as she approaches the underground; an off-duty taxi driver not only drives her, but refuses to accept any fare for doing so.[54] Buoyed by the compassion of friends and strangers, Julie is rendered capable of affirming that, in words borrowed from Etty Hillesum, 'Despite everything, life is beautiful and full of meaning.'[55]

Ultimately, however, the violent and untimely nature of Jenny's death becomes a stumbling block in Julie's parish ministry. Less than a year after her daughter's death, Julie attracts global media attention by resigning from her post as parish priest with these words: 'It's very difficult for me to stand behind an altar and celebrate the Eucharist, the Communion, and lead people in words of peace and reconciliation and forgiveness when I feel very far from that myself.'[56] Unable to forgive the bombers and, hence, unable to preach forgiveness to her parishioners, Julie seeks to fulfil her calling in alternate forms of ministry, finding life and hope through employment on a youth community theatre project.

Her own questioning of the Christian motif of forgiveness leads to a BBC documentary in which she meets other bereaved parents.[57] She converses with a couple from Northern Ireland who publicly forgave the loyalist paramilitaries who murdered their son and for whom that forgiveness has become a burden that they must reassert daily. From this, Julie argues that being held hostage to forgiveness does not bring peace for the survivors.[58] Similarly, she records the guilt of a mother who knows that she has not forgiven, but was pressured by her church into announcing that she forgave the perpetrators of a knife crime assault that killed her son. Julie's response to these encounters is to assert that imposing forgiveness is morally wrong and is far from life-giving; furthermore, she insists that some acts should not be forgiven.[59] In situations such as hers, where there is no repentance or, indeed, no possibility of repentance and reconciliation because the perpetrator is also dead, forgiveness, Julie believes, requires humans to be greater than God. Thus, subsequent to the murder of her daughter, Julie reads the biblical passage 'Father, forgive them' with changed meaning; in reciting this passage she hands forgiveness over to God, acknowledging that she cannot forgive. There is no closure, no 'letting go' of traumatic grief; consequently, there is no neat and tidy path to forgiveness, peace and reconciliation. Yet, not forgiving, she explains, does not mean awaiting retribution as much as seeking understanding. Freed from the requirement to forgive, through her work as a chaplain, rather than a priest, therefore, Julie has discovered the means to embrace her grief and to continue living; in Maya Angelou's words, 'not merely to survive, but to thrive; and to do so with some passion ... and some style'.[60]

Recovering a Theology of Loss: Making Space for Darkness and Female Anger

From Julie's example, it seems that the inadequacy of a theology may not be fully apparent until faced with traumatic loss. In fact, the growing body of work categorized as trauma theology bears this out. Serene Jones' probing of the field originates from an encounter with a young woman suffering from post-traumatic stress disorder (PTSD) as a result of childhood sexual abuse; her enquiry develops as she grapples with the collective trauma of 9/11 (11 September 2001), when hijacked planes were flown into the Twin Towers of the World Trade Center in New York killing nearly 3,000 people.[61] Likewise, Shelly Rambo's exploration grows out of the ongoing trauma caused to residents of New Orleans struck by the deadly Hurricane Katrina in 2005.[62] Alternatively, Karen O'Donnell is left questioning theologies of motherhood and reproduction following the trauma of miscarriage; she finds resources severely lacking.[63] O'Donnell's primary aims are to rupture the silence on reproductive loss and refute any suggestion that such loss be considered redemptive; in this respect, new theological work is required to fill the void.[64] Contrastingly, Jones and Rambo embark on rediscovery and reinterpretation of extant sources in conjunction with lessons learned from trauma studies outside theology.

By paying closer attention to the trauma of those around her, Jones begins to question: 'How did the Lord's prayer sound to each of them? ... Did our collective words of thanksgiving to God make sense in the face of so much pain and loss?'[65] Pulled up short by the wounds of the traumatized, Jones is forced to consider whether the Christian imagery contained in liturgies 'reinscribes the violence ... rather than healing it'.[66] As a feminist theologian, Jones is concerned that the annual retelling of the crucifixion narrative might be repeating harm done to the already wounded. She is troubled by the possibility of abused women believing that their sacrifice has salvific potential, and yet she finds abused women identifying with Christ on the cross, empowered by the idea that there is solidarity between themselves and the wounded Christ-figure.[67] Unusually, though, she does not promote the resurrection as the promise of a happy denouement. Instead, she turns to Mark's Gospel and its ending in early manuscripts at chapter 16, verse 8: 'So they went out and fled from the tomb, for terror and amazement had seized them; and they said nothing to anyone, for they were afraid.' That is, having gone to the tomb to anoint the body of Jesus, the women, finding the sealing stone removed and a man in white robes telling them that Jesus has been raised, flee in silence. This ending is abrupt; it does not relay joy and glory. Nevertheless, Jones notes, *we like our stories to have satisfying conclusions*; in other words, 'We want stories that allow us to get on with things, as if there is an ultimate point to it all, a conclusion to the tale of human life that makes it worthy of living.'[68] Conversely, though, the after-effects of trauma are such that stories are disrupted; there is no linear progression to a positive finale. Rather than adding an extrapolation of good news to Mark's Gospel, with the original 'unending', Jones suggests, the sense of the messy and incomplete may speak to the traumatized imagination more effectively. A survivor living with the memories of trauma is embarking on a crooked path towards healing that might not ever be finished. The healing process is full of twists and turns that loop backwards and sideways as well as forwards; thus, she contends, for a time, hope is deferred.[69]

Delving deeper into this liminal space, Rambo cites the words of Deacon Julius Lee, a New Orleans hurricane survivor: 'The storm is gone, but "after the storm" is always here.'[70] Lee's words clearly express the ongoing struggles of a post-storm community – homelessness, hunger, bereavement, trauma. Not only is it impossible to return to a pre-storm state, any life lived after the hurricane has dissipated is marked indelibly by its effects. Julie Nicholson similarly speaks of her life being divided along the jagged line of her daughter's murder: life before 7/7 and life after 7/7. While Anthony Walker's older sister, Dominique, refers to her life in two parts: BA and AA (before and after Anthony's murder).[71] Traumatized bodies retain scars: Julie asserts that she will grieve every day for the rest of her life. Yet, there is social and theological pressure to erase the trauma, to quell the grief, to find happiness. Socially, this compulsion can be likened to the rose-tinted glasses of Disneyfication, dispensing the warm, fuzzy glow of saccharin endings that sentimentalize past trauma. Theologically, this compulsion is fuelled by a reading of the Easter narrative as a continuum from death to life, from devastation to renewal. Rambo, like Jones, cautions, on the contrary, that reading the crucifixion–resurrection narrative in this linear fashion underestimates the inscrutable experience of living with trauma and risks glorifying suffering; she avers, 'Insofar as resurrection is proclaimed as life conquering or life victorious over death, it does not speak to the realities of traumatic suffering.'[72]

Opposingly, drawing on the work of Hans Urs von Balthasar, Rambo proposes that we recover a deeper engagement with Christ's descent into hell: 'not the victorious ascent out of hell, but the experience of absolute death and alienation in hell'.[73] Instead of glossing over Holy Saturday, instead of hastening from Good Friday to Easter Sunday, she endorses von Balthasar's preoccupation with the darkness that is the middle day. Correspondingly, reading the resurrection through the lens of trauma debunks the impression that death is surpassed; rather, the wounds of trauma are a constant witness to death. Likewise, the implication that love is sacrificed in death is not borne out by post-trauma survival; thenceforth, she argues, trauma compels us to reconceive of the relationship between love and death: love remains.[74]

Undoubtedly, both Jones' evocation of deferred hope and Rambo's focus on Holy Saturday offer more apt theological resources for traumatized persons than triumphalist notions of life conquering death. Nevertheless, what both theories lack is a discussion of anger. Even though Rambo acknowledges that 'smoothing over this day [Holy Saturday] is tied to a larger smoothing over of oppression, violence, and the injustices of history',[75] she does not develop a concept of righteous indignation. There are numerous biblical precedents describing acceptable anger as that which is appropriately directed towards injustice: God is frequently angry with the Israelites for their unfaithfulness (Exodus, Numbers); Moses is angry with the Israelites' constant complaining (Exodus); Samuel is angered by Saul's disobedience, David is angry with God for perceived injustice against Uzzah (1 and 2 Samuel); Jesus exhibits righteous anger in the Gospels' accounts of the cleansing of the temple (Matthew 21; Mark 11; Luke 19; John 2).

Noticeably, these angry biblical figures are male; we have little on which to draw if seeking to comprehend the emotions of women in the biblical narratives. Hence, we are obliged, as Renita Weems expresses it, 'to wrestle ... [them] from their presumably male narrators',[76] male narrators who did not consider women's thoughts and emotions to be of enough significance to warrant writing about them in any detail. In conjunction with the traumatic grief of the Christian mothers considered above, Mary represents the archetype of a mother whose son suffers a violent death, and yet the tradition has painted her as a passive actor in the Christian story; one who epitomizes meekness and submission encapsulated in the words, 'Here am I, the servant of the Lord; let it be with me according to your word' (Luke 1.38). Such an account is hardly a lifeline for mothers whose sons and daughters are brutally killed. Indeed, feminist theology has long critiqued the ideal of femininity exemplified by Mary, and if we are to escape the narrow confines of this portrayal, we need to use our imagination; perhaps this seems unorthodox, but we have no other choice. As Hilary Mantel astutely declares: 'Since the world began, men and women have held up the sky between them, but men have written the histories, and women have been, by and large, written out.'[77] In this vein, Jones creatively conjures the thoughts that Mary and another woman at the cross (Jones calls her Rachel) might be attempting to process; nevertheless, Jones stops short of imagining anger.[78] Naomi Alderman, on the other hand, uses fiction to expand Mary's agency to include defiance of Joseph and cultural expectation. In addition, she credits Mary with a range of emotions issuing from the bewilderment and hurt caused by her son Jesus who rejects his familial duties.[79] At times, Alderman's Mary is angry; this is not how we are used to conceiving of Mary and we cannot verify its authenticity. In the absence of testimony, however, fictional retellings fruitfully expand our perception of historical interpretations and chart a course out of the traditional quagmire.[80]

Patriarchal contexts have rendered anger a male preserve, an indication of masculinity; whereas, women have been constrained by models of femininity that valorize the 'softer' emotions. Especially in situations of injustice, though, women are rendered increasingly vulnerable if taught to passively accept suffering, to be meek and forgiving. On the contrary, women have an ample supply of injustices to be angry about and, as the #ChurchToo movement reveals, this includes Christian women. Thus, as Audre Lorde asserts: 'Every woman has a well-stocked arsenal of anger potentially useful against those oppressions, personal and institutional, which brought that anger into being. Focused with precision it can become a powerful source of energy serving progress and change.'[81]

A prime example of mothers eschewing the demand to silently forgive and, instead, invoking anger to pursue justice is presented by the *Madres de Plaza de Mayo* (Mothers of Plaza de Mayo) in Argentina. This formidable group of mothers, traumatized by the disappearance of their sons and daughters under military dictatorship in the 1970s and 1980s, rejected the social and theological construction of private motherhood by entering the public arena with their demand for answers. From the late 1970s, these distraught mothers began a weekly vigil at the Plaza de Mayo, a site of political and public significance in Buenos Aires, drawing attention to the names of the disappeared, demanding rights as mothers and holding the government to account for its human rights abuses. It was necessary for the mothers to engage 'a confrontational tone with official institutions' due to the fact that, Heike Walz attests, 'The idea of forgiveness had been abused and distorted in Argentina, because the churches encouraged the victims to be reconciled with their oppressors, without asking for repentance.'[82] Over time, unexpected female persistence and resistance, in spite of brutal punishment, resulted in the imprisonment of military personnel and the unearthing of information regarding the 'disappeared' children. In other words, as Lorde claims, 'anger expressed and translated into action in the service of our vision and our future is a liberating and strengthening act of clarification'.[83]

Counter to this, in patriarchal cultures and through androcentric theologies, women have been encouraged to suppress their anger; they are socialized to appease men and to proffer forgiveness. As we have seen, those very qualities have the potential to lead to the abuse of women, constraining their freedom under a dangerous and unfairly burdensome duty; whereas, accepting that women have a right to be angry and that forgiveness might be inappropriate, impossible or both, validates women's resistance and self-determination. Admittedly, anger can be destructive, but in the fight for justice it is an essential motivation, and in post-traumatic survival, it may be a necessity for existence. In Soraya Chemaly's words:

> [Anger] is actually one of the most hopeful and forward thinking of all our emotions. It begets transformation, manifesting our passion and keeping us invested in the world. It is a rational *and* emotional response to trespass, violation, and moral disorder. It bridges the divide between what 'is' and what 'ought' to be, between a difficult past and an improved possibility.[84]

From what we have learned above, it is not only the *Madres de Plaza de Mayo* who would agree with Chemaly's statement; it seems that Doreen Lawrence and Julie Nicholson would too, and they are not alone.

From Black Lives Matter to the Grenfell Fire and Cornwall Hugs

Sybrina Fulton is widely known as the mother of 17-year-old Trayvon Martin, fatally shot by a local homeowner while returning on foot from a 7-Eleven shop in Sanford, Florida, in 2012. The much-publicized trial and acquittal of the shooter was the catalyst for an outpouring of anger regarding systemic racism and loss of life that birthed the Black Lives Matter movement.[85] Reluctantly, Sybrina rose to prominence as a spokesperson opposing racial violence. As a committed church attendee, finding a route to healing through the trauma is for Sybrina intimately bound up with her Christian faith. By focusing on the words of Proverbs 3.5–6, 'Trust in the LORD with all your heart, and do not rely on your own insight. In all your ways acknowledge him, and he will make straight your paths', she has succeeded in coping with the ongoing pain caused by the senseless death of her son. Furthermore, she reaches out to other grieving parents through the Circle of Mothers, a support network she founded for women whose children have been killed by gun violence.[86] Despite believing that, as a Christian, she ought to forgive, Sybrina has been unable to do so and does not ask this of other bereaved mothers in the Circle.[87] Indeed, six years after her son's death, on the release of a documentary series entitled *Rest in Power: The Trayvon Martin Story*, during an interview at the Cathedral of St John the Divine in New York, she replies to the question of forgiveness with the following:

I know that in my own time … I have to forgive. But by the same token, I'm not at that point yet. I'm very honest with that. A lot of people ask me that question, and I'm very open and honest about it. I'm very real with my feelings, and I know I have not forgiven.[88]

Only a few months after the shooting of Trayvon Martin, Lucia (known as Lucy) McBath's son, Jordan Davis, also 17 years of age, was fatally shot through a car door at a petrol station in Jacksonville, Florida; the man who pulled the trigger objected to the loud music coming from the car in which Jordan was a passenger. Although the defence lawyer drew on the controversial 'stand-your-ground' law, the perpetrator was found guilty.[89] A few years after the conviction, Lucy successfully ran for Congress in Georgia with a campaign that promoted gun reform. At the trial, Lucy spoke these words to the perpetrator who murdered her son:

> I choose to forgive you … for taking my son's life. I choose to release the seeds of bitterness and anger and honour my son's love. I choose to walk in the freedom of knowing God's justice has been served. I pray that God has mercy on your soul.[90]

Lucy's Christian faith and her understanding of divine justice enabled her to see forgiveness as a choice, even though she 'didn't see any remorse … didn't see any humility' in the perpetrator.[91] Her ability to choose forgiveness in the face of trauma echoes that of Gee Walker and Marie Fatayi-Williams. Conversely, Doreen Lawrence, Sybrina Fulton and Julie Nicholson, equally convinced of their Christian faith, attest to their inability to forgive the perpetrators of the violent crimes that killed their children. Through the dual lenses of feminist theology and trauma theology, their narratives and the Christian motif of forgiveness can be viewed in a new light. Feminist theology teaches us that it is not always appropriate to ask women to forgive, it may even be injurious to do so; trauma theology teaches us not to rush past the descent into hell. Holy Saturday is a time for dwelling in the darkness, for grieving, for reliving the trauma; we do not know how long this period will last following traumatic events in our lives; we can remain; we do not have to expel the pain; we do not have to insist on forgiveness as a form of healing. Rather, anger may be the necessary motivation to keep living, to fight for justice, to engender change. By paying attention to the narratives of traumatized mothers, it is abundantly clear that, more than a requirement to forgive, humanity is conserved through deeds of tenderness from neighbours and strangers, actions that generate mutual empowerment.

For instance, as Esmé Page watched the shocking footage of the Grenfell fire on television, she immediately understood that the survivors would 'need a sanctuary, a place to be and to grieve … some kind of hope on the horizon'.[92] Unsure of how to fulfil this need, Esmé was buoyed by her Christian faith. Convinced that God was instructing her to proceed and remembering the words of Psalm 18.29 – 'by my God I can leap over a wall' – she prayed and then posted a request on Facebook. A plentiful supply of individuals and businesses responded almost immediately offering travel, accommodation and funds. As a result, hundreds of religiously plural and diverse survivors of the fire have enjoyed respite on the south-westerly tip of England. Reflecting on her interactions with the holiday guests of the Cornwall Hugs Grenfell project, Esmé observes: 'What moved me most was the courage of mothers determined to kayak or paddle-board with their children to give them fun, despite their own exhaustion and overwhelming grief.'[93]

Hence, from the Circle of Mothers to Cornwall Hugs, we encounter models of Christian empathy and kindness restoring faith in humanity and enabling small steps on the journey to healing; what is more, they are achieving this without requiring forgiveness or the suppression of anger. In Weems' words:

> We are frequently just a sister away from our healing. We need a woman, a sister, who will see in our destitution a jagged image of what one day could be her own story. We need a sister who will respond with mercy.[94]

References

Alderman, Naomi, *The Liars' Gospel*, London: Penguin, 2012.

The Archbishops Council, *Responding to Domestic Abuse: Guidelines for Those with Pastoral Responsibilities*, London: Church House Publishing, 2006.

Aune, Kristin and Rebecca Barnes, *In Churches Too: Church Responses to Domestic Abuse – A Case Study of Cumbria*, Coventry and Leicester: Coventry University and University of Leicester, 2018.

Aynsley-Green, Al, 'The Truth About Childhood Bereavement', *BMA.org*, 17 June 2016: www.bma.org.uk/connecting-doctors/b/work/posts/the-truth-about-child hood-bereavement (accessed 18 April 2019).

Batty, David, 'Doreen Lawrence: I Don't Forgive Stephen's Murderers', *Guardian*, 5 January 2012: www.theguardian.com/uk/2012/jan/05/doreen-lawrence-stephen (accessed 25 April 2019).

BBC Documentary, *Every Parent's Nightmare*, dir. Roger Childs, 2006.

BBC, 'Stephen Lawrence: Murdered Teen's Father Forgives Killers', *BBC News*, 15 April 2018: www.bbc.co.uk/news/uk-43775801 (accessed 19 April 2019).

BBC, 'Trayvon Martin's Parents on Path to Forgive George Zimmerman', *BBC News*, 24 August 2013: www.bbc.co.uk/news/world-us-canada-23822998 (accessed 27 April 2019).

Bonhoeffer, Dietrich, *Dietrich Bonhoeffer Works, Volume 4: Discipleship*, trans. Barbara Green and Reinhard Krauss, Minneapolis, MN: Fortress Press [1937] 2003.

—— *Dietrich Bonhoeffer Works, Volume 8: Letters and Papers from Prison*, trans. Isabel Best, Lisa E. Dahill, Reinhard Krauss and Nancy Lukens, Minneapolis, MN: Fortress Press [1953] 2010.

Booth, Robert, 'Stephen Lawrence's Father Says He Forgives His Son's Killers', *Guardian*, 15 April 2018: www.theguardian.com/uk-news/2018/apr/15/stephen-lawrences-father-says-he-forgives-his-sons-killers (accessed 25 April 2019).

Brotherson, Sean E. and Jean Soderquist, 'Coping with a Child's Death: Spiritual Issues and Therapeutic Implications', *Journal of Family Psychotherapy* 13, nos 1–2 (2002), 53–86.

Cantacuzino, Marina, *The Forgiveness Project: Stories for a Vengeful Age*, London: Jessica Kingsley Publishers, 2015.

—— 'Forgiving the Nazis is Incomprehensible – But It has saved One Survivor's Life', *Guardian*, 1 May 2015: www.theguardian.com/commentisfree/2015/may/01/forgiving-abuse-not-forgetting-auschwitz-eva-kor (accessed 19 April 2019).

CBS This Morning, 'Trayvon Martin's Mother Recalls Opening a "Pandora's Box" of Evidence 3 Years after Shooting', *CBS News*, 8 August 2018: www.cbsnews.com/news/trayvon-martin-mother-sybrina-fulton-may-donate-sons-clothes-to-museum/ (accessed 27 April 2019).

Chemaly, Soraya, *Rage Becomes Her*, New York: Atria Books, 2018.

The Church of England, *Responding Well to Domestic Abuse: Policy and Practice Guidance*, March 2017: www.churchofengland.org/sites/default/files/2017-11/responding-well-to-domestic-abuse-formatted-master-copy-030317.pdf.

Clute, M. A. and R. Kobayashi, 'Are Children's Grief Camps Effective?', *Journal of Social Work in End-of-Life and Palliative Care* 9, no. 1 (2013), 43–57.

Collins, Tim, 'Straight From the Heart', *Guardian*, 13 July 2005: www.theguardian.com/uk/2005/jul/13/july7.uksecurity23 (accessed 26 April 2019).

Diski, Jenny, *Only Human*, London: Virago, 2000.

Doka, Kenneth J., 'Helping Children Spiritually Cope with Dying and Death', *Huffington Post*, 25 March 2011: www.huffpost.com/entry/helping-children-spiritua_b_839764 (accessed 18 March 2019).

Fatayi-Williams, Marie, *For the Love of Anthony*, London: Hodder and Stoughton, 2007.

Field, Marilyn J. and Richard E. Behrman, eds, *When Children Die: Improving Palliative and End-of-Life Care for Children and their Families*, Washington, DC: The National Academies Press, 2003.

Garbarino, James and Claire Bedard, 'Spiritual Challenges to Children Facing Violent Trauma', *Childhood* 3 (1996), 467–78.

Harris, J. Irene, Joseph Currier and Crystal Park, 'Trauma, Faith, and Meaning Making', in *Psychology of Trauma*, ed. Thijs Van Leeuwen and Marieke Brouwer, New York: Nova Science Publishers, 2013, 135–50.

Hawthorne, Dawn M., JoAnne M. Youngblut and Dorothy Brooten, 'Parent Spirituality, Grief, and Mental Health at 1 and 3 Months after Their Infant's/Child's Death in an Intensive Care Unit', *Journal of Pediatric Nursing* 31, no. 1 (2016), 73–80.

Herbert, Ian, 'The Killing of Anthony: The Boy who Died because of the Colour of His Skin', *Independent*, 1 December 2005: www.independent.co.uk/news/uk/crime/the-killing-of-anthony-the-boy-who-died-because-of-the-colour-of-his-skin-517644.html (accessed 26 April 2019).

Jones, Sam, 'Vicar who Cannot Forgive Tube Bombers Quits Pulpit', *Guardian*, 7 March 2006: www.theguardian.com/uk/2006/mar/07/religion.july7 (accessed 29 April 2019).

Jones, Serene, 'Hope Deferred: Theological Reflections of Reproductive Loss (Infertility, Miscarriage, Stillbirth)', *Modern Theology* 17, no. 2 (2001), 227–45.

—— *Trauma and Grace: Theology in a Ruptured World*, Louisville, KY: Westminster John Knox Press, 2009.

Knight, Ben, 'Auschwitz Survivor Angers Co-Plaintiffs in SS Office Trial by Saying Prosecutions Should Stop', *Guardian*, 27 April 2015: www.theguardian.com/world/2015/apr/27/auschwitz-survivor-angers-plaintiffs-trial-forgiveness (accessed 19 April 2019).

Kor, Eva Mozes and Lisa Rojany Buccieri, *Surviving the Angel of Death: A True Story of a Mengele Twin in Auschwitz*, Terre Haute, IN: Tanglewood, 2009.

Lorde, Audre, 'The Uses of Anger' (1981), republished in *Women's Studies Quarterly* 25, nos 1–2 (1997), 278–85.

Luscombe, Richard, 'Michael Dunn Sentenced to Life without Parole for Killing of Florida Teenager', *Guardian*, 17 October 2014: www.theguardian.com/us-news/2014/oct/17/michael-dunn-sentenced-life-without-parole-florida (accessed 27 April 2019).

Lusher, Adam, 'Victim's Mother Renews Calls for End to Violence at Westminster Funeral', *Telegraph*, 24 July 2005: www.telegraph.co.uk/news/uknews/1494707/Victims-mother-renews-call-for-end-to-violence-at-Westminster-funeral.html (accessed 26 April 2019).

Macmath, Terence Handley, 'Interview: Esmé Page, Founder, Cornwall Hugs Grenfell', *Church Times*, 12 April 2019: www.churchtimes.co.uk/articles/2019/12-april/features/interviews/interview-esmé-page-founder-cornwall-hugs-grenfell (accessed 27 April 2019).

McClatchey, Irene Searles, M. Elizabeth Vonk and Gregory Palardy, 'Efficacy of a Camp-Based Intervention for Childhood Traumatic Grief', *Research on Social Work Practice* 19, no. 1 (2009), 19–30.

McIntosh, Esther, 'The Concept of Sacrifice: A Reconsideration of the Feminist Critique', *International Journal of Public Theology* 1, no. 2 (2007), 210–29.

Nicholson, Julie, *A Song for Jenny*, London: HarperCollins, 2010.

O'Donnell, Karen, *Broken Bodies: The Eucharist, Mary and the Body in Trauma Theology*, London: SCM Press, 2018.

—— 'Reproductive Loss: Towards a Theology of Bodies', *Theology and Sexuality* (2018), 1–14.

Office for National Statistics, 'Domestic Abuse: Findings from the Crime Survey for England and Wales, Year Ending March 2018': www.ons.gov.uk/peoplepopulationandcommunity/crimeandjustice/articles/domesticabusefindingsfromthecrimesurveyforenglandandwales/yearendingmarch2018 (accessed 25 April 2019).

Oliver, Mark, 'Cousins Jailed for Racist Axe Murder', *Guardian*, 1 December 2005: www.theguardian.com/uk/2005/dec/01/ukcrime.race (accessed 26 April 2019).

Rambo, Shelly, *Spirit and Trauma: A Theology of Remaining*, Louisville, KY: Westminster John Knox Press, 2010.

Sherwood, Harriet, 'Doreen Lawrence: Grenfell Tenants Faced "Institutional Indifference"', *Guardian*, 2 June 2018: www.theguardian.com/society/2018/jun/02/doreen-lawrence-grenfell-tenants-faced-institutional-indifference (accessed 25 April 2019).

Sormanti, Mary and Judith August, 'Parental Bereavement: Spiritual Connections with Deceased Children', *American Journal of Orthopsychiatry* 67, no. 3 (1997), 460–9.

Tansley, Janet, 'Anthony Walker Murder: Gee Walker will Clean the House on the Anniversary of Anthony's Death to Wash Away the Evil of What They Did', *Liverpool Echo*, 22 July 2015: www.liverpoolecho.co.uk/news/real-lives/anthony-walker-murder-gee-walker-9698515 (accessed 26 April 2019).

Terkel, Amanda, 'Obama Calls for Review of "Stand Your Ground" Laws after Trayvon Martin Verdict', *Huffington Post*, 19 July 2013: www.huffingtonpost.co.uk/2013/07/19/obama-stand-your-ground_n_3624594.html (accessed 27 April 2019).

Townsend, Mark, 'Dominique Walker: "I Wasn't Able to Protect My Brother – But Now I Can Help Other People"', *Guardian*, 10 June 2012: www.theguardian.com/world/2012/jun/10/liverpool-police-dominique-walker-interview (accessed 30 April 2019).

Walz, Heike, '*Madres* Appear on the Public *Plaza de Mayo* in Argentina: Towards Human Rights as a Key for a Public Theology that Carries on the Liberation Heritage', *International Journal of Public Theology* 3, no. 2 (2009): 167–87.

Weems, Renita J., *Just a Sister Away*, San Diego, CA: LuraMedia, 1988.

Williams, Delores S., *Sisters in the Wilderness: The Challenge of Womanist God Talk*, Maryknoll, NY: Orbis Books, 1993.

Willis, Ella, 'Stephen Lawrence's Mother Reveals She Cannot Forgive Her Son's Killers in Final TV Interview on *Loose Women*', *Evening Standard*, 18 April 2018: www.standard.co.uk/news/uk/stephen-lawrences-mother-reveals-she-cannot-forgive-her-sons-killers-in-final-tv-interview-on-loose-a3817601.html (accessed 19 April 2019).

Notes

1 Geraint Elfyn Jones, 'In Fond Memory' (personal copy).

2 See, for example, Irene Searles McClatchey, M. Elizabeth Vonk and Gregory Palardy, 'Efficacy of a Camp-Based Intervention for Childhood Traumatic Grief', *Research on Social Work Practice* 19, no. 1 (2009), 19–30, and M. A. Clute and R. Kobayashi, 'Are Children's Grief Camps Effective?', *Journal of Social Work in End-of-Life and Palliative Care* 9, no. 1 (2013), 43–57.

3 See, for example, Mary Sormanti and Judith August, 'Parental Bereavement: Spiritual Connections with Deceased Children', *American Journal of Orthopsychiatry* 67, no. 3 (1997), 460–9; Sean E. Brotherson and Jean Soderquist, 'Coping with a Child's Death: Spiritual Issues and Therapeutic Implications', *Journal of Family Psychotherapy* 13, nos 1–2 (2002), 53–86; Dawn M. Hawthorne, JoAnne M. Youngblut and Dorothy Brooten, 'Parent Spirituality, Grief, and Mental Health at 1 and 3 Months after Their Infant's/Child's Death in an Intensive Care Unit', *Journal of Pediatric Nursing* 31, no. 1 (2016), 73–80. Despite such studies, literature on miscarriage and theology is scarce: see Serene Jones, 'Hope Deferred: Theological Reflections of Reproductive Loss (Infertility, Miscarriage, Stillbirth)', *Modern Theology* 17, no. 2 (2001), 227–45, and Karen O'Donnell, 'Reproductive Loss: Toward a Theology of Bodies', *Theology and Sexuality* (2018).

4 Sir Al Aynsley-Green, 'The Truth about Childhood Bereavement', *BMA.org*, 17 June 2016, www.bma.org.uk/connecting-doctors/b/work/posts/the-truth-about-childhood-bereavement (accessed 18 April 2019).

5 James Garbarino and Claire Bedard, 'Spiritual Challenges to Children Facing Violent Trauma', *Childhood* 3 (1996), 467–78.

6 Garbarino and Bedard, 'Spiritual Challenges', 470, citing Bessel van der Kolk, 'Meaning and Trauma', paper presented at the Rochester Symposium on Developmental Psychopathology, University of Rochester, New York, October 1994.

7 Garbarino and Bedard, 'Spiritual Challenges', 470.

8 Garbarino and Bedard, 'Spiritual Challenges', 473.

9 Garbarino and Bedard, 'Spiritual Challenges', 474.

10 See, for instance, Kenneth J. Doka, 'Helping Children Spiritually Cope with Dying and Death', *Huffington Post*, 25 March 2011, www.huffpost.com/entry/help ing-children-spiritua_b_839764 (accessed 18 March 2019), in which Doka relays the account of a boy whom adults had tried to comfort by claiming that his friend died in a car accident because 'God wanted him to be an angel in heaven', with the effect that the grief-stricken seven-year-old was intent on acting in such a way as to attempt to convince God that he would not make a good angel.

11 Unless stated otherwise, all biblical quotations are taken from the NRSV.

12 Dietrich Bonhoeffer, *Dietrich Bonhoeffer Works, Volume 8: Letters and Papers from Prison*, trans. Isabel Best, Lisa E. Dahill, Reinhard Krauss and Nancy Lukens (Minneapolis, MN: Fortress Press [1953] 2010).

13 Dietrich Bonhoeffer, *Dietrich Bonhoeffer Works, Volume 4: Discipleship*, trans. Barbara Green and Reinhard Krauss (Minneapolis, MN: Fortress Press [1937] 2003), 44.

14 Eva Mozes Kor and Lisa Rojany Buccieri, *Surviving the Angel of Death: A True Story of a Mengele Twin in Auschwitz* (Terre Haute, IN: Tanglewood, 2009), 133.

15 Ben Knight, 'Auschwitz Survivor Angers Co-Plaintiffs in SS Office Trial by Saying Prosecutions Should Stop', *Guardian*, 27 April 2015, www.theguardian. com/world/2015/apr/27/auschwitz-survivor-angers-plaintiffs-trial-forgiveness (accessed 19 April 2019).

16 Marina Cantacuzino, 'Forgiving the Nazis is Incomprehensible – But It has Saved One Survivor's Life', *Guardian*, www.theguardian.com/commentisfree/2015/ may/01/forgiving-abuse-not-forgetting-auschwitz-eva-kor (accessed 19 April 2019). See also www.theforgivenessproject.com/.

17 Cantacuzino, 'Forgiving'.

18 See, for example, Desmond Tutu, 'Foreword', and Alexander McCall Smith, 'Foreword', in Marina Cantacuzino, *The Forgiveness Project: Stories for a Vengeful Age* (London: Jessica Kingsley Publishers, 2015), vii–viii and ix–xiii.

19 The Archbishops' Council, *Responding to Domestic Abuse: Guidelines for Those with Pastoral Responsibilities* (London: Church House Publishing, 2006), 2.

20 The Archbishops' Council, *Responding to Domestic Abuse*, 19.

21 The Archbishops' Council, *Responding to Domestic Abuse*, 20.

22 The Archbishops' Council, *Responding to Domestic Abuse*, 20; see Esther McIntosh, 'The Concept of Sacrifice: A Reconsideration of the Feminist Critique', *International Journal of Public Theology* 1, no. 2 (2007), 210–29.

23 The Church of England, *Responding Well to Domestic Abuse: Policy and Practice Guidance* (March 2017), www.churchofengland.org/sites/default/files/2017-11/ responding-well-to-domestic-abuse-formatted-master-copy-030317.pdf.

24 Church of England, *Responding Well*, 44. Slightly misleadingly, the document claims that women in abusive relationships are at risk of being murdered when, in

fact, they are most at risk when they leave. It is not entirely clear what practical steps the Church is taking to protect women and their children when they leave an abuser.

25 Church of England, *Responding Well*, 43.

26 Church of England, *Responding Well*, 44.

27 Church of England, *Responding Well*, 45–6.

28 For Emily Joy's account of the hashtag, see Emily Joy, *#ChurchToo* (blog), http://emilyjoypoetry.com/churchtoo.

29 Founded by Tarana Burke in 2006 to support black women and girls from low socio-economic backgrounds who were survivors of sexual violence, revived in 2017 in the wake of sexual harassment and abuse allegations in Hollywood; see *Me Too*, https://metoomvmt.org/.

30 While men also experience abuse, the Crime Report for England and Wales (2018) finds that women are nearly twice as likely to experience domestic abuse as men and four times as likely to experience sexual assault by a partner (although abuse, including male abuse, is likely underreported); see Office for National Statistics, 'Domestic Abuse: Findings from the Crime Survey for England and Wales, Year Ending March 2018', www.ons.gov.uk/peoplepopulationandcommunity/crime andjustice/articles/domesticabusefindingsfromthecrimesurveyforenglandandwales/ yearendingmarch2018 (accessed 25 April 2019).

31 Kristin Aune and Rebecca Barnes, *In Churches Too: Church Responses to Domestic Abuse – A Case Study of Cumbria* (Coventry and Leicester: Coventry University and University of Leicester, 2018), 7.

32 Aune and Barnes, *In Churches Too*, 60.

33 In drawing on the examples of traumatized mothers, I have deliberately omitted the names of the perpetrators of violence in the main text to allow the names of the mothers and their children to be the focal point. I am using 'trauma' as it is used in psychology: 'Typically, an event is defined as "trauma" when the individual's coping resources and meaning systems are overwhelmed, so the trauma survivor is tasked to re-create a global meaning system that is failing' (J. Irene Harris, Joseph Currier and Crystal Park, 'Trauma, Faith, and Meaning Making', in *Psychology of Trauma*, ed. Thijs Van Leeuwen and Marieke Brouwer (New York: Nova Science Publishers, 2013), 135–50, p. 139). Field and Behrman note that 'Mothers typically report more intense and prolonged grief reactions than fathers' (175) and that the link between post-traumatic stress disorder (PTSD) and the sudden, unexpected or violent death of a child or young person is evident but is under-researched (Marilyn J. Field and Richard E. Behrman, eds, *When Children Die: Improving Palliative and End-of-Life Care for Children and their Families* (Washington, DC: The National Academies Press, 2003), 174).

34 Robert Booth, 'Stephen Lawrence's Father Says He Forgives His Son's Killers', *Guardian*, 15 April 2018, www.theguardian.com/uk-news/2018/apr/15/stephen-lawrences-father-says-he-forgives-his-sons-killers (accessed 25 April 2019).

35 BBC, 'Stephen Lawrence: Murdered Teen's Father Forgives Killers', *BBC News*, 15 April 2018, www.bbc.co.uk/news/uk-43775801 (accessed 19 April 2019).

36 David Batty, 'Doreen Lawrence: I Don't Forgive Stephen's Murderers', *Guardian*, 5 January 2012, www.theguardian.com/uk/2012/jan/05/doreen-lawrence-stephen (accessed 25 April 2019).

37 Ella Willis, 'Stephen Lawrence's Mother Reveals She Cannot Forgive Her Son's Killers in Final TV Interview on *Loose Women*', *Evening Standard*, 18 April 2018, www.standard.co.uk/news/uk/stephen-lawrences-mother-reveals-she-cannot-

forgive-her-sons-killers-in-final-tv-interview-on-loose-a3817601.html (accessed 19 April 2019).

38 Harriet Sherwood, 'Doreen Lawrence: Grenfell Tenants Faced "Institutional Indifference"', *Guardian*, 2 June 2018, www.theguardian.com/society/2018/jun/02/doreen-lawrence-grenfell-tenants-faced-institutional-indifference (accessed 25 April 2019).

39 Ian Herbert, 'The Killing of Anthony: The Boy who Died because of the Colour of His Skin', *Independent*, 1 December 2005, www.independent.co.uk/news/uk/crime/the-killing-of-anthony-the-boy-who-died-because-of-the-colour-of-his-skin-517644.html (accessed 26 April 2019).

40 Janet Tansley, 'Anthony Walker Murder: Gee Walker will Clean the House on the Anniversary of Anthony's Death to Wash Away the Evil of What They Did', *Liverpool Echo*, 22 July 2015, www.liverpoolecho.co.uk/news/real-lives/anthony-walker-murder-gee-walker-9698515 (accessed 26 April 2019).

41 Mark Oliver, 'Cousins Jailed for Racist Axe Murder', *Guardian*, 1 December 2005, www.theguardian.com/uk/2005/dec/01/ukcrime.race (accessed 26 April 2019).

42 Tansley, 'Anthony Walker Murder'.

43 Tim Collins, 'Straight From the Heart', *Guardian*, 13 July 2005, www.theguardian.com/uk/2005/jul/13/july7.uksecurity23 (accessed 26 April 2019). Marie later published a book in which she questions the delays and bureaucracy that hampered the relatives in their quest for information; Marie Fatayi-Williams, *For the Love of Anthony* (London: Hodder and Stoughton, 2007).

44 Adam Lusher, 'Victim's Mother Renews Calls for End to Violence at Westminster Funeral', *Telegraph*, 24 July 2005, www.telegraph.co.uk/news/uknews/1494707/Victims-mother-renews-call-for-end-to-violence-at-Westminster-funeral.html (accessed 26 April 2019).

45 Julie Nicholson, *A Song for Jenny* (London: HarperCollins, 2010), 131.

46 Nicholson, *A Song for Jenny*, 146–9.

47 Nicholson, *A Song for Jenny*, 220–1.

48 Nicholson, *A Song for Jenny*, 160–1, 263.

49 Nicholson, *A Song for Jenny*, 274, 289.

50 Nicholson, *A Song for Jenny*, 281.

51 Nicholson, *A Song for Jenny*, 294.

52 Nicholson, *A Song for Jenny*, 148.

53 Nicholson, *A Song for Jenny*, 123.

54 Nicholson, *A Song for Jenny*, 125–7.

55 Nicholson, *A Song for Jenny*, 293.

56 Sam Jones, 'Vicar who Cannot Forgive Tube Bombers Quits Pulpit', *Guardian*, 7 March 2006, www.theguardian.com/uk/2006/mar/07/religion.july7 (accessed 29 April 2019).

57 BBC Documentary, *Every Parent's Nightmare*, dir. Roger Childs, 2006.

58 Julie Nicholson, Ebor Lecture, York St John University, 3 October 2018.

59 Nicholson, Ebor Lecture.

60 Posted on Maya Angelou's Facebook page, 4 July 2011.

61 Serene Jones, *Trauma and Grace: Theology in a Ruptured World* (Louisville, KY: Westminster John Knox Press, 2009).

62 Shelly Rambo, *Spirit and Trauma: A Theology of Remaining* (Louisville, KY: Westminster John Knox Press, 2010).

63 O'Donnell, 'Reproductive Loss'.

64 O'Donnell constructively explores theological resources for traumatized bodies in Karen O'Donnell, *Broken Bodies: The Eucharist, Mary and the Body in Trauma Theology* (London: SCM Press, 2018).

65 Jones, *Trauma and Grace*, 9.

66 Jones, *Trauma and Grace*, 65.

67 Jones, *Trauma and Grace*, 76–7.

68 Jones, *Trauma and Grace*, 90 (italics in the original).

69 See Jones, *Trauma and Grace*, 127ff.

70 Rambo, *Spirit and Trauma*, 1, 143.

71 Mark Townsend, 'Dominique Walker: "I Wasn't Able to Protect My Brother – But Now I Can Help Other People"', *Guardian*, 10 June 2012, www.theguardian.com/world/2012/jun/10/liverpool-police-dominique-walker-interview (accessed 30 April 2019).

72 Rambo, *Spirit and Trauma*, 7.

73 Rambo, *Spirit and Trauma*, 77.

74 Rambo, *Spirit and Trauma*, 111ff.

75 Rambo, *Spirit and Trauma*, 129.

76 Renita J. Weems, *Just a Sister Away* (San Diego, CA: LuraMedia, 1988), x.

77 Hilary Mantel, as cited by Anita Corbin, *100 First Women UK* (portraits exhibition, 2018 onwards).

78 Jones, *Trauma and Grace*, 101ff.

79 Naomi Alderman, *The Liars' Gospel* (London: Penguin, 2012), 'Miryam', 11–65.

80 Fictional accounts, such as Alderman's, and Sarah's imagined emotions in Jenny Diski, *Only Human* (London: Virago, 2000), take us somewhat further than Weems' and Williams' reconsideration of a biblical narrative from the perspective of a sidelined and misused character, namely, Hagar; see Delores S. Williams, *Sisters in the Wilderness: The Challenge of Womanist God-Talk* (Maryknoll, NY: Orbis Books, 1993).

81 Audre Lorde, 'The Uses of Anger' (1981), republished in *Women's Studies Quarterly* 25, nos 1–2 (1997), 278–85, 280.

82 See Heike Walz, '*Madres* Appear on the Public *Plaza de Mayo* in Argentina: Towards Human Rights as a Key for a Public Theology that Carries on the Liberation Heritage', *International Journal of Public Theology* 3, no. 2 (2009), 167–87, 184–5.

83 Lorde, 'The Uses of Anger', 280.

84 Soraya Chemaly, *Rage Becomes Her* (New York: Atria Books, 2018), xx (italics in the original).

85 Founded by three women: Alicia Garza, Opal Tometi and Patrisse Cullors.

86 See www.circleofmothers.org/.

87 In her first interview with the British Press following the trial, Sybrina claimed: 'As Christians we have to forgive … But it's a process, and we are still going through that healing process. We are still in the process of forgiveness. We know it's coming but we're just not there yet'; BBC, 'Trayvon Martin's Parents on Path to Forgive George Zimmerman', *BBC News*, 24 August 2013, www.bbc.co.uk/news/world-us-canada-23822998 (accessed 27 April 2019).

88 CBS This Morning, 'Trayvon Martin's Mother Recalls Opening a "Pandora's Box" of Evidence 3 Years after Shooting', *CBS News*, 8 August 2018, www.cbsnews.

com/news/trayvon-martin-mother-sybrina-fulton-may-donate-sons-clothes-to-museum/ (accessed 27 April 2019).

89 The perpetrator's defence did not rely on Florida's controversial 'stand-your-ground' law that permits lethal force in response to a perceived threat, but his acquittal led Barack Obama to call for a review of the law; see Amanda Terkel, 'Obama Calls for Review of "Stand Your Ground" Laws after Trayvon Martin Verdict', *Huffington Post*, 19 July 2013, www.huffingtonpost.co.uk/2013/07/19/obama-stand-your-ground_n_3624594.html (accessed 27 April 2019). The stand-your-ground law and the shooting of Jordan Davis is further explored in Marc Silver's 2015 documentary *3½ Minutes*.

90 Richard Luscombe, 'Michael Dunn Sentenced to Life without Parole for Killing of Florida Teenager', *Guardian*, 17 October 2014, www.theguardian.com/us-news/2014/oct/17/michael-dunn-sentenced-life-without-parole-florida (accessed 27 April 2019).

91 Luscombe, 'Michael Dunn'.

92 Terence Handley Macmath, 'Interview: Esmé Page, Founder, Cornwall Hugs Grenfell', *Church Times*, 12 April 2019, www.churchtimes.co.uk/articles/2019/12-april/features/interviews/interview-esmé-page-founder-cornwall-hugs-grenfell (accessed 27 April 2019).

93 Macmath, 'Interview'. See also www.cornwallhugsgrenfell.org/.

94 Weems, *Just a Sister Away*, back cover.

Index of Names and Subjects